Artist is a Verb

A Daily Reader to Support You in Building a Creative Practice and Inspired Life

Tish McAllise Sjoberg

Daily Artist and Expressive Arts Therapist

Art Helps Art Heals Press

San Diego

Art Helps Art Heals Press
San Diego, California
www. ArtHelpsArtHeals.com

Library of Congress Control Number: 2023918868

Author: Tish McAllise Sjoberg
Title: Artist is a Verb - A Daily Reader to Support You in Building a Creative Practice and Inspired Life

ISBN-979-8-9891373-1-2 Paperback
ISBN-979-8-9891373-4-3 Electronic Book

Cover art, interior design and interior illustrations by Tish McAllise Sjoberg
Author photograph by Michael S. Robinson

Disclaimer:

Though this book and having a Creative Practice can be therapeutic, it is not therapy. This book is not intended to replace therapy. If you have big feelings, memories, or sensations related to trauma or daily life, get regular mental health support. Adding adjunct creative therapy can be a great resource: Expressive Arts Therapy, Art Therapy, Dance Therapy, Drama Therapy, Music Therapy, or body-based Somatic Therapies. (Bring the product from your Creative Practice to your therapy sessions to share your story in the language of the arts.)

When it is suggested to follow your impulses and follow your pleasures, what feels good—know that included in that idea is always "and doesn't hurt yourself or others." If you notice you are getting impulses to hurt yourself, others or property, get mental health support to not act on those impulses. It is okay to ask for help!

All opinions expressed in this book are those of Tish McAllise Sjoberg.
This book does not replace the advice of mental health and medical professionals.

“Artist
is a Verb.
We don’t
become an
artist and
then do art,
we do art and
then begin to
feel like an
artist.”

Tish McAllise Sjoberg

Reviews

Good Reasons to Read This Book

"Between the covers of *Artist is a Verb* are more than 365 daily readings of encouragement, information, ideas, inspiration, support, and resources to living a life of making art on a daily basis. Tish McAllise Sjoberg doesn't just tell us how to do it; she shares how she created such a life for herself. She is a generous teacher, wise mentor, compassionate friend, and lively cheerleader. This book will be my daily art-making companion; I can't wait to begin."

—Judy Reeves
author of
A Writer's Book of Days,
Wild Women, Wild Voices,
and *When Your Heart Says Go*

"I just love this book. I will buy a dozen copies! Tish has given the world a gift with this book. It's a gift that we can give to ourselves, a tool to help us explore our own creativity one day at a time. And all this process asks of us is five minutes a day. Five minutes to draw or dance or write or sing or play with whatever creative impulse intrigues you. Tish's book shows you how to get into that practice and stay there, for fun and for life."

—Graham Yost
Film and television writer for
Justified, Silo, and *Speed*

Reviews

Good Reasons to Use This Book

"As a writer, I know very well how lonely the creative process can be. Despite the company of a fellow writer or a group of readers who are kind enough to offer their support, the actual act of making something where there was once nothing requires the creator to step into the wasteland, alone and untethered, battling the forces of inertia, doubt, and disillusionment. *Artist is a Verb* is a lifeline for the creator. It offers help, hope, encouragement, empathy, and a much-needed friend for the arduous, foolhardy, creative journey."

—Matthew Dicks
internationally bestselling author of
Memoirs of an Imaginary Friend: A Novel,
Storyworthy,
Someday Is Today,
and many more

"Whether you secretly long for a more creative life
or are a full-fledged working artist (or anything in between),
Tish's encouraging daily voice in your ear will guide you
to follow your heart's desire, and gently remove every obstacle
in the way of cultivating a creative practice.
Becoming a daily artist takes only five minutes a day.
But with Tish's inspiration, I bet you'll
find yourself doing much more."

—Donna Otter
Moth Storytelling GrandSLAM champion,
Expressive Arts Therapist, and daily diarist

Also by Tish McAllise Sjoberg

Scribble Art: A How-to Guide and Coloring Book

Dedicated to all the people
who have desire to show up
for themselves and creative expression.
I hope this book will help you
walk through any fears or challenges
so you can live the life of a creative.

And to my mother,
Dorothy Marie McAllise,
whose regret and death inspired my first
365 Days of Art project.
Thanks, Mom.
May you live on in an infinite number
of creative endeavors inspired by this book.

Contents

Never doubt
what 5 minutes a day
can add up to,
you are holding evidence
of it in your hands
as you read this book.

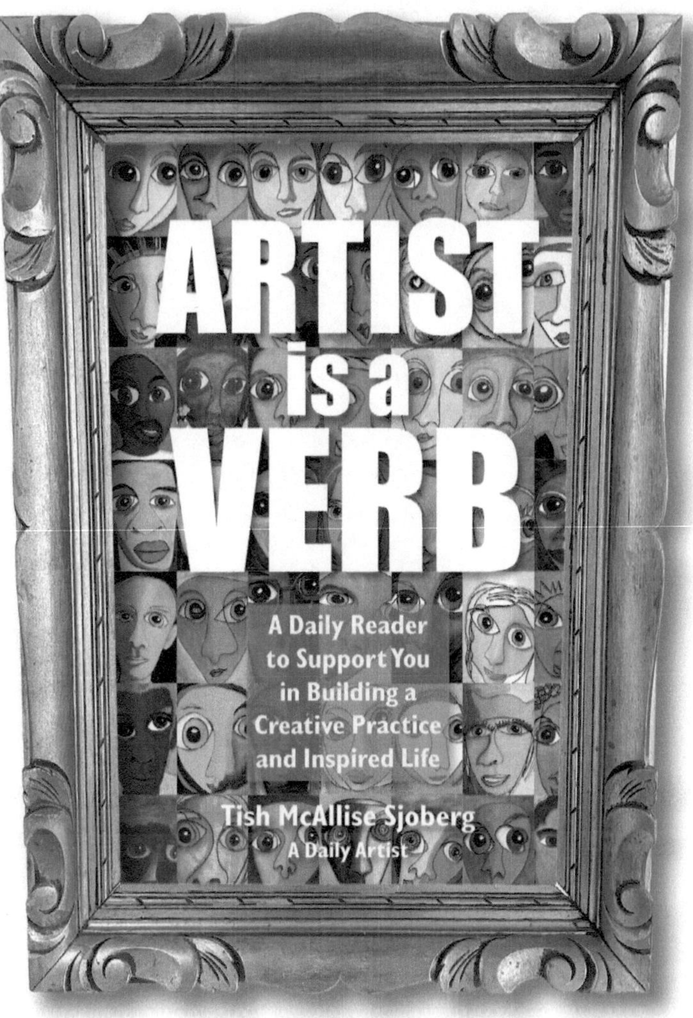

365 Days of Writing This Book

I spent at least three years writing this book as a daily Creative Practice, though the book took about ten years overall to create. Writing and editing it as part of my Creative Practice is what made it happen and helped me enjoy the process. My commitment was a minimum of 5 minutes a day. And, I could go as long as I wanted. It may not be perfect, but I got it done!

Preface

I am fascinated by the books we are drawn to, when we notice them and why. I often think of books as answers to prayers. Our heart or soul asks a question, or longs for some change, and then the book appears. Sometimes we go looking for the book, sometimes it finds us. Sometimes we are ready, we buy it and read. Sometimes we think we are ready. We buy it and it sits.

Something drew you to this book, called to you, because deep within you there is a longing to bring more creativity into your life. Listen to this call and see where it takes you. If you aren't ready to dive in, how about having the cover face outward on your bookshelf or nightstand? Let the conversation begin in this quiet, subtle way.

When I began writing this book, as my own daily Creative Practice, it was a book with a beginning, middle and end, but then the writing told me it wanted to be a daily reader. *A daily reader for a daily practice* you can read over and over. A small drop into your life each day.

There is no right or wrong path in this process. You cannot fail if you show up. And if you do not show up you are not failing, you are learning more about yourself and what keeps you away. You can even use this book without doing a Creative Practice. Maybe reading this book every day is your practice. (I hope at some point you can't resist and will be pulled into action!)

YOU get to create your own creative journey, decide how often you show up, and how long you will do it. YOU get to choose what you do when you show up. You will have opportunities to adjust, shift, and change to make this process work for YOU. There is no one to please, but rather an opportunity to follow what is pleasurable, what feels good for you.

You are not on this journey alone. This book is your companion, as are all the other people doing this same process, reading this same book. I may speak using we. When I say we I am thinking of you reading, and others who are reading, too. Though we are each on our own as we read, I am imagining we are connected to each other. We are all doing this together. Even though time has passed since these words were written and when you first picked up this book, I believe in some way we are having an intimate conversation in our heads and hearts.

Reading this book will not be a passive experience. Each day I offer you a resource to help you work through challenges that may arise in your process and keep going. Do the resources if they speak to you. And though it is a daily reader, there is an index for you to use often. If you are having a challenge with motivation, go to the index and find pieces on motivation. If you want to quit, look up "I want to quit" to gain the needed inspiration for you to stay on your creative path.

You were drawn to this book for a reason. Don't put off your longing to create one more day. Today is the day to begin. And by holding this book in your hands, you have begun. It is time to stop thinking, it is time to live a more creative and inspired life.

Artist is a verb. We don't become a painter by buying the materials, reading books, or watching videos. We become a painter when we pick up the brush filled with paint and touch the paper. We become a writer when we string letters, words, and sentences together. We become a musician when we combine notes and put music in the air. Dancers move their bodies and in drama we take on roles. Fashionistas express through what they wear. Chefs cook. Gardeners garden. An inspired life is created by being inspired.

Showing up regularly to express creatively is ultimately about living a more art-FULL life. Your life becomes the medium to mold and create. Though you may focus on the arts in this process, your entire life may feel the effects creatively. Artist is a verb. Dive into your verbness!

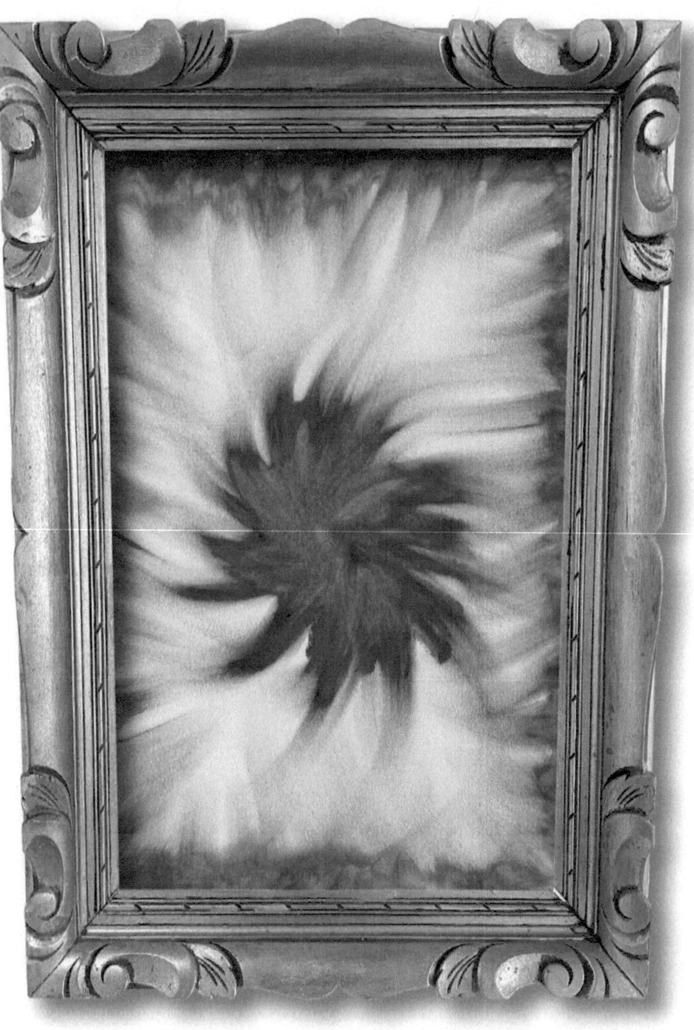

365 Days of Art—The First Year

I wanted to honor my mother's one year death anniversary with one year of art-making. I also wanted to fulfill a lifelong dream of becoming a painter. I realized early on that painting was too stressful for me and I would not make it a year. I decided to switch to oil pastels. It worked, and I grew my show-up muscle and my creative confidence.

You don't need any
creative experience
to get started.
Once you get started
you will grow your experience.

My Story
A Driving Force

About a week before my mother died, I asked her if she had any regrets. She said yes. She had always wanted to be an artist. Her confession washed through me with a wave of surprise and then sadness. I had seen little evidence of this desire in her life. She continued to tell me she had taken writing classes before my brother and I were born and she had hoped to someday take more, but never did. She also said she had wanted to be a visual artist. I did remember her and my dad taking a still life painting class together when I was seven or eight years old and how excited I was to see what they had done when they arrived home from their class. I also remember my dad giving my mom a gift certificate to a drawing class when I was in college.

A few months after her death, as we cleared through her things of seventy-three years, I found a sketch pad with a half a dozen drawings in it. I cried.

A year later, as my mother's death anniversary approached, I wanted to do a piece of art to honor her, but I had no idea what to do. I reflected on my own fantasy—when I was old and retired, I would become an artist, more specifically, a painter. I cringed at the thought, I too might die before ever realizing my dream. The honoring became clear. I would make one piece of art each day for a year, because I did not want one day to go by where the world, and I, didn't know I wanted to be an artist. My first 365 Days of Art project was born.

I decided I would do a small painting every day. I was going to fulfill my dream to be a painter right away. I knew if this was going to work, I needed to create a system. I went out and bought 500 sheets of letter sized acid-free card stock paper and painter's tape to tape the paper to a small Masonite board to keep it stretched when wet from the paint. It would also create a nice sharp border when the tape was removed. I shopped for acrylic paints and brushes and set up my "studio" in my small Queen Anne style desk that had belonged to my mother. I committed to 5 minutes a day for each piece, and, if I chose, I could work longer. I knew I could show up for 5 minutes a day. I would never be able to say I didn't have 5 minutes. When I began I kept short journal entries about my process:

Day One. 10/30/03. "I hadn't planned to begin today. Went and bought all my materials and set up my cozy little space. But how could I not start? It was all ready and waiting! How could I wait until Sunday? Forget the pageantry of waiting. Start now! My mother would be very happy. I am very happy. Two paintings today. Hooray!"

Day Two. 10/31/03. "I had 5 minutes to do my painting— and I did it! Shows me that time is not the issue! When I have everything set up it is a breeze—and it was fun. De-stressed me…"

Day Four. 11/2/03. "Mom day, the day she passed, one year ago today…The result? Acceptable. The real result? I did it! And I am on day four. Inspired by you, Mom. I love you. So many days you didn't express your desire to do art, your desire to express yourself. I willingly, I lovingly, I, with a full heart, take the torch and commit to carrying it forward, lighting my world as I go. Lighting the worlds of all those who wish to join. Thank you, dear Mother, for planting the seed of art in my heart. I promise to write my own story. Art is in my blood!"

Unfortunately, this was the beginning honeymoon phase I thought would last forever. But by day fourteen, the tide was turning and my little paintings had become grueling.

I hated painting. Each day I would sit in front of this blank white page and not know what to do. Why did I think I knew how to paint? It was clear if I was going to make it through this 365-day commitment, I needed to change things up. At the time I was slightly familiar with oil pastels and knew when they were smudged and blended with my fingers, they could look like paint. I liked getting my hands in on the process, so I shifted to oil pastels. It made a big difference, I kept going.

By no means was it easy. Many nights I would be crawling into bed, dog tired and realize I had not done my art. I would begrudgingly get up and do something. This led to a new realization—having changed to oil pastels, my art was portable. I created three art boxes filled with all the supplies I needed: one for next to my bed, one for my car, and one in my travel bag. I could do my art anywhere. Now I could crawl into bed and *do* my art.

I did miss one day. It was Thanksgiving and I was less than a month into the process. It was by no means an art-free day, our yearly gathering of friends and family prepared an artful meal, we salsa danced after dinner and then had a lively drum circle. My intention was to let my night's art be a response to this creative day. I woke up in the morning realizing I had not done it. I was devastated. Less than a month in, I had blown it. I wallowed for a few moments and then realized this was my project, I could make the rules.

I immediately did the "make-up art." From then on, I encouraged people to ask me, "Have you done your art today?" I would rather feel bugged, than miss. This was the only day I missed in my first 365 Days project.

Throughout the year there were unexpected gifts. Because my art was portable, I could take my art box to dinner with friends. After our meal, I would invite others to join me. I would tell them, "Just fill the page with color and shape, maybe express how you are feeling right now, or how your day went." Often people would remark they had not done art since elementary school. Sometimes my guest artists would be so excited they would frame their piece. I learned making art in community was very satisfying.

I also learned to keep things fresh by mixing it up. A couple weeks I did "art in the dark," turning the lights out and randomly choosing colors that would not reveal themselves until the lights came on.

I did a week of found objects, where I would find a discarded object, often on the sidewalk during my day, like a rusty nail or a scrap of trash, glue it to my page and then I would write something around the object it inspired in me, like a memory or a wondering about who had discarded it.

There were quite a few blind contour* drawings of my cat, because she usually sat on the end of my bed watching my nightly art ritual. When Sharpie brand markers came out with their new sets of fabulous colors, I switched to abstract marker drawings for a week or so.

After I went to Cirque du Soleil, I did a series of strange clown faces. I added watercolor to my art boxes and used those here and there. Sometimes I just scribbled and sometimes I would write bold statements like, "There is no art tonight!"

There was a point when my, "Oh $#*%, I still have to do my art" changed to, "I can't wait to do my art!" I had found my groove. Miraculously, I started to feel like an artist, even though I was just doing child-like colorings.

At one point I felt the need to honor the work and went shopping for special boxes to store my collection in—by the end of the year I filled three boxes.

---

*Blind Contour Drawing is looking at an object, photograph, or being and drawing without looking at your paper. When drawing in the blind contour fashion, the pen stays on the paper the entire time so the artist doesn't lose their orientation. I love these drawings because they are so quirky. For me, it is giving exquisite attention to something without needing it to look realistic. Most of my blind contour portraits are done with my eyes closed, often blindfolded, to ensure I am not looking, while I think of the person, characteristic, or emotion I am trying to capture. Blind contour portraits became my "easy way in" because I had my eyes closed. How could I be critical?

As the one-year mark approached, I felt pride in my process and in all the art I had accrued over the year. I also felt sadness because the year would soon be over. These feelings made it clear I needed to keep going. Maybe now I would be ready to paint? But what would I paint? Once again, the terror of the blank page was nipping at me.

I made an appointment with my Expressive Arts mentor, Pamela Underwood, and with her help, I laid out my year's worth of work on the floor of her studio. As I stood looking at all 365 pieces displayed together, I realized the *"work of art"* was not the individual pieces I showed up to do every day, it was the collection of the entire year. Showing up each day to do one small piece added up to a big "WOW!" I had created this huge colorful mosaic-like tapestry. I was overcome by its grandeur.

With Pamela's help, I slowly walked the rows, looking at each piece and pulling those I liked most. Sifting through the chosen pieces down to twenty of my favorites, down to ten, down to three and finally down to the one I loved the most: a blind contour drawing of my cat. This is where I would start with my painting year, drawing blind contour portraits and then painting them. I was ready for year two!

In honor of my mother, the first piece would be a portrait of her. I chose to work on large paper 20" x 28" that I purchased ahead of time, cut to size. I also used low-cost tempera paint rather than acrylics. I was trying to make the process as stress-free as possible: I would draw with my eyes closed, then open my eyes and paint with inexpensive paint on paper rather than canvas. It helped me keep my expectations low—it worked.

For this second year, my commitment was to paint every day, not to do a finished piece every day. It didn't matter how long I painted or how much I did—just one stroke of paint would be enough. Usually, one stroke would lead to another and another and before I knew it, I was painting for anywhere from fifteen minutes to hours. Yet, I knew I had the option of just one paint stroke. This was helpful when I went through large life events like having breast cancer. If I wasn't feeling great, I only needed to add one brush stroke and I also realized how helpful turning to my art was during this stressful time. I always felt better after I painted.

I tried to finish each painting in a few days or less, so I would keep things moving and not get caught in perfectionism. At the end of the year, I had more than 100 large paintings!

Something unexpected happened along the way. I realized a person doesn't become an artist and then make art, which is what I had been waiting for my whole life. In fact, I had this magical idea someone, maybe an art fairy would tap me on the head and designate I could start because I was now an artist. Instead, I did art and then began to feel like an artist—*Artist is a Verb™*. My art making practice began in 2003 and I am still going! At this writing, I am in my twentieth year, and rarely does a day go by where I haven't made time to express, either visual art, writing, or both.

Today, I am not as strict and am willing to miss a day or two here and there. It is more of an internal process, I don't like to miss because it is an essential part of my day and who I am. My creative time is an opportunity to process my day and be more present in my life. My Creative Practice is like my morning cup of coffee, it is part of my daily life.

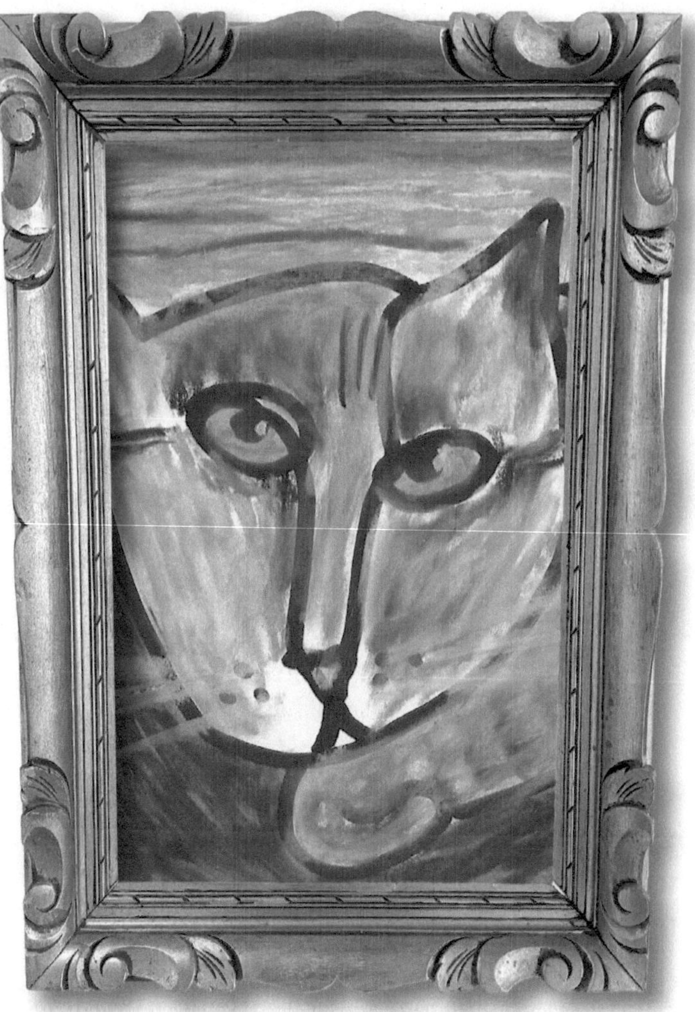

365 Days of Art—The End of the First Year

At the end of my first year I laid out all 365 pieces and found this to be my favorite, a blind contour drawing of my cat, Friday. This image inspired my next year's entry into painting large blind contour portraits. My confidence was higher, my show-up muscle was strong, and I was ready to paint now! Could I do another year? Could I stick with painting this time?

My Story

My Daily Art Projects

Here is a list of the 365 Days of Art projects I completed in twenty years. Completed for me was to take them a full year and show up most days. In general, I have missed very few days of doing something creative. I like having a project versus leaving it open, so I don't show up wondering what to do.

- ***365 Days of Art*** mostly oil pastels
- ***365 Days of Painting*** starting from large blind contour drawings. Commitment was one stroke of paint a day, no painting lasting longer than 3–7 days
- ***365 Days Painting*** people and pet portraits
- ***365 Days Painting*** people and pet portraits
- ***365 Days of Found Objects*** and writing about them
- ***365 Days of Narcissism*** small blind contour drawings, mostly of myself, adding colored pencil
- ***365 Days of Writing Artist is a Verb*** and other writing
- ***365 Days of Visioning Journals™*** collage, and painting
- ***365 Days of Visioning Journals™*** collage and painting
- ***365 Days of Visioning Journals™*** collage, and painting, I continue to do this process about 3 times a week
- ***365 Days of Scribbling*** (2nd try on this idea worked)
- ***365 Days of Manikin*** photos (2nd try on this idea worked)
- ***365 Days of Kick-Ass*** altered book, one page each day
- ***365 Days of Scribbling*** using the Scribble Kit
- ***365 Days of Blind Contour Portraits*** painting
- ***365 Days of Writing Artist is a Verb*** plus continue painting on my previous year's blind contour portraits daily
- ***365 Days of Writing Artist is a Verb*** plus painting daily
- ***Clean off the brush paintings*** each day I paint I do another painting or project cleaning off my brushes and palettes

My Story
My False Starts

Below is a list of 365 Projects I did not complete or what I call *false starts.* Most went for a few weeks to a few months. When I "quit" a project I would then move on to try something different—which means I kept going, I kept showing up, I kept doing daily art. False starts are an opportunity to learn what isn't working. Sometimes they were too boring, sometimes too ambitious. I learned to check in often and notice anything that was not working so I could problem solve to keep going. Some of these I did a second try incorporating what I learned and they worked, others I am still excited about and someday may try again.

- ***Junk wood sculpture***, add a piece a day—I ran out of interesting wood scraps and had challenges attaching them.
- ***Doodle a word a day***—I started this with my son when he was learning graffiti art and when he lost interest, so did I.
- ***Word a day writing***, using one word as a prompt—I didn't have a good plan and felt like I was floundering.
- ***Manikin photo a day*** and post it on social media—posting it everyday on social media was too stressful so I stopped. I tried it four years later and it worked, without social media.
- ***Collage a day***—too ambitious, too big, or not the right time.
- ***Different portrait ideas***—with found objects, as illustrations for a children's book, more realistic in oil pastels and ink.
- ***A poetic thought or quote about life a day*** while brushing my teeth—I loved this but didn't keep it up, not sure why.
- ***Large oil pastel piece every day with a blog post***—I did not have time for a large piece each day, nor a blog.
- ***A scribble a day***—tried again two years later and it worked.
- ***Where is my heart today mini drawing***—was not engaging enough, wasn't crazy about the process or the results.

Not every project made it the distance, but I tried things out and learned what worked and did not work. Sometimes what didn't work taught me the most!

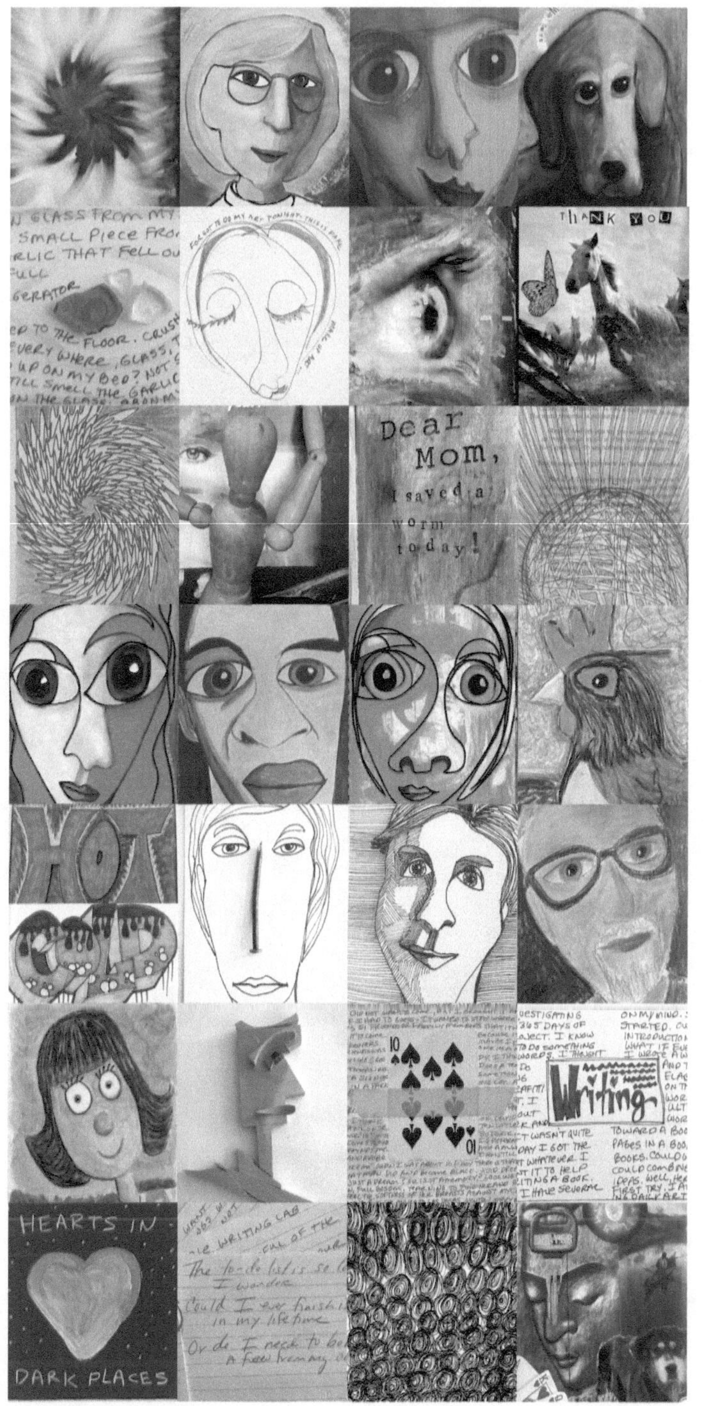
THANK YOU
Dear Mom,
I saved a worm today!
Writing
HEARTS IN
DARK PLACES

My Story
On My Way to a Whole New Life

Not only did my mother help me find my way to daily art through her own regret, I had another profound, life changing experience with her when she was dying.

I loved to be near her whenever I could and on this day as she was taking a nap—I sat next to her bed and swung my legs up so my feet rested on her bed gently touching her legs. A sweet point of contact as she slept.

As I sat, out of nowhere an idea overcame me. In my imagination I saw myself working with teenagers, using art to help them navigate their challenges. I was so surprised by the details in this imagining that I grabbed a pad of paper from my mother's nightstand and began to write it all down. It came complete with ideas of art projects we would do and the feeling sense of being with them.

After my mother's death, on my return home, I noticed a business card on my desk from a woman, Deborah Ogburn, whom I had met at a drum making workshop a month prior. Her title on the card was, "Expressive Arts Therapist." I immediately called her. She gave me details about the master's degree program she attended at the Expressive Arts Institute of San Diego and the European Graduate School in Switzerland. I learned that Expressive Arts Therapy is a discipline of helping and healing that uses the arts as its basis for discovery and change. The play through visual art, music, movement, writing, and drama helps open the senses, enter the imagination, and access a different part of our brain to find the resources that we hold inside ourselves.

Within a month after my mother's death, I completed the introductory intensive for the program and within two months I began their Expressive Arts Therapy Master's program. Add to this, the Expressive Arts Institute of San Diego was exactly one mile from my house. For the first time I felt passionate about my life. And alongside of that enthusiasm, I had a place to grieve my losses, using the arts. Not only had I lost my mother that year, a month before my beloved dog died and six months before my father died. Expressive Arts Therapy taught me how art could hold my grief and help me start a new story. I was off on a whole new trajectory in my life. The simple and easy stay-in-the-process-not-the-end-product approach helped me find my way into art and a whole new career.

It has been over twenty years since that story began. I initially worked in hospice with people who were dying and grieving—it felt natural after the loss of my mother, father, and beloved dog all in that short six-month period. I became comfortable with death and dying through my own experiences. I eventually worked with teens in different settings—pregnant and parenting teens, teens in foster care or experiencing homelessness, and teens with eating disorders. Ultimately, I decided adults were my niche and I continue to refer children and teens to my colleagues.

My idea for doing a daily art project to honor my mother began to form during my Expressive Arts training. Poet and classmate, Diane Gage, had begun a daily poetry project that planted the seed in me for a daily project. The idea to make it easy and tangible was inspired when classmate, Donna Otter, brought a stack of pre-primed cardboard to a class for a project. "Yes!" I thought, "If I prepare for a whole year ahead of time, I will be able to show up easier."

It is my own navigation through my fears to do art, using my daily art projects to support my life, and what I have learned as an Expressive Arts Therapist and Coach that I bring to you in this book. Although at this writing I am in my twentieth year of showing up to do art daily, I also feel I am just beginning. Every day there is an opportunity to learn something new. Curiosity leads me forward—I hope it will be your friend, too.

My Story

Paying It Forward

This book is born from my desire to support others to grow a Creative Practice that feeds them as much as food and water. If you have had a wish to express yourself regularly or a desire to feel like an artist, this book is here to help. I invite you to let the arts guide you toward living a more inspired life. I welcome you to this process and look forward to learning what works for you!

Any creative discipline is invited into this practice: visual art of any kind, movement and dance, improv, theater and drama, poetry and writing, and music—playing, writing, or singing. It can also be used for other creative endeavors like cooking, gardening, clutter clearing, interior design, fashion, thesis writing, a life project you have wanted to start or finish, and more.

Let these daily readings support you to build a Creative Practice that feeds your spirit and changes your life.

Disclaimer:

Though this book and having a Creative Practice can be therapeutic, it is not therapy. This book is not intended to replace therapy. If you have big feelings, memories, or sensations related to trauma or daily life, get regular mental health support. Adding adjunct creative therapy can be a great resource: Expressive Arts Therapy, Art Therapy, Dance Therapy, Drama Therapy, Music Therapy, or body-based Somatic Therapies. (Bring the product from your Creative Practice to your therapy sessions to share your story in the language of the arts.)

When I talk about following your impulses and following your pleasures, what feels good—know that included in that idea is always "and doesn't hurt yourself or others." If you notice you are getting impulses to hurt yourself, others or property, get mental health support to not act on those impulses. It is okay to ask for help!

I didn't start being good,
I began and I got better.
The surprise arrival was
I became more confident
and I started to feel like an artist.

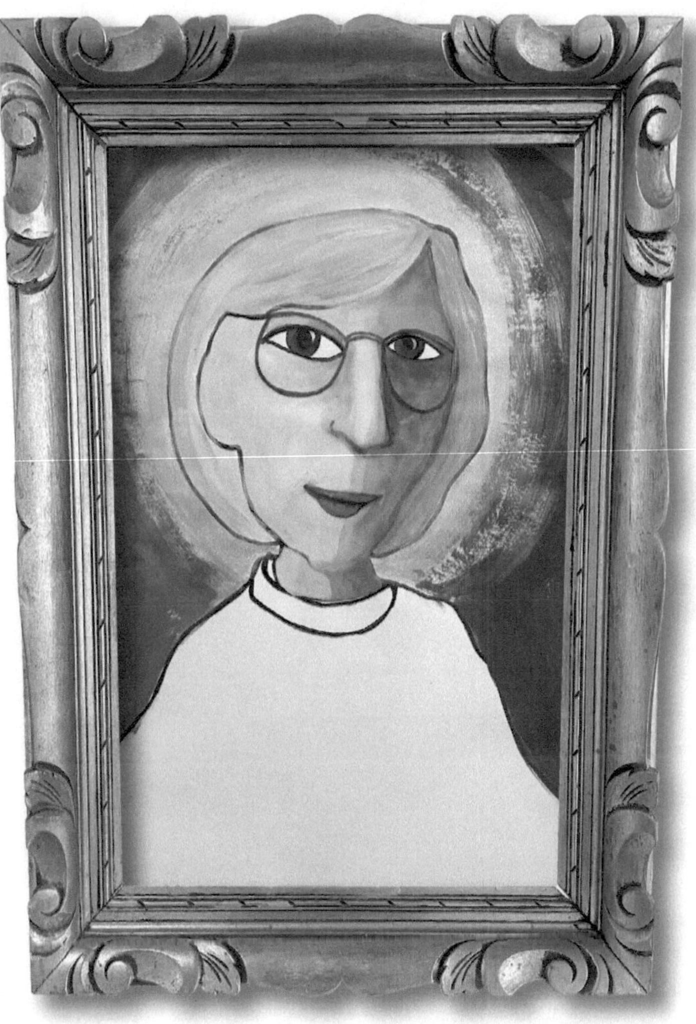

365 Days of Blind Contour Paintings

Large blind contour portraits were my easy way into painting. I drew them with my eyes closed or while looking at a photo, not looking at the paper (okay, sometimes I peeked) and then opened my eyes to paint. I found freedom in their quirkiness, which took away the stress of perfectionism. This painting of my mother was my first.

Preparation

What Is a Creative Practice?

When we answer the call for a Creative Practice we are honoring our desire to do something creative every day or with regularity. We routinely make time to take action to express ourself so it becomes an integral part of our everyday life. Or as I like to say, as important as brushing your teeth or having morning coffee, you won't want to go a day without it.

When our creative time turns into a practice we can also bring a new level of dedication to our showing up, if we choose. We are claiming a place in our life for creative expression and honoring it as essential to our well-being.

This devotion does not need to be a lot of time, 5 minutes a day can change your life.

If you choose, your creative time can also intersect with your spiritual time, family time, alone time, or create a mini-vacation in your day.

You get to make it up. And this book will support you to make it happen and keep going so you can reap the rewards of a more creative and inspired life.

Basic Steps for a Creative Practice:

1. Show up daily or regularly for 5+ minutes a day to be creative.
2. Have a project or idea for the time you show up so you don't have to think or get overwhelmed with not knowing what to do. Find something easy and enjoyable that you can get lost in if you have more time. Allow yourself to be in the process of expressing rather than worrying about the end product.
3. Grow your *show-up muscle* by showing up.
4. Make adjustments along the way so you keep showing up.
5. Celebrate that you showed up and notice what changes in your life by expressing yourself regularly.

Preparation
Reasons to Get Started

What called you to pick up this book? What invites you to begin a Creative Practice? Identifying why you want to start can help you show up. Why? On a day you do not want to take the time for your practice, you can remind yourself why you are doing this.

"Oh, that's right, I am doing this because I want to live a more alive life." Or, "because I have a story to tell," or "because I want to stay clean and sober."

The original reason I started was clear for me. "I will make art every day for a year to honor my mother's death and her regret she never became an artist. I choose to show up for my art because I want the world and myself to know I want to be an artist."

Find your own personal calling, write it down, and post it where you will see it. Revisit it as needed, your purpose for showing up may change with time, or remain as true as the first day you started. If you are not sure, here are some ideas that may spark something in you:

You have a longing to create. You have challenges showing up for yourself to make art. You have a desire to become an artist. **You want to learn to put yourself first in your life.** You own a lot of creativity books but rarely create. You want to honor someone who has died by making art. **You want to manage your anxiety.** You are depressed. You have major stress in your life. You have a health challenge. You are recovering from an accident or illness. You have chronic pain. **You are trying to stay clean and sober and need a new companion.** Your relationship is challenging or has ended. **A loved one has died and you are grieving.** You spend a lot of time alone. **You want to live a more interesting life.** Someone suggested you seem very creative. **Your work is stressful.** Your home life is stressful. Your life seems empty.

The walls in your home are empty. **You loved to make art as a child.** You want to be more improvisational in your life. You are too improvisational in your life and want to create more structure to bring a specific project to completion. You want to express your emotions through art. You feel lonely. **You have a really busy life and have a hard time taking time for yourself.** You are in therapy and you would like to honor the work you are doing through art. **You have art training but haven't been using it.** You haven't been creative since elementary school. You want to leave a legacy. You feel something is missing in your life. **You are wondering if you could become** a painter, a musician, a writer, a singer, an actor, a dancer, etc. **You feel you waste too much time.** You have retired and need to fill your day. You want to tell your story. **You need a meditation practice.** You need alone time. You need community time. **You want to build more creative confidence.** There has been a big change in your life. **You suspect it would be helpful.** You used to make art and you want to get back to it. You had a night dream where you were an artist. **You daydream about being an artist.** You have a friend who makes art and they inspire you. You have kids and want to make art with them. You want to be doing something while you watch television. **The world events are stressful so you need something hopeful to focus on.** You saw a movie about an artist and were inspired. You make your living in the arts and want to make art just for you. **You know showing up every day would be good for you.** You suspect you might be good at something but need to sit down and do it. You have had a trauma in your life and need to learn to relax your body. **Someone told you once you did not have talent and you want to heal that part of you.** You are inspired. You have 5 minutes in your day and you want to spend it creatively. You are ready for a good challenge. You don't want to die without writing your story or doing a certain creative endeavor. **You don't want a day to go by when the world and you don't know you want to be an artist.**

Preparation
Let's Define Art and Creative Acts

What is art? The definition I use at my studio and in my practice of *making things special* is inspired by the early work of Ellen Dissanayake. In her book *What Is Art For?* she describes what artists do as the behavior of *making things special.* This way of looking at art, as what we do when we make it, opens the doors wide for us to be creative. It can also help us be in the process of *making things special* rather than focused on the product and needing to make things look or sound just right. It can allow us to do what feels good, follow our pleasures, explore, and create.

How does this translate into your Creative Practice? If you are dancing, you are making your movements special, treating your body as special. If you are painting, you are making your paper or canvas special as you add color and shape. Writers treat words as special, bringing words and sentences together. Musicians create sound that is special and treat their instruments as special.

Making things special also allows our senses and emotions to get involved. I am thinking about a favorite exercise I like to do on the piano, exploring all the keys, the notes, to find the note that matches how I am feeling in the moment. When I find the right note, and I play it over and over, its vibration enters into me, and I can feel it. Just one note gives me so much pleasure. Imagine where we can allow ourselves to go if we bring this depth of presence into our creating.

The challenge can come when we want to make things *too special.* Suddenly our critical voice throws up roadblocks telling us it is not good enough, and it stops being fun. Be on the lookout and remind your inner critic you are here to *make things special,* not perfect, and to please stop interrupting. (Lots more about the critic ahead in your daily reading or refer to the index.) This is art-making to nourish you, not for commerce, critique, or others.

Preparation
Define What Art Is for YOU

Allow your definition of art to be personal and flexible. You do not have to paint the Sistine Chapel in 365 days or paint a Mona Lisa every week. Look at what is considered art for YOU, and what is doable for the long run, while also allowing room for change and growth.

When we look through the lens of making things special, the range of what is art can grow. Here are some potentially outside the box ideas to get you thinking:

Create a piece of art with the food on your plate (yes, play with your food!) using color, shape, pattern, and photograph it or create a quick sketch.

Let your appearance be special. Think of your clothes on your body as art. Wear a different piece of jewelry or head wrap each day. Take a photo or do a sketch of yourself.

Get rid of 5 objects a day toward clutter clearing and arrange them somehow that makes a special photograph or sketch.

Collect one found object a day in a box and at the end of the week or month create a piece of art with it all.

Hang a large piece of paper or canvas somewhere you walk by regularly. Have colored pencils, markers, or oil pastels nearby. Every time you walk by, draw one line, or write one word or sentence.

Let your home be your canvas. Look at one small area at a time, a wall, drawer, or section of your closet. Arrange it more artfully, look through your artist eyes.

Put a blank sheet of music paper at your music stand. Every day add one note to the composition. Play all the notes up until that day. This could also be a word a day for a poem or song, or a move each day toward a dance.

YOU get to define what art is for you and what contribution you want to make. Think of your whole life as art.

Preparation
Planning Your Creative Practice

This is the first step in your new creative journey. You get to make this up! Your Creative Practice can look like anything you would like it to look like. It doesn't even need to be in the traditional forms of art. It only needs to feel inviting and creative to you. Here are some ideas to consider.

1. Choose a modality.

Visual Art
Dance/Movement
Writing/Poetry
Music
Drama
Gardening
Cooking
Home Decorating
Inventing
Restoring Something
Sewing
Decluttering
Family Time
Letter Writing
Learning Something New
Or...

2. Choose a project.

I encourage you to create a project of some sort, so you are not showing up each time wondering what to do. *I don't know what to do syndrome* can be debilitating. The blank page can be stressful. If you have an idea ahead of time, it will make showing up much easier. Brainstorm some ideas of what you might like to do. Make it small—something you can do in 5 minutes if you need to, yet know, you can spend more time when you can. Do you want to do a drawing at each sitting? A dance each time you show up? You might look to your longings in life. Is there something you have been wanting to do and you could start it in baby steps, one day at a time, through this project? Write stories from your life? Mosaic the wall in your backyard? Remember, you can change your project or take it in a different direction any time if it does not fit. You are in charge!

If you are unsure of one thing to do, maybe one creative act a day, each day something different, until you find what makes your heart sing. You might make a list ahead of time of all the things you want to try, so you don't fall into *I don't know what to do syndrome.* (You could include a journal response to each creative act so you can track your exploration.)

3. What do you need for the project?

Make a list of all the materials you will need for your project. It can help to gather all the materials ahead of time. You can start with things you have. I have found it easier also to do all my visual art on the same size paper, so it feels like a collection. You might get yourself a journal to take notes in, especially if you use a modality which is not visual. In the journal you can make a log where you state what you did that day, or create a one-line poetic response or title to each day's dance you do, or meal you cook.

4. Decide how often you will show up.

I prefer doing things daily, so it becomes a habit like brushing my teeth. If you are not going to do it daily, I recommend choosing days, like every Saturday, or Mondays, Wednesdays and Fridays. I found if I said three times a week, I had a hard time keeping track of when I showed up. AND, if a number of times a week works for you, DO IT! This is your process!

5. Decide what time you will show up.

It can be easiest to connect your art making to something you are already doing regularly in life. For example, with your morning cup of coffee, before brushing your teeth, after meditating, right after dinner, or before you go to sleep. It might take a few tries before you find a just-right fit. For me, it depends on the project.

Usually I like making visual art at the end of my day, the last thing I do before brushing my teeth and climbing into bed. The right time revealed itself through trial and error. My first months I was often getting into bed, and realized I had not done my art. To make it even easier, I started doing my art in bed. Yet when I write, I prefer the morning or daylight. Almost always with a cup of coffee at my kitchen table, outside patio table, or the local coffee shop. Try a few times and see what works best for you.

6. What will help you show up?

As I mentioned above, find something to connect with your creative time. A connector helps us show up. You can also:

- Set reminders on your phone or in your calendar.
- Ask a friend to buddy up with you so you will remember.
- Post a sign, even put it on your pillow, so you can't go to sleep without remembering.
- Create an intention/project which is easy even when you are busy or sick. This can help you show up. (5 minutes a day, one stroke of paint per day, one sentence a day…remember, you can always go longer or do more.)

7. Write your Creative Practice intention in a statement.

You may want to put your intention for your Creative Practice in writing. Maybe you create a sign you post in the area you will be working to remind you and make this journey concrete. *I will paint for 5 minutes a day after the dinner dishes are done.*

8. Decide on a start date.

You could also include an end date if you want to try something for 100 days, until your birthday, 365 days, or until a project is done. Or who knows, this could be a practice you do for the rest of your life!

9. Get started!

Begin the action, the verb of creating. Read this book as you go for support to keep going. Put it in the bathroom or at your art table, desk, or your nightstand. Somewhere you will see it, read it, and then do your Creative Practice!

10. Final thought.

This book was written over many years, more than three years of the writing was as a daily practice. (Years seven, nineteen and twenty were 365 Day Writing projects, with many 30 and 90 day challenges in between, plus writing in my writing groups.) You will experience me writing in year seven, and then in year twenty, and anywhere in between. So enjoy knowing you are in the moment with me at different linear times of my process.

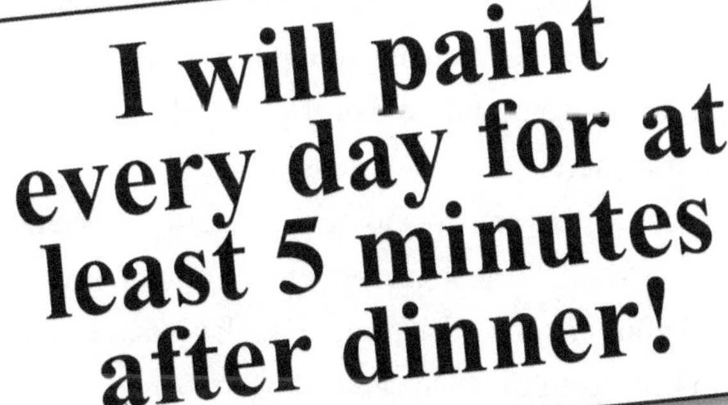

***Note:** If you work in the arts, you may want to have a Creative Practice that is separate from your work—art just for you.*

Preparation

Use This Book as a Resource

I am a resource-oriented person. I look for solutions and new ideas for challenges—thinking of obstacles as opportunities to grow as a human and as an artist. It has become an inspiring way to view my life, where the roadblocks that want to stop me become openings to something new.

I bring to you experiences I have navigated in my years of having a daily Creative Practice, thinking you may experience them, too. Always with the idea to help you keep going, to not stop, to create what could become a lifelong practice.

If this is your first time through the book or having a Creative Practice, you may want to read it in order, as you may be facing certain challenges in a predictable time. If you don't want to read it in order, you are welcome to read popcorn style, blindly opening to a page and letting it be a drop of inspiration in your day, or use the index to find what you need. Sticky notes and a highlighter could help you mark pages that call to you often.

At the end of each day's entry, I offer a resource, an offering of support, for you to take your process further, or a summary of what was said that day as a bit of wisdom to take into your practice.

On the day you read, you may not relate to the specific topic addressed, yet on some future day if you do hit this challenge, you know it is there.

The resources are prompts to get you started—change them however you want. Adjust each reading and resource in your mind to fit your creative discipline. Use the index to find extra support to keep your creative channel open.

Ultimately, I imagine you will begin identifying your own resources and trust yourself to find your way through challenges. When you do need a helping hand, let this book support you to keep going and showing up for yourself!

Preparation
Creative Practice Blessing

As you venture off onto this creative voyage...

May you have a love affair with your art.
May you wake each day with desire to spend time together.
May you begin slowly yet commit to know each other deeply.
May you bring enthusiasm and caring to each meeting.
May your time together be mostly pleasure with
just the right amount of risk.
May you keep each other company in darkness, as well as
dance when the light shines bright.
May you be honest and forgiving, knowing today's mistakes
can become tomorrow's new ideas.
May you show up consistently and not allow others,
or yourself, to pull you from your commitment.
May you honor each moment spent together
as the gift or the challenge it is,
and continue to show up for both.
May you share your anger, disappointment,
and sadness with each other
as well as your joys and delights.
May you listen to your art with an open heart
and follow the steps that are illuminated by it.
May you breathe in courage, exhale doubt, and know
just after things get hard, they usually get easier.
So don't quit.
Keep showing up.
Leave ample evidence you existed in this relationship,
in this marriage of creation.
Till death do you part,
or at least until you reach day 365.

Let this book be a conversation.
And this is the beginning
of the conversation,
a starting point.
I hope you experience a long
and satisfying relationship
with your Creative Practice
and with this book,
a relationship that will last a lifetime.
Get started, keep going!

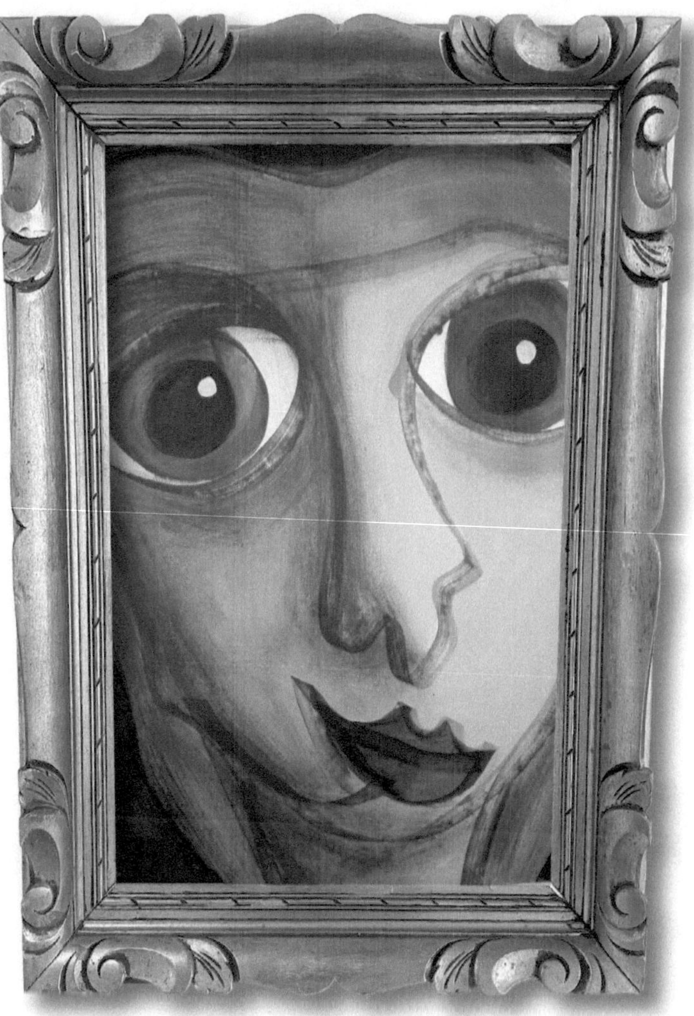

365 Days of Blind Contour Paintings

The blind contour portrait process that I stumbled into has become my style. I love using wide permanent markers that I can't erase or change. This gives me another layer of freedom from perfectionism. I loved the process so much I went three years, painting everyday.

Day Zero
Welcome to a Creative Practice Life

Welcome to the world of a daily or regular Creative Practice. It can be an exciting and scary time and might begin the biggest shift of your life—which could lead to a lifelong practice. You are at a moment where you have decided to move forward in a call to create and express. Be aware you may also meet resistance at its strongest.

The secret, if there is one, is to keep moving forward. Show up for the next day, no matter how small the advancement. Sometimes we have an immediate surge of creativity and sometimes, because we have decided to begin, there is a desert, the blank canvas is terrifying, the blank page mocks us, our blank mind feels impenetrable.

Know this—forward movement can be one word, one brushstroke, one note, one dance step at a time. Forward movement is taking action—doing something. It is not thinking about doing, it is the actual doing. If there is a thought, at the very least, write down the thought.

Resistance may mean you have not found the "just-right" fit for yourself. Yet, you don't know until you begin. So, today is about beginning. Think about the expression you want to commit to and take the first step. Don't worry about tomorrow. Tomorrow will present itself when you get there. Show up, get started, ready, set, go!

Resource: No worries about whether your journey is going to work or not, simply show up and start! Bon voyage!

Day 1
The Conflicting Start

There is something exciting about the first day of my Creative Practice projects. I come with so much hope and excitement. Imagining how much fun it will be, how I will excel at the project I have chosen. Imagining how much I will grow and change as I progress.

And right next to my excitement can be small niggling or sometimes monumental fears. Will I like it? Will I be good at it? Will I show up? Will I stick with it? What if I hate it? What if I tell people I am doing this and then I fail?

Your role in this process is to keep showing up, no matter what fears may try to stop you. Whether you plan to show up every day or on some other regular schedule, plan for your success. Make your commitment easy enough to stick with, knowing you can exceed what you say you will do if you want.

Keep today's creative expression small and simple. My commitment is usually 5 minutes a day, because I know I cannot tell myself I do not have 5 minutes. I know I do.

Stay with the excitement. Keep it simple and celebrate that you started today!

Resource: In this first day, are you noticing anything you need to simplify? What did you love about today? Prep for your next day.

Day 2
Loving It? Or...

You had an idea. You prepared. You showed up to begin. And you found your way back today. If you are feeling pleasure, take a moment to notice the good feelings you have. Notice the sensations in your body, your emotions, and your spirit. Take a moment to mark those feelings in your memory so one day if you don't want to show up, you can remember how good it can feel.

Or...maybe you are not loving it. Maybe you are feeling tension in your shoulders, experiencing a creative block, or feeling lost or afraid. Take a moment and allow yourself to breathe. Our breath is our biggest helper in the creative process. We tend to hold our breath or take shallow breaths when we are unsure. Conscious breathing can help us relax and be open. Another helper is to take a moment to close your eyes and clear your mind before you begin. Make space for the creative.

It doesn't matter what you do when you show up, especially in the beginning. It matters that you made an appearance. You are building your *show-up muscle* first. You have plenty of time—the rest of your life—to grow creatively and get better at your craft.

Whether you are loving it or not loving it, I encourage you to take a moment and congratulate yourself. You started. Relish the enthusiasm of beginning. Don't worry about tomorrow or the days ahead. The gift is starting.

Resource:

Breathe—Take a few minutes to breathe before you start.
Clear—Clear your thoughts, imagine them floating away.
Prepare—What is your first impulse, first idea to start?
Start—Jump in! Act on that first impulse and then the next...

Day 3
"I Don't Have Time." Is It True?

The most common excuse for not answering our desire to be creative is "I don't have time." We will rarely HAVE time to be creative, instead we need to MAKE TIME.

This is why 5 minutes a day is a magical number. We can always make or find 5 minutes. And it can be inspiring to see what we can create in 5 minutes. The key is to have less expectations for that time. Keep it simple.

We start with 5 minutes because we can't say no to this small investment. We may also learn this short amount of time keeps us out of overwhelm. Remember, in the beginning we are growing our *show-up muscle*, if 5 minutes gets us to show up, we are on our way.

Having a system can be helpful so we can jump right in and don't use our precious time to setup. I created art boxes with everything I needed for my project—nothing extravagant, just enough to get me started.

If we can pair our creative time with another activity we are already doing, we don't have to find more time. Maybe your creative act happens while you drink your morning coffee or your evening tea. How about making art on your lunch or afternoon break at work or in the evening while you watch the news?

A writer in my writing support group realized the best time to write was after work, sitting in her car before she went into her house, knowing when she went in, she would get pulled in multiple directions. Get creative as you learn to carve out time for your Creative Practice. You may find time in unusual places.

Resource: Find 5 minutes. Try different times of day to see what works best. Grow your creative life 5 minutes at a time. And yes, you can stay longer if you choose.

Day 4
But, I Have No Space or Money

If we wait until we have the just-right space, or the just-right materials or equipment, or the just-right time in our life, we will never start. Start where you are and make it work!

Next to no time, not having enough physical space or enough money to buy materials are the excuses I hear the most. Often, we THINK we need more than we really need to create.

I need a studio to dance. How about dancing in the space you have? A year of door jamb or chair dances, or outdoor dances?

I need an art studio, an extra bedroom, or a garage to make visual art. Is that really true? Most of my visual art projects have used a small box, small fold up table, or a small wall.

I have no space or money for a piano or other instruments or equipment. Use a free electronic app for now, it can still help you build your practice, grow your *show-up muscle* and hone your skills. Tell your friends what you need, you may find something for free! That is how I got my piano.

I don't have a theater group I can meet with or a stage. Do monologues in front of your computer, camera, or mirror. Put out a call to find another actor to work with you when it is possible.

I don't have the right desk, table, computer, pen, paper. Writers just do it, they write.

Looking for everything to be perfect could be a way of putting off your dream or desire. It could be the voice of fear.

Think minimal to get yourself started. What can you do with what you have? Let this be part of your creative process.

Resource: When you feel the desire to have something better, make a wish list for the future. For now, make it work with what you have. Check out BuyNothingProject.org, or other resources like this, you could find what you need for free.

Day 5
Everything But...

So, you need to do laundry, walk the dog, clean the refrigerator, scrub the toilet, do the dishes...instead of your art? Or before you can do your art? Why is it suddenly all the things we hate to do are more inviting than taking time for ourselves?

When we make a commitment *to* ourselves to do something *for* ourselves, it is amazing what can come up to keep us from the doing. Procrastination can be a sign there is fear or overwhelm between you and your project.

It can be scary to take time for yourself, especially if you usually put everyone else first, think you might fail, or you are worried you won't know what to do, or...or...or...

I have found that structure can be helpful. Here are a few ideas to get you doing what you say you are going to do:

Put it on your calendar. Either your written calendar or your digital calendar. Set a time to show up. Set a reminder.

Bookend. Call a friend and tell them you will be working on your project for the next 5 minutes (or whatever time you decide) and you will check back with them when you are done.

Set your timer. You can start with 5 minutes and work your way to longer. During this time, you cannot get up and do anything but what you set out to do. Turn off the ringer on your phone. Tell your kids to not disturb you unless they need to call 911. When the timer goes off reset it for more time to keep working or you can call it a day. Make yourself the priority.

Resource: Figure out what is between you and doing your art. Finish the sentence, "If I take time to do my art...." Do you need someone's permission to show up? From who? Is it someone from your past? Or from yourself? Make art about whatever you discover. Then think of other resources and make a plan.

Day 6
Will I Forget?

As I write this, I am on day six of my 365 Days of Manikin project where I am taking a photo a day of my longtime friend—a wooden artist manikin. I have held onto Manikin since college as a constant reminder that someday I would become an artist. I tried the project once before and made it a few months, but then I kept forgetting so I abandoned it, or should I say abandoned him. Four years later my love of this project never left so I decided to try again. On day six and actually for the last three days, I have had the sudden, startling thought, "Oh no! I forgot!"

I hadn't actually forgotten, but the fear of forgetting has been at the surface. With styling and snapping the photos, they only take 5 minutes, so it can be easy for me to think I forgot. My resources to help me remember are reminder signs posted throughout my home, office, and car. And my friends—I ask them to ask me how it is going. On the evening of day ONE, as I was crawling into bed, my Sweetie asked if I had taken my Manikin photo. I hadn't! I jumped up and made it happen. I almost forgot to begin!

Reminders help. Set up reminders on your devices, put a sign in the bathroom where you brush your teeth, on your pillow to see before you crawl into bed, or in front of the coffee pot, so you will see it when you first get up in the morning. Ask a friend or family member to check in with you. In the beginning you may need help to strengthen your Creative Practice *show-up muscle*.

And, if you do forget, remember, you are making this up. You can treat the missed day however you want. Mostly, be gentle with yourself so you will keep going. No one wants to be creative under the rule of a tyrant!

Resource: Make a list of ways to remind yourself to show up. Do what is on the list!

Day 7
Creative Preparation

There are certain things I do to prepare myself for creative time. I think of it as transition time. Transitioning from my daily life to my Creative Practice time.

For me, to write, which is often in the daylight, I need a cup of coffee or tea—which somehow helps me feel more grown up. I also clear off the kitchen table of any paper piles to create the illusion that I am clutter free. I often have a healthy snack, like carrots, close by so I can crunch and think between sentences.

Visual art, which is regularly at night, is a little different. I usually change into my paint clothes or don my well-worn red paint apron, put on my paint speckled shoes, pull out my art table, and gather up my various journals or projects. I often have a plate filled with apple slices, cheese, and nuts nearby. Again, it helps me think.

Lately, I have begun to take some quiet time before I begin, a few minutes of meditation to clear myself internally. In this time, I sometimes get an idea of what to do next with my art.

What do you need to get started? Turn off the phone? Turn on music? Close the computer? Close the door and hang a do not disturb sign? Send the kids to a friend's house? Set a timer? Honor the uniqueness of what helps you show up and look at it as transition time.

Resource: Honor transitions. It can be hard to jump from one thing to another without a pause in between. What do you need to do to prepare before you get started? Make it simple so you will get to your art!

Day 8
Follow Your Next Impulse

*Follow your next impulse** is my golden rule for the creative process. We don't need to know where we are going or what we are doing, we just need to know the next step, the next impulse. When we sit in front of the blank canvas, what is the first impulse? When we get stuck or feel stalled, what is the first idea that comes? When we don't like what we have done, what aren't we liking? Be specific and listen for what needs to change.

Often people tell me they have no impulse, they don't know what to do. I wonder, is it we have no impulse, or maybe we don't yet know how to recognize the impulse, or we don't know what to do with the idea once we get it? We may think it is too weird, or hard, or doesn't make sense. We judge it as not good enough, or it is too subtle, too small, or unexpected.

The challenge becomes listening. Are we willing to listen? Are we willing to listen so closely we can hear that small quiet voice? The tiny next step, "Oh, I want to use orange." No impulse is too small, yet we might need to listen closely for the small prompt. As we build a history of following our impulses, we learn to trust ourselves more.

Resource: If you are not sure what to do next, close your eyes and sit quietly. Wait for an idea or impulse to come. If you still don't get something, get up and take a walk, dance, or do something physical. If you still don't have something, make art about the not knowing. Nothing then becomes something.

---

* *The impulse we follow does not want to harm self or others. It is a small voice for our greatest good and the greatest good of all. If you do get impulses wanting to hurt or harm, get professional support. Allow the attention and healing. (A valid impulse may be to tear up our work on the way to reconstructing it in a new way. If that is the case, I suggest you take a photo or make a copy first.)*

Day 9
It Has to Feel GOOD!

If what you are doing does not bring you pleasure, how can you get yourself to show up? Creating art should not be a punishment. Create a practice that fills you up, feeds and nourishes you. No one else can tell you what feels good. They may be able to tell you what they like aesthetically, but you need to follow what feels good for YOU to create.

Make art for you, not for anyone else. Make art that is satisfying, so you will look forward to showing up. You may need to experiment and try lots of different things to find your way to pleasure. And, you may need to make changes along the way so it will continue to feel good. If you find yourself avoiding your creative time, look at what may need to change. It could be a small adjustment that stands between you and enjoying your process.

Think pleasure! Follow pleasure, what feels good! Have pleasure be your goal! Don't give up until you find what works for you. And know, sometimes solving creative challenges like this can be pleasurable!

Resource: Are there any changes you need to make in your project to make it more pleasurable? Look at your process and your attitude. Give yourself creative compassion as you get started and find your way to what feels good. If you are feeling pleasure as you play, notice what you are doing that feels good so you can call on it in the future if needed. And, celebrate the sensation of pleasure.*

---

* *When following pleasure we are following that which is for our greatest good and the greatest good of all. If you get pleasure from hurting or harming yourself or others, or if you have been taught that pleasure is a bad thing get therapeutic support. Allow the attention and healing, you do not need to do this alone.*

Day 10

Emotional Intelligence for Artists

Emotional intelligence is defined as "skill in perceiving, understanding, and managing emotions and feelings." (Dictionary.com) Through art making we can come up against our critical voice, disappointment, fear of success, fear of failure, joy and excitement to be creating, and other subtle and strong emotions. As we learn to stay with our feelings and stay with our art, we can grow our emotional intelligence.

Years ago when I took painting classes, I would get overwhelmed because I didn't know how to handle my feelings of incompetence—I would leave the class after one or two times and never return. This repeated, with the same results each time. I wondered, "Don't the teachers know how stressful it is to make art?"

When I took African drumming and dance classes, I had never moved my body in such a free way or created sound so compelling and emotional. I would tell the teachers, Paulo and Charmain, "We should have therapy afterwards." I was having so many feelings of vulnerability. We did go out to eat as a group after class, which was like therapy. I was able to stay with this class because the bonds I created with the teachers and other students helped me feel safe. Had this not happened, I am sure I would have run.

When I was introduced to Expressive Arts Therapy, I finally felt affirmed for all my feelings and learned it was natural.

Let us grow our emotional artist intelligence so we can meet the big feelings and stay with them, express them in our art, rather than abandoning our art or under-expressing.

Resource: If you feel a wall going up, the "I want to quit" message, check in to see what is happening emotionally. Can you stay with the emotions, express them or ask for help?

⇨ *If traumatic memories or sensations arise, be sure to get therapeutic help.*

Day 11
Track Your Progress

You may want to track the progress of your Creative Practice. You could mark off the days on a calendar when you show up. You could include a brief sentence about what you did. Or a journal entry in a notebook. Looking back on a log can be satisfying.

In the case of visual art or writing, you have the actual piece that can be dated. Remember to date them! I forget often and am always disappointed when I look back and don't know when I did something.

For dance, music, drama, ongoing visual or writing projects, a log can be fun to look back on to see how many days you showed up and what happened.

When I began my ongoing painting practice, my commitment was one stroke of paint a day. (I don't think I ever did just put one stroke of paint; art is too seductive.) I would take a photo each day to track my progress.

In the beginning, I also kept a journal with thoughts from the day as I painted. I did not log in every day, and soon found it too overwhelming and let that part go. Dating the front or back of my art with a few words I was inspired to write, what I would call the "Title" for that day, was doable. I do love looking back and reading what I wrote so I can remember where I was when I did the art.

Resource: Find what works for you. Here are a few ideas.

- Date your work.
- Keep a log with the date and a one-sentence summary.
- Keep a journal with an entry of how it was to show up.
- Take a photo every day showing your progress.
- Do a video or audio check in.
- Mark a calendar when you show with a brief summary. Or…

Day 12

Set the Timer for 5 Minutes

Five minutes. Set the timer for 5 minutes to see what can be done with a 5-minute contribution to your creative expression. The idea is that you can take longer than 5 minutes if you want. And, if all you can do for the day is 5 minutes, you have been successful. I encourage you to set a time so you can get a clearer idea of 5 minutes.

Another option is to create a piece *in only 5 minutes.* To have a finished piece in 5 minutes. This can make the challenge a little different.

You could also attach the 5 minutes to another activity. Sing while you do the dishes, dance while you cook dinner, do a little improv in front of the mirror while you get ready in the morning, or doodle while you are returning phone calls.

Sometimes the possibilities can unlock and start pouring forward when we set a small timeframe. It can help us steer clear of perfectionism. Being able to say, I only had 5 minutes or I did this in only 5 minutes can be liberating.

Well, my timer just went off, this was my 5 minutes. And look, in just 5 minutes I got my muse aroused and happy. Granted, I will take more time to go back and correct the many spelling and grammar mistakes as well as edit content. But I did do it!

Now it is your turn, go forth and spill something from your creative brain *for 5* or *in 5* minutes. You might be surprised what can happen. You could also do multiple 5 minutes throughout your day. Yes, 5 minutes can turn into 5 hours, just be careful you don't overdo it, we want you to come back tomorrow!

Resource: Find a timer, set it for 5 minutes. Ready, set, go!

Day 13
Creative Practice as Relationship

I hope you will think of your Creative Practice as a relationship. Let your practice be your lover, your child, or your friend. Like all relationships they take time to grow. We meet, and we spend time together. Like all relationships, if we don't give it our attention, it will not survive.

Relationships evolve and change. They go through cycles and phases. Sometimes we feel closer, sometimes more distant. We may experience love, hate, complacency, irritation, excitement, disappointment, anger, stagnation, growth, comfort, soul connection, and breakups. All these can be present in your relationship with your Creative Practice.

You are partners—you and your art. So, let's look at some stages your relationship with your Creative Practice might go through.

Attraction. Before any relationship can begin there has to be an initial attraction. The attraction of you to your art form or your project. What brought you together? When did you first meet or see each other? What is the hope this relationship will fulfill in you? Remembering why you came together could help in times of trouble.

Eros. This is the fun stage, when our excitement is high, we have been struck by the arrow and we are in love! The eros phase helps assure we will keep coming back. Art making, just like lovemaking, can increase the brain's production of dopamine, oxytocin, and endorphins, increasing pleasure and decreasing pain. Pleasure can also be a little scary—are we allowed to feel this good?

Reality sets in. You go out on a first date and there are fireworks. The second, third, fourth, all good. You date for a few months and things start getting rocky, you start to question what you have gotten yourself into. You may wonder if eros has worn off and you start noticing everything that bugs you. You might even question if you are good enough for this relationship or notice it is a mismatch.

Staying connected. To grow a relationship, we must stay connected and deepen our connection. We notice what is working and not working and talk about it. Are we paying enough attention to each other? Is the relationship feeding us? We stay curious, ask questions, we listen and make adjustments, we experiment and find what helps us go deeper. We have the harder conversations with ourselves and our art.

Commitment. Eventually our relationships want commitment. This is when we see how willing we are to move forward. Do we want to be with our art every day? Just on the weekends? Long term or short term? Are we going to remain friends or become lovers? Or even, sadly, break up? Can we renegotiate the relationship?

If we can think of our Creative Practice as a relationship, it can help us to navigate the ups and downs easier and help us feel more connected to the process of making art and why we need each other. I am not just doing art, I am being there for and with myself. I acknowledge this is an essential relationship in my life.

Resource: Create a love story for yourself. Think about when you and your art met, what attracted you? What is your hope for this relationship? If your connection doesn't seem deep enough, revisit your intention for starting your Creative Practice, can you take your original intention deeper?

Day 14
I Don't Have Talent

I don't have talent. I am not an artist. I am not creative. These are probably the statements I hear most from people. The first thing I wonder is, how much have you trained, practiced, or played in the arts? We understand we need to learn math, science, or finance, but we think we should KNOW how to make art without learning.

I get it. I had a vision of being a painter. I even took a few classes that I did not like at all because I was faced with my not knowing. Mostly though I was waiting for the art gods to tap me on the head and make me an artist. Instead, I took on a *365 Days of Art* commitment and an amazing thing happened, I began to feel like an artist. I do art—I feel like an artist. What a concept!

In his book *Outliers,* Malcolm Gladwell suggests 10,000 hours of practice could turn you into an expert. If you practiced your creative discipline 8 hours a day, 5 days a week, 52 weeks a year, you could reach mastery in about five years. Or, with your Creative Practice, you can take the rest of your life to learn and grow creatively. You don't have to rush, you get to wander and explore forever. Remind yourself you are improving by doing.

A Creative Practice is just that—practicing every day. You *will* get better, more comfortable, and more confident. If you quit, you will never get to these good feelings. So, keep going! Right now what is most important is to build your *show-up muscle*.

Resource: If you are unhappy with what you are creating, see if you can find joy in the process, in showing up. Play can be a great way to improve your craft. Play has no rules or destination. Play follows what feels good, follows the next idea or impulse, it is *in the moment exploration*. If you want to learn techniques, watch videos, or take classes. Just keep showing up!

Day 15
Trust the Process

The slogan, "trust the process" has been around for a long time. It is used in recovery programs. It is the name of a book on art making by Shaun McNiff. It is a way of life.

What does it mean when we trust the process in our art making? So many times I have heard, "Oh, I screwed it up" when a *mistake* is made. In the arts, *mistakes* can lead to the best outcomes because they get us thinking outside the box.

I am painting and I accidentally drip paint on my piece but don't see it before it dries. If I trust the process, I see it as a surprise arrival and get to decide what to do with it. Rather than cover it up, maybe I let it inspire me. Do I add more drips? Do I turn it into a tear? Rain? Do I add drippy texture to the background?

The painting does not turn out as planned and it becomes a piece more unique than I may have imagined. The challenge gets me out of my normal routine and asks me to try something new. This holds true for all the arts. I am not a trained pianist, but I love to plunk around and improvise. Instead of giving up, because I couldn't play well, I followed my love for the piano to where it wanted to take me, improvisational play.

Had I not trusted the process I might have torn up my painting or never played the piano again. Trust your longing. Trust the impulses that arise. Trust the *mistakes.* Follow the surprise turns your creating provides. Your best work could come from your *mistakes* or those unexpected left or right turns.

Resource: When things don't turn out the way you want or a *mistake* happens, make a list of at least three new turns you could take. "Trust the process" often means staying out of the results. Remember, you have the rest of your life to grow your creative self. Following the unexpected turns may be growth.

Day 16
I Am Not Allowed to Fail

An important teacher in my life, Lael Greenleaf, talked about the importance of letting children learn for themselves what works and doesn't work. She gave an example of a child wanting to take their bike to the beach. Parents know you can't ride a bike in the sand, so they say no. Her idea was to let the child take the bike to the beach and learn for themselves.

When my son was six and having challenges adjusting to a new school, I suggested we go to the beach before school—lo and behold, he asked to bring his bike! "Yes!" I responded. It was a dream come true; I was going to be able to witness this experiment in action.

The spot we were headed for had a cement sidewalk running the length of the beach near the parking lot and he did ride there. Soon he was racing off the edge of the sidewalk, getting some height and then planting his bike in the sand. He then dragged his bike down to the water, where the sand is hard from the waves washing up and began riding back and forth on the hard sand! He beamed with delight as he sprayed seawater behind him.

Is our aversion to making mistakes in our art, failing or making something ugly, because we haven't had enough opportunities to fail and problem solve? Experimenting is an essential part of the creative process. Having things work and not work is part of learning and finding new ideas. When you are feeling afraid or stuck, ask yourself what am I afraid of? What needs to happen so I can play and experiment and make mistakes?

Resource: Look at your history of play and experimenting. Were you allowed to figure things out on your own or make mistakes? Let your Creative Practice be a place to experiment.

Day 17
It Doesn't Have to Be Perfect

"Perfection is the voice of the oppressor, the enemy of the people. It will keep you cramped and insane your whole life, and it is the main obstacle between you and a shitty first draft."
—Anne Lamott, *Bird by Bird*

The joy of a Creative Practice is knowing you will be growing a body of work, and you will be learning along the way. You do not start as an expert. You acquire expertise as you put in the time. Understanding this can release you from the pressure to make great art every day.

I have noticed when we only make art once in a while, we have this desire to create something amazing. When we show up every day, or regularly, we have the freedom to make art we don't love because we know we are going to show up again tomorrow and keep growing.

As I mentioned in my introduction, at the end of my first *365 Days of Art* project when I laid all the pieces out, I realized the real art was the entire body of work together. Each individual piece was mediocre at best from my viewpoint. But as a grouping, it made a statement! It also prepared me for year two where I did ask more of myself aesthetically. I was ready, because my daily art muscle was strong, and I knew I would show up. Now I could focus on acquiring new skills.

The message is to show up, wherever you are in your learning process, and to put in the time to grow your artist self.

Resource: If your critical voice comes up, remind yourself you are at the beginning of your journey. You have the rest of the year—and the rest of your life—to learn and get better.

Day 18
It Is Okay to Test the Waters

It is okay to test the waters—to try something new and not know how it is going to turn out. It is also okay to try something, dislike it, and decide to do something else.

You are in charge of your process. You are the captain of your Creative Practice boat. It does not have to be hard. If it is hard, you may not keep going for a whole year or however long you intend to practice. As the song says, "Row, row, row your boat gently down the stream."

It can be easy—make it easy. Especially in the beginning. It can be hard enough to remember to show up. If you feel stressed by what you need to do when you show up, you may stop.

After you are rowing your creative boat gently down the stream, and are creating regularly, you could add more challenge into your project. It is good to have a plan that excites you, but not one that is too stressful or too hard.

Finding the place between interesting enough to show up and simple enough to show up may take some experimenting. In my first year of daily art, I had wanted to paint because it had been my dream. I soon realized it was too stressful to paint and I would never make it a whole year. I changed to oil pastels and that worked. I still got vibrant colors, and I could blend them to look paint-like. It was interesting enough and simple enough. Allow yourself to experiment!

Resource: Notice if anything is feeling either too overwhelming or too boring and what adjustments you can make to get you more excited about showing up. You can even keep a list of "future ideas" for your Creative Practice. You don't have to do them right away, and you won't lose track of them either.

Day 19
Devotion Versus Discipline

While listening to a podcast interview with Eric Maisel, creativity coach and prolific author, I first heard the idea of devotion versus discipline. I had never thought about it, yet he was voicing what I experienced in my own practice. Just seeing the words written here offers two different feeling senses to me.

Discipline feels like a have to, a grin and bear it, you better or else task. While "Devotion" feels like an act of love, a blessing, even a spiritual practice. Looking the words up I find these definitions:

Discipline: Set of rules or regulations, strong tie to military. I must be disciplined and show up every day for my art.

Devotion: Profound dedication. I have a deep devotion to my desire to make art and want to show up.

If I am devoted to my desire to make art, I want to show up because it is meaningful. This is my hope for you, your relationship with your art will be meaningful. And if it is not, continue to show up to figure out what needs to change, so it can be a positive, loving experience.

Please, don't ever use your Creative Practice to beat yourself up. *Oh, I didn't show up, I am so undisciplined,* subtext, *I am a bad person.* If it is not working, it only means you haven't found your personal way in. If your Creative Practice feels like a ball and chain around your heart, revisit why you are doing it. Are you trying to prove something to someone else, or is it a devotion to yourself? What if your time could be a profound dedication to yourself through art? What would help you step into this gift?

Resource: If your Creative Practice isn't nourishing you, what needs to change so it is not a task needing to be done but an act of love you get to do?

Day 20
But Doesn't It Take Discipline, Too?

People say I must have great discipline to show up every day to make art. Like I have some supernatural power. I tell them it is the same power they have to brush their teeth every night or make coffee every morning. It is part of the fabric of my life.

Prior to my first daily art project, I needed external deadlines. I often waited until the last minute. Back then I enjoyed the adrenaline rush from a deadline.

What was different with showing up to my Creative Practice? First, on a pure brain level, it is easier for me to show up every day than to show up once or twice a week. I forget when it is a now and again thing, doing something daily makes it easier for me, not harder. I did need to grow my *show-up muscle*, which took about three months.

Secondly, I was in touch with the heart, spirit, or soul reason I was doing my project. It was a devotion to my mother who had never fulfilled her dream of becoming an artist, and to myself, wanting to feel like an artist. This was an irresistible invitation to keep going. Or was I fear driven? Did I too fear I could die without realizing my artist dream?

Maybe the discipline was to set up an easy system, gather supplies, set reminders, and ask for people to help me. The discipline was the investment in myself to help me succeed.

I want to give you permission to be kind to yourself, not demanding. Use the idea that feels right for you—discipline, commitment, devotion, promise, prayer, or vow. Cultivate self-love by showing up. If you don't show, don't discipline yourself, devote yourself to finding what works.

Resource: Be kind to yourself with just the right amount of *keep going* push and encouragement. Follow what works for you.

Day 21
The Power of Nothing

I sit to write and today there is nothing. No idea, no motivation, no desire. What now?

Start where you are. Start with the feeling of nothing being there. Start with the first words that come to you: "Tonight there is no art..." Or the worry: "I am screwing this up now..." Or the reality: "My mind is blank..." Or the body sensation: "I feel lethargic, heavy, unwilling to move..."

The truth *is* a starting place. Today there is nothing for me and I write to you about there being nothing and how to get through. I started, I stated what is, and now something is happening. In the arts, nothing *is* something. The dance of nothing may be imperceptible to some, but to you, the dance of nothing can be cathartic.

The key is to *believe* nothing is something. Nothing is the beginning, not the end. Nothing places something in motion when we *show up* and acknowledge it. Nothing is not a measure of our commitment or talent, but a temporary state.

Just as the earth needs to go fallow to regenerate, changing up your art may be a way to step away. If my commitment is to paint, maybe I write today, and maybe the writing is on canvas or maybe it will be added to my canvas on another day. I have no dance in my body today, but maybe I dance a pen on paper. I have no monologue for my video blog today so maybe I sit silently in front of the camera and record stillness and silence.

Never doubt the power of nothing. Sometimes it holds a gift in its expression. Embracing and relaxing into nothing becomes something. You never know where our showing up will lead.

Resource: Rather than getting stressed when you show up to nothing, name it, relax into it, and see where it takes you.

Day 22

Oh, No! I Forgot to Show Up

In my first year of daily art, I forgot to show up less than 30 days into my 365 day commitment. It was Thanksgiving, I had an artful day with family and friends, but I forgot to do my specified daily project before I went to bed. The very moment I woke up in the morning, I remembered. I was so angry with myself, knowing I couldn't take it back, and I was so committed to showing up every day. I reminded myself the reason I wanted to do this project was to "not let a day go by where the world, and I, didn't know I wanted to be an artist." And it was still true. Missing a day helped me commit even more. I could have given up because I was unhappy with myself, but that would not be congruent with my mission.

I chose to keep going and I did make up the missed day right then when I remembered. I realized I am in charge and could make the rules. The idea is not to be superhuman. We get sick, we have obligations, and we do the best we can. The idea is to be committed to our creative life.

Forgiveness helps us keep going. It also gives us space to look at why we missed and problem solve. I missed because I had a really full day and when I got home, I was tired. What could I do to make sure I remembered to do my art before I went to sleep, especially when I was tired? I decided to make a little sign to put on my pillow when I made my bed in the morning, so I would see it when going to bed at night. Be creative with your reminders, until your daily art muscle is strong. Remember, the idea is to create a practice, not a life-or-death sentence.

Resource: When you stumble, think of what you want to do with the stumble, and keep going! What kind of reminders can you set up to increase your chances of remembering and showing up?

Day 23
The Blahs

Sometimes the creative energy is just not there. Maybe you didn't get enough sleep, or you have big things going on in your life and the overwhelm is turning you into a couch potato. Having an ongoing project can help. You could define ahead of time what is the least you can do that will still be a step forward. For example, one stroke of paint on the canvas, or play one song on the guitar, or write one sentence, or glue down one collage piece, or sing one song, or dance while you brush your teeth.

Having a way to show up and be successful even when you don't want to show up makes the verb of artist easier. Granted, you still need to show up, but showing up is easier if you don't have to think about what to do. Preplanning for the days when your creative energy is low can be helpful. "I need to set the timer for 5 minutes and start scribbling."

I have found even when I am having a blah day, if I can get myself to show up, I can do something of small significance. I showed up, I did something. Often, I feel better after I show up and when my art doesn't kick away the blahs, it can be cathartic to have an expression of them.

If you have these days more often than not, maybe it is time to make some changes in your project or in your life. Is the project the right fit for you right now? What adjustments can you make? Or does your life need adjustments? Get help for your mental or physical health? Make changes with your work, home, or relationship? Our Creative Practice can be an indicator for our life.

Resource: Plan ahead for the blah days, what is the least you will feel okay doing on your project? If every day is a blah day, look at what needs to change.

Day 24
Finding Our Truth

Our Creative Practice offers us the opportunity to explore the truth of who we are. We set down the mask we may have put on in childhood or currently put on for our work or our grown-up life—and express freely. Each day we have our 5 minutes, one hour, or however long we take for ourselves, to not care what the world wants from us and to uncover more of ourselves through creative expression. We get to be with ourselves with no expectations, no strings attached, no goals except to show up and keep going.

Our art invites us to play like we are children, to explore outside the box, to surprise ourselves, and even express what seems inexpressible.

With each day we get to know ourselves better, more intimately. We watch ourselves prepare, problem solve and create. Our creation is evidence of our time spent. Take notice of who you are today, your future self may not recognize you.

Resource: Take a moment and create a portrait of yourself, in your art form or through a selfie. Write about how you see yourself now. Who are you today as a creative? What are your challenge areas? Where do you hope to grow? Put this somewhere so you can look back on it at the end of our year together to see if anything changes.

Day 25
Saying Thank You

Have you thanked your art for what it brings to your life? Have you thanked yourself for showing up? Have you thanked whatever you believe is the source of your creativity? Have you thanked your world that enables you to show up and be creative?

It is a gift to have a Creative Practice. In many places in the world where there is so much suffering, creativity needs to be used for getting through the day—surviving. The fact that we can take 5 minutes, an hour or however long we take to be creative, is a privilege to appreciate.

Honoring this privilege may create an extra motivation to show up. I remember the moment in my first year of 365 Days of Art when I transitioned from *"Oh no, I still HAVE to do my art..."* to a new realization and new attitude, *"Oh, yeah! I GET to do my art."* And the excitement that was created as I shifted from it being a burden or something I almost forgot, to being a gift I could open each day when I showed up.

Resource: Explore what you have to be thankful for that enables you to have a Creative Practice. Maybe you want to create a ritual of appreciation, say a little thank you each time you show up, to begin or end your time.

Day 26
Come Together for Support

I have discovered three truths in my years of daily art.

One. Building the *show-up muscle* can be challenging. When we feel accountable to someone else, we are more likely to show up. We also have the opportunity to support each other with reminders and problem solve challenges.

Two. Making art can be a solitary process—an internal process. Having others to share our experience can help us feel connected to something greater outside of us. It can help us feel more like we are making art in an atelier, in community, offering us the inspiration of others.

Three. Having support can help our practice feel more alive. Sharing our art and our process we get encouragement, feedback, and our art lives outside of our small bubble and begins to have a life of its own, even inspiring others!

When we have a supportive community we inspire each other, learn from each other, and together we find solutions to common challenges. Maybe most importantly, we no longer feel alone. The act of creating can be a lonely sport, community helps.

Resource: Begin to build a community of creatives. Find others who want to create a Creative Practice or are creative in their life. Come together to support each other. We live in a world where it is so easy to find community. Send a message to friends, post a challenge on social media, create a private group to share your processes. Turn to the back of this book in *Follow-Up Resources* where I give you ideas to create an ongoing support group.

Day 27
I Want to Give Up

I recently found myself thinking, "What am I doing? There is no way I can figure all this out." I wanted to give up. I wanted to quit. Interestingly, I started out very motivated and excited. The motivation and excitement helped me make progress. But then I shut down and went to doom and gloom.

Having done my own Creative Practice long enough I was able to see what was happening and catch myself. I realized it was time to stop. I had done enough for the day.

If we understand that wanting to give up is often a sign of overwhelm or fear, usually because we can't see the next step or the step we are trying to take is too big, then we can see it as a sign that something needs to change—not to give up. We can ask ourselves what the smallest thing we can do that would still be making progress. Remember, adding one more note to your song/score, or one more brushstroke to your painting or one more sentence to your book IS making progress. Allowing a small step to be enough may help you keep moving forward.

If we let ourselves look at the big picture, we can quickly feel overwhelmed. Part of our creative process is to rein our thoughts back to seeing what small next step we can take, which could be as simple as congratulating ourselves on the step just taken and being done for the day. This is what I did.

The next day when I woke, I was able to see the tiny next thing to do. I was back in the process. (Writing this right now!)

Resource: When you are feeling overwhelmed step back to notice what just happened. Are you tired or hungry? Did you do enough for the day? Are you unsure of the next step? Did you do something you didn't like and now you don't know how to fix it? Write down a small next step that will still make progress.

Day 28
I Don't Know What to Do!

Not knowing what to do can be a huge obstacle, or so we think. Sometimes we put the not knowing up like a roadblock. The question becomes, do we not know what to do, or is it an excuse to not get started?

There is safety in saying "I don't know" and in not doing. If we don't begin, we may critique ourselves for not doing anything. Yet if we start, we may realize we don't like what we are doing or even scarier, decide we are no good at it or talentless. We can turn it onto ourselves with an even stronger critique. Fear of failure may live underneath not knowing what to do.

We are here to learn a different way of being in the world. Not judging or critiquing ourselves but being supportive and compassionate. Focusing on our process, not the end result.

How about getting started with the first impulse we have? For example, you want to do photography. Don't wait to get a nicer camera or better software. Don't wait until you have the perfect idea. Simply go take a photo, with your phone, your tablet, your old camera. Take a photo of the first thing that attracts your attention. Do this for a few days or a year. You then get the idea to photograph people in the act of daily living. Next you realize you want to take a bigger risk and photograph those impacted by homelessness in your neighborhood and learn their stories. And so on and so on. This process could take a lifetime.

If we GET STARTED with SOMETHING, the next something will show itself. The starting point is just this, a starting point. You have the rest of your life to grow your craft, grow your confidence, and develop your artist self.

Resource: Do something. Do anything. It does not need to be the perfect project, just a starting point.

Day 29
Is It Magic?

Over all my years of having a Creative Practice, it has been proven to me over and over—if I am feeling depleted, too tired to do art and I do it, I am reenergized. My apathy lifts, I feel grateful. After experiencing this often enough, I began to trust it. Show up, it will help.

Maybe it is magic. Or maybe it is my soul saying thank you for taking the time to express. Maybe it is physics or math, *"Life + art = a better life."*

When at my worst, I think this time it probably won't work, and lo and behold, it works.

I admit, sometimes I even get mad because I want to wallow, I don't want to feel better. I do my art and darn it, I feel better. Once I am on the other side, I do not want to go back to my wallowing state. I am grateful.

Recently at my studio we had an inspiring show by artist Luz Clayton who had been dealing with depression. Medication was not working. In a moment of clarity, she turned to art. Art was the medicine that worked for her. She began creating on her phone, because she had her phone with her at all times. Working digitally gave her immediate results. Art helped.

Stay with it. Let the magic of creative expression work in your life. It probably won't hurt and it could help.

Resource: Practice showing up even when you are too tired or feeling too lousy to show up. See what happens. Take notes. Be curious. If you can't do a lot, do a little. It may or may not be actual magic, but it certainly can be magical.

⇨ *If you have challenges with depression, get therapeutic help. You do not have to navigate it alone. Medication may help and it can be accompanied by art.*

You made it to day 30,
celebrate, it is a big deal!
And, keep going.

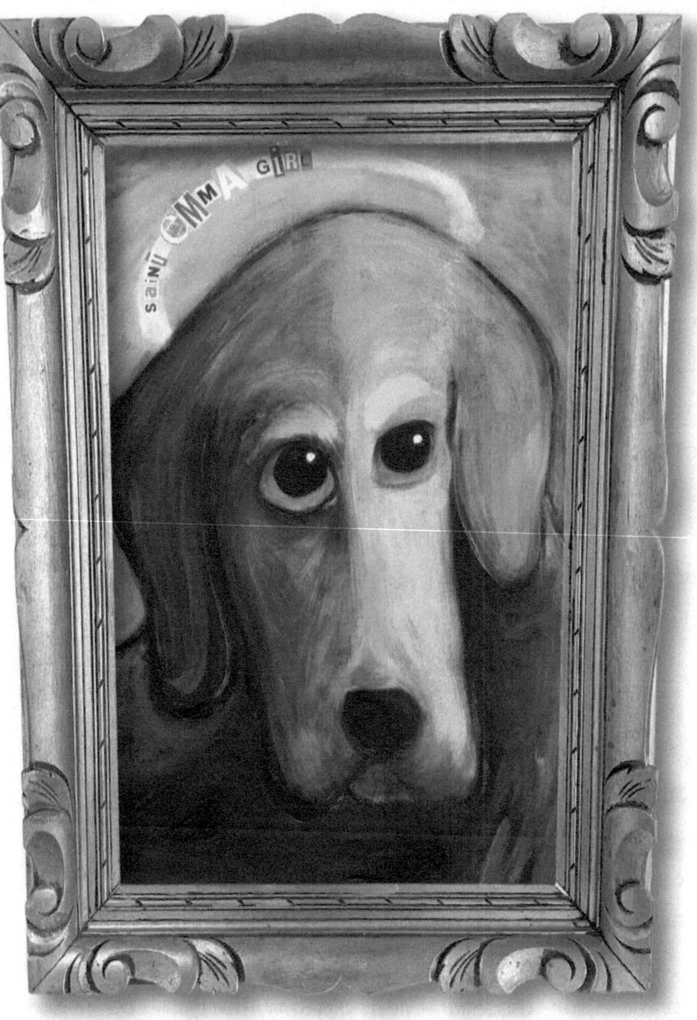

365 Days of Blind Contour Paintings

As my confidence grew in painting I created a portrait of a friend's dog, Emma, who was dying. This opened the door for quirky blind contour pet portrait commissions and selling my work. After a few years, I decided I wanted to make art for myself, not as a business.

Day 30
Celebrate Thirty Days!

Thirty days is a big deal. It means you started and stayed with some kind of Creative Practice. A big shout out to you! You are beginning to create a habit that could stay with you for a lifetime. Thirty days can be the point where you are remembering to show up more easily. Your *show-up muscle* is getting stronger. You know what you need to do. You did it!

Thirty days is a point where you can begin to see a small body of work being created. You have something to show for showing up. Check out what you did!

Thirty days can also be a slippery moment where you may want to stop. It can be inviting to think, "I made it thirty days, that's enough." And before you know it, it is a memory.

In case you have any ideas like that, I am here today to tell you to keep going. You have not even begun to experience the great feelings ahead. Let this become a lifelong habit, not a short-term test or challenge. Artist is a verb. Keep creating.

Let your Creative Practice be with you in sickness and in health, to keep your cup full. Let it be with you as the world changes around you, your constant dependable companion. Let it be with you to express the challenges life brings you or be a vacation from those challenges. Allow it to help you grow your creative confidence, grow your skill level, and remind you that creative expression is your birthright as a human. It is one thing that separates us from other mammals and living creatures. Keep making things special!

Resource: Celebrate you have gotten to day thirty! If you have thoughts of giving up—what needs to change so you will keep going? Make adjustments and recommit for thirty more.

Day 31
I Am Overwhelmed

The overwhelm of life and my to-do list can often send me the message *I do NOT have time for art making.* This is the exact thought I had just before I sat down to write today. Forcing myself to take 5 minutes to write before I start my day, I sat down and began. Listening to my own counsel, I started where I was, and thus this entry began. As soon as I typed out the first sentence, I could feel my overwhelm begin to fade, my body begin to relax, and I took a deep breath. Whether it is writing or painting, for me, if I start where I am, the process is helpful because I have given voice to what is happening: I am overwhelmed.

So, I sit and I write, for 5 minutes.

The message *there is not enough room in my day for ME,* can run me into the ground. Time to feed my creative spirit is time building my reserves and helping me stay balanced. Physical exercise feeds my body, creative exercise feeds my spirit. Not only does showing up—no matter what—keep the artistic process and project going, it also keeps *me* going. I feel better now than I did when I began.

When we are overwhelmed is when we *need* art the most.

Epilogue: I wrote for 5 plus minutes and then walked, made my breakfast and wrote some more. I started my day with *me,* feeding my body and spirit. Now I am ready to start my workday.

Epilogue 2: I ended up getting everything that really needed attention, done. This evening I had a thought, *"Wow, I love my life!"* It all began with a 5-minute commitment.

Resource: Create a way to make small art so you can do it anywhere, in any amount of time. Have art available wherever and whenever you need it to help you through overwhelm, stress, and other difficult moments.

Day 32
You Are Going to Get Better

Whatever it is you are committed to doing, if you keep showing up, you will get better at it, just from showing up each day. When your art becomes a practice, and you keep at it, you will increase your skill level. The more you write, sing, draw, play, or express, the easier it will become, and chances are, you will improve.

The word *practice* has different meanings. Most notably in athletics, we practice regularly to get ready for the big game, we are training because we want to be prepared. Musicians practice to learn new material. The same can go for all art forms. The more we practice, the more we work with our craft, the better we get at what we are doing.

Practice can also be a (daily) commitment to something for the betterment of ourselves. We create a meditation practice or a yoga practice, meaning we will show up regularly. And, if we show up every day, not even intending to improve or do things more challenging, we will grow because our *show-up muscle* is stronger and things get easier.

Whether we become an expert or not, by having a Creative Practice we get the benefits of expressing ourselves and the opportunity to advance our skills.

So keep going and know by showing up, you are getting better at whatever you are doing!

Resource: Think about what having a Creative Practice means for you. Why are you doing this? To get better? To show up regularly? To express? To relax? Knowing your expectations of yourself is helpful. Journal or make art about this.

Day 33
Last Minute Art Is Still Art

"Last minute art is still art. A few minutes before sleep is still a few minutes. I showed up, even for a moment. I may not love what I did, it may not be award-winning or even good. But it is one more day of exercising my muscle of showing up. I am grateful I did what I did." —Tish, *Year One Journal*

The above was my art one night. And, in reading it now, it doesn't feel like nonsense or a waste of 5 minutes. It actually leads to something of substance. Allowing ourselves to move slowly on a project, to do it imperfectly, to do what we can, not what we think we should, is growing our artist self.

Create a culture of affirming your efforts. Give yourself credit for showing up, even when it is for just a moment. Build on the moments.

If your critic voice comes up take notice. Whose voice is it? Is it someone who taught you it wasn't okay to go slow or work at your natural speed? Maybe they expected huge accomplishments from you and huge steps were all that counted. Only home runs were acknowledged, not walks or base hits.

And, if you notice last minute art is becoming your normal, check in to see if it is okay with you. Is it satisfying your desire to create? If it is not feeling satisfying, look at what may need to change to have a more pleasurable experience.

Resource: Practice gratitude for showing up, however that looks. And if you need it, how can you offer yourself gentle pressure to grow your practice? You can bring any explorations about your Creative Practice to your Creative Practice. The arts help us process things in a different way than thinking.

Day 34

How We Use Our Time

Time is an elusive thing. It is manufactured by humans. Though nature has seasons and cycles, the advent of schedules and time-pieces (clocks and watches) being synchronized started with the arrival of the train. The Industrial Revolution had us working in shifts, meeting quotas and moving further away from the natural rhythms of nature. As technology increases, it seems our schedules become more and more filled. We fit more into our day. More emails, text messages, phone calls, and binge watching. We can get from here to there faster, so our to-do list grows.

Why is it so hard to take time for ourselves, for the things that feed us, nourish our spirits and give us pleasure? Is pleasure overwhelming for us? Have we been taught to feel guilty about taking time to do things that make us feel good?

Do you put everyone and everything else ahead of your own desires, so you have no time for yourself?

The gift of beginning with a 5-minute-a-day commitment is 5 minutes *can* be guilt free. 5 minutes *can* be a sign of putting yourself first. 5 minutes *is* enough time to do something, and 5 minutes *is not* too overwhelming.

This week I sat outside to write for 5 minutes, which turned into more. It was pure pleasure. Even in the city, I was surrounded by nature, crows fighting, squirrels chattering, songbirds, and the sweet sound of my fingers typing. I claimed my time.

Let time work for you, rather than against you. As my mother used to say, "You don't find the time, you make the time."

Resource: Set your alarm for a time of the day to take your 5 minutes. Show up, walk through any feelings like guilt or overwhelm in taking time for yourself or feeling pleasure. Pat yourself on the back for putting yourself in your schedule.

Day 35
Am I Lazy?

Why am I not doing my art? Am I lazy? Unmotivated? A slacker? A sloth? A loser? A failure?

No! Here is my thinking on creating (and life). If it is not working, you have not found the just-right fit. Something is not right. If you beat yourself up, it could mean you care. You have a longing to be creative, yet something is not working. Maybe you don't have enough information, the parameters of your practice or your project are not right. The time of day is not right, the materials are not a good fit. Something is off. Beating yourself up is probably not helpful, but an exploration could be.

My first year of 365 Days of Art I did one week of found object art. I loved this week so much I wanted to do a whole year of found objects. It took me three years of not doing it to finally figure out what was off. When I realized what needed to change, the project ran full speed for a whole year with no regrets. The shift? A little voice said, "Go smaller." I took it from an 8.5" x 11" piece each day to a small 4" x 6" piece every day.

Could this realization have come a moment sooner? Maybe, if I had thought to brainstorm reasons why I wasn't getting started, or had just gotten started to test it out for a while longer. New information can come in the doing, rather than in the thinking. (I did do daily painting while I was waiting for this realization.)

When the idea is there, and it is not picking up speed, don't get down on yourself, be curious, look for what needs to change.

Resource: Finding the just-right fit is important, and you can only find it by testing it out, by doing. Brainstorm with yourself or a friend about what might need to change so you can get traction. Continue to brainstorm after each adjustment if it is still not working. Journal and make art about being separate from your desire.

Day 36

Letting Ideas Evolve and Change

Maybe you have experienced having an idea and struggling to make it fit your expectation. You try to make it work, almost using force, but it doesn't want to comply. Imagine being in relationship with someone who wants to force you to be who they want you to be. This usually does not turn out well.

The same goes with our art. When we use force, we are not in relationship. If our desire is to be in relationship, we must be good listeners, good observers, and good at going with the flow, going with our art. The creative process asks us to trip over surprises and wrestle with our ideas. The creative process does not celebrate sameness and detailed instructions; it dances with unplanned detours and surprise guests.

The difference is being in the process of art making rather than focused on the end result. Following our next impulse, not forcing the next idea. The relationship with our art can be exciting, maddening, confusing or...(name an emotion). The more we allow the process to get messy and playful, the more we talk to our art and listen to what our art says, the better we will get at being in the creative process.

You might also look at the rest of your life. Are you feeling out of control anywhere? Could your desire to control your art be a by-product of feeling out of control somewhere else in your life? If this is the case, it is another great reason to get messy and playful. Let your creative time bring fun to your life. Or make it so easy you can feel in control.

Resource: Notice when you are struggling with your art, are you being too heavy-handed, trying to make it work? Allow your art time to be goalless, to be play time. Practice showing up with no ideas. Enjoy where it takes you.

Day 37
Until Death Do We Part

"I am told I may have a year to live. But really, I could go on for many—or only another 5 minutes. I don't know, you don't know, nobody knows, when they will exit...when our time runs out."

—Bob Findle, excerpt from his daily art project

Today I am thinking about Bob Findle, who was a regular at my studio. Inspired by a Daily Art Show we held, Bob started his own daily art project. Within weeks of beginning, he received a diagnosis, he was dying. Bob did not stop because he was dying. And, he had a great excuse. He continued because he was dying and had something to say. He started where he was: I am dying and I am making art from this place.

Bob's daily art went on for 107 days, to the point where he did not have enough energy, which was a few days before his death. Though he did not know it before he died, his daily art project culminated in a show at my studio. *The Art of Dying* inspired many. What a gift from him to give us a window into his process. It was an amazing tribute to see people take such exquisite time to look at each piece and read what was written. We cried, laughed, and were changed because this amazing man showed up for his Creative Practice.

We all have bad days, or maybe we are in chronic pain physically or emotionally, so every day is a challenging day. Our daily art gives us an opportunity to mark our days with something special, no matter how bad we feel.

Don't let life define whether or not you show up for your art. *Let your desire to honor your life be what helps you show up.* Arrive no matter how you feel—it may help. It helped Bob.

Resource: Show up however you are and do what you can.

Day 38
Don't Let Doubt Stop You

You were called to make art a regular part of your life. You have answered the call, I know, because you are here reading this right now. Maybe you had been thinking about doing this for months, years, or a lifetime. But right here, right now, you are doing it.

We often begin with a gung-ho attitude full of excitement and promise of what will come. And then, a moment comes where we start questioning ourselves. Doubt begins poking its finger into our creative foundation and tries to dismantle it. Doubt is a voice that can cause great damage and even stop us. Many a project has been abandoned because of doubt.

I think of doubt as the desire to do something really well and right next to it, the worry we may not do it well enough. How about we make a commitment, right here, right now, to do as author Anne Lamott says, *write a shitty first draft.* Let's commit to doing it however it gets done, knowing at some later date we can do a take two, get an editor to fix things, or a mentor to help us out. For today, allow your creativity to flow out of you, to not get stuck inside you, because of doubt.

Resource: When doubt shows up, recognize it. The gift of a Creative Practice is just that, you practice each day. As you continue to practice, your skill level will grow and your confidence will become stronger. Recommit so you will continue to show up. You may remind yourself why you started your project in the first place and reaffirm your desire. Desire transcends doubt.

Day 39

Building Muscles

When we start a daily Creative Practice, we need to build our *artist muscle* and our *show-up-every-day muscle*. These muscles don't get strong overnight. As with physical exercise, the time it takes to get in shape depends on how out of shape we are when we begin. If we have not been doing art for a long time or never (well, maybe in elementary school) then it may take longer to find our groove or even our project or direction.

When our artist muscle is underdeveloped, we can feel lost, anxious, and unfocused. The blank canvas can be our worst fear, the blank page the enemy, a blank mind a disaster.

When our artist muscle grows and becomes strong, we can usually show up to our art with more confidence and get going on something without much thought. We show up and start wherever we are, with whatever needs to be said, with whatever is on our mind or in our heart. If the project we are working on has not revealed to us the next step, then we spend time on another project. As we build our identity as an artist we become the verb, we become the action, we become art makers.

As our *show-up muscle* gets strong, even 5 minutes can help us stay in touch with our process, stay in relationship with our project. It is easy to pick up where we left off. When we take time off, we may need to refresh ourselves. It may take more time to find our way back. We may lose focus, and momentum.

Ultimately, your *show-up muscle* helps build your *artist muscle*. You become a stronger artist by showing up and practicing your craft.

Resource: Showing up for any amount of time is still showing up. Do something, do anything. Grow your muscles. Build your relationship with your art and with your artist self.

Day 40
An Interesting Thing Happened...

After two years of daily art making, I was faced with the task of writing my Expressive Arts Therapy Master's Thesis. School had always been hard for me and the idea of writing a thesis was daunting. Add to this I was a single mom, worked full time, and was in a relationship. It was during this process of writing my thesis I realized the unexpected benefits of having my Creative Practice.

My *show-up muscle* was very strong by this time and I transferred this same idea to my thesis. My commitment was to show up for at least 5 minutes every day, yet I could work longer if I wanted. I almost always could tolerate more than 5 minutes, and in fact, often went for hours, just like with my art. I finished my 125-page thesis in about three months.

When I opened my Expressive Arts Studio, I committed to 5 minutes a day of marketing. I spent years on this book writing 5 minutes a day, and in the later stages editing.

I have also used this tactic for exercising, keeping up with my finances and decluttering. So yes, we start because we want to live an artful life. The payoff becomes bigger when our *show-up muscle* is developed. I was never a get-a-little-done-every-day kind of person. Prior to this I was a last-minute deadline driven worker.

This process has changed me from the inside out, and it could do the same for you, too.

Resource: Once your *show-up muscle* is strong, notice if there are other areas of your life you could apply it toward. Keep your Creative Practice as the number one priority!

Day 41
Forget Inspiration

"First, forget inspiration. Habit is more dependable. Habit will sustain you whether you're inspired or not. Habit will help you finish and polish your stories. Inspiration won't. Habit is persistence in practice." —Octavia E. Butler, author

At this point in your Creative Practice, you may have experienced how the habit of showing up every day or regularly helps you be there to catch the inspiration when it strikes, or holds you until inspiration arrives.

A dry spell of inspiration can be painful if we need it to show up. We blame ourselves or this elusive *other* named inspiration. We build resentments or comparisons toward those who seem inspired, or toward our life and our loved ones who seem to be blocking our inspiration.

Having a "project" helps me when there is no inspiration. I know what I need to do when I show up. Then inspiration has the opportunity to come in through the back door. Or, I am content because I have my day-to-day project.

If I start where I am, for example, with my Scribble-a-Day project, I do the scribble of not being inspired. Doing this meditative act (or any non-thinking activity) is often when my inspiration strikes. Or maybe inspiration eludes me longer and longer, but my habit for showing up and putting pen to paper sustains me through the creative dry spell.

Honor the habit to show up, be persistent in your desire to create whether you are inspired or not. Whether you create the mundane or break through to a masterpiece.

Resource: Let go of the idea that you need to be inspired to show up. Keep showing up so you can catch inspiration when it arrives.

Day 42

The Gift Is to Notice the Impulse

Creativity is not a special gift that only belongs to the few. I have learned over years of art-making that creativity is following the impulses we get. We get a thought or a vision and take the next step this impulse suggests. The gift is in learning to listen to those impulses. We get impulses all the time, but in our busy life, or being brought up in a world of do as I say, we may have learned to disregard them.

By showing up regularly in our Creative Practice, we can also practice listening for those impulses. They may be whispers or fleeting thoughts we need to train ourselves to notice, take seriously, and not doubt their validity.

Learning to listen to ourselves and follow those impulses* and pleasures in our Creative Practice can lead to listening to ourselves in all areas of our life and, voilà! Suddenly we are happier, more connected to ourselves and others. Maybe we will even live longer! Or at least more joyfully!

Learning to hear our desire to use blue could open the door to hearing the tiny voice that says, "Slow down, take a nap." Or, "It is time to eat something healthy." Or, "Go to the doctor."

Growing your Creative Practice, growing your ability to listen for the creative impulses may just lead to a happier and healthier life!

Resource: Have a pad of paper near where you work to jot down the impulses you get as you work. Start following those ideas, accept them as gifts. Impulses are inspiration.

**The impulse we follow does not want to harm self or others. It is a small voice for our greatest good and the greatest good of all. If you do get impulses wanting to hurt or harm, get professional support. Allow the attention and healing.*

Day 43
Welcome Your Good Parent Self

We want to feel like an artist, which means, showing up. It can be necessary to call forth a more evolved part of ourselves to help. I think of this part as my inner *Good Parent Self.* I don't want to be forced but firmly and lovingly invited.

Most days my *Good Parent Self* says, "Yes, you DO have 5 minutes for your art, let's do it!" Over and over, I am reminded I cannot say no to 5 minutes. It is hard for any of us to say we don't have 5 minutes. We do have to snag the time though. 5 minutes can help us feel invited without too much expectation and help us build our *show-up muscle*. My *Good Parent Self* knows this.

Then there is the advanced self-parenting skill, when it is time for longer chunks of time. We have to be the good parent to say, devices down, dishes down, put yourself on the calendar today for at least one hour so you can fully be in relationship with your project. When I am creating longer, getting into the creative flow, seeing and feeling progress, I feel more grown up. I feel a maturity as an art maker where my art is not a hobby, but it is my longing realized.

You don't have to create big chunks of time every day, but often enough so you can feel yourself falling in love with your project or your medium. Like a relationship, time together is a necessary ingredient, you schedule time to connect, time to work through challenges and feel the joy of spending time together. Allow yourself pleasure and allow your *Good Parent Self* to come out and help you get there!

Resource: How could you be a good parent to yourself, hold the boundaries of creating time for your art in an inviting way? You could even name this part of yourself. Art Parent, Art Mentor, Fairy Art Mother, Father Art or...

Day 44
Do It Now!

One of the best words of advice I heard many years ago to ward off depression and anxiety was to get up when you wake up. The idea is, if we lie in bed, the world can start seeping into the tender place between sleep and wakefulness and ambush us with unfriendly fire.

I have found a similar thing happens with art-making. When I think about something too much, it is like lying in bed and getting ambushed by my critical voice. I have learned, when I think about doing something—do it. To not put it off and think about it—to jump in and get started.

When we take action, we get out of the thinking, critical brain and move into the creative brain. I have found the longer I put something off, the further it gets from me and the less likely I am to act.

Taking action right away starts the creative juices flowing. The action can be as simple as writing the idea down somewhere where it won't get lost. Recording the idea on voicemail, calling a friend and telling them. It can also be jumping in the deep end and getting started. Especially if it scares you!

Resource: Take action as quickly as you can, it doesn't have to be perfect, just get started!

⇨ *If you have challenges with depression, and can't get out of bed, get therapeutic help. You do not have to navigate depression alone.*

Day 45
Do What It Takes

We were talking at my *So, You Want to Write?™ Support Group* the other night about doing whatever it takes to write. One writer said they like to have a glass of wine while they write, another likes going to the coffee shop. Some people said they work better with others around, like in our group, and some liked writing when they are alone.

If you are having trouble showing up or finding your rhythm, don't give up before you have tried everything! Trust your desire to be a creative. It may take time and exquisite listening to find the just-right fit for you and your life.

If you want to give up, know exactly why—*I want to give up because I do not have the patience to sit and write.* Okay, you don't have the patience to sit and write, so how about standing while you write, or walking and recording yourself or find a time of day when you have more patience.

You try this and you realize, *I want to give up because I have no ideas*. Then join a writing group or class where they throw out prompts to get you started. Or, you create a list of your own prompts throughout your day, so when you sit down you have a place to start.

The more specific and honest we are, the better we can be at finding the adjustments that need to be made. This is not only the secret of a Creative Practice, but also a lesson for life. When we are specific, we can make changes. We can't do anything with, *"I hate it, I don't know what I am doing."* We can do something with not feeling confident, safe, or not having ideas.

Resource: Be specific about what *isn't* working so you can explore what *will* work. Stay curious.

Day 46
To Do or Not to Do?

Today I run the risk of not getting everything done if I sit here to do 5 minutes of writing. I am thinking ahead to my to-do list and need to get to an appointment. Today my desire to write is greater than my fear of not getting everything done—so I show up, I sit and write.

It helps to know I do not need to do anything miraculous or award-winning, but simply have the evidence and satisfaction that I showed up. The belief we need to do more, we need more time, we can't accomplish anything in just 5 minutes, can keep us from showing up at all.

When we do show up, we stay in touch with our project. It stays close to our heart, stays close in our mind as we review or look for the next step. It can be helpful to have a log or notebook nearby to write something about our 5 minutes. "Sat with my painting for 5 minutes and noticed I love the periwinkle blue in the upper right corner. Wondering if I bring some of this color into the lower left if it will create more balance?" Or, "played the first stanzas of my song today and noticed it felt flat, I want to liven it up a bit."

Remember, the step doesn't have to be big; it needs only to be progress. Giving a few minutes is giving our attention. Sometimes our 5 minutes of attention can be more laser focused than when we have more time.

Resource: Carve 5 minutes into your day to be with your project even if you are very busy. Think about what you can cut out, to put your creative time in. If you can't find 5 minutes, chances are something is out of balance in your life.

Postscript: I wrote, did what I needed to do, and was on time!

Day 47
Ideas Arrive in the Blankness

The most fertile time for new ideas is not always when we are sitting down to work or create. It is often the moments when our minds are resting, we are lost in the doing of something mindless. These moments can arrive in the shower, in the middle of the night, washing dishes, on a hike, sitting in the bathroom, walking the dog, or driving on the open road. And when this brilliance comes, we are often not near paper and pen to write it down.

Creating a way to capture our ideas can be easy today. We can speak to our devices, "Take a note..." Record ourselves when we are out and about, either with audio or video. Or send a text message or voicemail message to ourselves.

And there is pen and paper. Leave a small notebook in the bathroom, by your bed, in your car, or in your pocket.

If we write it down, we have a better chance of remembering because we took the time to capture it, and of course, we will see it again later. If you don't have a way to capture an idea, sing it or create a vivid picture in your imagination while you describe what the idea might look like out loud to yourself or to a friend.

If the only quiet time you have as a parent is in the bathroom, use it! If your work schedule is intense, use your driving time to imagine or record next steps. Using plane, train, and bus time as creative time is a personal favorite. I share a writing program between all my devices. When I get a new idea for a page in this book, I open a new file with a sentence or word to remind me.

I have heard we have a matter of seconds to write down an idea before we lose it. When I do lose one, I often say a little prayer for it to come back to me when I am ready.

Resource: Honor and create blank moments in your life. Plan ahead ways to capture ideas before they get lost.

Day 48
Do ANYthing!

It really doesn't matter what you do, it matters if you do something! I was just closing my laptop from what seemed like an endless number of emails to catch up on. Exhausted, way past my bedtime, and setting my computer on my side table I see the sign I made, "DO ANYTHING!" Damn. I pick up my computer and here I am, writing this so you can read it and maybe you, too, will do something (or shall I say, ANYthing!).

After more than 20 years of daily art projects, I know the value of "anything." Your holding this book in your hands or on your device is the result of many days of doing anything.

So, keep going! Get back out of bed or get off the couch and put a mark on the paper or sing a note into the air. You got this, even if you think you don't!

Resource: It doesn't matter what you do, it matters that you do something! Have a plan for these days, when you are exhausted, so you WILL show up. You just might find you stay longer than you imagined.

Day 49
Stakes and Mistakes

Sometimes when we begin a creative adventure, we may feel like the stakes are really high. Perfectionistic desires become strong and looming. We want it to be fabulous, original, and loved by everyone. With the stakes so high, fear of failure can creep in and keep us from showing up, trying something new, or having fun. What if we make a mistake? What if the whole project is a mistake?

If we take a different view, we can look at the imperfect or the mistake as a gift. When we don't like something, feel like we have done it wrong, or dare I say, failed, we open to our biggest creative opportunities. When we don't like what we have done then we can take big risks. We can try the thing that seemed too big or too scary, because there is truly nothing to lose at this point—we already don't like it!

What if in the creative process there is no such thing as failure? What if creative dislikes are invitations to PLAY BIGGER! What if instead of a sign of failure when you are not getting where you want in your project, it is an opportunity or even evidence of a desire to break out, do something unexpected, or get a little crazy?

And, if it ultimately wants to go in the trash, make a spectacle of the process. Video yourself lighting it on fire and see what you can make out of the ashes!

Resource: When you notice you are playing small because you are worried your art has to look good or be perfect—how can you play with the idea of lowering the stakes to enable yourself to make BIG mistakes and even get playful?

Day 50
Honoring Life Through Daily Art

Our daily art can be more than making art. It can be a diary of our life and a diary of the world we live in. As I write this the world is in rest and unrest simultaneously. The 2020 Covid-19 pandemic quarantine is happening and we are living a quieter life. And, at the same time, across the country demonstrations against the murder of George Floyd and racial injustice are in full swing. The takeoff of Space X is happening. All these events move me and become part of my Creative Practice.

The ability to track the events of our personal life as well as world events is the added gift of a daily Creative Practice. I learned along the way of many years of daily art practices that I appreciate when I add notes to my art so years (or weeks) later I can remember what was happening as I created this or that piece. I either write directly on the art or on the back of it, or when that is not possible, I keep a separate journal talking about my process and the state of my world, and the world. It does not need to be a dissertation, just a sentence or two to remind you what was going on.

Resource: If you are not already, for a week or two, make notations on your art, on the back of your art, or in a separate journal, to remind you where you were physically and emotionally this day. It could be a simple title for the day, “Feeling out of control.” Or, a sentence, “Felt out of control so I went to the park and danced a big dance in the grass.” Or a few sentences that are even more specific, “Feeling out of control, out of work and no money, I wanted to do a big dance, a screaming *get me out of here* dance, so I went to the park and felt like I owned the whole place. I feel courageous now, not scared.” If adding notes works for you, keep making notations, your future self will thank you!

Day 51
Creative Practice as Timekeeper

When I first began my daily Creative Practice, I had a journal where I wrote a few lines each day about my process. Soon though, it felt overwhelming. I stopped because I did not want it to get in the way of my showing up to do my art. I still have that journal and have loved reading the few entries I did make. In fact, some of the writing has made its way into this book.

I was also new in the process and I was sure I would remember everything anyway. I would remember why I did this or what was going on when I did that. As you can imagine, this was unrealistic and I did not remember everything.

Recently, when hanging my *5985 Days of Art Show* I noticed the more I knew about a piece, about the process of making it or what was happening in my world, the more I felt a connection. The pieces that said nothing became "just art" and I noticed I was not connected or even very interested in those pieces. In fact, my critical voice came up and was just looking at them for their aesthetic value.

At the opening of the show, I also experienced people reading the pieces with writing and some even commented to me how they felt connected to the pieces that included narrative.

Journaling can also be helpful in growing our emotional intelligence as an artist by processing the feelings that come up when we make art.

The lesson of this story is *whatever we can do to stay connected to our art, helps!*

Resource: Continue yesterday's writing practice idea. See if it feels good. You do not need to write a lot, just a few words or a few sentences.

Day 52
The Critic Is the Separator

The inner critical voice, in its lower form, is divisive. It lives to separate us from others, our self, our creative juice, our project, and mostly, from our aliveness. Noticing that the critic is trying to keep us away from something can be valuable.

My critic in its UNhelpful state has messages like: give it up; it isn't worth it; you are no good at it; nobody is going to like what you are doing anyway; you don't have time; it is not important; who do you think you are fooling; and so on!

If we put on our detective hat, we might be able to see what the critic is separating us from—why does our critic want us to stop? Here are seven reasons that I have experienced:

1. The critic wants to protect us, keep us safe from being hurt, disappointed or vulnerable.
2. The critic's voice may belong to someone else, someone from our past and we have internalized their voice.
3. The critic is scared, it doesn't know what to do next.
4. The critic is overwhelmed by the next step.
5. The critic starts thinking about what someone else might think of our work or starts comparing our work to another.
6. The critic may be scared of being critiqued.
7. The critic is a perfectionist.

Sometimes our critic's voice is so subtle, or we have lived with it for so long we don't hear it. Coming to the awareness that it exists is a first step. The second is to identify what we need.

Resource: When you are stalled on your project, or notice a negative voice in your head, take time to listen and observe. Write down or make art about your thoughts, feelings, and sensations to better acquaint yourself with your inner critic voices.

Day 53
The Critic as Our Protector

When our critic tells us we should not even try, or what we do is not good enough, it may be feeling vulnerable and trying to protect us—wanting to save us from hurt, disappointment, or failure.

If we can see our critic wants to protect us, to keep us from being hurt, what might change? We might reassure the part of ourselves that is worried it might fail. We can notice, is this tied to an experience from our past that needs some attention, some loving? Is it a reminder of another fail?

When I was young, singing in a group, someone turned to me and told me I had a terrible voice. My critic became my protector from this day forward, by not allowing me to sing in public, or when I did, I sang quietly or became a master at lip-syncing, especially for the birthday song.

My internal *Good Parent Self* might tell me it doesn't matter how I sound; it matters I feel the joy of singing. Or I might go take singing lessons so I can feel more confident.

I did take a singing class. I learned some helpful tools, like when we aren't confident, we tend to sing at a low volume. For our voice to sound good, it needs volume. I also learned the happy birthday song is one of the hardest songs to sing!

We could also look at the worst scenario—if no one likes my voice, what will happen? Will they hate me? Will I die?

After learning to turn my volume up and also learning if I hit the wrong note and hold it long enough it will become the right note, I began singing *Happy Birthday* in my loudest opera voice and invite others to join me. My critic knows—I got this, if we fail, we fail big and have fun. Now I am the protector of my critic.

Resource: What might your critic be protecting you from? How can you help your critic feel safer?

Day 54

The Critic as Someone from the Past

Once we begin to understand there may be a critic within us who interrupts our creative process, we can start listening to its voice or attitude. We can learn more about where it was born and who it may belong to—then confront this voice and hopefully, learn from it and let it go.

Was there someone in your life who criticized you and now you carry their voice inside you? The voice of the critic may have been an overt unhelpful statement you believed to be true, saying you were no good at something or you did it wrong. Or maybe the messages are so subtle it takes time to uncover them. It may have been a disapproving look, attitude, or fear you took on as your own. Possibly your art didn't make it onto the refrigerator, but your siblings' art did. Or you came from a family of artists and you never felt as good as them. Or you picked up the opinion art is not valuable, it won't pay the bills, or it is scary.

Fine arts majors have come to my studio after years of NOT making art. The critiques from school felt cruel and humiliating and those voices come up every time they create. Maybe you received messages not about art, but that you were not capable or creative.

Stay aware as you create. Listen closely to thoughts and review your life for a thread where something unhelpful may have happened. A moment where you shut down. How can you give this part of yourself some loving? How can your inner *Good Parent Self* create a new supportive voice? Don't let the critical voice win—take your creative power back by showing up, one day at a time.

Resource: Write a dialogue or create a piece of visual art, music, or drama with a conversation between your muse and your critic. Let them battle it out through your art!

Day 55
The Critic Doesn't Know What to Do

Through experience, I have learned that bouts of unkind self-criticism are often moments when I don't know what to do next. I feel I have stepped beyond my level of confidence and competence. I begin to question my talent. And yes, I may take it out on the art—the project becomes a failure or a waste of time.

What if allowing yourself to feel lost is part of the creative process? I have noticed when I feel the most lost, there is a breakthrough right around the corner. I am up against my growing edge.

Curiosity can be a great tool to get out of judgment and back into creating. Think of a young child when they are learning something new—they ask a million questions, they look closely, poke, taste, tear, and squish. They immerse themselves in the things they don't know.

Through curiosity we can reach out to others for help, take a class, watch a video, look through some books for ideas. Or even take a break, go on a walk, or meditate. If we come back to our project with a sense of curiosity, it can continue to have a life and who knows, could become something beyond what we imagined.

Allowing yourself to be a beginner, and knowing you have the rest of your life to learn and grow creatively, opens doors. Expectations that we should know everything, slams doors shut.

It might be easier to abandon your project but stepping away to be curious and learn could be more life affirming and help you grow your artist self.

Resource: If you want to give up and realize it is because you don't know what to do, allow yourself to be in the discomfort of not knowing. Then, take a break, do an alternative creative act, or ask for help. Come back and see if anything changes or comes to you as a *tiny* next step.

Day 56
The Critic Might Be Overwhelmed

The critic can rear an ugly head when it is overwhelmed. Maybe the step we are trying to take is too big, scary, or stressful. Maybe our idea is bigger than our ability or asks for more time than we can give. Maybe the rest of our life is overwhelming and instead of supporting our life, our Creative Practice feels like one more obligation.

The critic tells us it is not worth it, it is not helping, it is too much, you don't know what you are doing, crawl into bed instead of being creative. If we can break our process into smaller steps, we can be fed again by our practice.

My first year of daily art I dedicated to my mother who had died a year earlier, I began with the idea I would paint every day. It ended up being so overwhelming I could feel myself wanting to give up. My critic continually stated the obvious, I didn't know what I was doing. If I was to make it through a year, I needed a BIG change. I switched to oil pastels, which I had some understanding of and a year later, my creative confidence had grown—I was ready to paint.

Two things helped me through this critical moment. First, remembering why I was doing the project, to honor my mother, helped me stand up to the negative voices. Next was the knowing I needed to make it less overwhelming. The way to answer overwhelm was not to buck up and get through it, it was to break it down to a smaller, easier, more manageable process.

Learn to notice the body sensations and messages of overwhelm, so you can create a new compassionate plan.

Resource: Don't give up, be WITH your overwhelm, make art about it or dialogue with it. Find a simple, less stressful step you can take that would still be showing up.

Day 57
The Critic as Comparer

In an instant we can move into a place of comparing ourselves to another, or many others. We listen to a story at an open mic and suddenly think ours isn't good enough. Or at a painting class we are happily painting in our bubble and then look to see what others are doing and have a sudden attack of "mine isn't good enough." We may start imagining what someone else will think of our work and become embarrassed, it may tap into old art wounds or shame.

We might even utter words out loud like, "Yours is so great, mine is terrible." When our inner critic is comparing itself to others, no one wins.

When I say, "Yours is so great, mine is terrible," I diminish myself because I use this comparison to put myself down. You, who I have just compared myself to, could lose also. Imagine how it might feel to have someone tell you your work makes them feel terrible about their own self.

The solution is simple in idea, but maybe not in action—to shift your brain one degree from comparing yourself to others to allowing yourself to be inspired by others.

` When you notice someone else's work is good, rather than comparing yourself to them, ask, *"What about their work inspires me? What can I learn from them, what can I take and make my own? Is it the color palette, the shapes, the sounds, or a feeling?"* You could talk to them, find out where they learned their craft or if they can show you how they did this or that.

The critic wants to separate us from others—when we compare, the critic wins, when we are inspired, we all win!

Resource: When you find yourself comparing yourself to someone else, ask how this person can inspire you. Take the inspiration and make it your own in some special way.

Day 58

The Critic Is Scared to Be Critiqued

Your inner critic may fear the outer critic in others. Worrying what others will think of your work is a sure way to create stress and stop your creative process. Sometimes the person isn't even there in real life, but they may have a place in your head. Or, maybe there is a fictional audience you imagine experiencing your expression and worry what they will think.

Do we become the critic so we are prepared for what someone else might say? Or do we give up or never start, so no one ever gets the chance to critique us? Does this moment become an abandonment point—abandon the project or idea so the work does not progress to a point where someone could comment?

Ask yourself if you could be guilty of giving up on something rather than taking it to completion, a point where it can be seen or heard, because you are afraid of being critiqued? Could this be the reason many of us have a graveyard of unfinished projects?

When we notice ourselves fearing a critic outside of us, where can we get a reality check? It is important to have support in our lives for our creative adventures. People who will give us encouragement to keep going, who want to see us finish our projects and lovingly help us when our critic or the fear of someone else's critic takes over.

Surround yourself with people who support you with a gentle loving presence. And learn to be a gentle loving presence for yourself. When you are afraid of what others might think, give yourself the reassurance that you get to do whatever you want and you do not have to please anyone else.

Resource: Create a team to support you, not critique you. Support to keep you going when times get tough. And grow this in yourself, too. "We got this! No worries what others think, this is for us!"

Day 59
The Critic as Perfectionist

Most of us live in a system that encourages perfection. Our schools celebrate top grades, perfect attendance, and award winning accomplishments. Our work environments credit top performances and high achievement. Yet, the creative process is about trying new things, which includes embracing failure.

When our critic comes up it could be a sign our perfectionist is alive and worried about not being perfect, not doing it just right. Our perfectionist wants us to quit if we are not good at something, because it does not want to be caught being imperfect. Even more insidious, the desire to be perfect may keep us from *ever* getting started.

If you think perfectionism is alive in you, the act of showing up to be creative can begin the healing. Use your art to express your desire to be perfect, the payoffs, and conversely, what might live on the other side of your desire for perfection. Is it someone's love or approval you are trying to win? Or, are you trying to avoid someone's disapproval?

Art-making is messy. The materials can be unwieldy. The process can be chaotic. The results are hit or miss. What if we meet the part of us who is afraid of making a mistake and show them sometimes the *mistake* becomes the gift. The *mistake* takes us in a new direction. The *mistake* becomes the doorway to something new and maybe exciting because we are entering uncharted territory. Creativity asks us to be bold and try new things!

Resource: The perfectionist is usually more interested in what others will think than whether we are enjoying ourselves. As you create, constantly bring yourself back to the process. The feeling of your fingers on your instrument, the sensations of creating, and give your perfectionist time off.

Day 60

The Critic as Our Helper & Friend

Once we understand more about our critic and what they may be up to—protecting us, keeping us safe, or carrying on an unhelpful legacy—we can attend to ourselves. We can begin to cultivate a compassionate inner voice to hold the part of ourselves that feels unsure, unloved, or unresolved. We can listen deeply to what we need to learn or transform.

If we choose to keep going, rather than give up; if we stay in conversation with our critic rather than letting it win the boxing match; if we sit knee to knee, looking in each other's eyes; we may find something new, not only about our art but about ourselves, or our life. If we ask our critic to be specific, we can DO something, we can create change.

A simple example: In my *Paint to Music™* class I noticed a newcomer had walked away from their painting and was pacing the gallery area. I went to them and asked if there was anything they needed. They started spilling out how they were not an artist, why did they come here, they hated what they were doing, and they would leave but they came with a friend. I suggested we go look at their painting. I asked them to tell me specifically what they didn't like or what was happening when they walked away. It turned out it was because the colors were mixing and turning muddy. They weren't bright anymore, they were dull. I honored their struggle, suggested they were in the throes of their first artist lesson and learning color theory. We discussed some options to bring the desired brightness back, and how to express the feelings of creative despair they were feeling. They finished their painting, and most important, came back the next week.

When we can get specific about what is going on—I don't like the color, my mother is in my head telling me I am doing this wrong, I just compared myself to someone else, I feel out of control, or I am in way over my head—we can take action that keeps us going rather than believing the unhelpful messages that want us to quit.

In its higher form, the critic can be our helper. "I don't like it," the critic says. We learn to respond, "What does it need? What do you need?" We listen for a response. "It needs more blue," "I am feeling scared," or "I need to ask for help."

Once we get in touch with our critic, identify it, and listen to what is going on under the unhelpful messages, we can begin to create change. When we know our critic may want to keep us safe, we can decide, do I want to stay safe? Do I want to live the smaller life my critic keeps me in, or do I want to take a risk? Will I play it safe or move out of my comfort zone? Do I want to grow through this and even grow out of this unhelpful message? And sometimes the answer will be, "Today I will play it safe." When you do need to play it safe, make a plan to do it different tomorrow or next week. Make the conscious choice rather than letting your critic choose for you.

The lower-form critic beats us up, berates our efforts and makes us want to quit, or not show up fully. The helpful critic wakes us up to a new idea to make things better or do something different. The secret is to bring compassion, to help ourselves to lovingly move out of suffering and into expressing. Then, the helpful critic can actually become our muse!

Resource: Your art, and you as a human work of art, deserve to find your compassionate self-talk voice, your inner *Good Parent Self.* Art-making is the place where our critic can show up the strongest and where we can practice healing those critical parts of ourselves that can show up in other areas of our life, too.

Day 61
The Critic as Doorway to Change

The critic can be our biggest helper because it can become our signal something is not right in our life. Because art-making is a place where the critic shows up so immediately, the two are a great team to help us grow.

Often when we get critical about ourselves or about another it is because something is going on under the surface. When we notice it happening, it is our cue to check in to see what is going on. Maybe our cup is not full and we are feeling depleted. Perhaps we are not feeling safe in the world because of money, relationships, work, or other life issues. Or, we are just not feeling safe as we make our art. The critic can rear an ugly head when something touches an unresolved past experience, or we are in the throes of change or uncomfortable transition. Other faces of the critic can be fear, anger, anxiety, and shame. The critic can also hide behind our unhealthy behaviors. When we reach for a drink, or food, or blindly turn to another numbing activity, has the critic just arrived and we want to avoid it?

Once we are clear we have a critic, the healing can begin. And once we get better at listening for our critic or noticing the feeling sense of our critic if there are no words, we can begin to respond rather than react. When we react we might quit, say unkind things to ourselves or others, blame our art or ourselves. All those messages we have talked about: I hate it, you don't know what you are doing, give up, leave, hide, fight, or numb out—can be indications we are reacting.

If we can observe what is happening, slow down, take a breath, a walk, or do some calming exercise, we can come back and more easily respond to the upset. Responding is looking through a caring and curious lens, it encourages us to take the next step. It is the growing of the compassionate inner voice.

Recently an artist at the studio mentioned she does not have a critic when she makes art—she feels free and expressive. And then the conversation turned to other people seeing her art and this is where her critic shows up. When she thinks about others seeing her work, she wants to cover up her truth, cover up anything revealing. She is worried about other people's judgment of her, the art maker, who the art is about—they may think she is too dark, too over-the-top, too depressing. The gift is that she has this place—art-making—where she can express completely without judgment. The next step is to heal this area where the fear of criticism from others lives. When she wants to cover something up, she can notice what is going on inside and ask how can she soothe the fears. She could look at where the "don't be dark" voice originates and reclaim it through expression and the cultivation of her compassionate inner voice who says, "It is okay to be you."

When we have a Creative Practice, we then get to explore what is coming up, through our art. Don't let your critic stop you. Instead, let it open the door to new insights, the possibility of change—and use your practice to express it all! Sing it, dance it, paint it, sculpt it, write its story, express it. The critic can be the muse who keeps on giving.

Resource: Learn to notice your critic's arrival and ask it "what do I need right now?" Attention to those parts of ourselves and the reframing* of the messages through our art can be big medicine.

**Reframing of the messages—Moving from an unhelpful message like, "You don't know what you are doing, give it up!" to a kinder, more useful message that can help us move forward like, "I am scared. I need to ask for help."*

Sometimes being patient
for the answer to come is a good idea.
Yet if the waiting keeps you from getting
started or continuing, brainstorm ways
through or around the challenge so you
can be creating. Do something else while
you wait for the answer.

(You made it over 60 days,
celebrate and keep going!)

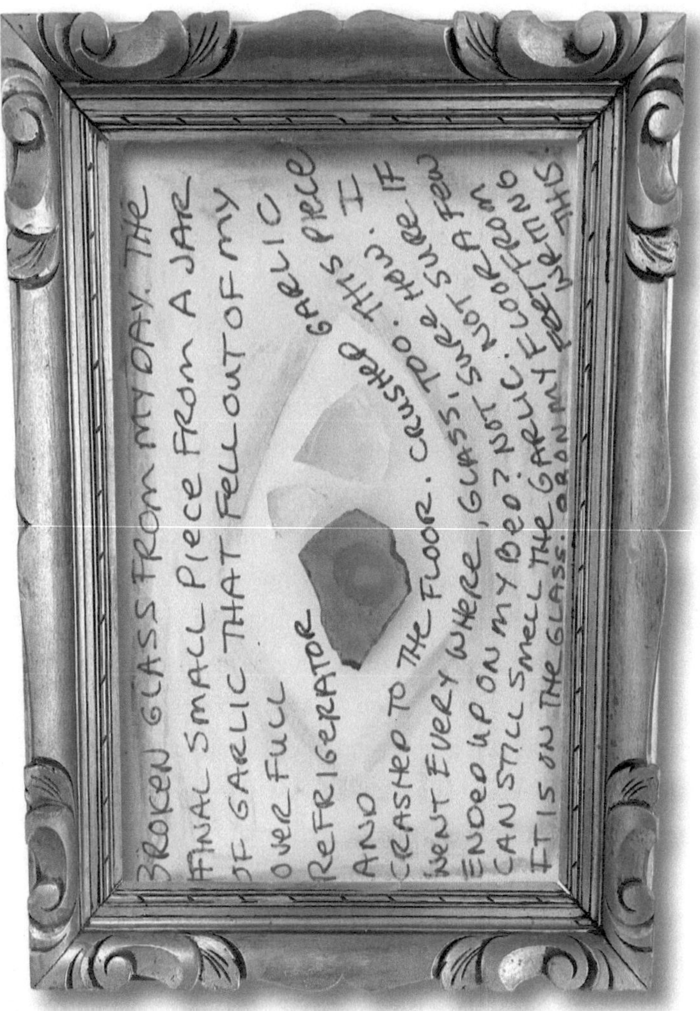

365 Days of Found Objects Realized

A favorite in my very first year review was a week I did of found objects. On many occasions I wanted to start it as a project but it never felt doable. One day when I saw some glass bobbles on the ground a little voice went off in my head, "Go smaller." I did and it worked! I loved every day of this project. This became an important learning about not giving up on an idea, but brainstorming what may need to change to make it work.

Day 62
Documentation I Showed Up

Some days showing up isn't the delight we originally envisioned for our daily art journey. We may have had visions of it all being easy and fun. Then reality set in and we have hard days. Hard to show up or showing up just under the wire. Almost forgetting. And then there is the day we forget completely or stomp our feet and do not show up on purpose.

When we get through those days, still showing up and adding one more small addition to our project, there is a feeling of accomplishment that ups our energy. I showed up, even if I didn't want to, even if I didn't make magic. I showed up. The alternative? Not showing up, not following your dream, not staying in the creative conversation, not feeding your spirit's call to express. Not living an art-filled life, one day at a time.

Every day we get to choose. In a perfect world, we would always choose to keep going. And, we will not do it perfectly because we are human. The idea is not to do it perfectly, but to tip the scale toward self-expression and creation.

Keeping a journal about your process can be helpful to get feelings out, track your challenges, get angry, celebrate, or remember moments of wisdom and growth. I have been amazed, when I look back, to see what I have written. "Wow, I wrote this?" or "I forgot how difficult this time was."

If keeping a journal gets in the way of showing up, don't worry about it—if it feels too hard, the scales could tip to not showing up at all because it is too much. A journal could also be good if you are a performance artist, to track your journey and *show-up muscle*. See what works for you.

Resource: If writing about your process helps, do it! It is great to look back at the process later. If not, it's okay to let it go.

Day 63
Ask for Help

Getting help is not a sign of failure—quite the opposite. It is a sign of deep desire and care of self.

A.R.T.S. Anonymous (Artists Recovering through the Twelve Steps) meetings can help you get unstuck, inspired, and supported when needed. I found A.R.T.S. Anonymous when I was in my 20s. It was a great tool to look at my avoidance, work with my confidence, and meet other creatives who were trying to get started or keep going. Back in those days I identified as a "passion seeker." I was looking for my creative passion. I did not know what it was yet, but I hoped it would exist for me, someday.

There are plenty of other ways to get going and build creative community: Julia Cameron's book *The Artist's Way* is a tried-and-true experience, or check out books like Austin Kleon's *Steal Like an Artist,* or work with a creativity coach, or take classes.

I would highly recommend getting together with other artists and want-to-be artists, not trying to do it all by yourself. You might even do a group with this book. Get together once a week, read a page, discuss it, and then make art!

We can talk about making art, buy books about making art, buy supplies for making art, but it is by doing we learn the most. Make art to learn how to make art. And, knowing others are on the same path, having the similar insecurities, inner critic, time challenges, joys and exhilaration can be helpful.

At my studio people often say there is something helpful about making art in community—it is inspiring and motivating.

Resource: Check out ArtsAnonymous.org for informative reading and try a meeting if it feels like a good fit. Create your own art-making support group, check out the meeting ideas and format in the *Follow-Up Resources* section at the end of this book.

Day 64

Art Reflects the Times, Our Times

"How can you be an artist and not reflect the times?"

—Nina Simone, singer

Art reflects the times, our times. We do not need to think beyond our own heart or the news headline for an inspiration of what to do each day in our Creative Practice.

In my Expressive Arts studies, we looked at how art is at the forefront of change. Through movies, television, comedy, books, visual art, songs, and stories we learn new ways to be, both creatively and in the world. When we present a new idea through the arts, it can be accepted and tolerated in a way that opens us up rather than causes defensiveness. We can present a point poignantly. As the saying goes, a picture is worth a thousand words.

When I write this, the world is at a new understanding of racism and other *isms*. My daily art includes a processing of new things I learn about black, brown, and indigenous history, white fragility, white supremacy, and capitalism. Through my art I process the world around me as well as share my views on human rights in my own creative way.

Years ago, I read a study about art and stress in communities. When times are stressful for a society, they often fall back to their native art, what is familiar. Likewise, when things in the bigger world or your own personal world are stressful, if you resort to drawing flowers or whatever you doodled as a youngster, let it be okay. My latest 365 Days of Scribbling project has included scribbling a flower for unarmed black lives taken by police as I learn about them. I use my art to process what I am learning, calm myself, and keep my Creative Practice alive and relevant.

Resource: You hold power in your creative expression. Use your creative gifts to help create change within your self and the world.

Day 65
Art as Meditation

Sometimes, I begin my art-making time with a short 5-minute meditation, just long enough to clear my mind and listen for a next step with my art. It could also be considered transition time from my daily life to my creative time.

For many, a still, sitting meditation can be difficult. The reasons for this can be many—trauma, anxiety, restless legs, or preference. I have found art-making can become a beautiful meditation. Movement, music, the visual arts and even poetry can all be forms of meditation.

In its simplest form, Art as Meditation is exquisite attention to the process of creating. It is how we use our art form that helps it become a meditation—slowing down, putting our attention so completely on what we are doing. The pen on the paper when scribbling, your body as it dances, the brush as you paint, your fingers on the piano keys as you play, or your voice as you sing. Slowing yourself down so nothing else exists but you and your creating. Closing your eyes can engage other senses and help us be in the moment. And, remember to breathe, slow intentional breaths.

We can even use repetition as a way to meditate—leisurely drawing the same shape over and over or playing the same series of notes over and over or doing the same body movement over and over. Anything that gets us out of our thinking brain.

The gift of Art as Meditation is not only have you meditated, and have those good feelings, but have something to show for it!

Resource: Try meditating before you start your art to transition into creative time. Or, use your creative time as a meditation. Watch my YouTube video *Scribble Meditation—The Meditation You Can See.* Or turn to *Day 122* and read the Scribble Meditation there. Imagine how you would use your art form as meditation.

Day 66
So Much Pulling on Me!

"It all seems hard! So much pulling on me! How do I let things go so I can show up for my art?"

This is me trying to show up for my art. I planned a writing and painting weekend retreat at home. I started with a meditation to try and clear myself. It did not work. Instead, I am here with so many things swirling for my attention, mostly my endless to-do list.

As I write a solution comes. I will make a list of everything that is swirling: texts I need to answer, emails I need to check, paperwork for a project that needs to be turned in, announcement to design for a new show, and on and on.

The list has been made. I am now breathing deeply. Letting it all sit on the to-do list that I can pick up after my weekend. It is time for me. I will begin. And if any other mental diversions come, I will write them down and come back to my breath and begin again.

When we write things down our brain isn't trying to hold onto them, instead the paper can hold the list and our critical thinking brain can relax so we can be creative.

There will always be something important to do—and even unimportant things whittle their way in front of our creative time. Making our creative time a priority is good care of self. *And creating the boundaries to make sure we create is another muscle to be strengthened.*

Resource: If you have a lot pulling on you for attention, before you begin your art or while you are doing it, make a list of all the things you have to do and will get to *after* your art time.

Day 67
But I Have Kids

Having kids was my mother's reason for not pursuing her dream to become an artist. By the time my brother and I were grown and out of the house, I can imagine she was so separate from her dream it never happened. Not having pursued becoming an artist was her biggest regret when she was dying. I don't want anyone to live or die with this regret.

No matter how many kids, no matter how much is going on in life, we must take time to put ourselves first, even for 5 minutes. Art-making is a perfect vehicle for this self-care. Not only are we CREATING something new in the world, our brain is producing serotonin and dopamine, the feel good, happiness and well-being chemicals. Having too little serotonin and dopamine in the brain is linked to depression. Art-making is a prescription for well-being.

When you hear yourself wavering because you have too much on your plate, remember my mother, who never got back to it, and remember you CAN make 5 minutes to play. And, if you can't do something in 5 minutes in your Creative Practice, rethink it, simplify it, find your way back to 5 minutes of scribbling—on paper, with movement, with words, with music, with improv, or… And you can always go longer.

Make art as if loving your life depends on it.

Resource: If you are not getting to your art, don't give up on the idea, rework your project to make it more accessible. If you don't have an idea of how to change it, sit quietly each day for 5 minutes until you get an idea. (Maybe lay out your project in front of you as you meditate on it.) The key is to still take the 5 minutes, to continue building your *show-up muscle*.

Day 68
The Best Laid Plans

In my more than nineteen years of having a Creative Practice, I have worked with everything from doing a large 36" x 48" oil pastel every day to adding one drawn line a day to a piece of paper. Being honest, neither of those extremes went the distance.

At some other moment in time they might have flourished, but in those moments, my momentum was stalled and abandoned.

The daily art process needs to be a flexible system so it can evolve with our muse as well as our life. Had I been flexible enough I might have seen that finishing a large drawing every day was not realistic. What I did at the time was to go smaller and smaller each day so I could finish. But then I lost what I was originally excited about—working BIG! I was too close to the situation and I couldn't see it. Now it seems so simple. If I knew then what I know now, I would have allowed myself to work with one big piece for one week or month, finishing 52 or 12 pieces rather than 365. What a relief this would have been!

The project I began with one line a day was during a time I was traveling. I thought it would make things easy, and it did. But when I got home, it was too simple and not engaging enough. I don't even know what I did with it. I never looked at what I could have changed. I just quit.

It is necessary when we are not loving our art, to step away and evaluate—on a heart level—what is happening. We cannot afford to lose our Creative Practice momentum, but instead we can lose our attachment to a project looking a certain way.

Resource: Be in constant conversation with yourself (and others if you need help) to follow your needs on a project. Step away and be curious. Getting others involved can help us find a new perspective we may not see on our own.

Day 69

Moments of Upset as Creative Muse

When we are angry, sad, grief-stricken, frustrated, prickly, bitchy, enraged, defeated, or any other strong emotion—that is the perfect time to be creating.

Grab your emotions and express them through your Creative Practice. If we learn to use our emotions to express, they can propel our art forward to authentic and original places we may not have imagined going. And through the healthy expression of these emotions we can increase emotional and physical health.

Those expressed emotions can also take us to deeper places within ourselves that are looking for healing. The anger at my partner, when worked with in my art, reveals the anger I had at my father when I was seven. The grief I am feeling about making a mistake might be exposed as the need to be perfect to stay safe.

When we express, there are opportunities for several things to happen. First, we get the feeling out so it can move through us. Second, we get to see our expression in a way that can bring us healing in the moment as well as a possible healing of the past. And third, we have an expression of an emotion we can share with the world, if we choose. The world needs examples of healthy creative expression, and when we share that expression, we give others the permission to do the same.

Resource: When the feelings are big, especially the ones the world might frown upon, express them through your Creative Practice. Check in after you have expressed and notice if anything changes, even a tiny change. Also note if there is any new information about this situation that could be helpful. Get help if you need support to get through big feelings, trauma, and old wounds. You don't have to do this alone.

⇨ *If traumatic memories or sensations arise, get therapeutic help.*

Day 70
Art Wounds

Many of us come into the creative process with art wounds, a moment when something happened and shut us down creatively.

My most obvious art wound was with singing, being told I had a terrible voice and not singing for many years. (See Day 53, The Critic as Our Protector.) It was helpful for me to learn the concept of the art wound and find compassion and understanding for myself and others.

My friend and colleague, Michele Lyons, had a visual art wound. In elementary school her teacher held her art up for the classroom to show how she had done it wrong. From then on her visual expression was met with a feeling that she was not good enough. Later in life she owned dance as her primary creative expression. As she grew confidence in her dancer self, her visual art became simple expressions of dancing bodies. She had found her way into visual art by expressing what was important to her.

My son seemed a natural at the trumpet when he was young. When his teacher started a children's orchestra, he got overwhelmed. He was so afraid he would play the wrong note at the wrong time, he gave up and never played again. I tried to help him understand everyone was learning and it was okay to make mistakes, but he was having none of it.

Sometimes our art wounds don't seem like a big deal because we didn't really love playing the trumpet anyway. But what if the shutdown shows up in other areas of our life? We don't try anything new or stop doing things we are not great at, because we are afraid of awakening feelings of shame from the past?

Resource: Scan your life, is there an art wound somewhere? Make art and/or journal about it. Are there any threads connecting it to your Creative Practice in any way?

Day 71
The Antidote to Art Wounds

Creative expression can be a vulnerable experience. We are sharing a part of ourselves that may be unconscious or deeply personal. If we get critical feedback or have a negative experience when we are in this vulnerable state, we might shut down our creative self in order to keep from being hurt. An art wound can be when we get separated from our creative expression or the love for our expression becomes dulled.

Some forms of art wounds could be: teacher or peer critiques; going professional and all the fun being squeezed out; hoping to win the love of a caregiver by creating perfectly; being called out for expressing in a nontraditional way; having an anxiety attack before a performance with no one to support you; being made fun of; or no one appreciating the gift of your creating.

Ultimately we want to take our power back and grow more confidence in sharing our expression. Here are a few ideas you could play with to create some healing and compassion:

- Make art about your wound and what the healing might feel like. Rewrite the story with a healing next chapter.
- Write a letter to your younger self who experienced the wound offering that part of yourself what you didn't get.
- If your tendency has been to hide creatively, take baby steps toward going bigger, louder, and bolder.
- Find safe places to be supported and tell your story.

Resource: Take steps toward honoring and healing any stories you have lived that have resulted in you shutting down creatively. Seek professional help if you need it. Most importantly, keep showing up to your Creative Practice. There is no greater healer than to continue to show up for ourselves.

Day 72

Don't Stay Stuck in the Yuck!

One of the gifts of having a Creative Practice is working through what life hands us more quickly. If I am upset about something and play with it through my art or use my art to take a vacation from it, I get relief. My body relaxes, my thoughts organize, my spirit finds lightness, and often I receive information about a next step to take.

Sometimes I find myself wanting to stay in the yuck. It feels good to be angry. It feels good to have emotions. It feels good to be immobilized so I can justify doing nothing. Maybe it is a different kind of aliveness I am feeling and I want to hold onto it.

Recently when I was doing some research on hate, it was startling for me to learn that the same hormone, oxytocin, is released in the brain when we are feeling hate, as when we are feeling love. Maybe it is some sort of chemical rush that I am enjoying when I am angry?

It can be a short distance between big feelings and feeling like a victim; for me the muckiest of yuck. Art-making is taking action, which can be a necessary ingredient for moving forward and not staying stuck in the yuck and instead, being energized by it. Bring it to your writing, your visual art, your music, your Creative Practice and see what doors open.

Resource: When you have big feelings, or the absence of feelings, turn to your Creative Practice to move you through whatever is going on.

Day 73
The Blank Page

If you have moments of fear, worry, or concern when you stare at the blank canvas or the blank page—welcome to the world of being an artist. As creatives, this is what we sign up for—the unknown—the world of endless possibilities and no sure-fire ideas.

There are some artists who have found their groove, found their style, practiced for years, grown their talent and show up with an idea and then execute it. In my experience, the people who get to this place naturally, without major work or practice, are children and artists with developmental disabilities. I believe it is because they are masters at following their impulses, and the ideas as they come to them. They don't question if it will work, if it is the right choice, or if it will turn out okay, they just keep following what feels good. They are not thinking, they are doing.

When we can approach the blank page, take a moment to listen for the first impulse, and start, without worrying where we will end up, we are on our way. It took me a year of making art every day, showing up 365 times, to begin to get this idea—to listen to a simple impulse like, choose red. We all have our very own path to take. We all have our own art wounds, life experiences, and aesthetics to influence our journey.

The secret of the blank page could be to enjoy the journey. Enjoy the learning of what doesn't feel good so you can find what does feel good. Please, don't give up because you haven't found your way yet. If you have gotten to this page, you have arrived to hear me say, "Keep going!"

Resource: Listen for the impulse and notice what feels good. Don't complicate it, let go of expectations and do it. You don't need to know where you are going or what the final result will be, you need only to listen for the next step.

Day 74
I Have Arrived

Today as I sat to write I did a short meditation before beginning. I imagined a blank page before me and asked for words to get me started. "I have arrived" was what came and becomes my prompt. I wonder where it will lead us today?

My first thought—when did I arrive at feeling like an artist? I don't think it is a one-time event. For me it comes and goes. Often when I am starting a new project and am wandering through the unknowns, I think, "Yes, this is what it feels like to be an artist." I have an idea, a direction, but don't know the specifics of the journey. Then I step into action that could take me anywhere. If I imagined a recipe, it might look a little like this:

45% excitement about the idea of expressing myself.

45% fear about what I am going to do, how I am going to do it, and how it will turn out.

10% the ever-changing teeter-totter moving between trust and distrust in the process.

This small 10% defines the difference for me of what happens next. Will I lean toward distrust and squelch the whole idea because being scared wins out? Or will I do it, show up and feel like an artist (writer, singer, musician, actor, dancer) because I allow my expressing voice to be louder than the voice to stay safe.

This is the moment when I feel I have arrived, I feel most like an artist. It is when I trust failure more than I trust safety. I feel more alive living in the risk, knowing it could end in disaster, and I keep going. And of course, it could also be magical or anything between disaster and magical!

Resource: When the voice comes up and says *I can't*—imagine moving your body toward an action to begin. Then do that action. This is the verb of being an artist.

Day 75
Words to Create By

Dancer Martha Graham wrote this to dancer Agnes DeMille in 1943

There is a vitality,
a life force, a quickening
that is translated through you into action,
and because there is only one of you in all time,
this expression is unique.
And if you block it,
it will never exist through any other medium and be lost.
The world will not have it.
It is not your business
to determine how good it is;
nor how valuable it is;
nor how it compares with other expressions.
It is your business to keep it yours
clearly and directly,
to keep the channel open.
You do not even have to
believe in yourself or your work.
You have to keep open and aware
directly to the urges that motivate you.
Keep the channel open...
No Artist is pleased...
There is no satisfaction whatever at any time.
There is only a queer, divine dissatisfaction;
a blessed unrest that keeps us marching
and makes us more alive than others.

Resource: Post this and read it often to remind you to keep going, keep your channel open and live an expressive life!

Day 76
Am I Valuable Enough?

"It is not your business to determine how good it is; nor how valuable it is; nor how it compares with other expressions. It is your business to keep it yours, clearly and directly, to keep the channel open..." —Martha Graham, Dancer

Taking the time to create is not easy. Our lives are busy, we may have many things pulling on us AND, we may not believe we are valuable enough to take creative time.

My Sweetie, Michael, just told me a passionate vision he had and I urged him to write it down. We talked a bit more and he said he was going to let it sit for a bit and write about it later. I gave him a very insistent, "No!"

When we are feeling impassioned, when the muse hits us, when the channel is open, we *HAVE* to stop, follow, and *DO* something. I have been there—feeling excited, not taking the time to honor it, and then later it is gone.

Michael was willing to stop and write about his passionate vision in the moment. He put it ahead of his to-do list. The dinner will wait, chores will wait, the dishes will wait. If your baby is crying, yes, go to them, and then bring them with you into this passionate moment. What a great role model for those around us, "Hold on folks, dinner will be a few minutes late, I have to run and write down my idea!"

When you tell the world you are unavailable while you capture a passionate moment, you are understanding your role in the creative process. What a beautiful example of following the impulse and creating space for the unique expression to come through you—to keep the channel open. Yes, you are valuable enough!

Resource: Make the time to create when the muse arrives!

Day 77

Is the Process Valuable Enough?

"You do not even have to believe in yourself or your work. You have to keep open and aware directly to the urges that motivate you. Keep the channel open." —Martha Graham, Dancer

What is the value of having a Creative Practice? In the Preparation section of this book, I listed reasons to have a Creative Practice. If you haven't, I encourage you to find your own reason so you can use it as a reminder to keep going. And, your reason might change. You may have begun because you have something to say, something to express. And now you realize it is an essential part of your self-care or recovery.

Your critic may use the tactic of telling you that your creative process is not helpful, that you could be doing something more valuable with your time. It may say many things to stop you from showing up. Remembering why you decided to have a Creative Practice can help build your resolve to keep going.

If you still don't value the process of showing up every day to make art, maybe your critic is worried you are not going to have something "good enough" to show for it. Maybe you are looking through someone else's eyes at what you are doing and imagining they will be judging you.

Allow the time you take to be what is significant. Honor that you are valuable enough to spend this time devoted to yourself and being creative, no matter what the outcome of the process. Your real commitment is to keep the channel open and follow the impulses that come, the urges that motivate you. The way to keep the channel open is to show up, so you are available and ready.

Resource: Judgment closes the channel, curiosity and being available keep it open. Stand up for yourself and your commitment.

Day 78
The Negotiation

In my late 20s I quit smoking through a 12-step program. I learned as soon as I start negotiating, I lose. As soon as I allow myself to begin thinking about buying a pack of cigarettes, if I don't stop the thought in the moment with something like, "Oh that's right, I am no longer a smoker, " then the negotiation will continue until, possibly, I am smoking.

What does this have to do with a Creative Practice? I have experienced similar negotiating with my Creative Practice. Being older and wiser I have new information about the negotiating.

So here is how it might sound:

"I don't really feel up to doing my art today."

"I could skip one day."

"It wouldn't hurt anyone, no one would even know."

When I begin to have thoughts like this I check in and ask myself, what is going on for me where I don't want to do art today? Usually it comes down to feeling overwhelmed with something in my life, feeling overwhelmed with my project, my project is boring, or my space does not feel private enough to make art.

When you have these moments, ask your artist self what you need today? What do you need so you WILL show up?

As I say often, I have never shown up and been sorry I did art! I am always grateful. Remember, your creative time is self-care, it fills your cup and helps create a life that is fulfilling.

Resource: As soon as you notice the negotiating, take a moment to close your eyes, breathe and ask yourself, "What does my artist self need right now?" Give attention to whatever comes up. Make the changes needed and make art. Even allow your art to be an expression of what needs attention.

Day 79
Negotiate to Win

I was talking to a friend today who is doing a writing project. She told me she found herself negotiating out of showing up to write. Her writing is important to her and is also her way of earning her income. Not showing up has consequences. Today she said her negotiation led to: if you sit down and write, when you are done you can go out to breakfast, a favorite thing to do. She negotiated to stay in, rather than negotiating to get out of doing it.

This led me to thinking about the negotiating that can happen around our Creative Practice. I like to think the joy of showing up is the reward, but sometimes it isn't. Sometimes it doesn't feel like it will be fun or a joy. Sometimes when we are up against a hard part of our project or life feels hard, we need an incentive to show up. If checking off each day on your calendar is not enough, if making progress on your project is not enough, if being sure you don't miss a day is not enough, figure out what will make it enough. If having a small scoop of ice cream after you are done helps you get there, helps you build the *show-up muscle,* then do it! If watching a movie while you do your art gets you to show up, do it! If it helps to play your favorite music while you do your art—or wear your lucky boots—do it!

Negotiating to win means there is no losing. Maybe you only work on your new song project for three minutes instead of your usual allotted time. You still showed up and you stayed in relationship with your project. Three minutes is still showing up.

When you feel yourself not wanting to show up, put on your negotiator hat to find the win!

Resource: Sometimes negotiating is okay. Less is better than nothing. And when we can't feel the internal rewards, external rewards are okay now and then.

Day 80

Start Where You Are in This Moment

I say it often: "Start where you are," because it has never failed me. There are a few reasons for this.

First, if you don't know what to do, you don't have to go far. Simply check in with yourself, and ask what is going on for you right now? This is where you start. I don't have enough money to pay the bills, I make art about this and the feelings that go with it. If I have a headache, I make art about my headache. If I had a really bad day today, I make bad day art. Starting where you are in this moment, with whatever is going on for you, gives you unlimited inspiration. A bad day can become a creative treasure!

Second, starting where you are can get you ready for something else. I notice in my writing I cannot concentrate on my book if I am thinking about something else. Yet, if I write about the something else, I can clear a space for my project. Maybe I have to scribble out my anger before I can work from love.

Third, starting where you are is therapeutic. Making art about where you are can bring a new perspective or new ideas. Just getting to express "it" can be a relief.

Lastly, but probably not finally, starting where you are keeps your work truly yours. It keeps your expression authentic and real. And, when we have been through something and express it, we inspire others to do the same.

When we can show up authentically to our Creative Practice, we want to make art. Why would we want to show up when we are feeling crummy, unless we get to express feeling crummy? And once you have expressed it, notice, what is there now? Is there space to begin something new?

Resource: Practice checking in with yourself, notice where you are, and make art from this place.

Day 81

Ideas to Keep You Going!

Where do we find inspiration when we are showing up every day and need 365 inspiring moments? Here are some of my favorite ways to get inspired:

1. Start where you are. Check in, identify what needs to be expressed, and express it.

2. Look around the room for an object—what do your hands want to touch? Let the object, its characteristics, or the memories it holds, be your starting point. Maybe the object shows up in your story or your painting or is the jumping off point for a song or something creative.

3. Take 3+ minutes to close your eyes and meditate. Once you have relaxed just a little, imagine a blank page in front of you. What are the words, colors or images that appear on the blank page? Start with what arrives.

4. Scan your day and identify the most important, least important, most surprising, most boring, or most challenging moment and start by expressing one of these moments.

5. Open a book to a random page and point, let the words or image your finger finds be your starting place.

6. Close your eyes and let a memory from the past come to you. How can you incorporate this into your project?

7. What person wants to come to you today to be with you in your art-making? Close your eyes. Imagine they are there with you, and that they have something to tell you.

8. Let "I don't want to do art" or "I have nothing to make art about" be your starting place. Express it and see what comes.

Resource: When you feel uninspired look around you or inside you until you find something inspiring. Follow the impulse that comes. No worries about where it will lead.

Day 82

Disruptions and Distractions

Even though I have had a Creative Practice for many years, I still have challenges staying put in my seat. As I write this, I have claimed a writer's afternoon of three hours. Before I began, everything was done—I walked, made coffee, my house is clean, the dog is fed. Here is what is happening:

I wrote a text to my writers' group telling them I was starting my writer's afternoon. I moved a few writing pieces from one folder to another. I read and edited the Preface. I wrote. I got up and grabbed a few books to look at who published them, could they be a good fit for my book? I wrote another text. My glasses were dirty, so I cleaned them with special glass cleaner. Now I am writing this.

And though I am writing, I look out and the dog wants in, the door is open, but he is old and gets confused sometimes. I get up to help him. Now I am cold, I need to go get my favorite furry sweater and while there I see I still have my walking shoes on. I change into my comfy shoes.

Now I am back writing. Disruptions can be a way of avoiding what we are doing, or they could be our rhythm. Sometimes the disruptions can be my thinking time. A time to plan the next action.

I have learned that when I am unsure of what to do next, if I get up, when I return, I usually have an idea.

Your job as a creative is to notice if you are finding disruptions to keep you away from your project or are they part of your flow?

Resource: Is there anything you can learn from your distractions? Are you avoiding something? Is what you are doing too overwhelming? Do you need to create boundaries around your creative time? Or are the distractions part of your natural process that keeps you moving forward?

Day 83
Distractions to Avoid

Yesterday I talked about how distractions can be helpful for me, to keep myself making progress on my projects. But sometimes the distractions keep me away from my project. The question I always ask is: Does the distraction keep me in the process or take me out of the process?

The telltale signs for me of when disruptions are taking me out of or away from my project are: Irritability when I get disrupted. Not coming back when I get disrupted. Losing my place and not remembering where I left off. Not getting started because I get distracted.

One way to tell what is going on is to pay attention to what is happening inside you. For me, there is a difference in the feeling sense when I am distracted to keep going, versus distracted to avoid. When I am distracted to keep going, there is a level of excitement or inspiration. I may not know what to do next and I come back.

Disruptions to avoid are different. I don't come back. I accept offers to keep me away. I don't set boundaries. If I am irritable because I get distracted, I know I am not setting boundaries. I am putting others first. Our Creative Practice may be a mirror for the rest of our life. If we have challenges putting our self first and taking time for ourselves, it will show up when we start a practice.

Setting boundaries can be easier than you think. Announce to your world you will not be interrupted. Turn your phone off, close and lock the door. Period. It is your job to make your time sacred.

Resource: Teach your family and the outside world that this is your time and there are no negotiations. If you start negotiating, not holding the line, they will know. If you let the outside world in, they will know you are not serious.

Day 84
Practice in Setting Boundaries

A big shift in my life from having a Creative Practice was building the skill of setting boundaries. To show up to my art every day, I needed to make the time for myself and not let anything get in my way.

I learned early I needed to say "NO" to anything keeping me from my art, so I could say "YES" to my art. I said no to housework, the to-do list, and to interruptions from my son. It was helpful for me to realize my first year that my best time to create was in bed before I turned out the light. It was time I already set aside for myself—to go to sleep!

I also learned I could share my art-making time. As I shared in the introduction of this book, during the first year I had an art box in my car I would take to dinner parties or other social visits and invite others to make art with me.

When I began my first year of painting, sometimes my eleven-year-old son joined me, or he did homework alongside me, or sat watching a mutually agreed-upon show while I painted—my studio was in our living room. It was agreed, this was my art-making time. Interestingly, it was not as easy for me to paint in front of adults. I needed alone time.

With my writing it is easier to get distracted because it is harder for people to see this is my Creative Practice time. It isn't easy setting boundaries, but it is a great skill to strengthen. Whether it is saying no to people or a to-do list, if we are going to be successful in our Creative Practice, we need to claim our time and not let everyday life get in our way.

Resource: Who or what do you need to say NO to, so you can say YES to your Creative Practice as well as to your life and self?

Day 85
Excuses

The most obvious excuses keeping us from our art are connected with our to-do list. I have to finish this job, meet a deadline, do laundry, clean, go shopping, take care of this person or that person before I can get to my art. And often, we never get to it. We are learning to set boundaries, take charge and sit down for 5 minutes or more and not allow anything or anyone to interrupt us.

How about the internal excuses though? How do we deal with: I have foggy brain, I can't think clearly, I am feeling depressed, I am tired, I am overdone, I am sick, I am not feeling creative, and so on. These excuses, the unseen ones, may be even more challenging—and we need to make boundaries here, too. Commit to SHOW UP NO MATTER HOW YOU FEEL.

After you build the *show-up muscle* it can be easier. I absolutely *show up no matter what* because this muscle is strong in me. I learned if I don't show up one or two times, it gets harder to show up the next time and the next.

So, plan for those days where it is hard. Allow yourself to do *just enough.* Plan for success. My current project is a blind contour portrait every day and paint it if I can. Occasionally, I only have it in me to do the 30-second drawing. At some point in the future when I have more in me, I go back and add paint. Or I do more even though I think I can't, and I usually feel better after!

Why is it we often avoid the things that help us the most? Do we think we don't deserve to feel better? Or we are not worthy of giving time to ourselves? Or do we just forget that it helps?

Resource: Show up no matter how you feel—you began this project to be in service of your life, showing up even when you are not up to it shows your devotion to yourself. And, if it arrives, receive the gift of feeling better!

Day 86

Excuses, Excuses, and More Excuses

Over the years of my daily Creative Practices, I find myself making excuses for why I can't show up. Most often I am too tired—I have been too busy and need a break. There is also a whole list of others. I don't know what to write. I am not feeling well. I have too much on my plate already. It is too cold or too hot. I don't have the right materials. I am blocked as to what to do next. What I am doing is terrible. I got a better invitation. The list can be endless.

What I know is, when I do not listen to the excuses and I show up anyway, progress is made. The progress can be as little as knowing I showed up and putting in my 5 minutes or as big as getting excited about what I just did and painting, writing, or doodling for hours. The challenge is to deflect the excuses and get to it.

I challenge you this week to NOT make excuses or complain about your art and just do it. Sit with the discomfort when you show up to the project you have committed to and make progress despite the discomfort. Find a journal or piece of paper to put next to you and make notes about what comes up, what feelings, ideas, and messages. Just track them, don't get caught up in them, just notice. You could even make art about the feelings and sensations.

We will investigate this more tomorrow, too. You will have an opportunity to understand what could be a new layer below the surface of excuses.

Resource: Practice tracking your excuses and the feelings present when you show up anyway, see if you can gain any new information about yourself or your Creative Practice.

Day 87
Getting Beneath the Excuses

When we take the time to explore our excuses for not wanting to show up, we have the opportunity to learn more about ourselves. Beneath excuses or complaints, you may meet discomfort. As suggested yesterday, if you have a little notebook, you can track this uneasiness. Notice the discomfort. Where do you feel it in your body? Are there any messages attached to the feelings? Write this down, *AS YOU DO YOUR WORK,* not instead of doing it.

In my own process I came up against my lack of confidence, my fears of failure, and my fear of success. My mother had always wanted to be an artist—if I succeeded, would I take anything away from her? There was a lifetime of story I had to unravel to own that it would be okay for me to be successful.

Sometimes we even realize that feeling good, feeling excited, feeling pleasure, feeling present in our body, or taking time for ourselves, is uncomfortable.

If we can learn to stay with the sensation, the discomfort or even the pleasure, we can grow our tolerance to it, get through, and even thrive while we are in it. The creative process is all about handling the sensations of discomfort and pleasure. If we stop avoiding, we learn we can handle it and get through our discomfort, even for just 5 minutes in the beginning. And we can grow our capacity to hold the uncomfortable feelings with time.

And, you *must* show up and be *in* the process of creating.

Resource: If you haven't yet, get a notebook to place beside you to take notes and journal about the discomfort that arrives as you create or think about creating. Stay for a little bit longer than you want to, not as punishment but to discover and learn from what may lie beneath the discomfort. And, yes, write down the good feelings, too.

Day 88
The Only Excuse Is Death

I keep little notebooks to jot down interesting or important thoughts for this book, my other creative projects, and life in general. I found one of these notebooks tonight and there were surprises in it. Notes passed back and forth with my sister friend, Michele, at a silent retreat. I found ideas written in the dark of the night that I can barely read. Then I saw this: *"The only real excuse to not make art is because you are dead. Every day of being alive needs creative time."*

This note is a little treasure in response to a recent creative dry spell. I have not been feeling excited about my visual art or my writing, feeling tapped out and even trapped by my practice. Because my *show-up muscle* is strong, I know I am not going to give up, but I am showing up with less energy. Being reminded that my life does not go on forever, offers me a different perspective. Knowing today I *can* do art changes how I look at my time.

Again, I am reminded of studio regular Bob Findle who began a daily Creative Practice just before learning he had terminal cancer. He did not allow his diagnosis to stop him—instead it fueled his desire to use his Creative Practice to process, escape, and communicate his journey. His last daily art piece was created about a week before he died. Death was not an excuse for him, it was a reason to keep going.

Explore your own excuses to not show up—are they valid? Could you show up in a small way, even though you don't think you can? If it is too much to commit to your creative self, until death do you part, could you commit for one more day of 5 minutes? And then recommit one day at a time?

Resource: Today you are alive! What can you do to express your aliveness to yourself and the world?

Day 89

Allow the Becoming

We live in a world of instant gratification. This kind of culture can suggest we need to be good at things and if we are not, we should give it up. If we don't have instant results of expertise, we think it is not meant to be—if it was meant to be I would be good at it and it would be easy.

What if you gave yourself permission to be in the "becoming" rather than the arrival? Becoming means showing up and putting in the time and not knowing where you are headed but knowing you are going in the direction of learning. Becoming means knowing it will take time to understand and gain expertise. Though some have natural talent, even those with natural talents need to practice. And a practice is just that, continuously showing up to practice a skill so we get better in the creation, and better at listening for the next impulse.

What if you dared to jump in as a beginner and allowed yourself to fail, to not be great? What if you allowed yourself to ask for help and support? What if you gifted yourself the freedom of becoming?

What if you let go of the idea you have to be good at something and embrace the idea you can enjoy the process no matter how the end product turns out?

Can we create practices for ourselves where we can explore, experiment, and enjoy rather than perform? Can we be present in our body and our process rather than caught in thinking we need to produce a perfect, finished product?

Resource: Are you allowing yourself to be in the becoming, to be imperfect and learning? What can you change, even just a little, to be fully immersed in the freedom of creation and not worry about the quality of the product?

Ninety days
of showing up is a
Celebration!
Do a little celebration dance!

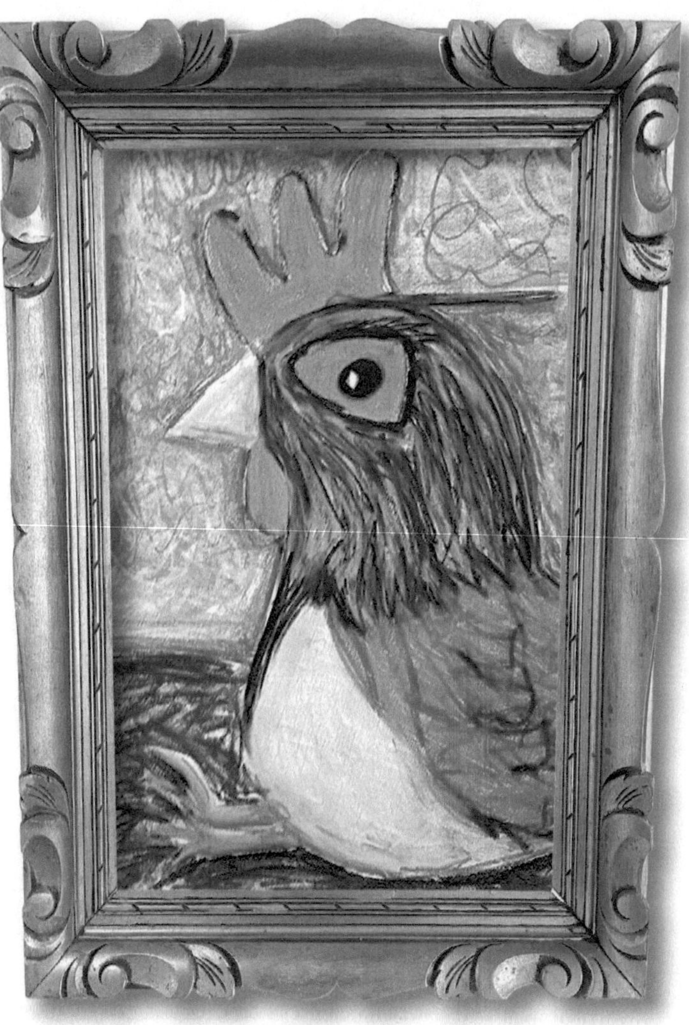

False Starts

I had lots of projects that seemed like great ideas, but once I got going did not go as planned. This rooster was the beginning of a large oil pastel a day project. Each day the images got smaller and smaller. Had I been better at brainstorming maybe I could have done one a week rather than being so ambitious wanting to finish one a day. Learn from your false starts and carry the learning forward.

Day 90
What Changes in 90 Days?

I often see life coaches offering 90-day challenges. In some twelve-step groups for addiction they encourage 90 meetings in 90 days. In numerology the number 90 means infinite potential. I have heard it takes 90 days to create a permanent change in our life. I have found when at all possible, my Expressive Arts groups are 12 weeks, which can be around 90 days, so people can settle in, bond, create strong community, and grow their creative confidence.

It was at about the 90-day point of my first daily Creative Practice when I started trusting I would show up and create. I had worked out some of the kinks that made it hard for me, and my *show-up muscle* was getting strong. It was also about this time I started feeling just a tiny bit like an artist. I made art—I felt like an artist. Being honest, I wasn't feeling like a talented artist, but I was trusting when I showed up I would pick up an oil pastel and look kind of like an artist!

In 90 days, we can build a connection to our project—we are growing our relationship with it. When dating, often it is that three-month mark where eros wears off and our real self begins to show; the honeymoon is over.

That said, I have noticed 90 days being the point where I often realize something is not working with my daily practice plan. I have learned I usually need to go deeper or find a way to make it more engaging if I am going to keep showing up.

Resource: What has changed for you in these 90 days? What may need to change to continue forward? And, celebrate! You made it to day 90!

Day 91
Day 91 on Day 91

As I write this, serendipitously today I am 91 days into my current Daily Blind Portrait Painting Project, and I am working on day 91 in this book! The real gift is that I am feeling like a painter again. I look forward to the end of my day which is my painting time. It even motivates me to get home earlier so I will have more time for my art. It has been a good process so far, and I have needed to make adjustments and can feel more coming.

Through these 91 days, I have negotiated and rearranged my art area to make it less cluttered and my paints more accessible and organized. I began setting some boundaries of what can be in this area, not everything from every life project I am working on—just painting materials.

I bought some new paint colors and I threw out paints that were old, dried out, and unsatisfying. Why was I using them?

I am also noticing I am unhappy with the ergonomics of my work area. I may need to rethink my chair so my back is supported.

I have the idea I will need to play and experiment more to keep myself engaged if I am going to continue for a whole year. I will start a file of inspiring artists and paint styles. I know from experience if I don't take care of these small things, they will snowball and continuing could get difficult.

Remember, everything is changeable, make adjustments so you will stay with it. Don't weed out your practice, weed out what is not working with your practice. Don't use the negatives as a way out of this adventure you have chosen. Let them help you create a better experience.

Resource: Continue to be aware of what is working and what is not working. Look through your creative eyes for fine tuning so you will keep going!

Day 92
Start with What You Notice

I feel my feet on the floor as I avoid putting words on the paper. I can't be barefoot at home, no matter what time of year. Even in the summer the concrete under my floor seems to make my bones ache. A chill sets in and then wants to become an illness. Even today, on a day with the temperature in the 80s, I have my slippers on to be a barrier between sensitive feet and the cold cement under the linoleum.

This is what I do when I show up and I don't know what to do. I write or do visual art about what is there, what I am noticing in the moment. It is still a creative act, even though it may not be in line with my project and what I think I am supposed to be doing. Like today, writing this book.

And yet I find a way for this writing to gently curve toward my book—telling you when you don't know what to do, start with what you are noticing.

Resource: When you don't know where to start, start with what you notice. Use your senses to do the noticing—what are you feeling, seeing, touching, tasting, smelling, and see where it takes you.

Day 93

When You Want to Give Up

Yes, there will be times when you want to give up. I have had them and I found my way back. If your practice is not working, allow that something needs to change. This is not the time to beat yourself up, but quite the opposite. It is the time to listen to yourself closely. How can you open your heart again to the desire to live a creative life? Here are 10 ideas that may help:

- Revisit your list of why you wanted to do this project or make a list now of five reasons why you started.
- Look through what you have done so far, not to judge or critique, but to honor it.
- What is hard about your practice? Is the project wrong? Are your expectations too big or is it too boring?
- Find one thing you enjoy about the process and see if you can build on it.
- Talk to a friend or mentor about how it is going and wanting to give up.
- Write to the part of you who wants to quit, and let it answer, continuing the dialogue back and forth.
- Always remember to start where you are. If you want to quit, make art about wanting to quit.
- If you need to, take a day off. Step away to see what needs to change. And, set a time to come back!
- Is there another idea calling you? You don't have to stick with something that is not creating joy or pleasure. Switch your project and see if it helps.
- Have compassion for yourself. You are getting to know yourself better, allow yourself to be human.

Resource: Keep reading and highlight what is helpful so you can return to it as needed. Make your own list of what helps!

Day 94

Negative Chatter to Nurturing Talk

Negative chatter is often connected to old feelings of being less than, not good enough, or comparing self to others. These messages can go back to comparisons in family, school, bad experiences with a teacher, abusive childhoods, art wounds, and more. The patterns may be laid out early; art-making can help us hear and heal these voices.

When I hear someone talk negatively about themselves, their art, or their abilities to do art, I admit, I react. I have an actual physical feeling of a stab in my heart. How can we help ourselves change negative chatter to nurturing talk? Does encouragement work? Can our change come from an outside source? Or do we need to do the work inside? I think it is a combination of both. Encouragement and safety can help us try a new way.

Here are a few ideas you could try to help turn negative chatter into nurturing talk:

- First and foremost, start noticing when it is happening. Sometimes we are so used to it, we don't even notice.
- Don't discount it with, *I didn't really mean it, or I was just kidding.* Words have impact, hurtful is hurtful.
- Notice, whose voice do those words or feelings come from? Someone or something in your past or present?
- Practice lovingly reframing the negative thoughts or words, "You suck at this!" can become, "Are you worried what someone is going to think? Let's look for what we like in it together."
- Practice paying it forward, use nurturing talk with others, so you can practice it with yourself, too.

Resource: What nurturing talk would you like to hear? Practice it with yourself and ask others to say it to you, too.

Day 95
Act as If...

Okay, maybe you are showing up but you are not feeling like an artist or an accomplished artist. We have such big expectations for ourselves—when we are just starting. Allow yourself to practice in your practice! ALWAYS remember you have the rest of your life to learn and grow creatively. We are never done!

This reminds me of five or more years back when a trained painter friend, Therese Rossi, was coming to my open studios. It looked so effortless when she painted. I would watch her and think, "She is what a painter looks like." Soon after I began my *leftover paint journals* and I practiced holding my brush and dabbing the paint on the page like I saw her do. It was such fun *pretending* I was a painter.

Though I had been painting for years, I did not look like her. Pretending I was her as I played with color, pretending to be a confident seasoned painter worked, mostly because I wasn't thinking, I was having fun!

Flash forward to a few nights ago. (I am drawing a blind contour portrait every evening and then painting it.) As I finish with a color on my brush, I take it to the facing page in my journal and do a *leftover paint page.* And at the end of my process, I use up any extra paint from my palette on those leftover paint pages. As I work, I notice I no longer think about painting like my friend Therese, instead, I paint like me! I had found my way.

Pretend you are the musician you love, or favorite author, or a favorite actor or dancer as you do your daily performance. Act as if, until you find your own way!

Resource: Allow yourself to pretend, to follow, to act like, you never know where it will take you!

Day 96
Art as Savior—Art Helps

People tell me often that art saved their life. I have witnessed it happen as someone wants to self-harm or feels suicidal and turns to their art to help them get through. Art helps us tolerate and manage discomfort longer; when we need relief, art can help. In addition, we have something to show for it. We lived through it, and we have evidence of our journey through.

I first learned this when I was working through #metoo issues in my twenties. Feelings seemed too big for me and were centered in my body. I wanted to self-harm to make them stop.

At this time, I did not consider myself an artist, but I did have some acrylic paints. I spent hours with a tiny paintbrush painting tiny strokes of paint on a piece of furniture. Tiny strokes of paint that mirrored the damage I imagined doing to myself to relieve these intense feelings. I did not harm myself. Instead, I painted thin lines, over and over until I was too tired to hold the paintbrush any longer. By this time the ferocity of the feelings had subsided enough to let me get some sleep. The next morning, I felt somewhat better. I was able to reach out for help and as I tell this story today, what seemed so big then is now a manageable memory. My art saved me that night.

That experience was long before I studied Expressive Arts Therapy, long before art became an integral part of my life, but somehow, intuitively I knew to reach for a paintbrush and paint rather than harm myself. Art was my savior, art helped.

Resource: When feeling overwhelmed or challenged by strong emotions and the desire for self-harming, alcohol, drugs, or suicide, go to art. How long? Until you feel relief. Get outside help to support you, too. Call 911 if needed. You are not alone.

Day 97

Missed a Day, Skipped a Day

I accidentally missed a day on Saturday. I jumped right into my day, and it was a full one, with a new show opening at the studio and a concert after. I went until I was exhausted and fell into bed. I didn't realize I missed my writing until the next day. Again, another full day. It wasn't until midnight when I was already in bed I remembered I hadn't shown up again.

This time I made the choice not to write. I had spent my day in a creative splurge. I had been working in visual journals for the past few months and was on a creative joy ride. Writing is more work for me—brain work. I have to think. At this late time of night, I had no brain power left and decided taking two days off was not a failure; it was okay to step away.

This morning, Monday, as I write, I question myself—was it a negotiation I made in the night to make it okay? My answer was "no" last night. And today I agree, and I see a place for an adjustment. What if I still wrote on the weekends but I made it creative writing, or improv poetry? Or I incorporate writing into my visual journals rather than at the keyboard? If I accept this idea, I did write this weekend. And I had a prolific outlay of creative energy. And I feel relief.

You make the rules. You decide what the parameters are. This is your project.

Remember, *the goal is to keep going and grow a Creative Practice you love,* that you can't live without, that feeds your spirit—not to have a ball and chain around you weighing you down. It is important though to know when you are *negotiating to get out of doing* or *making an excuse* that could turn into stalling or ending your Creative Practice.

Resource: This is your Creative Practice, allow for change.

Day 98
Sit Quietly, It Will Come

"I don't show up because I don't know what to do."
"I show up and I don't know what to do."

If either of those statements are true for you, sit quietly, it will come. If there was a magic pill to take, it is simply showing up, ready to listen. Listening in a world where we are bombarded with information can be one of our most difficult tasks. How do we listen to know what to do next?

It is said listening is an active experience. In communication when we are practicing active listening with another, we hear what is said and then we offer it back to the other as evidence we have heard them. With our creative process, we sit quietly. We wait patiently for an impulse to arrive. And we show we are listening by following the impulse when it arrives.

In the creative process, active listening is hearing the impulse of what to do and following it with action. And accepting the impulse may be small. Sometimes we are so busy looking for the big gift, we want to find our passion for something that will change the world, and we miss the small gift of "pick up the pen" or "fill the canvas with red" or "start at middle C on the piano." Yet, if we can learn to follow those small impulses, one after another, they may lead to something we feel passionate about.

When the small ideas come your way, show you are listening by taking action, and see where it takes you. I assure you it WILL take you somewhere!

Resource: If you feel lost or unsure of what to do next, sit quietly and listen. Then, act on what you hear.*

**Listening for the impulse actions are those that do not hurt ourselves, others, or property. They are for our greatest good.*

Day 99

The Gift of Not Liking Your Art

Part of the creative process is to notice what is not working or makes us unhappy. Sometimes this leads to a simple change, sometimes the dislike calls for a major overhaul.

In my Wednesday night *Paint to Music™* group when someone doesn't like what they have done I often tell them to throw paint at their piece. Put all the feelings of disappointment into the throwing. Use their whole body, not just a sprinkle of paint but throw it with all the gusto they have. Suddenly they are in relationship with the piece they don't like. Their anger or distress has transformed it. Or maybe they do a separate process to get all their displeasure out so they can come back and view the piece they are not liking from a different perspective.

Sometimes the dislike doesn't even have to do with aesthetic desires. For me, it can be influenced by my bad day or learning my car needs a costly repair. If I express the emotions, no matter if they are about my art or not, I can come back to a more centered place to make creative and life decisions.

Another challenge is when we are trying to shape our art into something it does not want to be. We need to listen. What is the work wanting rather than what are we wanting. Maybe the 300-page book wants to be a short story, or the pop song turns into a church hymn. Could the ballet become a hip hop number? Don't worry about where it ends up, just take the dissatisfaction and make a BIG statement with it, rather than cowering away and getting smaller.

Sometimes the expression of the emotions, naming the dissatisfaction and even stomping away, opens the creative channel.

Resource: When you are feeling unhappy with your project, think of three BIG things to do. And ask, what does IT want?

Celebrate
ONE HUNDRED
days!

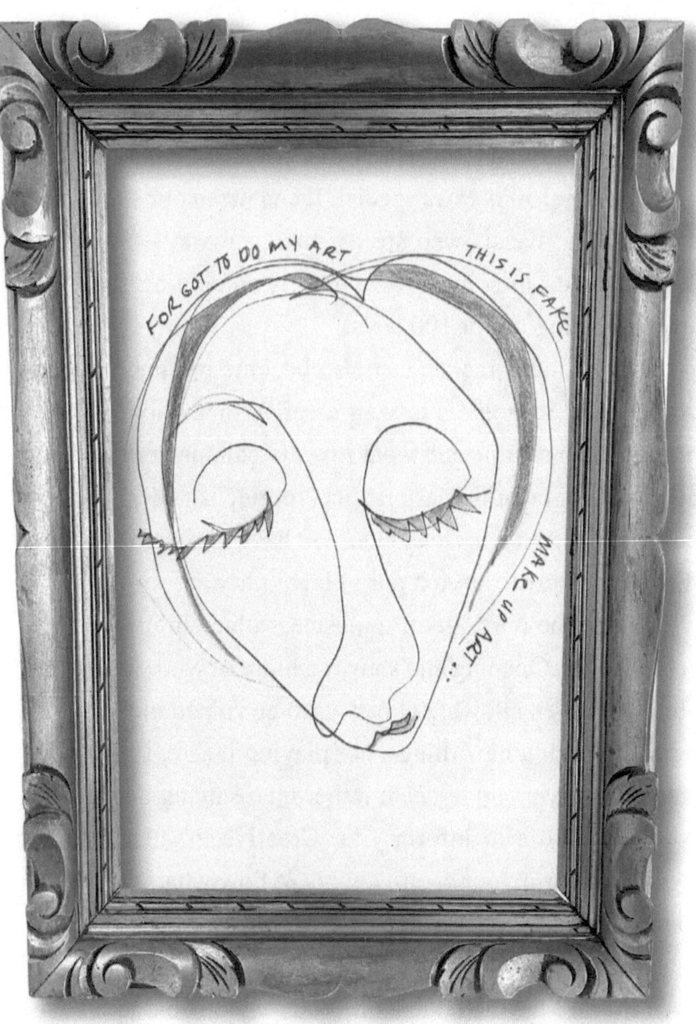

365 Days of Narcissism

A blind contour pen drawing each day, mostly of myself, thinking about how I was feeling or what I was processing from my day. About 100 days in I wanted to quit because it wasn't interesting. I decided to add colored pencil to the process, just little bits here and there. That small change took the process from boring to satisfying.

Day 100
Celebrate with Vulnerability

You made it to day 100! Every day we show up, I would call a gift, and day 100 is extra special. It can mean our *show-up muscle* is strong. We showed up, we made a mark, left evidence of our existence in some way. There is something empowering about showing up for 100 days!

And yet, our practice can also become routine. I encourage you to bring awareness to your creative time. Noticing when it becomes too routine and what I would call, unemotional. In the beginning of creating our practice, routine is good—we want to build our *show-up muscle*. Once we have mastered showing up, it could be time to stretch our vulnerability.

Almost the opposite of a muscle, vulnerability is letting go and relaxing. Opening and showing more of who we are through our work. Even allowing ourselves to be vulnerable with the materials by trying new things, not playing it safe. Expressing the emotional layers underneath rather than staying on the surface. Allow your life to inform your Creative Practice. Allow the world to inform your creative work. Allow what you care about to inspire your creative time.

Notice when you are feeling flat in your process, in the doing, even if you love the end result. You may be able to take things even further. Though we are not doing our Creative Practice for others, when we bring vulnerability to our art, our art becomes more compelling to ourselves and to the viewer.

Resource: Celebrate 100 days! This is a great marker of progress and a good opportunity to explore more vulnerability. Is there anything you can do to celebrate and also take more risks, be more vulnerable in your creating? You may also brainstorm any challenges so you will *keep going.*

Day 101
Art as Essential Self-Care

Have you noticed yet, *art helps*? Sure, there are frustrations here and there, but for the most part, I usually feel calmer, more centered and happier after my creative time. No matter how little time I can take, I notice a shift. I hear the same from others, too.

Yet, we still tend to NOT make time to be creative or we save it for when we do have time, which might be once in a blue moon, or never. How about changing the view, and instead of seeing your creative time as icing on the cake or squeezing it in, thinking of it as *essential self-care*?

Art-making can be a meditation, a prayer, a chance to quiet the mind and calm the body. The number one thing I hear people say after making art in my groups is how relaxed they feel. Who doesn't need to relax? Or feel inspired? Or recharged? Or accomplished?

When I play the piano, my whole body drops down into the keys, it is like I become one with the piano. When I dance, my body forgets everything except the sensations of the movements. Notice what your art form offers you.

If you have stress in your life, if you have trouble making time for yourself, let me give you permission to put your creative time in the category of essential. It is okay to do things that feel good, it is okay to take care of yourself, it is okay to put yourself first—front and center—for 5 minutes to an hour a day. And, if you have a hard time accepting this, I am happy to write you a prescription. The art doctor says a little art a day helps keep the blues-stress-anxiety-irritation-boredom-blahs away!

Resource: Where is art-making in your priorities? Is it a pleasure you get to do only if you have earned it? If so, try on the idea it is an essential necessity, and your health depends on it.

Day 102

Art as a Mirror for Self-Care

I experience my daily Creative Practice as a mirror for self-care. I like to write in the morning and paint or do visual art in the evening. This morning as I sit down to write I don't want to. I begin to negotiate and try to talk myself out of it. I note I am feeling a little blue this morning so there is no desire to write. Taking stock of my situation I have to admit I went to bed too late last night. My Creative Practice helps me to see my unhelpful behavior. The same becomes true when I don't allow time at night for my painting. It usually comes down to working too much or vegging in front of the television.

My Creative Practice feeds me, so when I am not doing it, I know something is out of balance in my life. My art is not just a place to work *with* what is going on in my life, it is a magnifying glass to help me see something *is* going on. How I show up to make my art becomes an indicator of how my life is going.

Yes, sometimes we need to veg in front of the television, or we have a night out with friends and get to bed too late. But when it continues, and our creative expression suffers because of it, what do we do? I say, start where you are at. If you are tired because you drank too much, make art about it. If you are overworking, make art about working too much. The gift is that the art becomes the solution. We show up no matter what. We see ourselves more closely, and maybe this will lead to change, or just showing up to our art is the change.

Today I wanted to negotiate my way out of my art because I didn't take care of myself, and as I write, I care for myself. That is magical in my world.

Resource: Don't let the reasons you think you can't take time to be creative get you out of creating, let it be the focus of what you create.

Day 103
Does Art Always Help?

I am the spokesperson for *the idea, art helps.* Because this has been my experience...okay, is that true? Does it always help? I admit, maybe it doesn't help every time, but most of the time. There may be those occasions where making art doesn't seem to help at all. I may be feeling blue, I make art about feeling blue, and I still feel blue. Or I try to escape by painting the ocean and sailboats, I still feel blue.

The gift is, when we are feeling miserable, and make art, at least we have something to show for it. We have this creative expression to mark our dark day. Or an entire series of work about extended dark times.

Currently the world is going through Covid-19 quarantine. It is a highly emotional time. Deep loneliness, desperate financial times, and this invisible thing in the air. Having a Creative Practice through times like this can offer a sense of accomplishment, expression, and emotional release in the midst of the stresses. Plus, we have an artful diary of our time to look back on.

With a consistent Creative Practice we know we will show up whether it helps or not. And, what seems like it is not helping today in the moment, might reveal itself in the future when we reflect from a different vantage point. Maybe it will have something to say to us that we couldn't see when we were in the darkness. Like, "Wow, I made it through, I did it! Art really did help me cope."

Resource: Take notice if art helps. Often, we want big changes, but shifts are made in small increments. A little more relaxed, a tiny bit happier. Or just a noticing, oh, I took a nice deep breath, or I was smiling while I was working, or I finished and did the dishes for the first time in days.

Day 104

Make It Easy on Yourself

It is natural to *want* to create a masterpiece. I noticed when I was not making art regularly, I had an expectation for my art to be great. And when this didn't happen, I was disappointed and would use it as evidence I was not an artist. When I began my first daily Creative Practice, I loosened up. I had fewer expectations because I knew I would be showing up every day. So, if today doesn't go well, there is always tomorrow, and the next day, and the next. This was a shift in attitude that brought me closer to feeling like an artist than I had ever felt before.

Remembering that no day needs to be particularly earth shattering, and the true aesthetic revelation is in the body of our work we create over time, can free us up to be more fully in the moment of creating. Let the critic take a vacation while we enjoy the satisfaction of showing up.

This said, make it easy on yourself, you do not have to paint the Mona Lisa or write the next Pulitzer prize-winning novel. What you need is to show up and do something to feed your creative spirit. Make it easy, inviting, and even playful so you will not waiver. You can always add difficulty after you show up. I say I am going to write for 5 minutes, I can always stay longer.

Whatever you need to do to make it easy on yourself, it is okay. Your Creative Practice is there to give you life energy. Let it be easy and fun.

Resource: The creative process is not meant to drain you. If your practice is not life giving, rethink it, make adjustments so you will enjoy the process and keep going.

Day 105

Push Through the Difficult

"Disciplined practice has to do with a commitment of time, energy, and attention. More than anything else, discipline has to do with sticking to something past the point where it becomes difficult or frustrating or challenging."
—Catherine Hyland Moon, *Studio Art Therapy*

When my son was young, he excelled at many things right from the start. At some point there would be a moment where it got hard and he had to push himself through the hard to get better. This was the moment he would often give up or move on to something else.

Committing to a Creative Practice can offer us the opportunity to push through those hard times, to not give up when we might normally want to quit.

For me, the desire to stop or quit is a tight and grueling place, almost like I am giving birth, in this moment giving birth to this book. I am in one more contraction of doubt and the unknown. Even in my twentieth year I need coaching.

If I could name one tool that serves me most in continuing onward when I am feeling like it is too hard, it would be breathing. To breathe my way through. A contraction is a natural part of giving birth, helping a baby into this world, helping bring my book into this world. I find relief in my breathing.

While breathing I remember past lessons of wanting to quit because it felt too hard, and if I continued on, there was often new growth, elation, even a sense of *kick ass* on the other side.

Resource: What can help you move through the difficult? Breathe, make a phone call for support, read something inspiring? Use your Creative Practice to process your pushing through.

Day 106
Shitty First Draft

Author Anne Lamott is famous for giving permission to write the *"shitty first draft"*—to hold back on judgment, critique, and editing until you get this *shitty first draft* written.

This process can transfer to any discipline: writing, painting, dance, drama, music, or whatever creative adventure you are taking. The idea is to let it flow, do not inhibit the flow with editing but enable it to come through raw and original. The shaping and editing comes later.

I call it *the download,* allowing yourself the gift of letting your idea come to life in physical form. Stay in the creative brain. Let your analytical editor go on vacation.

We need our analytical editor brain, we want it in our creative process, but not right away. It is difficult to stay in the safe creation zone when our brain jumps into examination.

I have seen too many projects stalled because the creator jumps back and forth between creating and editing and can't get the idea out. It can become a grueling process that is abandoned.

Put off the *shaping* and *editing* process for a day or week or more, so your work is not too precious and you aren't as attached as when you created it. Once you have some distance, then you can go in with your editor's eye, looking at what is working and not working. The shaping may take many revisits. This entry for example has taken days to finalize, and it may not be finished yet!

Resource: Let whatever wants to be expressed download without edits. If it is a struggle to let go and not edit simultaneously, this may be your perfectionist jumping in to save you. Can you start to grow the muscle to wait—a little at a time? Wait just a *little* longer, then a little bit longer than that, and keep growing your download time. Remember to breathe.

Day 107
Reflection on Your Creative Time

It can be a gift to learn to reflect on our art-making in a non-judgmental way. What could this look like?

1. *Look at the process* you have used. What has been pleasurable? Could you build on this? What has not been pleasurable, and can you do less of this? Was there a moment where something exciting happened? Were there any challenges? How did you get through the challenges?

2. *Now look aesthetically* at the product you have created. What are you liking? What is working? What does it need more of? What does it need less of? What wants to change?

3. *With the idea of shaping* the art, imagine the next steps you could take with your creating. What could happen next?

4. *Honor how you spent your time,* set your art, a photo or script some place where you can see it, so it can speak to you if it wants. If you are not liking what you did your first impulse may be to hide it away. Instead, keep it out, ask it, what does it need, and listen so it can tell you!

5. *Does another form of art want to be created in response* to what you have done? Does the painting want to be danced or the poem need music? Does the photo need a story written? Or maybe the photo wants to be painted abstractly.

6. *Start a log of your making time.* Dedicate a notebook or journal to your Creative Practice. You can give a title to the day's product or process, answer the above questions or journal about your process.

Resource: These can also be helpful questions when you want feedback from others. Telling them what you want from them in the form of feedback increases the chance of getting what you need, rather than too general or unhelpful critiques.

Day 108
Is It THIS Easy?

If life is a bowl of cherries, my bowl is filled with rotted fruit. Today I woke feeling high anxiety and desperation about the world around me. I feel powerless to do anything that could amount to any kind of change. I want to throw in the towel and scream about it all being too hard. I look out the window and the sun is shining, the leaves are fluttering in the wind, the sage is blooming purple. The dogs of the neighborhood begin their chorus announcing the approach of the mail carrier.

Wow. This was an interesting experience. I was going to write about the sun shining and how beautiful the day looks outside, while I am feeling dark on the inside. But instead, as I began to look out my window and name what I saw and heard, something shifted. Could it all be this easy? My brain began to focus on the beauty outside my window. My attention shifted away from my challenges to the beauty.

I don't profess it to be this easy, yet I just experienced it. You are in real time with me. Let's dissect what happened:

- I woke feeling anxious and dark inside.
- I thought, I need to write about this.
- My writing led me to look outside to compare my insides with the literal outside world.
- I looked out the window, and I ALSO wrote about what was happening as I looked out the window.
- I was looking through my senses and my artist eyes.
- I wrote and I began to feel the power of creating.
- My dark place shifted and I felt relief.

Resource: What if it really is this easy? What if the act of experiencing and creating, bringing our attention to the tiny moments, and capturing them through the arts, can help?

Day 109
What Excites You?

Having ideas about what to do when we show up can be a challenge. Having an overall theme can be helpful. Maybe you check in every day, what excited you during your day or what felt unfinished? Then take this to your Creative Practice. I did one year of *"Kick Ass Moments"* where I looked to my day, found something *kick ass* I did or participated in and made art about it. By doing this I learned that often the *kick ass moments* were small moments I may have overlooked.

If we can plan a theme ahead, it can cut back on the stress of what to do when we show up. And, you can change it any time you want. If you don't like it, do something different. Or if you get inspired by something new, try it!

In my first year of daily art, I sometimes did weeklong themes to enliven my practice. A few of my favorites: Sharpie doodles when Sharpie came out with fabulous new extra fine colors, found objects I would then write about, art in the dark where I turned the lights out and scribbled, strange characters after going to see Cirque du Soleil, and blind contour drawings because they were easy.

We never know where the excitement is going to lead. It may be a whim and lasts a moment or it may open doors toward deeper creative exploration. Scribbling led to my *Scribble Art* book and the Scribble Kit. Blind contour drawings became six or more years of projects, and has grown into my recognizable style.

If something catches your interest or excites you, follow it. If you don't have the time or space to do it right away, write it down. I have a little book where I keep my ideas, so if I can't act on them in that moment I can catch them for later.

Resource: What excites you can be breadcrumbs to your passion. Take notice, follow them, or make a note so you don't forget!

Day 110

I Donated All My Art-Making Books

In my pre art-making life, I bought book after book about art I was going to make, someday. It mostly never happened. Or I tried once and never did more. I loved looking at the photos, but I rarely made anything. Making art felt as scary as being a surgeon.

Here is the thing, when you want to become a surgeon, you KNOW you need a lot of education and you get it. You are taught not to get emotional, follow the procedures, think fast on your feet, and you are pushed out of the nest when you are ready.

With art, there is the idea it should come naturally. Because I WANT to do it, I should know how. No one, not the art schools, art classes, or the books prepare you for the out-of-control feeling you can have creating art. No one tells you your critic will come ROARING forward. No one tells you the act of creating will open things inside that make you feel vulnerable and inadequate.

When it doesn't come naturally, making art is an act of bravery and courage. To put music in the air when you can't take it back, to be witnessed painting, dancing, or reading something you wrote takes bravery. Art-making can be taking off a layer of protective armor.

Back to those books. Once I began my daily Creative Practice and learned to follow the next impulse, I donated all my books. I no longer had the desire to look at those pictures and learn someone else's way. I preferred to muddle through and find my own path, or to learn from making art in community and be inspired by others in real time. *Artist is a verb*, it is the doing, not the looking. You CAN do it, too! The more you do, the easier it will get!

Resource: Stop looking, start doing. *Artist is a verb,* create!

Day 111
Bravery and Courage

I think of bravery and courage as two qualities necessary for those of us on the creative path. Bravery is the initial quality to jump into something new or back into something that may or may not have worked at another time. Courage keeps us in the game. Think of a long-distance runner. Bravery says yes to the race, and courage helps us to stay in the race.

It takes bravery to start a Creative Practice. To answer a call to express yourself regularly. To say "Yes!" to yourself, be willing to rearrange your life and commit to take this time for yourself. To say "Yes!" to walking into the great unknown of the creative process where delight and disappointment may greet you at any given moment.

It takes courage to show up every day. To say no to the things wanting to pull you away and continuously say yes to this call. You were called, you bravely said yes. And now you courageously continue to say yes, one day at a time.

The etymology of the word *bravery* is to *be daring.* To *dare* to have a Creative Practice. To *dare* to become an artist, musician, dancer, writer, actor, or other creative.

The etymology of the word *courage* comes from the word *"heart."* We move forward *with heart,* we show up each day *with heart,* we express our *heart.*

Honor the bravery it took for you to carve out this idea for your life and honor the courage to take action on this idea every time you show up. Dare to move forward with heart!

You are on your way, brave and courageous one.

Resource: What words might (en)courage you to keep going? Post them somewhere. I have a message on my keyboard, *"GO FULL OUT, live the writer you are!"*

Day 112
Encouragement

Encouragement can help us push through what feels hard, try something new that may feel scary, and help us feel hopeful when we are not seeing our own progress. A loved one cheering us on to stay in the game.

Encouragement is essential to keep us going and feel supported. Having just one person to encourage you on your Creative Practice journey can be helpful. And asking for help is necessary because no one knows what we need until we tell them. Maybe ask someone to check in to see how you are doing, or find someone to create a Creative Practice alongside you so you share the experience. Tell your supporter what you need from them, try it out, and allow for adjustments.

There can also be a level of accountability for our own good when we let others in on our process. Because we don't want to *fail* or be witnessed in a *failure,* we show up. A more positive reframe could be, by having someone we are accountable to, we show up when we might easily choose not to. Someone is on our team and cares.

There is also internal encouragement. When we learn to celebrate ourselves and our baby steps, we build our internal muscle of support. When we take time to honor the steps we take, we grow our confidence and need less approval from the outside world.

Resource: Let us celebrate today, in this moment we both showed up to this entry in this book. I showed up to write it, you showed up to read it. It takes a village to encourage self-expression. The act of creation, making art, can be lonely internal work. If we surround ourselves with supporters who witness our journey with love, and be this for ourselves, too, it can be life changing.

Day 113
Everything I Do Looks the Same

As a mentor, a common topic I talk about to creators is to notice what feels good and follow those pleasures. When someone complains all their work looks or sounds the same my first question is, "Do you enjoy doing it?"

When you feel the desire to change things up, it can help to look at where the idea is coming from. Is it internal, are you bored and feel the need to mix it up, go bigger or smaller, brighter or quieter? Have you investigated the subject matter long enough and are longing to do something new? Have your skills progressed to a point where you are ready for more challenge, or do you want to learn new techniques? Do you have a desire to break out of the mold and go somewhere new?

Or is the desire to do something different coming from the outside? Are you worrying about what someone else is thinking? What the world wants, what will sell, what will get you attention, versus what you love to do?

It is okay to get pressure from the outside to grow and change, yet we need to be sure it aligns with who we are as an artist.

Try something new because you want to, because it excites you, and because you feel drawn toward it. Not because you feel outside pressure or you are looking at yourself through someone else's eyes.

If you create the same kind of art, over and over for the rest of your life, and enjoy the process, it is okay. You have a style. It is okay to do what feels good. This is *your* creative life!

Resource: If it feels good and you enjoy doing it, keep going! When you want to change things up, look at why you want to make the changes. Is it your true desire or is it because you feel pressure from outside? Follow YOUR impulses. Stay curious.

Day 114
Creative Despair

You are at the mercy of your life. Your critic, your depression, overwhelm, anxiety, or other happenings have taken over and there is no inspiration, no energy, no resources. The idea of showing up feels like it takes more life force than you have and throws you into overload. What do you do? How do we allow for these periods of lulled energy without abandoning our Creative Practice?

Once again, I say, start where you are. If you feel like a blob of nothing, begin there. One thing I love to do is to lay on the floor of my studio. I lay with my back on the floor, legs pointing north, arms open wide to each side, allowing the weight of my body to sink into the cool hard floor. Allowing myself to be depleted. Sometimes I begin to sing or chant a word or sound. Sometimes I yell, scream, or lay silent. Almost always, I can get up and do something, even if it is to write, *today there is no art.* Allowing myself to go to this lifeless place in a unique way, helps me feel more alive. Meeting myself where I am at—with what I need.

It seems helpful to give attention to what is, rather than trying to get myself out of it. Somehow, the attention creates movement. I am writing this right now because I am in one of those places, and just imagining doing my process, my body eases. These words are flowing when what I tried to write earlier was a major struggle. I start where I am and there is movement.

Resource: Always start where you are, then check in, what does your body want to do? Curl up in a ball? Sit on the edge of a stream? Grab a large piece of clay and pound on it? Whatever it is, do it or imagine doing it and see if anything changes.

⇨ *Get therapeutic help if you need it. You do not have to navigate despair alone.*

Day 115
Creating a Safe Space to Create

Creative time needs a safe place to explore new things because when we try new things we can feel vulnerable. How do we establish safety so we can generate authentic art and even *fail*? How do we create a protected space for ourselves? What is it you need to feel secure and encouraged in your creative explorations? Let's look at physical space, internal space, and community space.

Physical Space. When I began my first daily art project my art was small and I could work anywhere. It was also small enough so the world could not easily see what I was doing. When year two came and I was painting on large paper and did not have a private space to paint, I felt vulnerable. Not only were my paintings out for everyone to see, but when I painted, if anyone else was watching I would freeze up. I had to get bold and ask for alone time or schedule my painting when no one was there, until I grew my confidence. What do you need? You could even create in your car, at a friend's house, or at the library. Be creative.

Internal Space. How safe do you feel inside your own head and heart? Can you work without berating, critiquing, or having expectations? We need a safe place within to try new things that may not work. Cultivating a caring inner voice is essential to a positive long lasting Creative Practice.

Community Space. Having a mentor or creative community to give you positive and caring support is important. If you are not feeling safe, ask for what you need, ask for the kind of creative feedback you want and if this doesn't work, find a new creative community or create your own.

Resource: Feeling unsafe can shut us down, whether it comes from inside or outside. Create a positive supportive space to keep you going and set boundaries if needed.

Day 116

Start a Creative Idea Wish List

The blank page can be a game ender for many, not knowing what to put on the blank page or what to do in the blank time set aside to create. We can always start where we are, check in to how we are feeling, or notice what is right there at the forefront of our life. What if we want more? It is helpful to keep a file or notebook of creative ideas for those moments when the idea factory is closed. An idea inventory we can refer to for a bit of help.

When writing this book I would open a new document each time I had a new idea. I could go back and give it attention later when I had more time. I found those idea entries became what I looked for when I had no brain power to come up with something original in the moment.

Great ideas can come when we least expect them. Get into the habit of writing them down immediately before they are lost. I know from personal experience if I don't capture the idea quickly, it will be gone forever.

Often the challenge point isn't we don't want to be creative, it is we don't have the creative spark in the moment to figure out how to use our creative time. Sometimes we need someone to tell us what to do. This is why taking a class can be helpful, someone will tell you what to do, give you a prompt or homework assignment. Or go find your own prompts. Do an online search in your area of creative expression. Look for writing, dance, improv, musical, and visual art prompts or challenges. A small prompt can kickstart our process. Our job as artists is to break the code of the blank page! Find what works for you!

Resource: Anything can be a prompt, and ideas can come anytime. Write down your creative ideas and wishes so they are available to you when you are feeling blank.

Day 117
Allow Yourself to Get WILD!

Tonight in my writing group we had a prompt about being wild. As I wrote what it might feel like to be wild in my life, the normal constriction I feel lifted. Living wildly with my art would mean not caring what others think and even brazenly ending sentences in prepositions! I would make wild strokes of colors without caring why. My space would be wildly messy, at least for a moment.

Why don't we live more wildly in the world? Who thought wild should be tamed? Who clipped your wild wings, was it school, family, or a specific experience?

What would it be like for you to get wild with your art? What would happen if you didn't care for a moment—you lived out loud, really loud? What if you tried it once a week or every full moon or eventually, every time you show up? What would change if you made fierce statements with your practice?

In my studio we have a paint room where people are invited to get messy, throw paint, let paint drip, and spray all over, sometimes even onto themselves. I created this room after years of working at sites where I had to be tidy and never let it look like art was happening there. I was clear with my studio I wanted a place for people to get messy. Maybe if we all had a place to get creatively messy, we would not need to get messy in other areas of our life. Often people are timid at first, and then they SMILE!

Let's make a pact, right here, right now, to allow ourselves space to get creatively wild. Color outside the lines, sing louder than expected, tell the stories we fear would be wildly judged.

Resource: Look for a place or time you could get a little wild. You can work your way up the wild scale slowly. Tell someone you did it or invite someone to join you!

Day 118
Make a Gift

Austin Kleon, author of the books *Steal Like an Artist* and *Keep Going,* suggests if you are stuck with your art, make a gift for someone.

For the first half of my life, this was the only way I made art, by creating gifts for others. I would make all my own holiday and birthday gifts and cards. It was my reason to make art. Birthdays and holidays also gave me extra deadline pressure motivating me to show up.

For some reason it wasn't okay to "just" make art for myself, but if I was making a gift, it was okay. Once my daily Creative Practice began, I became the receiver of the gifts, each day a new arrival. And then the art started giving to others. My collage journal pages and my "Clean off the Brush" paintings became backgrounds for my yearly calendar gifts. Collages and scribble art became notecards for friends.

If making art for yourself feels selfish, or you have no room to store it or no desire to keep it, make it for others. Do giveaway projects where you leave art around your neighborhood for people to take, or create your own Tiny Free Gallery for giveaways. Hand your art with an encouraging message on the back to strangers as you go through your day or deliver it to hospitals and nursing facilities for staff and patients. You could do it anonymously or use the art to build relationships with your community. Or try both so you can see how each feels.

And for the performing arts, share your gifts with the world, we need you! Sing from your front porch, dance at the park, or...

Resource: How can your gift of creating begin to be a gift to the world? Sign up at AustinKleon.com for Austin Kleon's email for his regular inbox gift of *10 things worth sharing.*

Day 119
Art in the Dark

What happens if you limit your senses when you make your art? An easy experiment is creating art in the dark. What changes when you don't know what colors you are using? When the notes you play travel through darkness? In the dark no one can see how your body moves as you dance. If I close my eyes as I write, do the words even find their way to the lines or will I be able to read what I have written?

Sometimes I get my best ideas at 3:00 a.m. in the dark. I know if I don't write them down, they will be gone by morning. Sometimes I can barely read the chicken scratch. Sometimes I get brazen, feeling so sure I will remember I don't write it down, and usually by morning it is gone. Things slip away in the dark. The edges are softer, it becomes a mystery of sorts.

Sometimes the dark is not knowing where the story is going or where the painting is headed. Sometimes the dark is blindly pulling a word from a hat or color from your box.

Creating is metaphorically the perfect place to practice being in the dark, the unknown. When we let go into the creative process we don't know where we are going to end up and if things will work. We must constantly respond to the materials and to our aesthetic desires. It can get easier with practice.

And slowly we may even learn to live in the unknown and uncertainty of our life, too.

Resource: Explore making art in the dark. Literally turn off the lights and see what happens. (You might need a little preparation if you are using messy materials.) Or you can simply close your eyes, though it might not be as fun! Notice what is different when you limit your sense of sight.

Day 120
Making Dark Art

In my writing support group tonight the idea of needing permission to tell our dark stories, the sad, the grief, the trauma, the angry, or simply, whatever is not happy, was a topic of discussion. We live in a time of social media where people share everything great, even though we know it can't always be sunny. This lopsided sunshine may contribute to feeling isolated when our own world is not so cheery.

"Don't tell your unhappy truth" is an underlying message we learn. With the best of intentions, my mother would say, "If you can't say something nice, don't say anything."

The arts are our tool to share all the parts of ourselves. Yes, we hope for a hero's journey, to come out the other side changed. And sometimes we are in the midst of the discomfort and need to express our own personal hell. In tonight's writing group we witnessed one person's honest story opened the door for others to share their own difficult stories.

If we start where we are, and something raw and dark is there, how can we give it the attention it needs and deserves? Maybe we need to spend hours, weeks, or years with darkness and maybe naming it will be enough to move on. As captains of our own Creative Practice ships, there is no one to tell us what we can and can't do. Our practice offers us a safe place to express.

When we can give voice to those vulnerable places, we might become more compassionate toward ourselves and available to see the good in our life. Staying in balance is important. Purposefully create space for beauty so you can keep your life in equilibrium.

Resource: Make time for honest and truthful art. If you notice something feels big, ask for help through therapy or a support group. You don't need to carry it all on your own.

Day 121
Art and Anxiety

Often being too anxious can be a reason for not making art. What if instead, we brought our anxiety into our art-making and used it as inspiration?

Anxiety is full of energy, swirling, frenetic, and active. Even when it is at a low-level discomfort, it is packed with sensation. I see anxiety as energy wanting to be expressed. I want the anxiety out of my body because the discomfort is so strong. Focusing it toward art can result in amazing work. When I really connect with my anxiety I can fill the page quickly, working at a swift pace. My love for scribbling was born from wanting to express my anxiety and get it out of my body.

I know that many therapeutic approaches are to calm the anxiety. I find in my own process my body wants to express it and this helps me to move into the calm. If I can do a scribble, paint, or dance to meet the same frenetic energy as how it feels inside me, then, once I have expressed it, I can begin a calming scribble or other exercise. The scribble can help when I need to deal with it immediately. Also, my art becomes evidence of my discomfort—seeing the expression of it gives me a sense of satisfaction.

Anxiety can also tell me there is something I need to attend to, a step I need to take. By doing my anxiety art, I can get ideas of things to do to relieve my anxiety. Often it is an action I need to take, like making a phone call or completing a task. When I get below the discomfort of the anxiety and listen to what may help, and do it, I start to feel a sense of control, which I think is what my anxiety ultimately wants.

Resource: We all need to find the way art helps us. What is yours? Make a little sign and post it to remind you. "Feeling anxious? Turn up the music and dance!"

Day 122
More on Art and Anxiety

As I mentioned yesterday, art is always where I turn when anxiety arrives. I encourage you to do the same. Rather than reach for the pill, the drink, the food, or other mind-altering substances, reach for art first.

Another secret when working with anxiety, or any big emotion, is to bring your attention so fully to the moment of creation that nothing else exists. Here is an example of what I do. I am the queen of scribbling and I promote it because everyone can do it, all you need is a pen and piece of paper. Maybe pick up a pen and grab a piece of paper right now and do it for yourself as you read.

My pen meets the paper...my attention is at the small point where my pen meets the paper...nothing else exists... just the point where pen meets paper...I follow the point as the pen begins to move, doing a dance on the paper...nothing exists but the point. I listen to the sounds the pen makes. I continue to follow the line. Not worrying about making something from it, just follow the point where pen meets paper. I notice the texture of the paper, the smoothness or roughness of the line and the meeting of ink to paper. I become one with the line as it comes from the pen onto the paper. If I lose the connection, I remind myself to slow down and be with the point of meeting. I continue longer than I want, continue through the discomfort, until I feel naturally, slowly complete. Not because I want to be done, but when I feel complete.

When done, notice what has changed.

Resource: You can do this with any art form—be one with your fingers as they touch the guitar strings. One with your feet as they dance or walk. One with your hands as they weed. One with your voice as you sing or read poetry. This can naturally slow you down and take you out of thinking and into experiencing.

Day 123
Schedule an Art Retreat

I have found it important to schedule my art into my day. I encourage you to set an alarm, put it on your electronic calendar, set up reminders, whatever it takes to show up. Think of it as your dream job you are investing time into.

My commitment is 5 minutes a day. Which is all I *have* to do, but I can always go longer, and I usually do. And, occasionally getting through 5 minutes seems hard.

I also schedule *Art Retreats* once a month. A time where I have nothing else on my calendar I have to do. It could be a writing retreat or a painting retreat and is often both. I imagined I would go off somewhere for a day or weekend, or even an entire week. Financially that is not feasible, so I do it at home or house sit.

I encourage you to honor your desire to create by carving out a day or two for yourself to *live the life of an artist.* You do not have to work on one project all day. You can do this and that and back to this again. For example, maybe you are having a writing retreat. You can work on your book, write a poem, write a letter to a friend, do a writing exercise from a prompt, or write a gratitude list. Cook a great lunch, take a walk and notice what you see, go to a free neighborhood park concert, paint, write more, go for a night hike, write before you go to bed.

The only rule I make for my *Art Retreats* is to start and end my day with my art and trickle it throughout. Nothing more. My desire is for it to be a fun adventure of what is next, not a to-do list of what has to be done.

Find what works for YOU. And, you won't know until you try. What keeps the pleasure meter high enough for you to keep coming back? If you are a caregiver you may need to get help.

Resource: Look at your calendar and schedule an art retreat.

Day 124
Perfectionism in Disguise

Today in one of my groups a participant told the story of a writing project he started 26 years ago and abandoned. He was back with hopes of reigniting it. The story has stayed with him all these years, but he had put it away because he was worried he couldn't write it well enough.

Perfectionism can be disguised as many things. It can be our critic blasting us with negative messages about our creative endeavors. On the other end of the perfectionist spectrum, it can be giving up or never beginning because we think we can't do it well enough. The latter message may also be hidden subtly in messages like I don't have the time, or I can't afford it, I could never do this, or only certain kinds of people can do that. Perfectionism may be at work when we can't make a decision, so we are left in the in-between, non-committed state.

Perfectionism can also make the process so stressful and so miserable because it can't be less than perfect. How long can we keep this up? It becomes a death sentence for our creativity.

Anxiety can be perfectionism in camouflage. Again, the stress of needing to measure up, be good enough, do it right.

Perfectionism kills our excitement and enthusiasm, too. Think of a time you had a great idea that excited you, and then the next day or week you felt disconnected from it and dropped it or let it fade into the background.

Perfectionism works hard to keep us safe. Safe from failure, looking bad, and possibly losing the love of someone we depend upon. Our Creative Practice helps us test and change this story.

Resource: Practice purposeful imperfection. Consciously allow yourself to be imperfect. Test your perfectionist one small step at a time, so that part of yourself will see you will survive.

Day 125

Expression Not Perfection

A regular at the studio, Danny Sullivan, just passed along a story to me that I loved. He heard the cellist, Yo-Yo Ma, muse about how hard he worked to play the perfect concert. In the middle of that perfect concert, he realized he was bored. Perfection wasn't the object, he realized, but expression was. He wanted people to FEEL his music. Danny related it to his own process as a musician, how much happier he is if he plays a song where people are amused or sing along with him, than if he plays it note perfect. "Expression, not perfection," he called it. He added that he still needed to practice, but it put a different spin on his attitude, his intent.

This got me wondering once again about perfection. Not only can the perfect specimen be boring, trying to aspire to perfectionism can be boring, too. It may keep our creative voices silent. Perfectionism may be our way OUT of expressing. We will never be good enough, never meet the standard to show our gifts to the world. So the world will not have it. We retreat into the belief we can't do it; we are not good enough. We hide behind it as a reason to NOT share our work, or not progress, or even quit.

As an artist, I think of myself as a channel. When I am open, I can listen for the impulses and follow them. When I am caught in perfectionism, I may not trust the impulse or myself. Perfection feels stifling, expression is inviting.

If you have a perfectionist streak, what can you do to make the process more important than the end result? Could you allow your Creative Practice to be a place to experiment with messy, unfinished curiosity rather than excellence?

Resource: Follow curiosity and interest, expression not perfection. Practice being strange, weird, and creating imperfect art on purpose. Honor the feelings that arrive through journaling or your art.

Day 126

Let Art Get You Out of Your Head

The worst of the world may live in our head in the form of worry, doubt, uncertainty, and distractions. The gift of our Creative Practice is it can help us move from our head into our body, and even to our heart. As humans our brains have evolved to a point where we can easily be unbalanced.

Technology lessens our attention span and puts us in a mode of instant gratification. In a moment we can access the world—the good and the bad, the hopeful and the catastrophic. We can be in touch with loved ones, disasters, or the latest information on everything. This sends us in many different directions intellectually and emotionally.

The arts help us slow down and enter into our senses, which are a gateway to being more fully in our body so we can stop analyzing and start feeling. The arts move us from left brain critical thinking to right brain creative. We can be curious, try new things, and grow a rich internal life.

Rather than thinking our way through things, the arts can be the place to go when we need answers. In addition to doing research, take your question to the arts, or even better, let go of the question while you create. Do your Creative Practice. Then, after you have lost yourself in the process of creating—in the sounds, sights, smells, and the kinesthetic noticings of touch—ask your question and let the art, your process, and your more fully present body inform your answer.

In a world where we can't always know what is true, having our body fully engaged in our decision making is important. From there we can discover what is true for ourselves.

Resource: How do you know when you are unbalanced? Start to take notice. When you are, go to the arts for a vacation.

Day 127
Surrender Moments

Surrender—Step Away from Your Art.

When your project feels drier than the desert, when it is not fun, or when things are not working, surrender and step back. Take a break.

When there is no love there. Take a break.
When you absolutely hate what you are doing. Take a break.
When your heart is closed. Take a break.
When your critic is sabotaging you. Take a break.

This break could be:
Expressing why there is no love.
Expressing why you hate what you are doing.
Expressing why your heart is closed.
Expressing the feeling of the critic or saboteur.

Or, run around the block, punch a pillow, organize a drawer, clean the toilet, meditate, call a friend, or write a letter to an enemy. (Not to send.)

And most importantly, come back and try again.
What looks different now?
What needs to change?
Keep going.

Resource: If you are beating yourself up or your work, step away, breathe and take a break. It is just a break, which means, come back, it is a surrender *moment,* don't give up forever!

Day 128

Depression, Grief, Illness, Lethargy

Some days just getting out of bed feels like too much. I get it. Doing what you have to do is more than you can bear. And yet, our art time can be a beacon in this dark sky. Even 5 minutes can shift something. One challenge we can have is an expectation of a big shift, a big change. If we can learn to pay exquisite attention to our body, we can begin to notice subtle small changes.

Follow my own experience. *My heart is heavy, my body is heavy, my arm and hand are too heavy to even lift my pen. But I do. My eyes close so I do not need to use the energy to see. I begin to scribble on the paper. It is a slow, heavy scribble that meets me where I am. It tells the story of my sadness. My eyes open and there it is in front of me. I notice, though it felt heavy when I was doing it, it doesn't look heavy when I open my eyes. In fact, it looks light and wispy. At first, I am disappointed but then I like the idea. I begin to add color and instead of the dark colors I originally envisioned when my eyes were closed, my hands choose lighter, brighter colors. I surprisingly spend a long time coloring. What shifted? I feel soothed. When I was coloring I thought of a few things I want to do today. I take my time, and I get up and begin an easier day.*

Maybe it is not always this dramatic, but more than once I have experienced in myself and in others the turning to our art when we are down, shifts of feeling from overwhelm and dread, to love and care for self. Art-making and self-expression are essential to our physical, mental, and spiritual health. Though sometimes *doing* seems too much, when we can *do* art in the simplest way possible, shifts can happen. And get therapeutic help, too!

Resource: When you are depleted is when you may need to create the most. Find the smallest expression you can do.

Day 129
Keep It Simple

A Reminder.
Keep it simple.
Don't confuse yourself.
Follow the next small impulse.
Don't worry about where you are going.
Or where you will end up.
Trust your impulses.
Trust your ideas.
Trust yourself.
Show up.
Keep
it
simple.

Resource: Simply follow the next impulse. You don't need to know where it will take you or where you are going. Notice if you are making something complicated and it is hanging you up. How could you simplify what you are doing to make it more accessible to YOU?

The creative process often starts
with a small impulse or idea
and needs to be acted on right away so it
doesn't get lost. Write it down!
Who knows where that small idea
could take you!

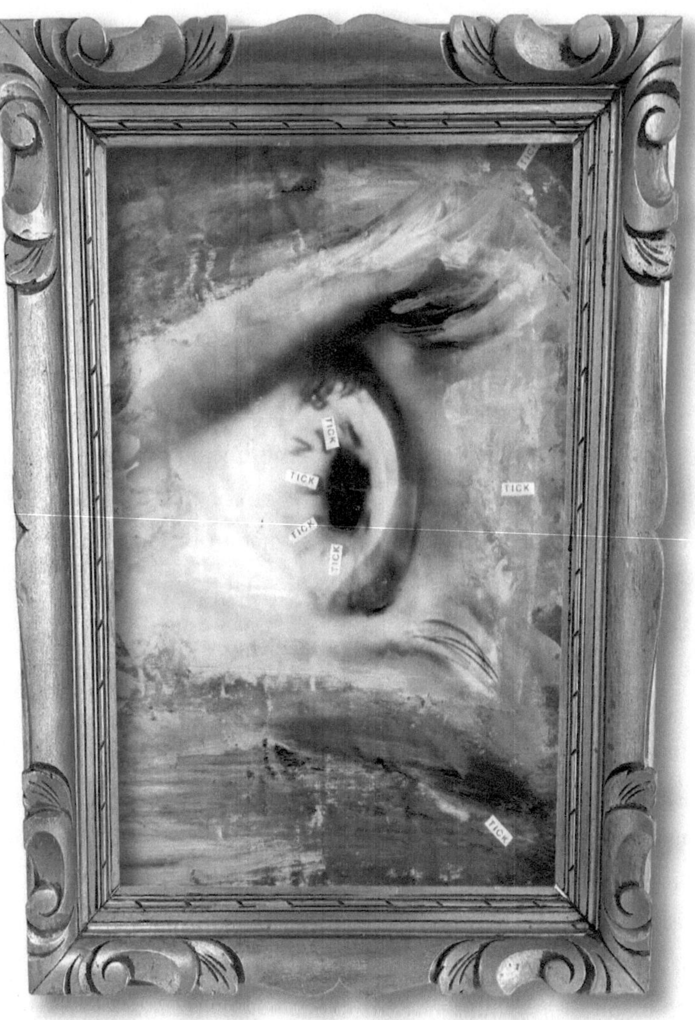

365 Days of Visioning Journal™

I wondered, rather than doing a vision board once a year, why not set an intention and check in with it each day for a whole year? I couldn't wait to get home every night and work in my journal with collage and paint. This was a daily practice for at least three years and I have led groups in the process for at least ten years.
I have over 40 finished journals and counting.

Day 130
Overworking Our Art

I showed up today to work on an entry I have been struggling with all week and just can't seem to get right. As I opened my laptop my belly got tight, and I felt dread. It was a sign. A sign it is not time. I realize, I am overworking it. I need to set it aside, come back to it later. It is not an excuse to give up, but to get a little creative distance.

Art isn't a science. Some days we are motivated and in the flow where it all comes easy, and sometimes it is a struggle. We can't turn creativity on and off. And, a part of creativity is problem solving. Sometimes taking a break is what problem solving needs.

With my painting, when I look at what I am working on and there is NO impulse or excitement, I move on. I look for something else wanting my attention or start something new.

Eventually, I am able to revisit the challenge and get a next step. Magically it is happening right now. A painting I have not liked for months—I try this and that, and it doesn't get better. Just now I have an idea for a next step. I trust the same will happen with my writing challenge.

I believe if you don't like something, it probably isn't done, so don't give up or abandon your work. We never know when the inspiration is going to hit. And, when we don't like something, it offers us an opportunity to try something new and maybe outside our usual box, since we don't like it anyway we have nothing to lose. Who knows, maybe this crossroad can create a doorway to our best work.

Resource: If something is not working, set it aside and go to something else. Place it where you will see or think about it on occasion. Revisit it when the next impulse arrives.

Day 131
I Will NOT!

I will not write today.
I will not pick up my pen and allow thoughts to find form.
I will not open my computer and type or write.
I will not allow myself the time to feed my spirit by writing.
I will not allow something to gel and become meaningful.
I will not allow expression of any kind.
I will not be creative and find a way around or out of this.
I will not do anything.
I am much too tired.
I am much too overwhelmed.
My brain is too foggy.
I have no ideas.
I have no energy.
I have no desire to say anything.
So what will I do?
I will say nothing!
You can't make me.
End of story.
Finished.
Done.
The end.
Maybe I will write tomorrow.
Oh, I just wrote this.

Resource: Give voice to the *"I don't wanna, I hate it, I don't have to"* and see what happens!

Day 132
A Modigliani Moment

It was a chance meeting on a rare weekend I had to myself maybe three-quarters into my first 365 Days of Painting. The movie "Modigliani" caught my eye, and painter Amedeo Modigliani became my muse for the weekend.

The tragedy of his alcoholism and the dark struggles of his story opened my heart. His paintings—long necked figures with empty eyes inspired me. As I watched the movie, I painted myself. Could I merge his style with mine? How would these long-necked figures translate if they were combined with my blind contour portrait style? Could my signature large eyes be influenced by his vacant eyes?

I struggled as I painted using a different color palette and style. As I stood back to observe my final piece, I had one of those defining moments. After an afternoon of struggling, it dawned on me *I have the rest of my life to learn and grow as a painter! I was not going to "become" a painter, it was not an end goal. I did not have to figure anything out or even get particularly good at anything...it wasn't about getting anywhere! It was about allowing myself to be wherever I was, and knowing if I kept showing up, I would probably get better at painting.*

Tears flowed when I had this idea, deep sobs even. It was a release, the deep revelation I did not have to be perfect, I did not have to get there. Instead, I could enjoy the process—experiment, explore, and uncover what I enjoyed doing. And yes, if I wanted to do more realistic painting I could practice. What a relief.

Modigliani died at the age of thirty-five, yet he lives on in me through our afternoon of painting. Thank you.

Resource: Remind yourself when your critic is unhelpful—you have the rest of your life to learn and grow creatively!

Day 133
Practice Means Practice

Having a Creative Practice is just this, we are practicing regularly. As with anything, the more we practice the better we get. If you are thinking you are not "good enough" at whatever you are doing, it is not time to give up, quite the opposite, you are in the perfect place to keep practicing!

Perhaps it started with the industrial revolution, where rather than handmade imperfect beauty, we became accustomed to perfection. Our handmade plates were replaced with mass produced dinnerware each looking the same. This uniformity, this perfection became normal. Now when we are not great at something from the get-go, this becomes evidence it is not what we are supposed to be doing. Or we are miserable trying to attain perfection.

Rather than looking through the lens of how good the outcome is, I encourage you to notice how pleasurable is the process. If it feels good, keep going no matter how it looks or sounds. If it doesn't feel good, and you have ruled out your perfectionist having an investment in the end product, look at what needs to shift or change. Remember my first year? I started wanting to paint, but it was too stressful, so I switched to oil pastels, then I could relax and enjoy the process. After a year of practice with oil pastels my creative confidence was strong enough to try painting and this time it worked.

Having a "practice" means practicing to get better at something. Not to know it all before we begin. Enjoy the process, and know you have the rest of your life to keep learning and getting better.

Resource: How can you allow yourself to be wherever you are in your creative journey without expectations or being hard on yourself? How can you practice with love?

Day 134
What Calls You to Go Deeper?

You are making progress, you are showing up, AND, you are having an inkling to do something more, something different, something new. Maybe you are feeling bored, or you are inspired by something you saw or heard. Or maybe you want to reveal something more personal and vulnerable.

How can you answer this call in some small way? Taking a step toward it. Growing your practice slowly, letting it evolve and change, but at a pace that keeps you moving forward.

A challenge for businesses can be growing too fast and not being able to keep up. The same thing can happen when we are building our Creative Practice. If we go too big or deep, too soon, we could shut down the whole process, feel overextended, overwhelmed or overexposed—then want to hibernate from our project. You know yourself, listen.

Whatever the call is, maybe to shift to a new medium or spend a longer amount of time, or express a vulnerable story, know you can always fall back into your comfort zone. You are making this up, there is no right or wrong way.

The ultimate goal is to keep showing up. A little discomfort can be motivating, it is sometimes what we need, and too much discomfort can stop the whole train. Make adjustments as you go, push yourself a little and be sure you stay on the train!

Resource: What small new step can you take to continue forward on your creative journey to help keep your process fresh and alive? How could you make your work more authentic to you and your unique voice?

Day 135

I'm Stuck! I Don't Know What to Do!

After a nine-month hiatus from writing this book, I am back trying to get my groove. The hiatus began because I couldn't see the next doable step. Everything seemed really big. I had written a lot and I didn't know what to do with all the writing. Where was I going? What the heck do I do with all these bits and pieces? I didn't quit, but instead, I allowed myself to move to another project, *Scribble Art,* a small picture book I completed to publication.

As you can tell by holding this book in your hands I did find my way back and found a solution. And, I kept my Creative Practice alive and going through other projects. I didn't give up my Creative Practice because I was stuck, I did other projects until I became unstuck.

In a perfect world when we get overwhelmed, we would sit back and ask ourselves what is the tiniest next step we can take to move us forward and keep going?

Life and the creative process don't always work this way. Sometimes we need to take a break from what we are doing so we get a different perspective.

Having another project to turn to can help keep our Creative Practice alive while we are working through what needs processing. As a painter I often have more than one painting going at a time so when I am stuck on one, I can turn to another. Remember, it is all about the process, keep showing up, and eventually you will get somewhere.

Resource: Make a list of other projects you could turn to if you need time away from your main project. Do SOMETHING. Trust your process and keep the *show-up muscle* strong, even if the commitment to your project wavers, don't let the commitment to your Creative Practice waver, keep going.

Day 136
Teach an Old Dog a New Trick

I recently renewed my daily writing practice to work on this book. I have had a strong practice on and off over the years, committing to 5-minutes minimum, every day or 5 days a week. At certain points, I have gotten stuck, didn't know what to do next, and abandoned the project.

Last week I started a writing challenge in my writing support group to help give me the structure to get back on track. The first week I showed up two times and felt a creative high afterward. Then my work got busy and I forgot.

Last night I looked at the system I had used to get started and fine-tuned it a bit. The two days I showed up I had set my open laptop at the kitchen table (my favorite writing place) and opened my writing program before I went to bed, so I would see it in the morning. My rule was no emails or other electronics before I did my morning writing. What caused me to forget on day three? I got busy with my life and though I set my computer out the night before, I glazed over it in the morning, not remembering WHY it was there. It had not become a habit yet.

In my fine tuning, I have now created a little sign that says "write" to put on my computer to remind me WHY my laptop is out. It is amazing how fast a good commitment can fly out of my consciousness.

I also decided to tie my writing to something that I always do, feeding my pets. I will write 5 minutes BEFORE I feed them. This way, they will become part of my team. I don't want to look at their sad eyes waiting for their breakfast for too long, so I better show up and write. As I write this my cat is meowing and my dog is looking at me wagging his tail—feeding time!

Resource: Keep trying new things and changing things up.

Day 137
My House Is a Wreck

There are a never-ending amount of excuses. I can't make art, my house is a wreck. Or, I can't allow myself to make art because my home, car, finances, relationship, family, work or whatever, need me more.

When we give our excuses more power than our art, it can be a powerful sign we are not in balance. Often people think they need to earn creative time. When the house is clean, the homework is done, the bank accounts are balanced, then I can do my art. Then the reasons keep getting bigger. After the taxes are done, once I lose ten pounds, or after the new grand baby graduates from high school. Or the reasons go deeper—if I was more talented, if I was better at it, then I would be worthy of the time to spend with my art. How can I justify this time when I am just a creative wanderer, beginner, or not earning a living at my art?

Putting our creative time last can be poor self-care. Conversely, putting our creative time on the front burner is a win for everyone. If we keep putting ourselves last, our life force will get dimmer. Having a Creative Practice assures us we will take time for ourselves. Usually when we take time for ourself to be creative, the rest of our life gets more of us—our attitude toward the chores of life changes. Our creative time is the oxygen mask feeding us first so we can then go back to life and do what we need to do with more presence and maybe a better attitude.

When I am showing up regularly, I feel more creative and I start bringing creativity into other areas of my life, too. The gift keeps giving.

Resource: If you put your Creative Practice last, and don't get to it, I challenge you to switch it up. Allow yourself to go to your art no matter what else is going on. Does anything change?

Day 138

In the Process & Out of Expectations

Staying in the process helps us stay out of expectations. Expectations can crush the creative spirit. Expectations can be fuel for our critic. Expectations can lead us to things needing to be perfect. Expectations can take the joy out of our process.

What does it mean to be in the process? Process orientation is about enjoying the making and noticing what is going on in the making. Noticing through our senses—how the paint feels going onto the canvas, what it smells like, the vibrancy of the colors. It can also be noticing our impulses, *"Oh, I want red."* We follow the impulse and then the next impulse and the next. *"I want to add more color there. I want to move the paint with my hands. I want to play music and dance while I paint."*

When we are in the process, we are in the zone of being curious and playing. Creating without the worry of where this will take us, and what it will become. The expectation is to show up, fill the time with what feels good, and make progress.

Resource: Listen closely for the impulses when you are playing today. Notice, is it easy or hard to follow them? Do you question the impulses or do you say yes to them? Also, allow yourself to be aware of your senses. What are you seeing, hearing, smelling, touching, feeling on your skin, and feeling in your body as you create? Begin by practicing this in your creative endeavors and soon you might be able to live your whole life this way.

Day 139
Example of Being in the Process

Let's imagine you start walking every day to get exercise. You decide you could take ten photos while walking as a Creative Practice. Being in the process you begin without a destination and without expectations. There may be things you know: you are going to walk for 30 minutes; you are going to bring your camera, and you are going to take 10 photographs. As you walk, you begin to notice the things catching your eye: the flowers, the shadows on the street, the kids playing. You proceed not worrying about why you are taking the photos or what you are going to do with them. You simply listen to the impulses as they arrive.

You notice along the way you are drawn to taking photos of urban decay. You sort out all the urban decay photos and put them in their own album. You play and convert one to black and white and realize you love this—you convert them all to black and white. At the end of the year, you are feeling sad about your 365 project being over and a poetic line swims through your head as you take a photo. You realize you now want to write poetry for your photos and a plan for year two of daily poetry is born.

Year two ends and you have the idea to create a performance piece for your community—the photos are projected on the back wall and your poetry is spoken.

The desire to take photos and get exercise was your beginning but then you traveled creatively to places you may have never known you would go. Or, maybe at the end of the year you simply have 3650 photos, your body is healthier from walking 30 minutes a day, and you are emotionally happier from getting out and doing something creative. You have made friends along your walk routes and know your neighborhood better. Still a win!

Resource: Being in the process opens us to next steps and surprises!

Day 140
In the Results, Not the Process?

The idea of staying in the *process,* rather than the results, is to keep you moving ahead, keep showing up, and not getting stalled in perfectionism. Being in the results leads us to having expectations of our work being great—it will win awards, it will be good enough for this show or that performance, or to be published. In a Creative Practice like we are doing here, the gift can be, if you don't like something you did today, you can try something new tomorrow. There is not so much emphasis on the result because tomorrow you can do it differently.

Signs you have jumped off the track of being in the process and into the lane of results could be:

- Feeling disappointment
- Hearing a critical voice inside you
- Tightening of your muscles
- Holding your breath or breathing shallow
- Forcing an idea or forcing the process
- Wondering what someone else will think of your work
- Thinking something is not good enough
- Not wanting to show up

Make it your mission to listen closely and stay on the *process* track. There will be a time ahead to shape and edit your work. But during this year, practice staying out of the results.

Resource: Be mindful for signs of jumping out of the process and into the results. Notice, are you following your impulses or questioning them? If you find yourself knotted in the results, get up, take a walk, take a break, breathe, and come back with new eyes, to being in your senses, and being present to the process.

Day 141
Gift, Not Obligation

Do you show up for your Creative Practice feeling a sense of duty and drudgery? In the beginning and throughout our 365 days this can happen. It can feel like one more thing on our to-do list. We may hold our practice with fists clenched, saying I HAVE to do this—maybe even with an eye roll or discouragement in our voice. Seeing it through the eyes of doing, making, and giving, rather than seeing our Creative Practice as a gift.

If we can relax into our commitment, hold it gently rather than gripping it, then it can become a sweet love affair and we can shift into, "I get to do my art!" We can then be open to receive the gifts of our creative time. The calming effect, the processing of our day, the chance for expression and allowing our creativity to flow. The walking toward a dream of seeing ourselves as an artist.

If your art is feeling like a drudgery, step back and look at what needs to shift or change. Your Creative Practice is not meant to be a punishment. It is meant to be a supportive gift YOU create and receive each day.

Resource: Notice if you are having the "I *have* to do my art" attitude. If you are, look at what you need to do to shift your project or your attitude. Or simply practice saying, "I *get* to do my art!" Fake it until you make it!

Day 142
Profession or Practice?

I have done both—made art to earn a living and made art for the love of making art and to feed my creative spirit. My art sales and profession grew from my daily practice. This may be a story you hope for or have experienced.

About two and a half years into my daily Creative Practice I painted a portrait of a friend's dog who was dying. A year later I was having a one-woman show of my daily art. In the show I included this dog portrait. At the show opening someone loved it so much they commissioned me to paint their dog. From there it took off, and I was becoming known for my quirky animal portraits.

Something changed when I started doing commissions. What used to be fun, became stressful. Instead of showing up to my art to feed myself, I was showing up to please someone else.

I don't want to discourage you from making a living doing your art, but to encourage you to always have a Creative Practice for YOU. Even if you decide to sell the work you create during your Creative Practice time, your work is FOR YOU, FIRST. Don't worry about it looking good enough to sell.

If you are already working at your craft or plan to go pro, let your Creative Practice be a separate process, for you and only you. Let it be for the pleasure of creating for yourself.

I offer you this idea so your Creative Practice is considered sacred time for you. It is about serving your own creative need, allowing you a space to experiment, rant, and do what you want—not what the world wants. (And yes, maybe this inspired, original and raw work could find its way into your working artist time.)

Resource: Let your Creative Practice feed you and only you. Does anything change when you think of doing it for your eyes only? You may choose to bring this attitude into your working artist time.

Day 143

Use Art to Change Your Life

Those feelings of irritation, crankiness, or even anxiety that can come with being in a relationship, a bad day at work, or the stars not lining up in this moment are great times to go to your art. Get it out, express it, let it be raw and prickly. Don't hold back.

I often hear people say they are waiting for their life to even out so they can make art. I offer you the contrary. It is when life is uneven, prickly, and full of potholes that turning to a Creative Practice can be the most satisfying.

If you are waiting for the perfect moment to start your Creative Practice or get back into it—there is none. Do it now. Don't wait for your life to change so you can do art, *use art to change your life!*

Resource: When we don't want to take time to be creative it is often the time we need to be creating the most, or when it will help us the most. So, get to it. You life does not have to look good to do art and your art doesn't have to look good either. Let it reflect and express your life.

Day 144
Finding Your Own Rhythm

After being in my visual journal group for almost six months, one of the participants got so excited. She announced to all of us she had figured it out, "It takes two sessions for me to finish a page!" Her challenge had been comparing her process to others and trying to rush to finish. She finally understood her rhythm was slower, she needed longer. When she had this realization, she relaxed and began to enjoy the process of creating.

Over the years it has taken me to write this book, I have had friends write and publish their books and be on to the next one and the next. Maybe I could have powered through my writing, but it has evolved in its own time. When I first started writing I had a different book in mind. A book with a beginning, a middle, and an end. Then the writing revealed it wanted to be something different, it wanted to be a daily reader. It wanted to be an ongoing touchstone, to help creatives keep going. It took time to get here.

So, I started over. Editing what I had written into smaller daily pieces, writing new entries, one at a time. I don't know when I will finish. What I do know is that I like the rhythm I have found, that keeps me moving forward.

Let your creative process be YOUR creative process. You do not have to please anyone but yourself. If you want to add one note a day to your musical score, yes, do it. If you want to paint one stroke a day, yes, do it. If you want to spend the rest of your life writing a book, one sentence or paragraph a day, yes, do it. And enjoy yourself as you go.

Resource: If it isn't fun, look at your process. Are you trying to meet someone else's expectations? What if, instead, you allow yourself to feel nourished by showing up and by what feels right for you to do each day?

Day 145
Your Life on Art

"Think of the arts as an activity that changes your biology, emotional state, and enhances your mental well-being. When the arts become a regular practice—the way you might improve nutrition, increase exercise, and prioritize sleep—you unleash an innate tool that helps you navigate the peaks and valleys of your inner life. And the best news is that you don't have to be great, or even good at making art to experience the benefits."
—Susan Magsamen and Ivy Ross, *Your Brain on Art*

I am an artist and an Expressive Arts Therapist, not a scientist or a quantitative researcher. I have witnessed over and over the transformative effects of creative expression of all kinds. I believe wholeheartedly in the power of the arts to change us, and that showing up every day or on a regular basis can increase the arts to a superpower.

What a gift to have neuroscientists actually study the arts effect on the brain and the body. Hallelujah to Susan Magsamen and Ivy Ross who have inspired and collected so much information and data in their groundbreaking book, *Your Brain on Art,* proving scientifically that yes, art helps. Even being in aesthetically pleasing spaces can have positive effects on us.

So if pleasure is not a good enough reason to show up for your Creative Practice, let knowing you will have a healthier brain and body inspire you to keep going!

Resource: Remember as you create that your brain is also creating new neural pathways and dopamine—the happy chemical! As you go through life notice moments where you feel uplifted—there is a good chance your senses were activated by something aesthetically pleasing through vision, sound, taste, touch, or smell.

Day 146
Who Am I?

In the process of creating a Creative Practice we get to know ourselves. We learn if we are a rule maker, a rule follower, a rule breaker. If we fly by the seat of our pants, or if we have challenges with perfectionism, long-term relationship commitments, or attention deficit.

When we show up to create art regularly, we get the by-product of learning more about ourselves, what makes us tick, what makes us resistant. We not only sign on for a deeper relationship with our art, but also a deeper relationship with ourselves.

If I had taken an interior snapshot of who I was emotionally on day one of my first 365 Days of Art project it would be timid, unsure, and excited. At the end I felt confident in my ability to show up, even with the art materials I was using. Before I started my daily art projects, I didn't know I was a person who was glad for the routine of showing up every day. I learned every day was actually easier than once a week or 3 times a week. I liked the structure, and I liked to be able to adjust the structure when needed to keep going.

How about you? What are you learning about yourself? In the review, it is not about beating yourself up or even giving yourself a free pass to quit. It is about learning more about yourself and adapting your practice to what you learn. When we fit our project more closely to who we are in this moment, we have a better chance of continuing and enjoying the process.

Resource: Do a review of yourself, how have you grown and changed so far? Does anything need to change in your practice to keep up with your growth?

Day 147
Be Fully with Your Art, Even Bad Art

Be in relationship with whatever you are doing and let it be authentic. If you dislike or even hate your work, give the dislike a voice. Keep following it until it leads you somewhere satisfying. My teacher, Paolo Knill, told me when I sang a note off key and quickly silenced myself, "No Tish, don't stop. Hold that wrong note long enough until it becomes the right note."

My belief is, if you don't like it, it isn't done. Maybe it needs to change shape, change genre, or be deconstructed and turned into something else. If you turn your back, nothing will change. If you stay connected, something will change.

When we don't give up, the conversation continues. Get more information. Why are you hating it? Art-making has a direct line to our emotions, when we stay engaged, we have an opportunity to learn and grow. Maybe the hate is connected to worrying what someone else will think. Or maybe a childhood art wound has been activated. The voices in our head often don't belong to us, they belong to a teacher, a parent, a sibling, an ex, or society. It could be work or money worries crept in and are coloring our perspective. We can't untangle the emotions unless we stay with them. If you need to, give yourself a break and come back later. Or ask someone for help.

Once during a commission painting, I was ready to give up, give back the deposit, say never mind and quit painting. The fear of failing was big and I did not want to face it. After struggling for too long, I asked my twelve-year-old son to take a look. He remarked, "The background is too dark." I lightened it up, it got better, I completed it, we were all happy and I kept painting.

If we give up, we will never know. Face your art demons!

Resource: Stay in conversation with your art, don't give up!

Day 148
You Are Ready to Quit?

Oh no! No, no, no! Don't accept this voice that wants to quit. This project you have chosen is WORTH continuing. Maybe there is a simple adjustment that needs to be made. Have you chosen something too big? Are you worrying it isn't good enough and thinking about what other people will think? Maybe you don't know what the next step is and feel overwhelmed? Are you doing what you think others want you to do, rather than what you want? Maybe an old inner voice/critic is challenging you or doesn't think you are worth taking the time to create.

For today, do what you can and hold the question, "What needs to change so I can keep going?" Follow the ideas that come. If you are blank, show up like you planned, knowing that in the showing up something WILL shift.

You were called to this practice because you knew it would serve you in some way. Maybe you need to reconnect to your desire. If you keep going, you WILL have something. Don't worry if it is good or bad, show up to express yourself.

What if you kept going, blindly trusting you are on the right path? Often when it gets hard, the magic or the breakthrough is right around the corner.

Resource:

- If something is not working, look at what needs to be changed. (Not at giving up.)
- If there is a message in your head, write it down and journal on this message. Whose voice is it? Where did it originate? Dialog with that voice through writing or another art form.
- What is the smallest step you can take to continue moving forward?
- MARK THIS PAGE, refer back to it as often as needed.

Day 149
Art as a Way to Reflect on Life

Maybe our brains are lazy, but autopilot is, for most of us, the way we live. Just as our heart knows how to pump without us thinking about it, our mind takes us through our day without much energy needed to make decisions. We automatically get out of bed, put on coffee, say good morning, get dressed, etc.

Art-making can offer us the opportunity to embody our life even more—consciously living even in the mundane moments.

If I look at my morning as art, I might notice: I wake before my eyes open, I have never noticed this before, has it always been this way, my eyes waiting a moment before opening? I stretch slightly and sit slowly so I don't get dizzy. My first thought is my feet, looking for my favorite slippers so my feet won't get cold, summer or winter. My Sweetie is already up. He sits at the table doing *his* morning writing. My greeting is a quick kiss on the top of his balding head as I must get to the bathroom.

This small reflection could, yes, be brought to writing or poetry in more detail or less. A moment from it could be captured through visual art, drawing, painting, a photograph series, a film, a storytelling moment. We could do the dance or the musical score of waking and awakening.

When we can look through the eyes of our artist at our life, we can slow it down and find exquisite details in even the most mundane moments. Dare I say opening us up to more conscious living?

Resource: Slow your autopilot moments down to see what really exists in them. How would you capture them or share those moments through your Creative Practice?

Day 150
From Creating to Shaping

If we are making art daily, at some point what we have done begins to become a body of work. Even with 5 minutes a day, those paragraphs become stories, the paint strokes finish paintings, and the music becomes a song or composition.

There is a point in the creative process when you may want to take a look at what you have been creating and begin to shape it. Think of shaping as looking at what you have created through a squinted, soft focus eye. This is different from the sharp eye that is used to critique and edit.

In shaping you are looking over what has been done and noticing themes, what is finished and what needs attention. You can explore what you like and want to see more of, what is interesting and essential. You might ask if there is emotional connection or passion. You could rearrange things, find what goes together, and even get new ideas for the progression of your work.

Shaping sends the work in a direction; the destination could still be in the making. Or it could begin to define what the project is becoming.

Maybe you are thinking, "I need to be critiqued. If all I hear is good supportive feedback, how will I ever hone my skills?" To that I say, yes, there will be a time for editing but at a later stage. When in the creative process anything goes. The sky—any color sky, is the limit—meaning limitless! Once you have created and stepped away for a while to get some distance, bring your shaping eye. This will support your art form to become better. And, if in the future you want to take your art public, then you can find an editor or do a sharp eye critique.

Resource: Practice looking at your art with the soft focus eye or ear of shaping. Look for what you want to do more of and what you like.

Day 151
Shaping Invites Curiosity

I am a believer in being in the process as we work and refraining from critique as best we can while we are creating. There are times when we want to review, shape, and edit. I encourage holding off editing until the work sits for a while so you can get some distance from it. More times than I can count, I have witnessed people say they hate what they did, and then look at it later and realize they like it. And conversely, asking for a critique when the work is fresh and personal, the comments can shut down the creative process. Allow some time to pass from the creating before going in to tamper with the product.

Here are a few ideas I have learned along the way when going in to shape. These ideas can also be used instead of a "critique" in a group setting, or when you ask others for feedback.

1. Start with what you like, what feels good, what you are attracted to, what pleases you. We are so trained to look at what we don't like first—try to shift your way of looking.
2. How can you build on what feels good, what you are attracted to, and what pleases you?
3. What isn't working, what might you want less of, what might be distracting or confusing, overdone or uninviting?
4. Can you let go of or shift what is not working?
5. Ask what you can bring in new? How could you surprise yourself or your audience?
6. Is the project leaning toward a new direction?
7. Does the project need a "take two," doing it differently, or can you continue as is?

Resource: Rather than critique, look through the eyes of curiosity and kindness in the process of shaping.

Day 152
Shaping and Being Shaped

Shaping, molding, and editing is an ongoing process, not a one-time event. First we create the *"shitty first draft"* (Anne Lamott) and get the idea expressed. Then we have the opportunity to go back and look at what has been done with new eyes. I often imagine I am someone else as I look or listen.

When I did my first year of writing this book as a Creative Practice it began as a book with a beginning, middle, and end. As I tried to shape the order of all the topics it was so confusing and such a challenge I abandoned the project for a year or two..

And then I returned. Here is what I wrote on that first day back: *"Today I sit to face the challenges that stopped me. I commit to open my writing program which I haven't been with for a while and am not even sure I can find—and start writing for ten minutes...I showed up to get reacquainted with my old friend, and with the process of showing up. I showed up and wrote what I needed to write. Big breath, big sigh, I am grateful."*

A week later, the book told me what it wanted to be. It wanted to be *a daily reader—a daily reader for a daily practice.* This was a perfect fit! I am emotional as I realize if I hadn't renewed my desire to show up and shape this book, it would not have a life.

Listening to what our art wants to become is an important step in the shaping process. Sometimes we want to force it into the form we have in our mind, and even abandon it when it doesn't conform. Go into the shaping process looking at what is working and not working for YOU, and also allow for what is working and not working for your ART.

Resource: Remember to be in relationship with your art as you create, shape, and even edit. Treat your work as a friend you are collaborating with, listen and see where it leads you.

Day 153
Stop Thinking, Start Doing

Have you noticed how relieved you feel when you start doing something you've been dreading? You spent so much time thinking about it, feeling the weight of it, beating yourself up for procrastinating, then once you finally start, you think, "Why did I make such a big deal about that?"

Years ago I took a training on social anxiety. The workshop leader's main tool was to go out and do the things you are afraid to do, bring a notebook and take notes on all the sensations and thoughts in the doing. *I notice my palms are sweaty, I feel my heart racing, I don't want to look anyone in the eye.*

When we become the observer of what is going on it helps us take a step away from the situation and from our anxiety or fear as well.

This can work with creating, too. How often do we buy the materials, tools, or instrument and then let them sit because it feels too stressful to actually use them. Or we have a story or project in mind and continually push it away because we are sure we aren't ready. What if instead we take the smallest baby steps we can and as we take action, we jot down what we are feeling and thinking. We become the observer of what is happening.

In the late stages of this book I started a journal to track the fears, doubts, and revelations I am having as I get closer to publishing. When my fear flares up or my confidence wanes, I write about it in this special journal and it helps me keep going. When I get specific, I can gently hold my fears, and offer myself a baby step to take action, and do it.

Resource: What is something you have wanted to do but haven't started? Try this process of doing and logging what is happening as you do. Be curious and maybe even have fun. Think of yourself as a science experiment where you are the subject and the scientist!

Day 154
Struggle Versus Strive

If our Creative Practice is an ongoing struggle, we are in a danger zone. We can start to ask ourselves, *Why do it if it doesn't feel good?* When we are feeling unfulfilled more than nourished, it is time to make changes.

I am not talking about the good stress of trying something new. Yes, it might be hard, but you are shifting, changing, and growing in your ability. I am talking about a struggle that can lead to giving up or hating art-making.

Your Creative Practice should not be a punishment. If it is feeling this way, look at your process, look at your history, look inside to find what is happening. If you are using your creativity to abuse yourself, this is probably an inside job of reflection and healing. Maybe it is time to work with your critic and muse to see what they have to say.

If it is because the materials you are using are not working, do not be afraid to switch things up, take a class, or watch online videos to teach and inspire you. Remember, you don't have to be good right away, you have the rest of your life to learn and grow creatively.

Strive to be better, strive to work through your blocks and do what you can to let go of the struggle.

Resource: When it feels like a struggle or it is not fun, take time to figure things out, don't give up. Do the inner critic work or look at your materials and process. Often it is one small change that needs to be made, shifting the time of day or where you work or even your attitude!

Day 155

Creating from an Open Heart

My daily art is a survival tool. It is my place to process and regulate my day. I can get into the flow of creating and fill my cup. Sometimes I need help to stay with it—music or a podcast can help me to stay painting when I only want to do the minimum.

And then there are the days when my heart door is flung open before I sit to create, and I bring this vulnerable sweetness with me. I might read something, have an inspiring conversation, or an intimate moment opens me and there I am, in the love zone.

When I bring this feeling of love and fullness to my art, something is different. Something extraordinary. Yes, when I bring anger, overwhelm, uncertainty, and the day-to-day to my art there can be an opening—but when love is in the room, I am nourished, my cup is already full and it spills into my art. Versus needing my art to fill my cup.

I experienced this today, I read something written so eloquently and with such hope, I felt the hope, too, and began to cry. Bringing this to my writing and my painting is a blessing. Could this become the norm? Could normal be a place where my cup is full, my heart is open, and the gifts spill out, rather than creating while I am in the desert, waiting for the gift to arrive and quench my thirst?

What was different today? What helped me arrive already feeling full? A simple answer comes to me—I put myself first for a time and filled my cup. There are a million reasons why we can't put ourselves first, but there is one great reason for exquisite self-care—love.

Resource: How can you find the "love" place before you show up to your art? What gets you there? Slowing, spiritual practice, inspired reading or listening? Explore what works for you.

Day 156

It's Okay to Move Slow

We do not have many opportunities in our life to move slow. We have plenty of encouragement to hurry up, get things done, and as my mother used to say, "Don't dilly dally."

Yet my mother was also the master of moving slow. She took her time. She did not care (to my knowledge) who was standing behind her in the grocery line. However long it took her to get out her money to pay, return the change to her wallet, put the wallet back in her purse, she was going to take it, with no apologies. When I was young, this drove me crazy. Usually, it brought up anxiety in me. I was worried about the people behind us in line. But age softened me. I stopped worrying about others and started being in the moment with my mother.

A few days before she died, I was walking her to the bathroom. We moved at turtle speed, and I was right there with her, enjoying what I knew would be one of her last days on this earth with me. As we walked, oh so slow, I realized, "Wow, I could feel 'God' when I moved this slow." There was something magical about moving slow. When I move slow, my heart opens.

During my 365 Days of Painting, in honor of my mother, I dedicated a week to slow. I let my paintbrush move leisurely on the paper. How slow could I go? Each stroke began to feel like a prayer. I was imbuing so much presence into each dab of paint. I felt my impatience sometimes. I noticed circles were ovals when going at turtle pace. Mostly, I noticed my mind quieted when I allowed myself to go slow. Painting became a meditation.

Resource: I offer you the challenge of going slow. Slow down your movements, your tempo, your mind, even your ego. You don't need to rush. You don't need to cross a finish line. You can work on one piece for an entire year if you want! This is the love zone.

Day 157
Vacation

As I write this I am in *Creative Practice Heaven.* I am in the mountains for ten days. My time is mostly free of "have to's" and I am painting and writing for hours each day. I have a more spacious setup and I don't have everyday responsibilities to distract me—not even wi-fi.

In the past I have had daily art projects fit into small boxes so they were easily portable. Often everything I need fitting into a lunch box, you know, the kind with the plastic handles you may have used in elementary school.

This year though, I am painting a portrait every day with acrylics. When it was time to pack up my daily art for this vacation* I told my Sweetie to be sure there was room in the car for a jumbo bin. You know, the kind you use in the garage for storage. Four smaller bins of paint would fit in there with brushes, two journals because I was toward the end of one and would be starting a new one, and then I also brought a "finished" journal that had plenty of portraits still wanting more attention. Plus, extras I might need and would not want to be without, just in case.

And yes, if I needed, I could have brought just one journal, my black paint pens, and a small watercolor set. This time though, we were driving so I went big! And I am grateful.

Resource: Be sure your daily art is travel ready. It can adapt to no wi-fi or power outages and is simple enough if you don't have a lot of time, you can still show up, but if you do have an expanse of time, you can linger and wander in *Creative Practice Heaven.*

---

*It is also okay to take a vacation from your art on your vacation. You are making this up, you get to choose. Just be sure you come back and begin again so your break doesn't lead to stopping completely. (That can happen a little too easily.)

Day 158
Follow the Breadcrumbs

I have mentioned before, as a child, I spent time in the library looking at art books, figure drawing books most specifically. At the time I didn't think much of it. I lived in a small town and there was no art to be mentioned, or I didn't know about it. Granted, I looked at those drawings and paintings because they had naked women in them and I was curious. And, looking back I see it as my first adventure into the world of art.

As an adult I had an inkling I wanted to paint. Had it started in those young days in the library? As an adult I took a few painting classes but hated them and would quickly drop out. My disappointment in not being able to paint mounted. I puttered a bit on my own but then dropped it. Little did I know I just needed an easier way in. I needed to avoid overwhelm.

Once I began my Expressive Arts Therapy training and learned the value of beginning with simple easy techniques, learning to enjoy the process, and not worrying about the end product, doors opened. I began to find my way.

Maybe a dream of becoming the next great fiction writer becomes a love for writing political satire or short stories. A childhood tortured with ballet finds freedom in modern dance. A movie star dream is satisfied with local theater.

The secret is to NOT give up the dream. Follow the breadcrumbs, the curiosities, the longings, the attractions, and where you find pleasure. Investigate the heck out of them before you give up. *Trust your desire to do the art*, question the ways you are doing it until you find YOUR way.

Resource: Don't give up the dream, find a new way in. What small steps can you take to grow your confidence? And use this book to help. After all, I am writing the book I wished I had to help me!

Day 159
Unconscious Resistance

What pulls you away from your commitment to show up for your creative time? Why do you allow yourself to be pulled way? The reasons can seem valid: *"the kids need me"* or *"the dishes have to be done"* or *"this other deadline is more important."* Yet there may be some unconscious resistance underneath. Do you secretly not want to show up? Is there a part of you that thinks you don't deserve creative time? Does something feel hard and you don't want to come up against big feelings or failure?

When you notice you are allowing yourself to be swayed from your creative time, take a moment to look at what is going on. Find the thread and expose why there may be resistance.

Try the *IF Excuse Exercise.* Write at least 10 sentences repeating and finishing the sentence *"If I show up for my creative time..."* Be as honest as possible, and keep looking to see if there is a deeper layer, a more powerful unconscious influence at work. Here are some examples to get you going: If I show up for my art I will get behind in my work. If I show up for my art I will get in trouble. If I show up for my art I am being irresponsible. If I show up for my art I will be selfish. And so on.

After making your list choose one that feels the most potent for you. Make art with this as your prompt. Get to know your saboteur. Make friends with the part of yourself who does not want to show up, so you can walk through the not-doing to the doing.

Now do the same process as above with, "I WILL show up to my art because..." I am important, I have something to say, it helps keep me balanced, and so on. Post this list and read it often.

Resource: Keep exploring the pull from your commitment. You might also do a list, *"If I don't show up..."* as another avenue to information. Counter with your *"I WILL show up because..."* voice.

Not every day
is going to be a stellar creative day,
but if you don't show up,
you won't get a chance
to catch the great ones.

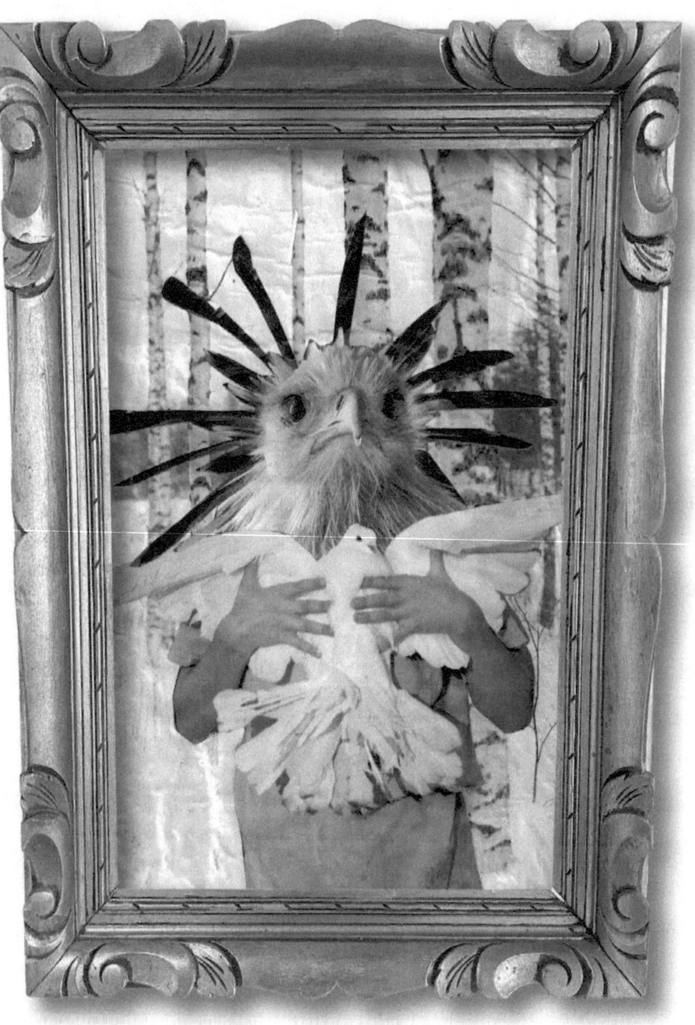

365 Days of Visioning Journal™

Having an intention with my Visioning Journals™ helped relieve the stress of the blank page. For the three-plus years I did it as a practice I was looking at bringing love into my life. Each day when I sat down to my journal I would ask where was I today with love or what did I want to express or grow about love? It was a way of being actively in relationship while I was waiting for my partner.

Day 160

Every Day Isn't Going to Be Stellar

We can have high expectations of ourselves, expecting masterpieces every day. Remembering this is a practice can help. We show up regularly to practice our craft. To practice showing up. To practice so we can get better. If our expectations are too high, we run the risk of wanting to quit when the results aren't good enough.

Some days we are going through the motions, doing only enough to say we showed. We do what is easiest or what takes the least amount of effort. And then some days we stay with it for hours. Trust it will all balance out.

The times that are the most worrisome for me are when my enthusiasm is low or absent for too many days. This is when I have to rethink things, look outside myself for inspiration, or change things up. Right now, I have raised my laptop to standing height—writing standing up rather than sitting down. It is just enough change to keep me here longer.

With my painting, I will look at other artists' work to find new color palettes. Or even look back through my own art to see what I like best to feel inspired.

Allow for the ups and downs of inspiration and creative energy. Just because you have some flat days is not a reason to give up, but an indication something might need to change. And it may not be in the art-making itself. Maybe it is changing the time of the day or place you show up or reaching out to friends to create together. If your cup is not full, rather than using it as an excuse to not create, see if your art can bring you the refill you need. You WILL have another stellar day, but if you don't show up, you won't get a chance to experience it.

Resource: If you feel flat, if your art feels flat, let it be okay, and look for ways to change it up.

Day 161
Art as Therapeutic Tool

Art-making is my go-to self-help tool. I am not saying it is to be used instead of therapy, but a great adjunct to it. I did a lot of work on myself in my 20s and 30s, individual therapy, group therapy, self-help groups, and reading books. In my 40s, I found Expressive Arts Therapy and began training in it. Ever since I have looked at art as helper. Art as balancer. Art as therapeutic.

Having a daily Creative Practice helps me stay current with my life. I make art about and from what is happening. Sometimes expressing feelings of anger or anxiety and then following with art about how I want to feel, balanced and calm. And sometimes my art is about what I want in my life—trying something on through my art to begin imagining what it might be like.

On the days when you are having trouble showing up for your art, remind yourself your well-being is at stake and creating art is therapeutic. Maybe something needs to be expressed, or maybe the act of creating will be helpful. Sometimes we might not want to show up because it feels too dangerous to express what is going on. Know you are always in charge. You can stop or change course at any time. Remember, you will probably feel better during the process and when you are done. It doesn't have to be an overt expression. A landscape painter could paint an angry sea or barren desert while a musician could play a chaotic or sad song.

If we check in with ourselves to see what needs to be expressed, we become exquisite experts on knowing, being in, and expressing our feelings. In other words, we become experts at being in the moment!

Resource: If you haven't used your art to express your feelings, try it. If you already have, keep going!

⇨ *If traumatic memories or sensations arise, be sure to get therapeutic help.*

Day 162
Art and Intimacy

In my studio I have a ongoing interactive poster where people can finish the sentence "Art..."

Many themes have been repeated over the years of this process and one that caught my eye today was, *"Art helps me say out loud what I can't say with words."* This made me think about the potential for intimacy with our art. Our art can be our greatest confidant and supporter. It can open us to new parts of ourselves we did not know. It can be a place to practice telling our truth.

Sometimes though, our art can be such an easy confidant we close ourselves off from the world. We never allow the world to see or experience these parts of ourselves. If keeping yourself separate from the world has become too easy, maybe your art is blocking you from growing intimacy in the outside world.

Intimacy occurs when we reveal something about ourselves to others. Once we learn to be intimate with ourselves through our art, we can then use our art as a bridge to the outer living breathing world of intimacy. We try it out in our art, so we can then share it with a human in our life—our therapist, our partner, a trusted friend. Perhaps we share the learning or maybe we actually show someone the art we created as we share our learning. A double layer of intimacy is created, sharing the idea and sharing the potentially vulnerable art.

Look at your life—is your art a way to avoid intimacy with others, or a bridge to create more intimacy? There is no right or wrong answer, just an exploration.

Resource: Share your art and your learnings from your art process with others who are safe. Be sure to ask for exactly what you want, *"No comments or critique please, I want you to simply listen and witness."* Let your art help begin new conversations.

Day 163
Art Helps Us Be in Our Body

Art-making helps us be more present in our body, with little effort. When we move into our senses, our attention shifts to what we touch, hear, see, smell, and taste. We are moving out of our thinking brain and into our feeling sensing body. This is one reason the arts are so helpful with trauma, because they help bring us into the present moment. We slow down, notice the feeling of the paint going on the paper, listen closely to the sound the brush makes. Our hands are in the materials, our eyes are seeing colors through our artist filter. Maybe we sing or play music as we work. Our art-making and our senses can be the bridge to our body and being in the present moment.

Aren't we always in our bodies? Yes, but to different degrees. More often we live from our heads, thinking, searching for intellectual answers. Our thinking can be a continuous loop, over and over having the same thoughts. And nothing really changes.

This week I was caught in a writer's loop, having the idea I am writing about right now, but not knowing how to communicate it to you coherently. Over and over I tried and it seemed to get more tangled, more unpleasant.

Today though, I settled in with a meditation, focused on my breath, the sensations in my body. I was able to see the looping tangle in my imagination in a new way. I sat down to write with new clarity. Now it feels pleasurable. I write, feel my feet on the floor, fingers on the keyboard, I am breathing, long slow breaths. I feel relaxed, not stressed like my earlier efforts. I have arrived into myself, the channel is open and I can listen.

Resource: Invite your senses into your Creative Practice. Slow down and bring your attention to what you hear, see, smell, taste, and touch. Notice if anything is different with your process.

Day 164
Remember to Breathe

My studio participants often mock me lovingly by saying, “Okay, I’ll remember to breathe.”

If there is one thing I want to leave with people, it is to remember to breathe. Our breath is the giver of life, and when we are tense, anxious, or even navigating normal everyday life, our breathing can become shallow. We don’t literally forget to breathe, but we do forget to take a deep breath. We take shallow chest breaths versus deep, fill the lungs and belly breaths. Often when we remember to take a deep breath, a natural sigh is expelled. The sigh may say, “Oh yes, I feel my body relaxing, I feel myself letting go of something.”

Our breath can be the most effective tool to move through our art-making process. When we don’t know what to do next, our breathing can become shallow. A few deep breaths can help our body to relax so we can remember to listen for the next impulse, not try to make something happen. Singers, wind instrument musicians, and dancers use their breath without even noticing. Combining those creative acts while we make art can be a great experiment. Dance, sing, or hum as you create. Or take moments to stretch. Our bodies want to take deep breaths when we stretch—it is an automatic response.

Allow, *“Remember to breathe”* to become a regular mantra in your life to help you get through and thrive. And, exhale, all the air out when you take your deep breath. Even add a sound to the exhale, or a musical note, and hold the sound or note as long as you can. I feel the good feelings as I write this, what a gift.

Resource: Remember to breathe. Ready, deep breath in, hold it for a moment, now let it out with a nice long, slow, sigh, sound, or musical note. Wait for a moment and repeat.

Day 165
Art to Release Frustration

Frustrations can add roadblocks to our day and to our hearts. We get irritated with a loved one, our co-worker, the art materials. Moving into the art to find relief can be a valuable tool.

Growing up, control became my drug of choice. Our household was at times out of control. I was young and did not understand what was going on. My father had challenges with anxiety and depression and would try to soothe himself with sleeping pills and alcohol. At some point I made an unconscious decision to take charge of my life. I would not use drugs to cope and I would take care of all my needs because I couldn't depend on others.

Today in the *last third of my life* (as writer Anne Lamott refers to it) I am inviting others to help, so I do not have to continue doing everything on my own. In trying to be in control, there is no time off and every detail needs my attention. Learning I can get help and let things be done in a different way is a great training ground for me.

And, I can feel frustration. It is hard to let go of control. In my head it seems so easy, in action it is not. I want to jump in. "No, do it this way... Don't do that..."

I don't jump in. Instead, I write to express myself. Instead, I paint to soothe my discomfort. I go inward to heal rather than outward to continue the pattern of doing it all on my own.

Turning to my art when frustrated (when I am not in control) gives me a chance to step away, comfort myself, learn more about what is going on and return with an attitude adjustment. I get to foster relationships rather than stay separate or alone.

Resource: What are the creative acts you do to help you reflect and release when you are upset? Scribbling is great because you almost always have a piece of paper and a pen nearby.

Day 166
Art and Anger

Anger is a motivating emotion. Someone steps on our foot (literally or figuratively) and anger says, "Stop, that is not okay!" Anger helps us set boundaries and create change in our life.

Yet when we don't process our anger in healthy ways it can be destructive. Anger turned inward or swallowed can be hurtful to ourselves and look like depression, addiction, eating disorders, low self-esteem, self-harm, self-blame, and feeling like a victim, to name a few. Anger turned outward in unhealthy ways can hurt others emotionally, physically, or destroy property.

Anger expressed in healthy ways, not hurting self or others, can inform us and lead us to create important changes, in our life and in the bigger world. Think MADD (Mothers Against Drunk Drivers), Tariq Khamisa Foundation, or the #metoo movement.

When I am angry I almost always go to scribbling. As I scribble with ferocious intensity, I begin to understand what is going on for me at a deeper level. Often disappointment or hurt lies under my anger. Once I have exhausted myself or the intense feelings subside, I can then begin to figure out what I need and take steps toward getting my needs met.

As an Expressive Arts Therapist I witness the power of the arts for expressing. Tearing things up and reconstructing them as visual art. Beating hard and loud on drums. Doing angry dances. Acting out a fantasy of what wants to be said. Singing angry gibberish songs, using made-up language without hurtful words.

The late Alice Eldred, an anger expert, used to say, "You need to express your anger every day to make up for all the days you weren't able to express it and every day to stay current with your life." This could be a 365 Days of Anger project! Any takers?

Resource: Don't be afraid of your anger, express it artfully!
⇨ *If your anger feels too big or overwhelming, get therapeutic help.*

Day 167

Will My Creativity Return?

Scarier than the blank page can be the feeling your creativity has left the house. A day or two can be navigated by doing enough to say we showed up, but when it seems like forever, what can we do?

Over my years of daily art, the creative juices have flowed and dried. I have dropped projects because of my lack of creative motivation, and I have gotten good at navigating those barren periods. The easiest way? Start where I am—name the barren place of missing creative motivation—and express this missing through the very art form that feels dull and dry. When I name what is going on, I am creating by naming it. Even with just the words—*there is no art.* Or an angry or lethargic scribble. Leaving a blank page in my journal noting there is nothing. Or write about there being nothing. Here is what I have learned about the dry spells.

I am burnt out. I have too much going on in my life, and instead of my art being a resource or a chance to refill, it is a burden. I must express the burnout.

I am overwhelmed. The overwhelm can come from the project, my life, or the expectations I have on myself to excel and be good. I must express the overwhelm.

I am depressed. I am flatlined in my life and somehow expect I won't be in my art. Expressing the anger I feel toward my depression can be a lifeline to inspiration.

I am happy. It sounds a bit ridiculous but somehow art making is easier for me when things are bad. I have been able to grow my *good-times-art-maker,* but it took attention and intention.

Creativity loves to solve challenges! Let it solve your challenge of no creativity. You might be surprised by its desire to help.

Resource: Instead of letting your dry days pull you away, allow them to inform you by becoming an honest expression of what is.

Day 168
Dropping Out Rather Than...

Today I got an email from Mary in my new writing support group wanting to drop out after our first meeting. This reminds me of myself when I wanted to paint. I would go one or two times and drop out. Why? At the time I wasn't very good at identifying my feelings, but later in life I could see I was overwhelmed and didn't think I was good enough or could be good enough. I had no one-on-one help to assist me in these big feelings, or even identifying what they were.

I called Mary and encouraged her to come back one or two more times to see if we could support her in continuing. Sometimes when we want to quit, it is because we are up against something important—a new learning, a chance to outgrow an old message, or an experience that is coloring our ability to participate. We often feel alone in the challenge.

Mary did return and finished the session confronting a strong voice in her head that said she needed to be grammatically perfect (she was an English teacher in early years). Being in her eighties, she had wavering health and a shaky writing hand keeping her from being able to focus. She learned that writing first thing in the morning rather than with a hot toddy cocktail in the afternoon was helpful! The stories she wrote painted rich pictures from her life and we felt gifted to support and witness her.

I can't make someone stay. I can't make you continue on your Creative Practice journey, but I can offer you support and ideas of what could open doors to new information rather than ending the journey.

When you want to quit something or change directions, here are some questions you might ask yourself:

1. Is there something scary about moving forward? What am I afraid will happen if I keep going?
2. Whose voice am I hearing telling me to stop? Is it someone from my past? Is it from a past experience?
3. Have I ever had an experience similar where I wanted to quit or change course? Is there anything I can learn from that past event?
4. Can I remember a time when I wanted to quit and I didn't? How did I keep myself going? Did anything help?
5. What is missing from my process? Is there something I could adjust just a little, either in my process or in my thinking?
6. Is it okay for me to be mediocre at this, or even fail? And if not, why not? What are my expectations for myself and where did they originate?
7. Remembering back to my original longing or desire to have a Creative Practice, can I reconnect to this longing or desire and create from this place?
8. Can I ask for help? Who can I ask for help? And if I have a hard time asking for help, why? Where was I taught it wasn't okay to ask for help?

After journaling about these ideas, see if you can move forward, just a tiny baby step.

Resource: Once you get more information about your desire to quit, voice this desire and what you learned out loud to a mentor or someone that you trust and see how it sounds when you speak it out loud. Sometimes we just need to say out loud to someone, "I want to quit!" Or maybe you need to talk it through with someone as your sounding board. And, of course, make art about it!

Day 169

Learn to Make Art Anywhere, Anytime

I just found myself cleaning the house and it got me thinking about our reasons to NOT make art or have creative time. People tell me they can't start a Creative Practice because they don't have a place to do their art. I hear the stories about the spare room or garage and how someday it will be a studio. Or there is no private space, or no quiet place, or no space, period.

Or there is no time. The kids need my attention, or I need to take care of my mother. Or I have too much work. Or my house is a wreck. All of these may be true, and we must learn to be creative within our life parameters. Otherwise, the next thing we know, a year goes by, multiple years, or worse, a lifetime. I don't want this to be you.

There will always be a reason, excuse, or inhibitor. Even when we get the "perfect" space or time we can still come up against creative blocks. If we can learn to make art ANYWHERE, ANYTIME, we will create a solid foundation for our Creative Practice and our life.

Let figuring it out be part of the creative process. If you can't find the quiet, the alone time or the perfect space, figure out how you can use what you have, or turn those negatives into your muse. The kids screaming ends up being a photo series, or you jot down family dialog and turn it into poems or lyrics. Dance in the driveway or paint on tiny paper. Using what you have is part of being an artist. Enough excuses or "good" reasons. If you are still sitting on the sidelines, it is time to figure it out.

Resource: If you are not showing up fully, let figuring out how to get yourself to show up be your creative act. You may have to try a dozen things before you find the right fit and the right way to hold yourself accountable. You are worth it!

Day 170
The Motivation of Pain and Suffering

May it be physical, emotional, or spiritual pain. May it be illness, addiction, a breakup, trauma, a separation from self or others, or an unhappy life. Pain can be a great motivator for change. And art can help get us through.

We often make changes for the better when we are confronted with loss. We get sick and we start eating better. We hurt our back and we start doing yoga. We fail a test and we double-down on studying or we change our field of study. When the pain or illness is serious, we make bigger changes. We begin to pray or meditate. We consult alternative therapies we might not have considered before. We ask for help from our friends and family.

Or we give up. We lose hope. We are overtaken by depression and despair. We isolate. We see no way out and do not allow anyone in. We shut down and lay quietly biding out our time.

Usually, it is a combination of both. We experience moments of motivation and moments of despair.

Art helps. Even if it is a momentary tiny shift, a glimmer of hope. Here are a few ways I have experienced art helping when we are suffering or in pain:

- Art-making is a vacation from the challenges.
- Art can be an expression of what it is like inside.
- Art can hold a vision of what life will be like after.
- Art helps us nurture a new identity beyond our suffering, the artist self.
- Art becomes a diary or journal of our journey.
- When making art, our bodies' natural pain relievers and happy hormones are released.

Resource: Turn to art as healer. It cannot fail to be helpful.

⇨ *Get therapeutic help, too. You do not have to do life alone.*

Day 171
It's Okay to Love Your Art

In one of my groups someone said, "I know you are not supposed to love your art, but I do!" I am not sure where this message came from, to not love her art, but I want to tell you it is absolutely okay to love your art. And, your art does not need to be museum quality for you to be in love. It can be simple, untrained expressions. It can even be unfinished, aesthetically unpleasing, or plain old ugly.

I encourage you to build a relationship with your art so you do love it. On good days and bad, in sickness and in health, in learning and in growth spurts.

When I can stay in the process of art-making, when I can revel in the time I get to spend with it, and the sensory feelings of doing the work, I am in love. The most common reason for me falling out of love or critiquing my art miserably is when I think about what someone else might think of what I am doing.

Our relationship with our art has to be strong enough to withstand the critic, internal and external. It needs to be committed and steadfast through the valleys, not just the peaks.

Allow yourself to fall in love. Whatever your process, no matter what the outcome of the product. Let yourself celebrate you showed up and you created something that would not have existed had you not made the time to create.

Resource: How is your relationship with your art? Are you in love? If not, what might need to change to grow the love? No matter where you are, celebrate you are showing up and creating!

Day 172

School's Unwinding of Creativity

The last 40 or more years have been a nail in the creativity coffin for the arts in schools. Experts decided the arts were taking kids away from their important learning and they needed to cut the budget. The arts were seen as frill or extra fluff—so on the chopping block they went.

Even prior to this, innovative and creative arts teachers were the few, most art was taught by general classroom teachers and they were often replicating one idea.

For the most part, schools were not designed to create free thinkers, creative problem solvers, or expressive individuals. In kindergarten my son was sent home with a "red card" meaning he had done something very bad. The reason stated was, "dancing in line to the library." I laughed, and the next day talked to his teacher asking what was bad about dancing in line to the library. She responded if she let him dance, everyone would want to dance. My response as you can guess was, "And what would be wrong with a dancing line to the library?" The worry was the kids would get out of control.

Things are changing ever so slowly. Project-based learning is finding its way into classrooms, where students create with their hands and use the arts to support their learning. Socratic circles help kids learn to discuss ideas and expand their thinking.

For those of us who came from those strict reading and writing backgrounds, letting go into the arts can also mean challenging ourselves to color outside the lines.

Resource: Do you have old rules telling you what is creatively right and wrong? Do those rules need to be deconstructed? If so, take a look at how rules may have been helpful and harmful for you. Now, invent a new creative agreement for yourself!

Day 173
Why Am I Doing This?

Remembering WHY you are doing this daily creative process can be the thread to help you show up and keep going. My original beginning was wanting myself and the world to know I wanted to be an artist. Then it transformed into becoming the painter I always dreamed of being. And then, showing up to process my day and my life. Later, I was dedicated to my art being my spiritual practice. One year it was about trying something new and expanding my skills. Now my Creative Practice is exploration to know what it is like to be in a Creative Practice to write this book. And the reasons continue to grow and change.

Reminding myself what my intention is for having my Creative Practice, keeps my fire lit. Helps me show up on days I don't want to show, when I think I don't have it in me.

After all these years though, I can sew all these together and I have a bigger reason for showing up. All of the above reasons and more have woven their way into the fabric of my life and created even more reasons.

I show up because this is my life, and my life is important to me. I never want to live less than this art-filled (even when it is just for 5 minutes) life. I love the artful evidence of my well-lived life. I want the calm brought to me by showing up and creating. I want the new ideas my mind opens to when I am not thinking but in the sensation of creating.

I began this journey because I wanted to become an artist. I continue this journey because it is the oxygen, the life force, of my life. It is more than the end product—I guarantee you.

Resource: Why did you begin your Creative Practice? What excites you about your practice and keeps you coming back? Create a gratitude list to refer to when needed.

Day 174

Balance of Body, Mind, and Spirit

We live in a thinking world. Spending so much time thinking can take a toll on our well-being. We get caught in worry, anxiety, and the desire to figure things out. We want to control our world and other people, too. Our evolved brain can take over, making us unbalanced. Art-making and creative endeavors can help us be balanced in the wisdom of our body, our mind, and our spirit. We can move from left-brain critical to right-brain creative, where new information can arrive.

When we are in the act of creating, we can slow down and be in the present moment, not lost in the regrets of the past or the worry of the future. We are working with our hands and noticing what we are touching. We are connected to the notes we play and listening with our musician's ear. We are feeling our feet moving across the floor and our muscles as they lift us up in dance.

When we are engaged in what we are doing, we can stop thinking, worrying, or catastrophizing. Instead, we allow our spirit to express. Instead, we are in creative mind inspired by this present moment. Instead, we allow our body to move and respond. Our reactive thinking can take a break. Mental exhaustion can be replaced with creative inspiration, even exhilaration.

In this space, impulses come, sometimes not even in words. I might see blue in my mind's eye, I hear a word or see an image in my imagination, I follow what arrives.

Resource: Within your Creative Practice, be present to what your body is doing, sensing, and feeling. If you find yourself thinking, especially thoughts of worry or regret, bring your attention to your breath, to what your body is doing. Learn what helps you feel balanced, less head-heavy and more light-hearted.

Our creative expression
can help carry us into
a healthier future.

Day 175
Reach for Art

If you are sober and are thinking of drinking, reach for art.
If you are clean and are thinking about using, reach for art.
If you want to get clean and sober, reach for art.
If you want to binge or purge, reach for art.
If you want to self-harm, reach for art.
If you want to stop any unhelpful behavior, reach for art.
If you want to be on your devices, reach for art.
If you want to scroll social media or shop online, reach for art.
If you want to contact a person you know you shouldn't, reach for art.
If you are angry, reach for art.
If you are turning things in on yourself, reach for art.
If you want to withhold from yourself or others, reach for art.
If you are overdoing and can't stop, reach for art.
If you are caught in perfectionism, reach for art.
If you can't turn work off, reach for art.
If you are overthinking, reach for art.
If you are thinking of smoking after quitting, reach for art.
If you are on the verge of going down a rabbit hole, reach for art.
If you want to eat sugar or unhealthy food, reach for art.
If you want to pull the covers over your head, reach for art.
If you feel triggered or activated, reach for art.
If you want to be destructive, reach for art.
If you want to blame or criticize, reach for art.
If you are feeling shame, reach for art.
If you are anxious or depressed, reach for art.
If you are suffering, please reach for art.

Resource: When you want to reach for unhealthy behaviors, reach for art instead. Let it soothe you until the craving is gone. If you are suffering in any way, reach for art. Art helps.

Day 176

My Muse Has Left the House

I don't know what to do. I am not inspired to do anything. Nothing interests me. I have no passion for anything. I don't know what I am supposed to be doing. Does any of this sound familiar? Does it feel to you like the muse is gone and there is nothing to inspire you? Does your creative energy feel depressed or repressed?

I used to think the muse was this giant exciting idea with all this information for a great creative adventure. And I would wait for it. And luckily it would come now and again. Often with a deadline, for holiday gifts or a birthday present I would make. But I wanted to make art all the time, not just for special occasions.

What I learned instead is my muse, my inspiration, is in this moment, right now. No matter how I feel. My muse IS this moment.

The secret is we have to know where we are in THIS moment. For example, if I am stuck in my head trying to think of what to do, I let this be my starting place. I make art about being confused and not knowing where to start. Maybe I paint my brain with big question marks. or compose chaos on my piano. I could do the dance of the thinking head. (I immediately get an idea!)

Our inspiration is inside us. So, rather than allowing the feeling of not being inspired to keep you from creating, create the art of not being inspired, of being depressed, of being depleted or whatever is there at the surface. Rather than waiting for the muse to arrive, nurture the idea the muse never leaves. It is THIS moment—wherever you are, however you are feeling, that is your muse.

Resource: Rather than looking outside yourself for inspiration, look inside. Start there!

Day 177

Let What Is Near You, Inspire You

If you are tired of starting where you are at, or looking inside you for inspiration, look right in front of you. Look around you right now. What is it your eyes find the most interesting? Let this be your muse. Put this object in the story you are writing or write the history of it in your life. Look at it closely and with curiosity.

Paint it, dance it, or create a monologue about it. Sometimes the most intimate stories are based around a tiny moment or object in life. Bring your object to life through your art so it does not get lost. I look around me and I see stories everywhere. The Christmas stockings still hanging, still full from the Christmas three months ago. The photos on my refrigerator, the ceramic masks hanging from the wall, or my mother's spoon in the dish drainer.

Open the nearest book or magazine and randomly pick a page and blindly point to a spot on the page. The image or sentence your finger chooses is your starting point.

Create about this day or time of year in your history or in world history. All around you are prompts to get you started.

Allow for the muse to be a tiny idea. A small moment. Those moments can be interesting if we can fullheartedly be with them.

Transform the idea the muse is going to be some fantastical experience, some manic burst of energy. Yes, these may come now and again, but mostly it is small, day-to-day moments that speak to us, if we are willing to listen. The muse is EVERYWHERE around you, asking you to take notice.

Resource: Look closely at your surroundings and life for your next prompt or inspiration. Bring curiosity to your relationship with it and see where it takes you.

Day 178

Honor the Evidence of Your Practice

How do you treat what you create? In my first year of daily art I made small letter-size pieces each day and they were stacking up. I wanted to somehow show that they were special. I found a lovely box to put them in to keep them safe. Each day I put my new piece in the box. By the end of the year I had filled three boxes.

The next stage of honoring my art was to begin framing pieces and hanging them on my walls. I was amazed at how a simple black frame would elevate the work. Even an abstract scribbly piece became "real art" by being framed and hung. I usually do my work in easily frameable sizes so frames can be bought at reasonable prices. I have artist friends who buy great frames at thrift stores and do their art to fit those frames.

If you are a musician, maybe you hang your instruments on the wall, frame the sheet music you complete or album art. Writers, frame your latest poetic endeavor or print out your story in book form for your coffee table. Dancers, frame a photo of you dancing or your choreography notes. Actors, frame a monologue you performed or a photo of you in a role. You can continuously rotate what you display so it is always changing, and you feel the freshness and inspiration of something new.

In my groups I encourage people to find somewhere in their home to display their art—to not leave it in their car or a bag, but to bring it out where they will see it. This also offers the art a chance to continue to speak to you.

Let your life be filled with the evidence of your craft. Take it out of hiding! Honor the art, and honor yourself as the creator.

Resource: Get in the habit of framing or displaying the evidence of your Creative Practice. When people walk into your home, let it be obvious that you are a creator. And, remember to sign your work!

Day 179

Sometimes It Is Hard to Get Here

My art is my happy place. Even though it fills my cup, I sometimes have a hard time getting away from my to-do list. Today I sat down to write, even donning my new fingerless "writing gloves" I bought to be a symbol to myself and others, it is my writing time. Sneakily, an email needed to be sent. This got between me and my writing. Then, hundreds of unwelcome emails I hadn't checked became a bottomless pit sucking me in.

Now I have arrived. And, my body is tight and stressed from this work. With you here with me I am going to do a very short practice, to see if it works. Let's close our eyes and take five slow deep breaths in, hold, with a slow, long exhale. Are you ready? Go.

What happened for you? I noticed those five breaths were not enough, I needed to sit quietly with my eyes closed for another minute or so, focusing on areas in my body needing to relax, just a little. One minute and I am now more present, and pleasant!

Transitioning into our art is important, especially when we live hectic, busy lives. In a recent podcast called "Hidden Brain" they talked about making things "frictionless" to get to whatever we are trying to create a habit around. For me, I got distracted by emails, which could be considered friction. If it continues to be a challenge, I could start doing my writing on my tablet, which does not have access to emails.

How can you ease out of those things wanting to pull you away and ease into the heart space of being creative?

Resource: Ease and transition are important to help us show up fully. Are there any adjustments you need to make or a process you could create to transition slowly?

Day 180
The Point of No Return

I have had many daily art projects, some of them were abandoned after weeks or months, some went the distance, a whole year. What was the difference? Those that went the distance, I stuck with, no matter what. Even when it did not feel like it was working. When I did stick with it, and made adjustments along the way, there would be a point where I knew it would not be an effort anymore, I was hooked. I call this the point of no return.

Last week was my point with this writing project. Somehow everything clicked and now it is no longer an effort to show up, instead I can't go to sleep at night without writing. I look forward to my time and I do not want to make excuses. It has taken me six months to get here.

I laugh, because the above two paragraphs were written almost seven years ago when I was writing every day as my daily Creative Practice. And yes, this project is still going, and I am in my second year of daily writing. I have no doubt I will complete this book. The gift of no return is knowing it will get done, I show up, I make progress, I get closer. I have gone through phases of being more involved and less involved. And, I continue. Some days I write a few sentences. Some days I simply read something I wrote and some days I write or edit for hours.

If I get caught in the idea this project has been going on for too long, I could feel defeated and pass another point of no return. The not returning and the book never getting done. Take care to allow yourself to be where you are, there are no finish lines. This is not a competition. Keep showing up, enjoy the process, and see where it takes you!

Resource: By reading this book you know I kept going and finished! Do you need to adjust anything so you will continue?

Day 181
Strange Days

What to do on a strange day? An off day. A day where creative energy is low. Today is one of those days. The sun hides behind a thick layer of clouds, so 9:00 a.m. and 3:00 p.m. look the same. I created an open day, nothing on my calendar until the afternoon. In theory it was going to be a delight. Writing time, painting time, work in my visual journal and maybe even call my brother.

But meeting the greyness of this day, I sit not wanting to do anything. I know if I give myself a push to get started, I could get something done. So, here I go...

It worked! I did create, and one thing led to another. I worked in my visual journal. I worked on another page for this book and here I am back to finish with you.

Getting started was the key. Yes, it took an extra push and I think feeling accountable to you, my reader, helped nudge me. What I created may not have been groundbreaking but the fact that I showed up despite gloomy skies and lack of creative energy—that is groundbreaking! I did it. I showed up and I am glad. The end.

Resource: When it isn't there, give yourself the extra kick in the pants to do it anyway. Don't worry about what you do, just do something. Do you have anyone you could be accountable to? Find someone in the moment. Call a friend, tell them you don't want to show up but you are going to and will call them back when you finish. It helps.

Day 182
The Artist as Witness to Self

We create, we stop, and then we look or listen. I have noticed when I step back from creating, my first thoughts are often critical. I notice what needs to change, what needs to be different. I can jump from creator to editor in an instant. Even when I set things aside for a day, often my first thought when we meet again is to begin a critique. Is this human nature—to constantly be aware of what needs to change, carryovers from days when our life depended on such vigilance? Or, if I name what is not working first, then when someone else sees it, I will be prepared by already seeing all its flaws?

What might change in our creative process if we trained ourselves—instead of looking through the eyes of the critic—we looked through the eyes of the witness first? We name what is there, "I see bold brushstrokes and motion."

The witness remembers the journey to this point, the struggle to show up, the frustration with the materials, the timidness of the process. The witness holds the entire experience and looks on without judgment. "I noticed you kept getting up and down." The witness may have a question for us. "What were you feeling as you got up and down?" Or, reframes the experience, "Who cares how it looks, it was fun."

The witness rests their hand on our shoulder letting us know they are there. They let us know with a gentle touch, "I see you. I hear you. I am with you."

Resource: What is your "go-to" with your practice? Do you jump immediately into critique? Do you dismiss your process or product as unimportant? Do you throw out reasons why it is not good? If you notice unhelpful patterns, try to be a kind witness. What changes when you step back with a gentle gaze?

Day 183
Sensory Living and Creating

Living as a creative we have the opportunity to live a more sensory life. We are using our bodies in different ways, to paint or dance or play an instrument. We are using our voice in a different way as we sing or act. We are creating from the right side of our brain, taking a vacation from the mundane everyday. We have the opportunity to fully move into our senses, embodying our experiences through art. The smells, the tastes, the kinesthetic feeling, the sounds, the visuals of life are accentuated, expanded, and enlivened.

And, if they are not, get your senses involved more purposefully. Slow down so you can be more present to the feeling of the paint going onto the surface. Feel inside your body the exquisite details of what is happening when you are singing. Notice the vibration of each note as you play or listen.

Today I offer you homework, and please, feel free to do it for the rest of your life. Purposely slow your attention down to the details of a moment. Notice how your hand feels on the door knob as you open the door. Feel the temperature, listen for the sound, feel the air on your skin, notice the smells as you pass from one room to the next. Do this as often as you can remember throughout your day. Then bring it to your Creative Practice—both to notice the smallest sensations of what you are doing mechanically as you create, and also to notice your internal state while you express. Is anything different when you bring your attention to your process so exquisitely?

Resource: The more we are present in our body, through our senses, the greater the presence we bring to our Creative Practice. Be with the tiniest details of your experience. You may want to write about it, too.

Our biggest job as creatives
is to keep the channel open.
Showing up regularly
helps keep the channel open
and helps us be available
when the channel is open.

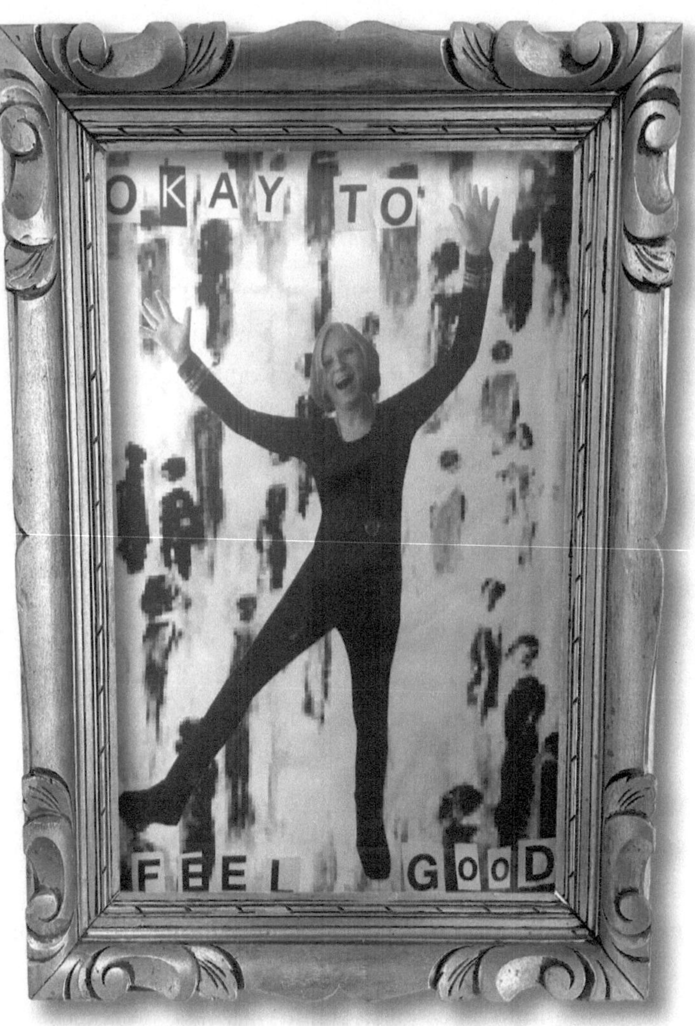

365 Days of Visioning Journal™

My Visioning Journals™ are also the place I can process my day. I might ask myself, what was unfinished or needs attention, how am I feeling or how do I want to feel? Sometimes I would express one or the other, or I would do both, express how I am feeling to get it outside of me, then express how I want to feel to inspire me forward. I did this as my Creative Practice for three or more years and continue to this day two or three times a week.

Day 184
Art Can Change the World

The arts are at the forefront of change. They pave the way toward new ways to be and new ways to think. The arts can change people's perceptions by introducing new ideas in creative ways. Sometimes using humor, sometimes using beauty, sometimes taking the old and tweaking it just a little, so we can get used to something new slowly. Or art can act quickly and shock us into reality.

If you can understand the power of the arts, you, too, can then be at the forefront of change. Think about movies, television shows, books, songs, visual art, comedy, music, dance, and how they all have pushed the edges of so-called normal to create new realities. We live in a world ripe for change.

What is important to you? Is it politics, the earth, domestic violence, addictions, racial or gender equity, children, dying, hunger, war, building community, or...

Whatever you feel strongly about, how can you bring it into your Creative Practice? How can you use your art as a change agent in the world? I create artful political mail I send to my representatives, hoping it will catch their attention. Today, with online avenues our messages can reach millions in a few seconds.

Your art is for you first. As you grow your artist self, be open to the possibility you can also create small and great change in the world through your creative expression. Explore and grow your creative voice to help create change.

Resource: What is important to you? Imagine bringing attention to it through your art. Try it, maybe dedicate one day a week or a month to a cause. For example, every Monday use your art discipline to address an issue in the world you feel strongly about. Share it through social media or mail it to someone who is working for this cause at a higher level, with a thank-you note for their work.

Day 185
Art Can Change Our Personal World

If you haven't already experienced it—art can change our own personal world, too. As an Expressive Arts Therapist I have witnessed the changes in the people I work with as well as within myself. How can you use your Creative Practice to bring your own awareness to something deeper and change your world?

During my Expressive Arts Therapy training I was dealing with big losses, the deaths of my father, my mother, and my beloved dog in a short six-month period. I learned firsthand how art can help. Most memorable was creating my own words to the song "Ave Maria" and singing it to my mother, Dorothy Marie. I painted portraits of my lost family members and through this spent time with them, grieving and healing.

In the last twenty years my Creative Practice has supported me through challenges like owning my own business, breast cancer, relationships, and working through moments when my buttons get pushed. My art helps me follow the threads back to the past and find new insights and healing, or just express what is there so I can move forward. I can even rewrite my story artfully.

Using art to help with life ties in directly with my number-one rule, "start where you are at." If we offer our art each day to what is there—what is asking for attention—we become more present in our life with the added opportunity to heal and change. This could be the simple idea of painting our emotional landscape or beginning with the musical instrument or notes that most closely express what is there. We can dance with our anger either with body, words, paintbrush, or other favorite tool—allow fine art to meet expressive art.

Resource: Invite your art to support and create change in your life—ask yourself what you need, what would feel helpful today?

Day 186

Resistance Can Be Our Friend

Resistance may show up in the form of feeling defensive, wanting to give up, turning our back on something, or lashing out. My resistance shows when something is getting too close for comfort and I am feeling too vulnerable. It could happen in a conversation with a loved one when they call me on something. And it can happen with my art when I am feeling close to something I don't want to look at—like I don't know what I am doing, I might fail, I am feeling lost or scared about the next step or sharing a part of my story.

My first step is recognizing it is happening—oh, I am getting mad at my art, I am hating it or wanting to give up.

Next is to look deeper. Why am I not liking it? Why do I want to throw it away or give up? Most often for me, my resistance comes when I start thinking what someone else might think if they saw what I was doing. Yes, this is when my critic comes up most often, too!

Finally, like a good parent, I look at how I could hold my own hand to keep moving forward. Just admitting I am having a challenge can help. Identifying the smallest step I can take and still move forward helps. I could share with someone what is going on, journal, or show up to my art to make one mark. In my personal relationships, when I can walk through the resistance or defensiveness, I feel closer to the other person. The same can happen with our Creative Practice. Resistance and defensiveness worked through can lead to new intimacy with our project.

Resource: When you get angry or apathetic with your art, look at what resistance might have to tell you. What can you learn about yourself and your project?

Day 187
Nature as Muse

Nature is the ultimate art form. Artists have tried to capture the power and beauty of nature since the beginning of time. From animals on cave walls to landscape paintings to using the landscape to make land art. Nature can not only be beautiful, but its beauty can also open the door for us creatively.

I am remembering how inspired I am after I take a hike or go camping. Resting in nature can revive me, can quiet the chatter in my brain. I can look at this natural world through my artist eyes and suddenly I have entered new territory. I notice the shape of a flower and how light and shadow play on its leaves. I want to smell it and touch its silky petals. Sometimes my camera wants to capture it so I can use the image later in my art or as inspiration for my art.

Researcher and author of the groundbreaking book, *Last Child in the Woods: Saving Our Children from Nature-Deficit Disorder,* Richard Louv, coined the term *Nature-Deficit Disorder* and says it contributes to *"a diminished use of the senses."*

If you are feeling stuck, unmotivated, or uncreative, go to nature. Take the time to consciously open your senses. What are you seeing? What are you hearing? What are the smells? Bring your nose close to the ground or the trees. Hold nature in your hands and be with it.

Even 5 short minutes in nature can change me, can help me take a deep breath, and help my body begin to relax. I start to notice what is around me. If I go to nature as my muse, to commune with my muse, I am never disappointed.

Resource: When you feel stuck, go to nature. Notice what calls to you as you enter the natural world. You may need to slow down to listen. Follow what calls to you.

Day 188
Where Do You Get Inspiration?

One of the hardest things as creatives is when we ARE NOT inspired. Those moments—or hours, days, weeks, months or dare I say, years—can feel like our soul has taken a vacation.

I have learned a great place to find inspiration is by playing in community. This was one of the guiding forces in starting my studio, to create community, and the given with community is "I know what I know and you know what you know, put us together and we can create anything."

And, a challenge when we work in community can be a tendency to compare ourselves to others. (Especially if we are just starting out, or in a creative desert.) I encourage you to shift your view, rather than compare yourself, allow yourself to be inspired by others, then take this inspiration and make it your own in some special way. As the originator of the inspiration, we get to know we are someone's muse! As the receiver, we create relationships with other artists and infuse them into our art. Everyone wins. Can it get any better? (Being inspired by another does not mean copying, stealing, or using work without permission.)

Though it can be vulnerable to create in the company of others, the risk can have a huge payoff—a community of mentors that keep inspiring you and help you grow as a creative.

Look for a community of creators in your area: open studios, community art-making events or classes. If you can't find a good fit, consider online artist communities or creating something yourself. For years I would have Art Night where I would invite people to sit around my dining room table to make art—all ages, sometimes our young art makers are the most inspiring!

Resource: Instead of hiding out when you don't feel inspired, try reaching out to others for inspiration. Create art in community.

Day 189
I Am Way Too Stressed to Do Art!

We ALL have these days, or weeks, or even months. It is important to remind ourselves in these moments of feeling "too stressed," that taking time to do our Creative Practice will help relieve our stress.

I know in the moment it may not feel this way, but I assure you it works. After being an Expressive Arts facilitator for over twenty years, the one thing I hear most from people after taking time to make art is, *"I feel so much more relaxed."*

Stress wants to squeeze us into a small tight space. Our art, whether we take two, five, or fifteen minutes, can help us feel more spacious and less cramped.

Granted, you might not want to pick up the complex composition you are working on, or the painting you are struggling with, or the script you are stumped by. Instead do something playful and improvisational, express the stress you are feeling, or take a vacation from it by doing something vacation-like with your creative time.

If you show up and you are not feeling just a little bit better when you are done, write me a letter and tell me how it didn't work! This is how sure I am of art helping. Mostly, keep going.

Resource: What can you do on stressful days to feel creative, be calmed, or express the stress? Small is okay, it says you showed up. If you notice you are having moments of feeling too stressed, too often, look at what may need to change in your life.

Day 190

Making Art in Troubling Times

The gift of a Creative Practice is we are training ourselves to show up no matter what. When times are good, when times are bad, when we are full of energy, when we are depleted. Our Creative Practice is there to support us. As I write this, I have just had a trying week or two. What I have wanted to do is crawl in bed and pull the covers over me. What I have done instead is bring all the emotion swirling in me to my visual journal. I had an interesting noticing today. When I crawl into bed I am often feeling like a victim, or the victim feeling grows. When I bring it to my journal I am taking action, I am not a victim.

Art has the ability to empower us. Through our art we can imagine the ending we want, we can slay dragons, express justice, and even be mean, rude, and irreverent.

Often just through the expression I am able to come back to reality with a new insight, or at the least, feel heard by myself. Then I know I can get out of bed and make it through one more day.

When our *show-up muscle* is strong, nothing can get in the way of our expressing what needs to be expressed. We can show up after a cancer diagnosis, a loved one's death, a pandemic, a fight with our significant other, or a bad day at work.

This is why we need to keep going. Once our art becomes ingrained in our life, it will be there to support us for the rest of our life!

Resource: If you feel like climbing into bed to get away from life, make your art in bed. Make your art before you lay your head down, even if it is for 5 minutes. Notice if anything shifts, even just a tiny bit.

Day 191
A Sentence a Day

I proclaimed to my writing group one night, "Even if you write a sentence a day, you will move forward on your writing project." Later in the evening I wondered, is it true? So, I decided I would take a week and write one sentence a day. Okay, I admit, some of my sentences are way too long!

April 27th. Taking a moment a day, to write just one sentence IS showing up to your practice—you never know what great idea might be living in one sentence.

April 28th. When I hear someone talk negatively about their abilities to do art, I react, I hate it, I want them to stop—what is the key to someone changing their negative chatter to nurturing talk?

April 29th. When doing a daily Creative Practice, I seem to notice the passage of time more, I am aware and awake, I have lived another day.

April 30th. Ideas whirling in my head are nothing until shared—when I write them down and someone reads them, do they become something more?

May 1st. What do you do if someone you love does not support your Creative Practice or project?

May 2nd. What do we do when our "less than" or "not good enough" shows up in our art process?

May 3rd. Anxiety can throw me into my art—looking for relief—maybe this is how the arts were born, the cave people were anxiously awaiting something.

Did I create movement forward? Yes, I went back to expand on some thoughts that have become part of this book. I even have a one-sentence notebook I continue to use.

Resource: Keep going on your project even if it is one sentence, one paint stroke, one note, one dance step, it adds up.

Day 192

Can You Take Your Practice Deeper?

I look at a Creative Practice as a relationship. You meet, you get to know each other, you bond. You are in a committed relationship, of sorts.

Think of your practice as a living, breathing being. Being in relationship with it means keeping your commitments. It means showing up when you say you will. It means honoring your time together, and even your time apart.

Notice how you are showing up in your relationship with your practice—are you giving it your all? Do you only have one foot in the door? Are you showing up authentically, being yourself? Or are you staying on the surface, keeping your art at a distance, or trying to be someone you are not?

If you are not fully committed, maybe an adjustment needs to be made in your life or with your project. Notice where you are withholding, ultimately you may be withholding from yourself—denying yourself a full and loving experience.

Keep going. Let the time you spend together help you grow a deeper relationship.

Resource: Look at where you can commit more or go deeper with your Creative Practice. Look at what might be getting in your way of honoring the commitment you have made. Celebrate your relationship, wherever it is, and know a little progress is still progress.

Day 193
Try New Things to Find the Right Fit

I am sitting at Open Studio right now and one of the participants, Carol, is painting in acrylics and just said, "I love working with acrylics!" Before, she had worked with watercolor and had not been thrilled. Prior to this moment she thought she didn't like to paint.

In my studio I try to provide a safe place for people to explore new things, so they can find their unique style, the expression that makes their heart sing. Art-making will not always be easy, but if we are doing something that brings us pleasure, that makes our heart sing, it helps us move through the difficult.

As a child, I loved my year or two of piano lessons with Mrs. Kristek. She died suddenly when I was seven. I never wanted to play again. Until age 40, when the desire to play came back. I tried lessons for a while and with time learned what I really loved was plunking around on my old 1930s piano. Though I can read music at a beginner's level, I prefer to improvise, it is like scribbling on the piano. I especially love playing duets with another improviser—it becomes an intimate exchange of notes. Maybe these sweet duets are a reminder of my time with Mrs. Kristek, sitting side by side at the piano with her, feeling her genuine love for me—no matter what note I played. I would have never found this way of playing, or this healing with my grieving young self who lost someone dear to her, had I not been willing to try new things.

Resource: If you haven't found the just-right fit, try something new. Maybe it is a new genre, a new size, a new material, or a new way of using the materials. If it still isn't compelling, keep trying new things. *Trust your desire to do the art, question the ways you are doing it until you find your way.* This may be a continual process throughout your lifetime, as artists we constantly need to be changing, to feed our creative spirit.

Day 194
What Do I Need?

Every time I sit down to my art I ask myself, what do I need? Then I follow this thread. My daily art has become a barometer for my life. If I need to get something out, I express it. If I need to calm myself, I find what will do this for me. Sometimes my needs do not align with my project, and I allow this to be okay. And often, once I meet the need, I can then move forward on my project.

I offer you this idea. Before you begin your creative endeavor, check in to see what you are needing in the moment. Does this need want to be expressed? Does an event from your day need addressing through your Creative Practice? When we can work with the deeper needs in our life our art can become more alive.

Another way in, is when we notice we don't have much energy for our project or we are not wanting to show up. This could be a clue something needs attention. I often notice when I am feeling frustrated with what I am doing, wrestling with it rather than in the flow, I may need to check in and see if something else is going on.

The gift of a regular Creative Practice is that our art supports us in living our life.

Resource: Let checking in before you start become a part of your Creative Practice. Or, when you are feeling uninterested, bored, or resistant toward your project, check in and see what else might be going on. Take it to your art, start where you are at, take care of your needs. Maybe it has nothing to do with your art—maybe you are hungry—go eat. Or you need to exercise, go walk. And then come back and be creative.

Day 195
Art While Consumed Elsewhere

How do you make art when you are feeling consumed elsewhere? I just went into the application I am using for writing this book and was unable to access my account. All I could do was quit the program, seethe, and worry! This is my writing time! I don't want to miss out, get pulled down the rabbit hole of figuring out some tech issue.

How do we continue with our art when something comes up taking all our energy or emotion in another direction—pulling us away from our art?

Once again, I say, start where you are at. Be with what is happening and express it. Embrace the challenges and detours of life as visits from the muse, and know you will solve them or make headway on them when you get back from your 5-minute voyage into your Creative Practice. Maybe it is not what you wanted to do, or what you hoped to do. But it is what is there. The arts offer us a way to respond to life. Allow yourself to use it as such.

As I write this, I have this worry going on in the background. Will I lose all I have done? Have I backed everything up? What if I do lose things? I want to scream. But I still write. I start where I am, and potentially this page will find its way into this book. If it does, you are witness to my sometimes rocky yet ultimately fulfilling process.

Don't let life keep you from your art. Let life inform your art—fuel it—be the muse to create it! No matter how out of control your life feels, the arts are here FOR you!

Resource: Allow yourself to make art from wherever you are in your life. Let your life fuel your creative time rather than steal it away.

Day 196
I Caught Myself Doing "It"

Today I marked my calendar as a writing day, morning to night. I had necessary business to attend to so it was almost 3:00 p.m. before I wrote. I worked for a bit and then suddenly was aware I was doing "it." I had gotten up and was cleaning the kitchen sink, instead of writing! I had mindlessly gotten diverted!

I did notice I was thinking about the entry I was working on, so I had not walked completely away. I know for myself sometimes I take breaks to do mindless things as I ponder my next step with my art. But this was not a conscious break. This was thoughtless wandering.

I laugh when I think of ways to keep me seated. Velcro on the back of my pants and chair? Shoes attached to the floor I slip into when I sit to write? A motion detector where an alarm goes off if I stand up? Figuring out what works for each of us can be as creative as our art.

I did try something new today. I set my phone timer for ten minutes. An alarm goes off every ten minutes (low volume) to remind me to get up and stretch, scrub the sink, walk outside or to return to my writing! And sometimes I just kept going without the alarm.

A proven technique, especially if I am having a hard time showing up, is to buddy up and work alongside someone else. We keep each other there. We can be together online, on the phone, or in person. I always love going to a coffee shop and having good coffee, good company, and writing, too.

Find YOUR way to stay at it. Let it be part of your creative process. Know tomorrow it might need to be something different.

Resource: What are some ways to keep you doing your art, rather than wandering off?

Day 197
Expressing the Night Dream

I have heard it said we try new things out in our dreams first. Things don't always match up to the real-life scenario, but the feeling sense can be similar. Last night I dreamt I took a bold step in my dream. I pruned someone's tree without permission, right in front of them. In the dream I was not apologetic about trimming off this branch I had determined was in my way.

As I sit here reflecting, I realize what was important in the dream—it was a bold move and I was unapologetic about it. I am immersed in social justice work. I have become a voracious student of Black history, learning what I never knew. I participate in a #saytheirnames project for women, men, and children who are Black and have been killed by police. I research one victim each week, paint their portrait and tell their story to others. I know I am making a difference in my own life, and maybe a small impact with people who see my work. Yet, I want to focus on something bigger to help create systematic change, and it scares me. My night dream helped me try out a bold step. Immediately I took it to visual art. I also brought the idea for this change to writing and dance.

Let your Creative Practice be a place to express your night dreams so you can learn more from them. Bring curiosity to them. What are they saying to you? Let each character or item have a voice. In my example of trimming the tree I could ask the tree what it wants to say. What was the branch blocking me from? Did the pruners want to say something?

Resource: Our night dreams can be fertile places for ideas outside the box. Bring your next night dream into your Creative Practice.

Day 198
Try It on Through Art

There was a defining moment in my life when I knew I was not finished with love. I had been divorced twice and had been single for quite a few years, thinking I could easily remain single for the rest of my life. Yet in a conversation with a friend I suddenly knew I was NOT finished. I knew I was on this earth to learn as much about love and relationships as I could. I knew I wanted more.

This awareness and a desire to try visual journaling dovetailed. I was going to create art every day about finding a healthy relationship. My journal would be my daily practice of love. I did this as a daily project for over three years and have continued consistently, though not daily, since. My intentions for my journals and my life change but almost always they can be distilled to love.

An amazing thing came from this. I wasn't hanging around waiting for a relationship. I felt actively involved in the process by being in relationship with my journal, my art, and myself. Every day I was checking into my heart, looking at what was getting in my way, what needed to be healed. Eventually I did find my partner, and my journal helped me with the life changes and challenges of making room for him in my life!

I named my process *Visioning Journal™*, and began offering it to others. The idea of envisioning where we want to be, through our art, can be a powerful process. We are actively involved in the creation of what we want to bring in, looking to the art for what we need and the next steps to take. Identifying what qualities we need to cultivate. The imagination is a powerful tool. If we imagine ourselves in love, we can actually feel love—our body does not know the difference!

Resource: What is calling you? What do you want or need to bring into your life? Practice embodying it through the arts.

Day 199
Art and Depression

When I wake up feeling blue or dark, dark blue, one of the last things I want to do is write, paint, or express myself. There is something about depression I want to keep to myself, own it, even stay in it. Depression is an evil mistress who wants to seduce me and keep me to herself.

Showing up to my art and myself is what she does not want. She wants me to stay down, stay inside, stay depressed. This is why creating a "practice" can be so important. When our art becomes a practice, we show up no matter what. It is time, we must do it. When the muscle of our practice becomes strong, it can stand up to and support us through depression, anxiety, grief, sadness, and anger.

Your Creative Practice moves from a longing to create and express, to essential self-care. If you don't show up for your Creative Practice, something is missing. Use your creative time to support you through depression, through anything life throws you.

Resource:

- No matter how hard it is to get yourself to your project, it is imperative you do. How can you support yourself to show up?
- Does your depression have something to say? Give it a voice. Don't edit this voice.
- Write a letter to your depression, Dear Depression...
- What can you do today to care for your depression, maybe even turn it from destroyer to creator.
- If you are not getting regular mental health support, do it now. And bring your art to add dimension to your therapy sessions. Adding adjunct creative therapy can be a great support, too. (Expressive Arts Therapy, Art Therapy, Dance Therapy, Drama Therapy, Music Therapy, to name a few.)

Follow what feels good.
Follow your pleasure.
Don't worry if it looks or sounds good.
The only person you need
to please is you!

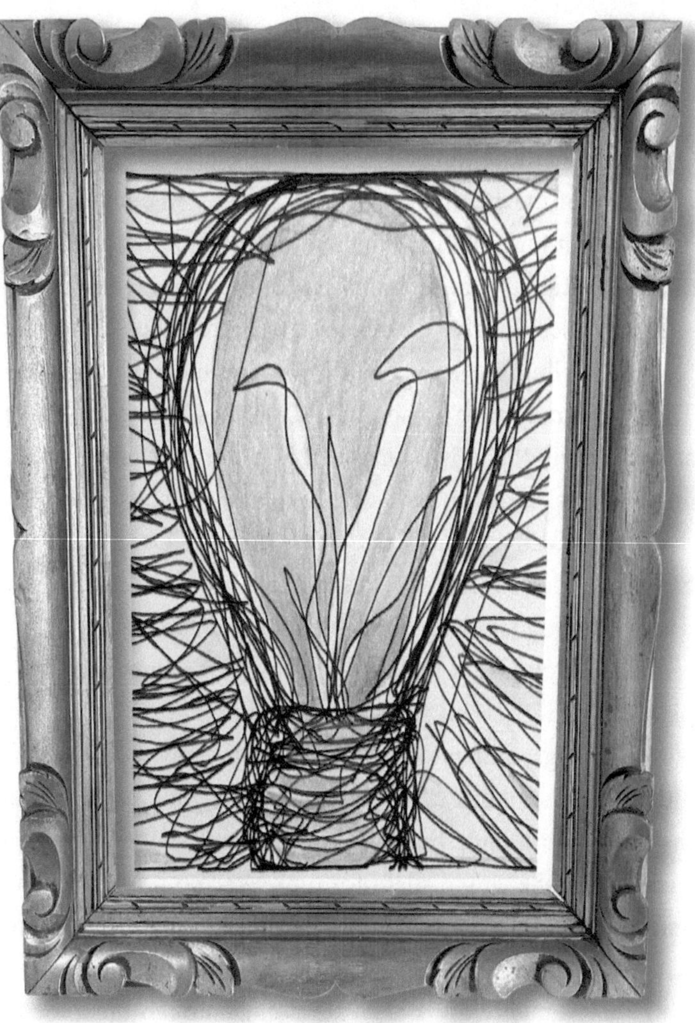

365 Days of Scribbling

I was having challenges with anxiety and scribbling became a way for me to express it and get it out of my body. I tried a daily scribble practice but let it go after a few months. A couple years later I wrote a book on scribbling called "Scribble Art: A How-to Guide and Coloring Book" which inspired me to try it another year. It worked! And that year then inspired a product, "The Scribble Kit"!

Day 200
Letting Go of Control

One of the hardest things in art-making is accepting we are not in control of the creative process. We can try to control it, bend it, or force it into submission, but it usually doesn't work and is often not ultimately beneficial or in our best and highest interest.

Yet gentle, sensitive listening can be more effective. We listen for the next impulse and then follow it through by taking action. The action may take some muscle. We might need to muscle away our critic who is telling us this is not the way to go, it is much too risky, or you will make a fool of yourself.

The impulses in our daily Creative Practice are not usually big. The impulse might say "use pink." Trying to control the situation I respond, "I hate pink! I am not going to use pink!" Receiving the impulse, I look through my pink paints and find the pink I like most. Then waiting for the next impulse, "Paint the whole background pink." Control might say, "No way, remember, I hate pink, I won't do it!" Receiving the impulse I paint the background pink, but I use an old, scratchy paintbrush, because it matches my disdain for pink. And so it goes, listening and following, listening, and following. I don't know where it will take me, but I'm in the process.

This is actually my story with pink. Through this process I remembered a pink bedroom, a pink dress, and my desire to dress like a boy, not wear pink. I began to make peace with pink. Today, I love pink in my painting and use it liberally.

If there is no impulse, sit quietly and wait. This can be hard. What if nothing comes? Letting go of control can also be a pathway to patience.

Resource: Practice sensitive listening, don't give in to that voice that is negative and demanding.

Day 201
I Am Not Enjoying My Project

Today I am not enjoying my Creative Practice. I am behind—which means I didn't get to it over the weekend and then another day and another. Now I feel like I have to play catch-up on my current project, 365 Days of Kick-Ass Moments—where I make a page in an altered book about a kick-ass moment from each day. I guess my kick-ass moment of today is admitting it isn't working. It is not fun. The spontaneity is gone. It feels grueling. All based on the fact that I am trying to *make up days.* As I write I see the absurdity, how can it be a daily project if I am making up days! Simply, my life changed and my commitment to my art wavered.

First, I am in a new relationship—when the weekend comes, I want to spend time with my Sweetie. Second, we share a small space, so making art when we are together seems complicated and vulnerable. Third, and most importantly, I let it happen. I take responsibility for not allowing myself and my art to be a priority. I know it is important self-care when I am in a relationship.

It happens to us all. It may be a relationship, it may be work, or kids, or caring for a parent. Life gets in the way of us showing up. I wonder how I could make adjustments so I can stay on track with my art. How can I make space in my new life for art and love?

I see I need to simplify. Adjust this project to fit my new normal daily life, weekends and relationship included. Reduce expectations so I can stay on track yet keep it engaging. For me, when it feels like a chore, it is not working.

Postscript: I decided I could not postpone days, just do *something* even if it is super simple. If all I have time to do is write the *kick-ass moment* down on the page, that is enough. It is working!

Resource: If you are not showing up, can you tweak your project to get on track, or tweak your life to include your project?

Day 202
Birth Takes Time

Recently I saw an illustration of an antique typewriter and it jogged a memory. In my mid-twenties I saw one of these relics at a yard sale and brought it home. My partner at the time asked me what prompted me to buy an old typewriter that did not work. I said, without thinking twice, "To remind me I am going to write a book someday."

Flash forward five years. My friend Mary O'Keefe O'Neil and I were putting together a series of workshops for our new-found organization *The Women's Creativity Project of Los Angeles,* and one was on writing. I was introduced to Natalie Goldberg's book *Writing Down the Bones,* which spoke to me in a loud and clear voice—there is a writer inside me.

I regret now I got rid of that typewriter in a downsizing move, yet it still lives in my memory. I now see my dream of writing this book began before I picked up my pen or tapped away on a more modern keyboard.

If you are still looking for your way to your desires or passions, whether creatively or in other areas of your life, keep going. Seeds have been planted along the way. Grow your *show-up muscle* to look at different possibilities, 5 minutes a day. Research next steps, 5 minutes a day. Try something new, 5 minutes a day. The key is to show up and do something. Listen for the internal impulses, and the external offerings you get from others, take them seriously and act on them.

I didn't start out writing a book. I began writing email newsletters for my studio with bits of wisdom. More than 10 years later, I am ready to publish, it's been a long labor of love to birth.

Resource: Don't give *up*, give *to* yourself. Artist is a verb and so is living. Don't wait for things to come to you, water your seeds.

Day 203
What Is Art For?

I mentioned at the beginning of this book Ellen Dissanayake's idea that "making special" can replace the sometimes overwhelming word *art.* In a recent conversation with Ellen she expanded, that in today's world we are *making ordinary reality extraordinary.*

As creators this gives us freedom from the art world that critiques and judges art. If we take this idea to each of our projects, maybe we are creating a special time to make art; we are making the paper in front of us special; we are making our words or our movements special; or maybe we are giving special attention to our music. Special is not necessarily the finished piece, it is the way we approach our art-making. Special is the verb of art-making.

In later writings, Dissanayake describes ritual ceremonies, which are composed of the arts, reduce individual stress about uncertainty, and join their participants in feelings of confidence and one-heartedness. In that sense, the arts, especially in community, can contribute to the survival of individuals and groups.

Years ago, two cancer research scientists were in my studio for an art-making event. We talked as we made art. I asked them, not wanting to bring work into their playtime, but also being curious, what had they learned about the cause of cancer. Their answer was one word, inflammation. They added that the leading causes of inflammation were stress and sugar.

When I make art, I de-stress. When I am not stressed, I eat less sugar. Maybe this does mean art-making will help us survive longer. And, if we do not live longer, we will have fun on the journey and leave evidence of our existence, through our art!

Resource: Think about your creative time as self-care, even healthcare. If the process is stressful, remember, you are only making things special or making your ordinary life extraordinary.

Day 204
Eustress, the Sweet Spot

Too much stress—distressed, overwhelmed, on the couch, can't move, immobile.

Too little stress—bored, unmotivated, on the couch, can't move, immobile.

The just-right amount of creative stress—gets you going and keeps you moving.

Living with creative anxiety or stress is surrendering to the chaos of art making where we don't know where we are going or don't have mastery over the process.

As creators we are often walking a narrow line between feeling overwhelmed or feeling bored. What we want is to be in the good stress. Stress researcher, Hans Selye, in the 1970s called it eustress, the just-right amount of positive stress to keep you moving forward, feeling fulfilled, but not too much to send you into distress. Healthy stress that moves you forward.

When I did my first 365 Days of Art project, I knew soon after starting that painting was too stressful this early in my creative development and I would never be able to make it 365 days. I needed to meet the fear of making art by making art—but not to overload myself. By becoming more highly sensitive to my own internal process I was able to keep myself out of distress and in the more motivating eustress by changing things up.

It is important as a creator to find where the sweet spot is in your creating, so you keep going. When you are in the flow, lose all track of time, and feel a sense of accomplishment, even if it is only a tiny step, this is good stress.

Resource: Notice your emotional state or enjoyment level. Do you need to slow down or amp it up? Learn to listen and build trust with yourself, knowing you are listening and will respond.

Day 205
Stretch Yourself

Once we become more familiar with eustress, finding the just-right amount of creative stress to keep us going, we can also begin playing and stretching a little at a time.

When we make art now and then or once in awhile, I think we can have big hopes and expectations when we show up. We don't make art often so it better be good or we won't show up again. We may go to something tried and true so we have a good process and outcome. It takes time to warm up and find our groove with anything, so if we don't show up regularly it may take us time to be ready to stretch and grow.

In comparison, when we have a Creative Practice and show up regularly there can be less importance on each piece. If something we do today doesn't turn out, we know that tomorrow we will be back and can try again. This can give us the freedom to go bigger, or do something outside our comfort zone.

In addition, when we are making art regularly we can make incremental changes, day-by-day small changes that stretch us slowly and can add up to something bigger with time.

Showing up regularly also helps us hone our craft, we literally get better at what we are doing and become more comfortable in the process of creating. The more we write, the better writer we become. The more we explore, paint, dance, create music, or perform the better we get, and the more willing we might be to try something new.

Resource: Ask yourself, "What could I do different to stretch myself and my craft?" Try to integrate a new material, a new idea, or take a different approach or viewpoint with your creating. Monitor your stress level, is it at that optimum where you will keep going? Or could you push yourself a little more or less?

Day 206
Working with Abandon

I used to have fantasies of "working with abandon." I imagined myself a passionate painter working on giant canvases, using paint liberally, leaving thick brushstrokes of paint on these surfaces, my clothing showing the evidence of my passion. Working in a studio that smells of oil paint and turpentine. No need to be tidy, no need to clean up. Allowing the dripped paint and messes to be the gift of the setting. I imagined I would paint all day with breaks to garden and eat healthy simple food, even have a glass of wine at lunch. A carefree life of an artist.

I have never lived this fantasy, but I have been able to reach a place of working with abandon. I have realized it is less an outside thing and more an inside letting go.

Yes, turning the volume up on my favorite painting music, allowing myself to spread my materials out in my tiny home and setting aside a larger block of time helps set the stage. But it is the not caring about what others think, or even what I think, and following my creative impulses even if I am not sure where I am going or what I am doing, that supports this feeling of freedom. Being outside my comfort zone just a bit helps me live my artist dream a little larger.

Working with abandon might mean failing BIG, and it also might mean trying something new or exciting. Let your inner artist self be wild and happy, even for a moment. As I write I realize I have a paint room at my studio for people (and me) to paint and get messy, so maybe I am living some of my fantasy!

Resource: What is your greatest fantasy as a creative? Write it down or make art about it. What can you do today to get just a little closer to this vision? What could you do that might be a little more wild and playful? How can you move from thinking to doing?

Day 207
Nothing to Lose

A project that has been abandoned can be a great place to practice working *with abandon.* There is nothing to lose, it has already been "rejected."

So, tear it up, rearrange it, make a sharp right turn with it, turn it upside down.

Or start something from scratch where you make a bold first step. Fill the "blank canvas" with something unexpected—unexpected by you! If you usually work small, work big. If you are a realistic detail person, go abstract! If you tend to be neat, get messy! If you are typically drawn to classical, think jazz!

Stretching ourselves like this makes space for surprises to arrive, and those surprises can be where we find new parts of our creative self. Sometimes what we avoid is what we *really* want, we may need to give ourselves permission to do it.

And, you can always go back to your *usual* way of creating tomorrow—another gift of having a regular Creative Practice!

Let go of worrying what anyone else will think, throw yourself completely into your project with all your senses alive. And do the unexpected! Ready, set, go create with abandon!

Resource: Can you remember something you have seen or heard, and thought, "I could *never* do THAT!" Try *that* now. Notice, are there any surprises? Feel the discomfort or pleasure of working outside your comfort zone. Is there anything you can do to keep yourself in the discomfort just a little longer?

Day 208

An Island in the Storm

The moment when all about you is falling apart, whirling in chaos, or suffocating you with overwhelm can be the best time to turn to our art.

It seems almost counterintuitive. How can I make time for my art when I am feeling so out of control or overextended? Yet when we go to our art, even give it 5 simple uninterrupted minutes, it can create an island of peace amidst the storm. And, in my experience, once I return to this outside world, I am changed. How I meet with the storm is different. I have expressed something, gotten something out, or I have taken a vacation from it all.

Even taking 5 minutes to close your eyes and imagine you are creating, without physically even doing it, can offer the good feelings of the doing. Imagine you are playing your guitar, or your brush is smoothing paint on a canvas.

You could even imagine you are doing your art on an island or in your favorite nature spot, bringing your artist eyes and ears to this nourishing environment. Our imaginations are incredible tools, and our bodies don't know the difference between doing something and imagining we are doing it.

Take 5 minutes in the midst of your life storm, create a safe place to be in the moment of creating, and see what happens. Maybe after a simple creative break from the turmoil you will return with a new idea and perspective.

Resource: When life gets crazy, step out of traffic and into your art for even a few minutes. Keep it simple, go to your favorite comfort art. Maybe it is something you did as a child, or a simple repetitive act like scribbling or coloring—something that does not take much brain power.

Day 209
Change It Up

When my son was in elementary school they would have backwards day, where you wore your clothes backwards. Changing things around keeps things fresh.

I did weeks of art in the dark. Removing the sense of sight made things very interesting (and sensuous).

I did a week of painting VERY slowly, where I moved my brush as slowly as possible. This even migrated into my days as I adopted moving slowly to everything, washing the dishes, sweeping, writing, and even driving.

Changing things around doesn't only pique your interest, sometimes you find a surprise that changes your style or approach. My artist friend and colleague Pamela Underwood says, "If you only paint what you know, how will you learn anything new?"

Notice if you are rigid in your style or process. Could you loosen up? Maybe introduce a new ingredient, hold your instrument in your non-dominant hand, or try a new genre. Possibly move the location where you usually practice to somewhere outdoors or to a friend's house.

Change the speed with which you do your art. If you are usually fast, today do things very slowly. Or if you usually create methodically, try being wild. How does it change the song or the brushstroke? Or up the tempo so you play the song at double time or create 5-minute poems. Limit the colors you use or the notes available or write with as few words as possible. Sing while you walk or do a dance in the checkout line. Let every day and every activity be a possibility for creating.

Resource: Change things up today. Change the time of day you do your Creative Practice, where you do it, or what you do when you show up. Maybe you implement a *change it up day* once a month!

Day 210
Keeping a Promise

The plane just took off as I head out for a holiday with family. I knew I would have hours on the flight and committed to using the time for writing. There is something so easy about writing when I am on an airplane. As I might have said before, I usually write with a cup of coffee because I feel more "grown up" and have the illusion it helps me write better. It is similar on an airplane. I have this grown-up feeling, as well as no real distractions—a recipe for satisfaction. (No crying babies nearby.)

So here I am, moments into the flight, seatbelt sign is still on, and my ears are adjusting as we climb in altitude. Getting my laptop out right away helps me keep my promise. *Do it now, don't wait for later because I may forget*—always works best for me.

The same can go when we are at home. Create first. Because when we put it off, sometimes we never get back to it. We get distracted, we forget, or we run out of time or energy.

If you can remember the promise you are making is to yourself, for yourself, for your greatest good, then it may be a little easier to accept the call to show up. Remembering the ultimate goal is to stay in relationship with your art and yourself, can help make showing up a priority. I find when I take care of feeding myself first, then the chores, the work, the less fun stuff of life, happens easier and more effortlessly—because my cup is full.

If a part of you isn't a believer, try it and see. If you create first, will it change your day?

Resource: Show up for your creative self first and see if anything is different. Notice when you break promises with yourself and gently steer yourself back to putting yourself first, so your own cup is full.

Day 211
Play Bigger

I connected the dots recently on a childhood trauma and how I am living smaller than I truly want. In the incident I was a joyous happy child, bouncing and squealing with delight. And then the trauma occurred. Though I have worked and healed much of this through my life, I still have moments where it is difficult for me to play and have fun. And when I do have those playful moments I can have a depressive feeling afterward. Recently it was pointed out to me in that incident I was playing big, I was playing full out. And when it all caved in, my body made an unconscious decision to play small from then on, thinking this would keep me safe.

Now I am wondering if I play small with my art? And what would it mean to play bigger? Most of my daily art is small, because let's face it, 365 pieces of anything can take up space. And, I do paint big whenever possible. Maybe I play small when it comes to what I do with my art. I don't promote myself as an artist because I don't do it for the world, I do it for me.

What could I do to go bigger, stretching in small steps? This book is a place where I play bigger one page at a time. With each entry I get closer to sharing it with the world. I have had several daily art shows, maybe I could reach out to a bigger venue to show my work? Or reorganize my art space to feel less cluttered?

How could you play bigger? Spend more time creating? Share your work with others? Invite others to join in, or create a Creative Practice support group? Maybe allow happiness and fun into your practice? Playing bigger does not necessarily mean size, it can be attitude, a feeling sense of taking up more space.

Resource: Notice if you play small. How can you play bigger in your Creative Practice and life? Try taking one larger step.

⇨ *When traumatic memories or sensations arise, reach out for therapeutic help.*

Day 212

What Would You Have to Give Up?

A friend asked me this evening what I would need to give up to have peace. The question was raised at her meditation Sanga. She said the number-one answer was fear. They would need to give up fear to have peace.

This gets me thinking about creative expression. What do we need to give up to be fully expressive? And with this too, I could see an overarching answer could be fear. Fear of failing, fear of not doing it right, fear of making a fool of oneself, fear of being judged, fear of being found out, fear of being vulnerable, or fear of going against what is considered normal. Even fear of claiming ourselves valuable enough to take the time to have creative time. Or maybe fear of owning we are an artist.

When we show up to create, we are looking fear in the eye. When we put music in the air or pen to paper we are taking action to support our creativity and we don't give in to fear. Yet, we may not be all in. We may play it safe, hold ourselves back. When I play it safe, I am not facing my fears. I am taking the easy way out so I won't disturb the fear monster. I don't want to wake fear because then I may be in discomfort. Fear most commonly lives in my body as anxiety. I would rather not awaken anxiety.

Yet, if I think about the times I have stood up to fear and did something I was afraid to do, it has not been anxiety who meets me in the doing—quite the opposite. I feel excited and alive. The anxiety is in the thinking about doing, not the doing. Maybe fear with creative expression is a signpost of where we need to go next. Rather than avoid what scares us, we take baby steps toward it, slowly confronting those scary activities, one small step at a time.

Resource: What are you afraid to do in your art? What baby steps could you take so you can look what scares you in the eye?

Day 213
What Would You Have to Give Up 2

Yesterday we looked at the idea of giving up fear (or outsmarting it), to be more fully expressive. Taking baby steps so we approach what scares us slowly or maybe jumping in fully in an inspiring moment.

Today let's look at what we have to give up to dedicate ourselves more fully to our craft or to the self-care of our creative expression. Having any kind of practice takes devotion and this includes our Creative Practice.

I currently have a painting practice going and I am also writing every day to finish this book, while working full time. I am trying to find bigger chunks of time so I can be even more devoted. What do I need to let go of to make this happen? The first and foremost is the need to limit my wasted time activities. In fact, I just got caught in two of them before getting myself here to write. Emails (a total suck of my time and energy even though they are necessary) and social media, where I go for self-promotion but get caught swiping.

I also need to give up putting everyone else's needs before mine. Give up saying I don't have time and make the time. Each day when I am asked to do something I need to decide, is this a good use of my time or could I be writing? Last night I needed to tell a friend I couldn't talk, I needed to write. I put my writing first. And, I absolutely have to give up my critic who taunts my ability.

This points to growing our Creative Practice roots deeper. To know when our life gets crazy we won't think about giving up what nourishes us most, this essential self-care. Maybe instead we can give up what makes our life crazy!

Resource: What do you need to give up to dedicate yourself more fully, grow your Creative Practice roots deeper and stronger?

Day 214
The Big Ideas May Not Come First

Often the desire to create comes before the ideas of what to create. We have a longing to paint or write or dance or play the violin but aren't sure where or how to get started. If you are reading this book and are still waiting to be struck by lightning to begin, or if you got started and it didn't seem to be working and you quit or are thinking of quitting, this entry is for you.

Let's take the example of writing. Often when people are considering my writing support groups, they say they *want* to write but they just don't know *what* to write. We often have this idea we need to know what to do before we can start. I say start writing and then you will know. And start where you are at, start writing about not knowing what to write. The actual writing will tell you what it wants, what it needs, and where it will go.

This is the idea behind the title of this book, *Artist is a Verb*, we do the verb, the creating, and then we become the noun, the creator. No matter what the genre of creating you want to do, it begins with taking action.

Great ways to get started in the beginning or when you are blocked are to follow prompts. Do an online search for art, writing, music, dance, theater, or creative prompts—there are plenty. Look at what other artists are doing and let them inspire you, or pick the first thought or idea and go for it. Follow the first impulse and then the next and the next. You don't need to know where you are going, you only need to know where to start, this first impulse. If it is not there, sit quietly and listen. Often there is something but we don't want to do *"that"* so we question or ignore it.

Resource: You don't need to know where you are going, just get going, do anything, keep going and I guarantee, your doing will become something. It could be a big idea born from baby steps.

Day 215
Waiting for the Idea

A dear friend went to film school many years ago and because of illness and life events was not able to follow his passion. I have encouraged him to get back to it. I sense his heart would sing if he did. He tells me he has no ideas.

I offer the homework to go take fifteen seconds of video every day. It doesn't matter what it is, just remember to do it. Fifteen seconds of anything. With his phone, not fancy equipment, using what he has. Put these daily videos in an album so he can access them easily when he is ready. I believe by the end of a year he will have an idea for a project. I would guarantee it.

This goes for all of us. If you don't know what to do, just start doing. If you don't know what to take photos of, go out and take photos. Your favorites will rise to the top and lead you.

If you don't know what to paint, paint everything and anything and you will find what you are liking most.

If you don't know what instrument to play, notice what attracts you and try it on. Try everything until you find what works. Don't allow the not working to be the point of giving up, let it be the place where you try something different.

Follow what feels good. Follow your pleasure, it will lead to what makes your heart sing. Never would I have imagined blind contour drawings would become my art form. It took me over a year to cement our relationship. A match made in trying something new!

Artist is a Verb means do it, and then become it. If you don't like what you are doing, change it up until you find what feels good. Never stop looking.

Resource: Do anything until you are ready to do something. Anything will lead to the something. At the most basic, make art about not knowing what to make art about.

Day 216
Patience and the Art Process

Though it would be great to create when we WANT, create on demand, create what we want when we want, sometimes creativity can be elusive. It strikes when it strikes, not a moment before. And, when we are in the habit of showing up regularly, there is a better chance of catching the wave of creativity. Even being like the magnetic moon and creating the waves ourselves.

Creativity can also be like an old-fashioned coffee maker, it percolates slowly, rather than the fast drip of a pour over, or the immediate results of a "pod" coffee process. When we show up regularly things can percolate.

A Creative Practice helps us cultivate patience for the ideas. We can do this while we wait for the inspiration to do that. We look through our Creative Practice lens at our day, at the world, always ready to be inspired. Art is part of our life. It is part of who we are. So even in the waiting to be inspired, we can be living an inspired life.

Sometimes I don't have time to do what I really want to do, so I do the bare minimum. But then the weekend comes when I can immerse myself completely and I am in a bit of creative heaven. Knowing this will be coming and creating space for it can take patience and boundary setting to make sure it happens.

It is those moments when I feel impatient, I am also most apt to think about giving up. Patience asks me to adjust, trust the process, know things will happen but maybe not on my schedule. I do what I *can* do while I wait for more. A 5-star chef doesn't create masterpieces every day, they can also prepare comfort food like mashed potatoes.

Resource: While being patient for a great idea to come, keep showing up, have an alternative idea to play with as you wait.

Day 217
Disappointment in Art Making

The arts are filled with disappointment. We try something—it doesn't work—we try something else—we don't get the result we want. The creative process is wrestling with the unknown because we can't predict the outcome, stay in control of the materials, or work at a talent level we may want. And then there is life, the total uncontrollable, affecting our creativity, too.

Through practice we can master the materials, master our instrument, our body, our abilities. But still, life remains unpredictable, unmanageable from a control point of view. Disappointment abounds. I have often found disappointment lays under the surface of my anger. I had an expectation for something and this expectation was not met, so I get critical and angry at the thing or person who let me down (usually not realizing at this moment I am disappointed). With my art I might want to quit, give up, tear it into pieces, throw it away, or deface it.

The gift of a daily Creative Practice is we also get to practice being with expectations and disappointment. I can hold better the duality of wanting it to be good and knowing it will probably not meet those high expectations. With time I have learned to better let go of expectations and just be in the process, following the next impulse, doing the next idea. How can I be disappointed in this? I move from needing it to be good to being happy it is good enough. When I meet with disappointment, I know I will be back tomorrow and have another chance. Either to take my disappointing piece further or to start new.

Resource: To move through disappointment, let go of expectations, or if you have them, let them be to expect to be delighted or surprised by *whatever* shows up!

Day 218
Expecting to Be Delighted

Disappointments and setbacks are inevitable when we set out on a journey. I want to pull back and lick my wounds when I am disappointed. I caught myself in this today. An entry I worked on for two days for this book disappeared. I immediately went into victim mode, "Oh, woe is me."

The arts are a spectacular medium for facing disappointment regularly since often things do not turn out like we expect. If we take our disappointments TO our art making, there may be more to learn. We also may find relief in the expression of the setbacks. There was a time in my life where I noticed I EXPECTED disappointment. I was curious about it (curiosity is an important part of the creative process, especially to counter our self-critic). I began noticing where expecting to be disappointed lived in my life. I found it everywhere. It probably had roots in childhood and not getting my needs met. If I expected to be disappointed, others would not disappoint me, I was already there.

I had a desire to repattern what I realized was a belief system that wasn't working for me. I believed I would be disappointed—I was a victim of my own thinking.

I did an experiment. What if I expected to be delighted, no matter what the outcome? Amazingly, instead of bucking up and not feeling, because I was expecting disappointment—I began to be more present in the process.

The expectation to be delighted became finding the delight in whatever the outcome. A failed relationship becomes a noticing that I stretched and did things different. The lost writing becomes this investigation into disappointment.

Resource: Investigate the role of disappointment in your life. Explore what happens when you expect to be delighted.

Day 219

Disappointment, a Call to Change

Disappointment can inform us we want more. Maybe I am not investing myself enough in the process, or maybe I am not investing IN myself. Maybe I am not doing something authentically. Maybe I need to ask for help or get a mentor. Instead of taking a risk to get what I truly want, I may live in the safer zone of disappointment because then I don't have to feel the discomfort of risk.

Often our response to disappointment can be to give up. In art and in life. I quit art classes because the teachers did not meet my needs for safety. They did not realize the immense fear I had when painting and my need to get it right. How would they know if I didn't tell them? They were not mind readers. What might have been different had I talked to the teachers after or during class?

In my own personal investigation of disappointment—the times when I was let down by circumstances, someone else let me down, or when I let myself down, the theme was I held back. I didn't say or do something, I could have gotten my needs met or expressed how I felt. And, disappointed was a familiar victim, woe-is-me feeling. I did not like this! So now the victim feeling became a signal I needed to metaphorically "Kick Ass!" (I did a collage and when I asked it what it was telling me, the message was: Don't hide, don't mope, kick ass!)

Rather than looking at disappointment as a cue to give up, instead look at it as an opportunity to take charge, make changes, and do a take-two to see if you can make it work better the second time around, or third, or fourth or 365th.

Resource: Investigate your disappointments so you can have an ongoing intimate relationship with them. Make art about them, too! What actions could you take?

Day 220
This Is the Place

This is the place you have dreamed of being—being creative in your life. Making your life more art-filled. Creating as a promise to yourself. How long has it been coming? How long did you dream of becoming a musician or a painter? A writer or an actor? How long did you think someday I just might—and here you are, one day at a time, one tiny bit at a time you are making it a reality. You have planted a seed and it is growing.

I had always been waiting. Somehow, I got the idea someday I would be an artist, not today, but someday. A moment would come when I would be tapped on the shoulder with a magic wand, by someone, maybe the artist gods or surely someone greater than myself, and it would be official, I would now do art because it had been bestowed upon me—I would now be an artist.

After the death of my mother and learning she had always wanted to be an artist, and she died before anyone tapped her on the shoulder, reality started to settle in. Not in a conscious you-better-get-your-butt-in-gear way, but in an unconscious stirring of my soul. If I was ever going to get there, I needed to start the journey, or I too would be on my deathbed voicing the same regret, confessing my own unrealized dream of being an artist. I could die before becoming a painter or living a writer's life.

Here I sit on top of my mountain of daily art, over eighteen years of it, living the life of a daily artist—the creative life that was once only a dream. Hopefully my last days can be spent giving gratitude for my life well lived.

Resource: Never underestimate the value of one sentence a day, one paint stroke a day, one note a day, one action a day. It adds up. And, if it does not feel like enough, do more.

Day 221
What Does the Artist Life Look Like?

In my twenties I had a vision of someday becoming an artist, the scene was what I would call late Georgia O'Keeffe. I would be old and retired by the time I would be able to live this life. I would have a small home with a garden and a paint studio. My home would be decorated with my art and fellow artists' work. My day would be a wandering life, writing with coffee in the morning, getting to my paint studio later, maybe some gardening and some creative house projects. It would be a bohemian sort of life.

Flash forward to today. I do have much of this in my life. I need to work to pay my bills, but my work as an Expressive Arts Therapist is part of my art life.

I am living my dream, which includes many things not in my youthful vision. Like my life being filled with creative messes, the organized chaos of paints, brushes, and endless amounts of creative ideas. The many boxes, folders, and piles of things that excite me and may be used in some project, someday. Paint on most of my clothes, even my Sunday best. Writing is tidier, or so it looks to the outside world. No longer are there typewriters with sheets of paper torn or balled up and thrown in the corner. The less obvious debris lives in files on my computer, in the cloud, in my backup hard drive, and yes, there are paper piles.

I am living the life of a daily artist. I don't usually sell my work, or even post it very often. Instead, I breathe in the verb of being an art maker. I breathe in the knowledge I am alive and I am doing it. And, I get to keep learning, keep growing, keep creating and asking, "What is next?"

Resource: Have you had a dream of being a creative? If you haven't already, write it down. Take notice of what still fits. What can you do today to step into it more fully?

Day 222

Move Out of Your Comfort Zone

It can be easy to get comfortable in our creating. It isn't bad since comfort is one of the reasons we turn to art. It can be a constant companion, an old friend we turn to. And, when we are showing up regularly for our Creative Practice it can be easy to get into a rut. Like a marriage, we can take it for granted, not invest as much energy into it, get lazy.

Changing things, just one degree, can bring us new insight, new experience, new thoughts, and even reenergize us and our practice. Stepping out of our comfort range, just a bit, can offer us a new experience.

When I paint, I love to paint on paper. I get overwhelmed by painting on canvas because I feel a sense of expectation, it needs to be good. I love the smoothness of paper, while canvas has irritating texture. One day I was introduced to painting on wood. It is smooth and it would help me up my game, move out of my comfort zone. I liked it. I did go back to paper, but I knew I had options.

Shift things up or down a notch. Just a notch. Change the key of a song you play or sing, use a different color palette, or cook with ingredients new to you. Write a poem instead of a story. Go to the art store and buy a new tool—keep things changing to stay engaged and interested.

Take your time. If we move too far, too fast, we can go into stress that can stop our forward movement. Just a tiny change helps us stretch, then we can adjust to the change and stretch again. Allow the craft of your art process to continue to evolve and grow, especially once you have mastered showing up.

Resource: Try something new. Notice, does it bring you pleasure? Do you need to practice it more so it becomes the new normal? Continuously look around you for new inspiration.

Day 223
Make Art Like This Is Your Last Day

A dear friend recently went through treatment for pancreatic cancer. He has gotten through and as of now, all is good. The statistics for surviving pancreatic cancer are grim, yet his outcome is enlightening. When spending time with him and his wife they remarked as to what has changed. After going through this experience, they live every day like it could be their last day together.

Years ago I read a book, *How Then, Shall We Live?* by Wayne Muller. It was with his help I first addressed the idea of knowing I am going to die and how do I want to live my life. We are all going to die one day. And we don't know when. Maybe illness leads us to death's doorway slowly, or it could be a sudden experience. Though we know it is inevitable, we are lulled by the idea it is far off into the future and we don't have to think about it—yet.

Talking with my friends got me thinking. What would happen if every day I made art like it was the last day I could do it? If I knew I could not make art again, I am guessing I would take more risks. I imagine I would tackle the important subject matter I might normally put off because it feels too hard. I have a whole file of artists who inspire me and I have wanted to make art with them as my muse. Would I tackle these ideas I avoid?

I often wonder about finishing this book. I don't know when I will take my last breath, will I finish before I die?

How about if we all do an experiment together. For the next week, each day show up as if it is the last day to leave your mark, to create. Let's see what happens!

Resource: Do the one-week experiment. In life and in your art, live like today is the only day you have. See if anything changes. Do you make different choices? Does the process feel different? You could keep a journal of your experience.

Day 224
I Dare You

Today in my writing workshop someone said they wanted to be more daring in their writing. This got me thinking about the word *"dare."* Remember when we were young, how we would dare someone to do something? Even double dare. Some of it was mean, like when I was ten at a birthday party and was dared to eat a piece of chocolate that ended up being an icky dog treat.

With age, the dares get more real. Life dares us to keep going during a pandemic, after the death of a loved one, to be vibrant in the midst of losing abilities from aging, illness, or accident. Getting out of bed when we are depressed or heartbroken is daring.

Life dared me the year I lost my father, beloved dog, and mother in a short six months. I answered this dare by doing Expressive Arts hospice work. Who better to know about death and using the arts to grieve? This book I am writing says, "I dare you to finish!" and I've upped it to a double dare.

The dictionary uses words like adventurous, courageous, and fearless to define *daring*. Yes, I think, daring is who I want to be—daring is the life I want to live.

Having a Creative Practice is a daring decision. To show up regularly to face ourselves—be intimately involved in witnessing our life, our limitations, being with ourselves in front of the blank page, at ground zero of the creative process, over and over is DARING! Confronting creative blocks and staying with it, not giving up is daring. Making art is daring, and our art can hold the emotional dares life flings at us.

Resource: To live daringly feels similar to living every day like it is your last. What is it you could dare to do so your life becomes bigger, more vibrant, or more meaningful?

Day 225

I Want to Take the Dare Back

The dare. It is easy to be dared when I am not asked to do something out of my comfort zone. When I was younger, I dared NOT to make waves, or have opinions, to NOT make art because it felt too risky and I had no training for taking risks. My upbringing was more about being a good girl and blending in, than standing out.

Life did dare me at unexpected moments. Daring me to move to California, to leave a marriage, to keep looking for my passion, and to create an Expressive Arts Studio in my community. But none of those felt risky. There was a sense of sureness, I was following the next impulse.

What happens though when the dare feels too big? In yesterday's entry I double dared myself to finish this book. What I may not have shared prior is this idea is scary, beyond my comfort zone. It is not really the finishing of the book, the craft of writing. It is what to do with it once I am done—put myself out there in the world to be rejected by readers, agents, publishers, or the world. It is safe when it is just me involved, but opening the door to the world?

I feel tightness in my belly when I merely think about publishing. I could probably make this project go on for another ten years if I hadn't just accepted my own double dare.

The gift of writing is I work things out as I write. And here I am at the end of the page realizing I am not ready for the risk ahead because I am not there yet. As I get closer to the next step, once I finish writing, I will be ready. If I am not, I will make the next step as small as it needs to be so I can face the risks ahead.

Resource: Notice if you are holding back because you are worried about a risk in the future. How can you help yourself stay in this moment, not jump into the future?

Day 226
Listening to My Body

I am dealing with a heavy feeling of expectation. I am going to explore it right now with you as I write this. Even in my twentieth year of daily art I occasionally have this dark feeling inside of me—my art is not enough. I am not doing enough. It *should* be better, more creative, more explorative, more original, more, more, more...

The feeling sense of this in my body is a weight in my chest. My heart feels constricted. I can't relax. I turn my attention to my breath. Take a few deep breaths and look out the window. Another breath. I make sound as I breathe out.

There I am, back in school, never being able to do good enough. My brain did not work the way it was being taught and school was a struggle for me. Always hearing messages like, "If you only applied yourself you would do better." This was before testing for learning differences. I was a hands-on learner and they were asking me to read and memorize. I take another deep breath and tears come as I think about the young me who didn't feel successful in school. So many expectations on me.

Do I want to put this kind of pressure on myself? Do I want to recreate this scenario in my life? No, I want to create an atmosphere of love and support, not expectations and the feeling I am not performing well enough. I relax just a tiny bit.

The tightness is now in my belly. This is good, tight belly usually happens when I am trying something new and feel unsure of myself. I tell myself it is okay to feel unsure. Let's go make art feeling unsure. No expectations, just celebration for showing up.

Resource: When it is not going well, settle into a quiet space and identify the sensations in your body. Be gentle with yourself and create art that soothes you, and maybe brings understanding.

Day 227

Exploration with Expectations

Yesterday's entry was about my feelings of expectations on myself to do better, do more, be more creative. I walked you through my process as I took a quiet moment to breathe and check in with what was going on. An old story of being in school and not being successful enough came to me. I was able to feel compassion for the younger part of me who suffered in school and realized I was reinjuring myself with my current expectations.

I then went to make art from a place of more compassion. And here is what happened.

I take time to look through what I have created so far, as I begin month four of my current project, a small blind contour portrait every day. Looking through the eyes of compassion, wonder and curiosity, rather than expectation and critique, I see the impossibility of my expectations. I look at what I have done as being a diary of my daily life. From this vantage, there is no need for perfection or greatness. I like what I see.

I notice I have stopped writing notes on my paintings to remind me where I was each day. Remembering how much I love to look back on those notes, I add words for what I remember. I go to a page only drawn in black paint pen and begin to doodle on it. I forget about expecting anything and follow the next impulse. "Oh, that's right," I say to myself. "Just follow the next impulse. If I do this, it can't be wrong." I relax into my process. Follow the next impulse. Simply follow the next impulse. I can follow the next impulse. And so I did.

Resource: When you look or listen to the outcome of your Creative Practice, approach it with curiosity, compassion, and wonder, not critique. Allow yourself to follow the next impulse, and not have to measure up or perform.

Day 228
You Don't Have to Be Good

Do you think if you do art you have to be good? Do you think you need to show and sell your work professionally? What if we get to be a creator, get to do what we love and not worry about how good it is? What if we don't have to monetize our love? What if we just love what we love to do?

Your expression doesn't have to amount to anything more than you loving it or loving the process of doing it. And you can still consider yourself an artist, musician, writer, dancer, performer. You may not do it professionally, but you are doing it. And, you can keep learning and growing. Creativity is not finite. We can never know it all. We can learn and change and find new ways to be in the creative world. We get to follow our pleasures.

I have sold my work and it is a whole different experience. If you want to make a living at art, you have to treat it like a job. Show up every day like you would at a job. It could be a great way to earn a living for you, or it could take the joy out of your process. (When our art becomes a business, creating the work is only the first step, you then have to market and sell your work.)

If you find yourself feeling like your work is not "good enough" to call yourself an artist, move your attention gently from looking at the end result to noticing how it feels to be creating, being in the process. As you are creating, is there a feeling sense of being an artist, living an artist life? Allow yourself to grow this feeling and take it in.

Resource: Focus on the feeling of making art. Are you enjoying it? Are you showing up? Are you having times where you get lost in what you do? Be with these good feelings. If there are next steps, they will reveal themselves when you grow into the next step.

Day 229
Death, Grief, and Art

Death can come in all forms. It may be the death of one from our human family, the death of an idea or belief, or the death of a time in our life. We are always in a state of transition from one thing to another. Our creating helps us honor these transitions.

I have experienced all kinds of death and grief in my life. The death of parents, pets, clients, heroes, and mentors. The death of jobs, careers, and friendships. The death of moving from a place that felt safe to a new town or city. Then there are the passages from childhood to adulthood to elderhood.

Death brings opportunity for new life. With every goodbye we make room for a hello. And there is grieving to do before we are ready for the new hello. The arts are the perfect vehicle for grieving, honoring, letting go, and transitioning. We can express and process through the arts all that is lost and begin making room for something new.

I am thinking of when my son was young and his father and I divorced. Every week when I took him to his dad's house I would drop him off with hugs and smiles and go to my car and cry. I would then go home with this heavy feeling and begin to paint. As I painted, I would process my missing of him and begin to reconnect with myself. When I would wake the next morning, I was ready to do life alone. It never changed. Every week was this process. My art held the transitions, all the way until he flew the nest.

If we allow them, the arts can be our companion through all the endings, big and small, which need attention. The arts can also fill the empty space left when life changes.

Resource: You do not have to suffer alone, your Creative Practice is here to support you through everything, including grief.

⇨ *If your grief is complicated or overwhelming, be sure to get therapeutic help.*

Day 230

The One-Week Experiment

"In life and in your art, live like today is the only day you have. See if anything changes." —Challenge from Day 223

Last week I committed to do the challenge I offered to you, to show up to my art as if every day was my last day. Because of this I tried painting in a new style I had wanted to explore. There was excitement to finally do it and a realization I might not have the patience to do it more than once.

My biggest noticing was being in the moment so much more exquisitely than *"usual."* Feeling my paintbrush on paper, choosing vivid colors, and not letting myself be distracted with other media as I painted. There were also moments of melancholy, if this really was my last moment, was I ready? Would ready mean living every day to its fullest, even when I am resting or can't finish my art?

I offered the Day 223 reading to my writing group also and gave them a writing prompt exploring if this was their last day to write, what would they write? Most wrote love letters to the people they would leave behind, revealing more of their love. It was sweet and heart opening to listen.

I may not be able to live like this every day, I even forgot during my one-week experiment. If I could live like each day is my only day even one day a week, what might change in my life? Could I grow this idea with time like I grew my Creative Practice and let it become my new normal?

Resource: If you didn't already, find time—minutes, hours, days, or weeks to live as if this day is your only day. Notice what happens. If you already did it, share your experience with someone. How could you carry this idea forward?

Day 231
I Am Not Ready to Die

As I muse after last week's experiment of making art like it was my last day, I am confronted with the truth—I am not ready to die. I have a lot of ideas I would love to explore, lots of creating and living to do.

Yet, my creative time and energy is limited, so I have to be thoughtful in how I use it. I don't believe our creativity is finite, but our hours in the day and our days on this earth are limited. Being clear and choosing how to spend our time is important. I do not want to die while being on my devices or on social media.

I have learned along the way not every idea is meant to come to fruition. Ideas are the easy part, actualizing the ideas takes a lot of time and effort. (I even created a book where I write my ideas down, so I can claim them, and not have to do anything with them.)

This is another reminder to choose my life. Don't let it get away from me. Follow my pleasures in creativity and in life. And I don't want to waste any of it.

I heard the phrase recently: It is only work if you don't like doing it. Is it possible to create a life you love living so it never feels like work? Like in our art, cut out what isn't working and expanding on what is working.

Today I am not ready to die, but if I knew my time was limited, how would I spend it? I would hope to be with the people I love and I would make art as long as possible, maybe I would make art with the people I love and then when I am too tired, turn it over to my loved ones and let them make art in my presence. Sing and dance me to my last breath.

Resource: We don't have to be dying to live each day as if it is our last. How do you choose to spend your life?

Day 232

Letting Go to Be Taken by the Process

When we find the flow or the groove of creating, it can be a high without drugs. Time stands still. We are so in the process daily life falls away and there is only this creative moment. I have heard when we are in the creative groove, the brain naturally releases endorphins and dopamine, which are feel-good chemicals in the brain—a natural antidepressant and painkiller combination. Similar to drinking or using drugs, without the negative effects.

What needs to happen for us to get to this place of creative flow? It may be different for each of us, but here are a few ideas that might help.

- Get in a space of following one impulse after another, don't question the next step, just keep going, keep following the ideas.
- Don't worry about where you are going, let yourself be as fully in the process as possible.
- Allow your senses (see, hear, feel, touch, taste) to stay awake.
- Allow enough time to get lost in the process.
- The critic is not invited. Stay with the creative process and postpone any critique to another time in the future.

I have had some fabulous flow art time, and the next day looked at what I did with a curious eye wondering where it came from—almost like being drunk and forgetting. Or, feeling as if my channel is open and the art flowed through me. These are times I am very happy.

Resource: Notice what happens when you get in the flow. Take a few notes so you can remember how you may help yourself get to this place in the future.

Day 233
Compassion for Our Art Wounds

"In seventh grade my teacher held my painting up in front of the class and criticized it. I felt horribly shamed." —Michele

"When I had my son I couldn't write anymore. The baby stole my language. I couldn't access the words once I became a mother. It took 10–15 years for them to come back." —Diane

"I remember my dad telling me I couldn't carry a tune in a bucket. I grew up thinking I couldn't sing." —Donna

"I shut myself down, I felt inadequate. My sister was the creative one, and I felt like I couldn't compete with her." —Lisa

"The message I got from my family was, 'Isn't that nice...but useless...it will be a nice hobby.' I felt apologetic for wanting to be a dancer." —Chris

"When I was ten, my singing teacher quit, he told me it was because I had no talent." —Karen

We are all wounded somehow. I think it is impossible to make it through life without scars. The arts are a place where we can feel the most vulnerable and naked. Add our wounding history and it is like we have no skin. Even the best intentions can hurt. Being sensitive to this we grow our capacity for compassion.

If you want feedback or support on your art let people know what you want. Before you give support to others ask them what kind of feedback or support they would like.

Resource: Compassionate and supportive feedback can help all of us to keep expressing and healing any past creative distress.

Your Creative Practice can be a place to invite others to join in.

Don't skip because you have company, invite your company to join you.

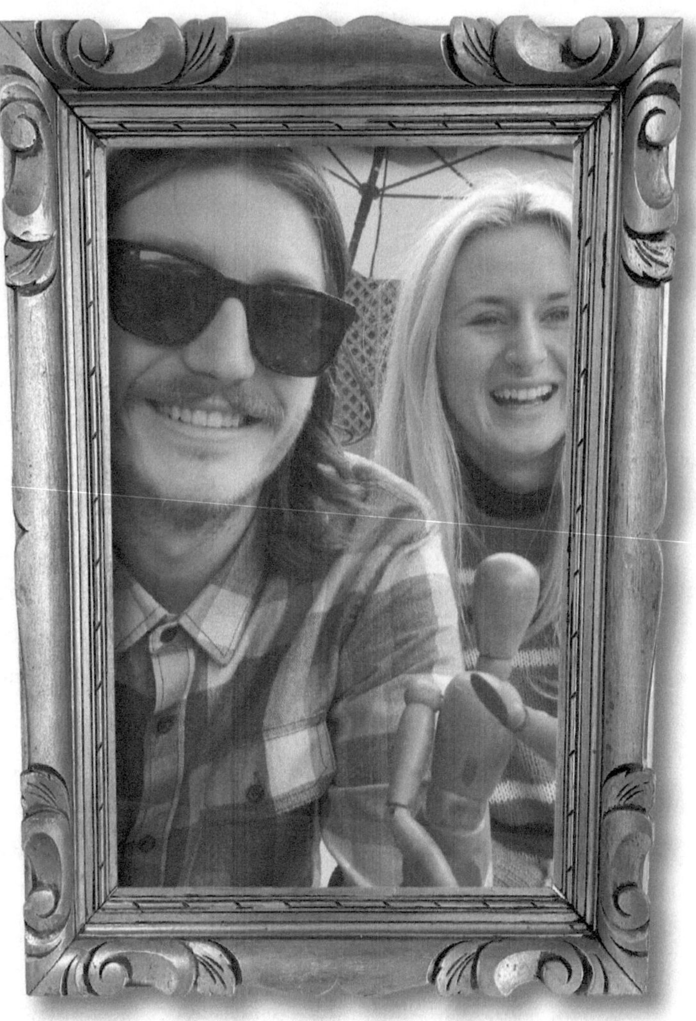

365 Days of Manikin

This project was a love and lost relationship. I went three months in a first attempt which included posting the pic each day on social media. The social media part was too hard, and instead of just letting that go, I let the whole project go. I tried again four years later without posting, and it worked! Except, I kept losing track of Manikin and missed days because he was lost. This was a great project to get others involved!

Day 234
Motivation—Keep Going

Our motivation waxes and wanes. And, motivation is a key to showing up. When we are doing things over and over it is natural they can begin to feel boring, dull, or uninspiring. I don't think of motivation as being the same with everyone. We have to learn what motivates us as the unique human we are. For the next five days we will explore some ideas you could use as motivators to show up, go deeper, or enjoy your process more. Revisit them whenever needed.

Change it up. Change things around as often as you need to so you will show up. Change the place where you are creating, change the project, do it in the dark, do it in the park, get creative.

Use different materials. During my oil-pastel-a-day project I would go to the art store and buy a new color or two every once in a while. Having a new color in my box helped up my excitement. Dancers could move their feet on the dirt, grass, water, or sidewalk rather than indoors. Writers buy a new pen or notebook.

Do art in the dark or by candlelight. Something as simple as changing the lighting can add interest, mood, or fun. Whether your project is musical, visual, writing, drama, or movement oriented, it can all work in a change of lighting.

Create an art retreat day. Once a week or once a month clear your schedule so you can have an art day. Wander through your day following the next impulse. If you can't carve out private time, let your family or friends join in and they can even help guide the day.

Resource: Know that it is natural for your motivation to increase and decrease. Notice when it decreases so you can help boost your motivation with what works for you.

Day 235
Motivation—It Has to Be Enjoyable

If our Creative Practice is not interesting or fun, why would we want to show up? If it is feeling too much like work, take a look to see what needs to change so your practice feeds you, not depletes you. Here are a few ideas to help.

Make it into play. With play there is no winner or loser. It's about following the next prompt without worry about the result. Watch kids play, they build a tower, knock it down, build again, knock it down, turn it into something else, and so on. Turn your painting upside down, create a silly rhyming poem, dance in a 4-foot area as if it was the cliff's edge, use your imagination to make it play rather than work.

Make a game out of it. Games are outcome related so if you need to get competitive to show up, do it. You can create a challenge for just you or include friends. Create a song using just 4 notes, a painting using 4 colors, a poem in 4 lines, or a monologue in 4 sentences. Sometimes when we have less to work with it becomes more interesting

Challenge yourself. Create personal challenges like: try three new drawing techniques in a month; finish one piece a week; explore how many words you can write in ten minutes. Set a deadline to finish something. Make it FUN, not stressful.

Take a class. Classes offer us new ideas and someone to help shape our work with the possibility to have a mentor. You can also do online classes, watch how-to and motivational videos, or look on social media for inspiring creators in your genre.

Resource: You can be in charge of your motivation by noticing how you are feeling and offering yourself something you need.

Day 236
Motivation—Remember Why

Our motivation can dwindle when things become routine or the call changes. Routine is good to help us show up, yet it can create a holding zone that can become boring or too easy. Sometimes we forget why we began or take it for granted. Revisiting and reevaluating our *why* can help.

Remember why you started. Reconnecting to our original desire to make art, to have a Creative Practice, can reignite our flame. When I started my Scribble-a-Day project it was because I was feeling intense anxiety and wanted to find relief. My physical discomfort was all the reason I needed to show up. If I missed a day, I might not find relief. Wherever your original desire came from, see if you can show up to honor it.

Create a new intention for moving forward. On the other hand, sometimes the reason we got started becomes obsolete or stale, so finding a new reason to continue can help. In fact, the Scribble-a-Day project ended because I was feeling better. I picked it up again at a future time when I realized it helped me stay current with all my emotions. Revisit the *Reasons to Start a Creative Practice* list in the front of the book to see if there is a more important or different reason.

Quiet time before you begin. Take 3–5 minutes or more of quiet, closed eye time before you begin. It could be meditation time where you follow your breath, relax your body, and clear your mind. Or ask a question like, "What is the next step for this project?" Take this question into your quiet time. Or it could be a prayer, "Help me find the strength to keep going." Follow the ideas that come to you. It might help your time feel more sacred and less mundane. Experiment!

Resource: Find the deeper helpful reasons to show up.

Day 237
Motivation—Get Others Involved

We can't do this alone. Humans need other humans. Sometimes in the arts we feel we need to do it on our own, or it is cheating if we involve others. Or we will be judged by others so we want to keep it a secret. Opening the door to others can help us show up, grow, and enrich our practice.

Invite others to get involved. Create a regular art night or jam session for your neighbors or friends. When we create in community, we can inspire each other. You could also start a Creative Practice support group with other creatives to get and give support. See the Follow-Up Resources section at the end of this book for a format idea and possible readings to create a safe space.

Bookend your creative time. Find someone you can call or text before you start and again when you finish. Bookending is great when something feels hard, or you feel stuck. It is added help when you bookend with someone who has a practice going also, so you can encourage each other.

Create creative partnerships. Check in each day or each week to share your work. Knowing someone is interested and is going to witness what you do can help push you to do your best or show up more fully.

Share your work on social media. You get instant feedback that can be rewarding. You can also build a following and inspire others. Be aware not everyone knows how to give feedback, so if you want people to comment, be specific about what you want. I recommend putting a copyright symbol and your name on work you want to protect.

Resource: Does the idea of bringing others into your creating sphere scare you? Think of one small step you could take to let others into your creative process.

Day 238
Motivation—Process and Progress

To keep our motivation high we must constantly be noticing what feels good and what doesn't feel good. We are called to be present in the process at all times.

Reevaluate to see if what you are doing is a good fit. Sometimes we commit to something only to find out we don't really like it or we are not ready for it. Our project may need a complete overhaul or just a little tweaking to make it fit better. Stay in touch with your pleasure scale. If it is not pleasurable most of the time, it may be time to revamp or go deeper so it feels like a better fit.

Take notice if your lack of motivation is really fear. Often fear is disguised as not liking something or wanting to give up (revisit the critic entries Day 52–Day 61). If you look closer, you may realize you don't know what to do next or the next step feels scary. Usually, the answer to fear is taking action. What do you need to do to confront your fear? Baby steps are always best because we can move forward slow enough to outsmart our fears and our critic.

Do something surprising. Deconstruct things you have done that you do not like and turn them into something else, combine them, change things around, do things different. This can be a way to get ourselves out of our everyday thinking and get back into the creative zone. Problem-solving motivation can be creative.

Celebrate each day you show up. Each day give a shout out to yourself for showing up and honor what you did, no matter how small. You might plan a gathering to celebrate major milestones.

Resource: Be in the moment, problem-solve and trust that you can get your motivation back.

Day 239
Feeling Like It Is OVER

Today I feel as if my relationship with my writing is over. Maybe because I am not feeling great. I need a certain amount of energy to be able to show up and do something. Today the best I can do is show up and give voice to this idea it might be over. Maybe my writing and I need a relationship counselor or a tuneup. Maybe a vacation from feeling like I have to show up.

The truth is my writing shows up every time I do. It is much more faithful than I am. Even when I show up thinking there is nothing there, something arrives. The same goes for my visual art, my drumming, or piano play. If I show up, my muse is in there somewhere, even if it is a short paragraph, a few notes, or a single stroke of paint.

It is five days later and I am not feeling much different about my writing, and the day after I wrote the above, I came down with the flu and have been sick ever since. I am truly not at my best. I have learned over the years to not make final decisions when I am in the highs or lows of life, to wait until I am on an even keel. The highs and lows may inform the decision, but they should not rule on it.

Update: Today I woke up ready to reengage with this project. The motivation is back. And though I only wrote this short update, it feels good. And yes, I get the interesting timing of this entry after five days of writing about motivation! This week I was in the trenches with motivation, and came out the other side.

Resource: When you feel like quitting, take a break, for a few minutes, an hour, a day, or a week. Or begin another project alongside the project that is giving you trouble. Don't make any rash decisions while you are in a lull phase. Talk to someone or write and make art about it and see if you get any clarity.

Day 240
Your Art History

When did your creative journey begin? Can you trace a thread back to your younger years where you can see something was sprouting? Maybe it continued to grow or maybe it went dormant until later or even until this moment.

What has your path been to unearth your creative self? What route did your longing take? Has it been there all along? Has it been calling you and you did or did not answer? Or, is it just being born? There may be breadcrumbs along the way—left or right turns, stops, starts, and even some U-turns after a dead end or being on the wrong road.

Maybe your life like mine has zigzagged toward art. Or maybe it came to you naturally when you were young. Or maybe you are a prodigy. Maybe you hit burnout and are trying to find your way back to the arts with heart rather than discipline.

My journey may have started in the basement as my best friend Barbara Gene and I made perfume or put on plays we had written. Or in our small-town library where I would look through art books, especially loving the nude drawings and paintings. It wasn't until my first 365 Daily Art project when I was 45 years old that I finally began to feel like an artist. This feeling did not come from creating amazing pieces of art like I thought I needed to do, but in showing up and creating. I am grateful for finally finding my way to what so clearly nourishes me.

Resource: Look at the creative thread in your life. Create a timeline of your life and the important creative moments along the way—up to today. Are there any people or artists who influenced you that you would like to honor? Can you find any surprises in your history that point to where you are today? Make a piece of art to honor your journey to this moment.

Day 241
Art and Self-Intimacy

When we are making art our life is our muse. The process of creating from our life helps us get to know ourselves and our internal workings better. Even when we are making art about the bigger world, our time spent with it is time with ourselves, too.

Sometimes when we are avoiding our creative time it can be because we want to avoid what is going on inside of us. The intimate connection we can have with ourselves when we slow down to create can be scary. Self-intimacy may be another muscle we have to grow.

Because intimacy needs safety, we also may need a private space or time to do our art. A space where we can more fully be with ourselves while we create. Having the luxury of a private space is not the norm. I share a 300-square-foot home with my Sweetie. We have found a nice rhythm, he goes to bed early so I have the later evening for my time, and he wakes early and has the morning for his time. If this is not available, I can scoop up my things and go out. Interestingly enough, creating in public where I can be anonymous, surrounded by people I don't know like at a park or in a coffee shop can help me feel safe. Lately I have learned a set of headphones can help me enter a more private world.

Don't let fear of intimacy with yourself or a lack of safety pull you off your creative path. Instead, look at how you can create more safety within yourself and your situation. And always remember to breathe.

Resource: Notice if your holding back or your blocks have to do with not feeling safe, start exploring the changes you could make. (If the lack of safety is because of your internal critic, revisit the critic entries Day 52–Day 61.)

Day 242
Art as Lover

My Creative Practice is more to me than doing art. It is a relationship. I bring everything to my art. When I first began, I brought my grief from the loss of my mother, father, and beloved dog. Then I brought the challenges of single parenting, changing careers, illness, and growing a business.

Many years of my Creative Practice centered around preparing for the life partner I had not met yet. I explored what I needed to let go of, grow, heal, and who I wanted to bring in, all through my art. My relationship with my Creative Practice, in retrospect, is an example of the relationship I was looking for in a partner and continues to be a relationship that teaches me to be a better partner.

My art is available. I always have my art-making tools close at hand to make it easy to show up, no matter what my day is like. My art is in a prominent place in my life, ready to support me.

My Creative Practice is a consistent long-term relationship. I show up every day. I initially set out on a one-year project—I never expected it to become a lifelong practice—until death do us part.

My art is expressive. My Creative Practice has been where I process my life: breast cancer, heartbreaks, empty nest, and even finding my Beloved and the work it takes to make room for him in my life and love better. My sharing is honest and authentic.

My Creative Practice is deeply intimate. I share my truth, my innermost workings in my art, I hold myself with love. I understand myself better. I can then bring that better me to others in my life.

Yes, my Creative Practice is training for love, to be more available, consistent, expressive, and intimate. I get to work through blocks so I can love more fully. What a great by-product!

Resource: If you are not fully "in relationship" with your Creative Practice, what needs to change so you can grow closer?

Day 243
The Gift of Creativity

I am reading a book, *The Choice* by Dr. Edith Eva Eger, a memoir of her life being Jewish in World War II and barely surviving the Holocaust. As I read, I cry, even on a crowded airplane. I cry for the atrocities humans can commit against each other and I cry for the creative spirit that can keep us alive in the atrocities of life. Edith, or Dicuka as she was called in her youth in Austria, uses her imagination to keep herself alive. She imagines her boyfriend telling her how much he loves her eyes and her hands. She imagines the future they will have if they both survive. She imagines herself dancing, twirling effortlessly in freedom. She imagines staying alive for one more day.

In my work with women who have been homeless, we look at how they used their creativity to help them survive—where will I sleep safely, where will I get my next meal. Now that they are safe, they can use their creativity to express, to create beauty, to imagine a long-term future.

I never want to lose touch with gratitude for having a life that allows me to create art. Art supports me through my day-to-day challenges and the bigger challenges life offers. Would I stay with it if I ended up living on the streets? If we were invaded by war? I would like to think I would leave some evidence of my existence everywhere I went. I don't know for sure. Can a strong Creative Practice survive anything?

Let us give gratitude for a life that allows art. Allows us to express and can support us through whatever life brings. Even if we can only create in our imagination.

Resource: Take a moment at the beginning of your creative time to give gratitude for a life that allows you to create. Pay it forward, contribute to creative programs in your area with time or resources.

Day 244
Is It Time?

I tell the story often about my desire to do a daily found-object project where I would find an object each day, write about it, and artfully display it. I had done a week of this during my first 365 Days of Art project and liked it so much I wanted to do a whole year. After some false starts three years later three blue glass gems caught my eye on the sidewalk. As I reached down to pick them up a voice went off in my head, "Go smaller." Originally my test pieces were 8.5" x 11". The new thought was to reduce the size to be less overwhelming. I began on this day using the blue glass gems I found and continued almost effortlessly for a year.

I say this to encourage you to be gentle with yourself, allow your projects the gestation time they need. And also, don't allow yourself to give up.

If there is a project you have wanted to do but haven't started, brainstorm what could be in the way of beginning. Maybe a change in the format or adjusting something a degree or two. In brainstorming, write down as many ideas as you can, don't critique them, just write them down—until one says, "Yes, this is it!" And begin. This same process can be used if you are feeling bored or stuck on the project you are already working on.

I didn't do nothing in those three years while waiting for the 365 Days of Found Objects project to finally come to life. I did three other years of daily art, preparing myself, growing my creative confidence, and my *show-up muscle.* Don't worry if it is the right project, keep going, keep building your *show-up muscle.* Creativity can't be forced; it can be invited, but it may arrive on its own schedule.

Resource: Brainstorm whenever needed. Ask others for help, another set of eyes and ears can be helpful. And keep going!

Day 245
Putting Off What Is Good for Us

We know showing up for our creative time is good for us. It feels great, we feel more alive after, there may be a sense of accomplishment, and we feel more balanced. Yet, allowing the time, even this far into our practice, may still be hard.

You may notice you are leaving your art for last when there is no time or you are too tired. The sad truth is we tend to leave what is important to us, even when it is for our own good, for last.

This is why, back when I started my first daily Creative Practice, I did my art in bed. I was always climbing into bed and remembering I hadn't done my art. Ultimately, I found I liked doing it at the end of the day in bed. It gave me a chance to process my day. I purposely decided to do my art at day's end.

The real concern is when we leave it for last and NEVER get to it. I am sitting here at 11:15 p.m. writing, because my newest strategy is to set an alarm for 10:00 p.m. every evening to remind me to write. I hit the snooze button at least four times before I finally started. It worked.

Do whatever it takes to allow yourself to have this time each day. If you need permission for this essential self-care, you have it. Turn the world off, let go of your to-do list and go have creative time. This is your time to serve and nourish yourself.

Celebrate you showed up, for yourself, for your project, and even for your loved ones in your life—because when your cup is full, they get a better you. Do a little dance, give yourself a high five, write in your date book, "I did it!" or whatever you need to do to feel the pleasure so you will keep showing up!

Resource: If you notice you have less and less time and energy for your Creative Practice, what can you do to get yourself there earlier? Set an alarm? Remember, art helps!

Day 246

I Tried to Not Show Up...

After over sixteen years of showing up regularly, and enjoying it most days, I still have those days where I just don't want to do my art. Today is one of those days. I am feeling blue and would rather eat, have a glass of wine, binge watch a show, or clean out my sock drawer, than do my art. And being honest, I did all those things and still haven't shown up.

I also committed to working on this book every day this week. I have fallen short of this desire, so I knew I needed to show up tonight. I thought I could combine the two—write, go do my visual art, and then come report back to you. So here I go. I will be back in five minutes, or so.

I am back, just under 16 minutes later. My daily art project this year is scribbling. Sounds easy enough, why avoid it? So, I scribbled and scribbled. I noticed halfway through I sighed a big sigh. I realized a difficult conversation I had with a friend earlier in the day had me feeling vulnerable and this is why my energy is low and I am feeling blue. Maybe it was this vulnerable feeling I was avoiding. My art gave me a place for it to be expressed. And, I must say, it helped. I feel a shift.

I am proof it can work. Don't talk yourself out of showing up. Trust your process, trust your project, trust yourself. And keep it simple.

Resource: When it is hard to show up, remember, you can tolerate it for 5 minutes and it might help. And, you just may stay longer. When you don't want to show up, maybe something needs attention. Let your art help you see clearer what that is.

Day 247
The Loss of My Muse

I've heard it said to write down your ideas as soon as they come, you have 10 seconds or so until they could be lost. When an idea comes, grab the nearest pen and paper and jot it down.

I have had small books on my bedstand for years where I jot down ideas, those elusive ideas that could be gone in a moment. If I am in the kitchen you might witness me repeating something over and over as I run for my book to write an idea down before it leaves me. These handy books are within arm's reach of where I do my daily art-making. As I have thoughts I might want to include in this book, I jot them down. Little quotes I could later expand into a larger entry.

This week, I went to grab these little idea journals, to get some inspiration for this book—and I could not find them. Panic screamed through me. I looked everywhere I could think of but couldn't find them. You see, my Sweetie moved in recently and we rearranged everything. My little treasure-filled books seem to be lost.

This leads me to this entry I may never have written, the loss of my muse. So once again, I started where I am at, and I found something new to say. Trust something new will always be there, or the old ideas we think are lost will come back—we just need to keep the channel open. And yes, I am still hoping to find my little books!*

Resource: Keep a notebook somewhere handy to jot down ideas. (You can also use your digital devices.) When you don't have ideas, be still, trust they will come, or go look in your idea book.

**Two years later I found my idea books during a spurt of spring cleaning!*

Day 248

Will I Run Out of Creativity?

Years ago, an artist attended the opening of an exhibition on Doodle Art at my studio. As part of the show, we had a community doodle table asking attendees to doodle. This artist stayed the whole evening, sat at the table, and never picked up a pen to make a mark on the table. He then came the next month to another doodle event, sat at the same table, and never made a mark.

I was perplexed. He claimed to be an artist and had even brought some photos of his work to show me. After viewing his work, which was quite textured and beautiful, I asked, "Why don't you contribute to the community doodle table?" He told me he saw creativity as finite and he did not want to waste his creative energy on something he didn't find meaningful. I had never heard this perspective. It had never crossed my mind I could run out of creative energy by using it.

After many more years of art-making and thoughtful consideration, I would say from my own experience it is quite the opposite. The more art I make, the more I want to make.

In my twenties and thirties I had a belief that I would not become an artist until I was old and retired. Maybe I thought I had to earn my way there? I am grateful this belief proved to be wrong.

This gentleman did eventually put a few marks on the table. Actually, he made something quite lovely. He would surely be appalled to know a day or two later a three-year-old came in and added her own scribble on top of his contribution.

Resource: Check in with yourself. Do you have any beliefs around creativity that may be holding you back or negatively impacting your ability to create? Any voices from your past saying art is not valuable or worthwhile? Make a list of what comes to you and journal or make art to see what more you could learn.

Day 249

What to Do with Disturbing Images

Sometimes when we are creating, we can come up against disturbing images that grab our attention. They can be visual images, written images, or ideas in our mind. They can be created by someone else or by ourselves. Coming up against these ideas, themes, and images can be scary, stop us, and have us turn away from them.

I want to propose rather than turning away from what is disturbing us, that instead they could become doorways to unfinished business or pathways to new information. If we can allow ourselves to be with them and not reject them, they may take us somewhere new.

This is not free rein to abuse* yourself with them, but when something upsets you—this is a form of attraction. Allowing time with it may lead to new learnings or new creative expressions.

Artists Francis Bacon and Frida Kahlo opened the door for everyone to say it like it felt, and it wasn't pretty. Sometimes the image might be benign to others but upsetting to us. Or vice versa. (I have an aversion to honeycomb patterns.) Allow your feelings.

Resource: One way to be "with" images that disturb us, and yet stay distanced at the same time, is to dialog with them through writing. You might ask the image questions like: Why are you here today? What have you come to tell me? I don't understand why I don't like you but am attracted to you also, do you know why? Where did you come from? Is everyone afraid of you? Why do you look so menacing/depressing/uncreative...? Has anyone ever liked you? Most importantly, be gentle with yourself.

**You know yourself. Don't send yourself into dangerous emotional places and trigger yourself further. Find a quiet way to learn more. It might be good to do this with someone you trust like your therapist.*

Day 250

Stop Making Things Complicated

We do it. We make things so complicated when they could be easy.

The make-it-complicated voice:

How am I going to find enough time?
How can I get this to unfold just right?
My house is a mess!
My project is a mess!
I can't afford a studio!
Do I write or do I watch a movie? I can't decide!
I don't have the just-right _______. (Fill in the blank.)
I can't figure this out, how do I get things to fit together?

The make-it-easy voice:

I have 5 (or 15 or...) minutes, let's DO IT.
Try it and then see what happens.
I can clean my house later, go make art.
My project wants my attention, go give it some.
I don't need a studio, get going right now, right here.
Do them both. Create for a bit, then watch my movie.
Don't wait for things to be perfect, do something.
Review what you created, then go for a walk. Return after.

I notice the complicated voice creates a scenario where I can't do ANYTHING, it seems impossible. There may be no answers, or the answers are a long way away. The easy voice seems like a wise part of myself that encourages me to DO SOMETHING, anything.

Resource: When you are not making progress, not in relationship with your project, what can you do that is EASY so you will keep going? Can you call up that wise part of yourself that wants to help?

Day 251
I'm Not Ready

"If you wait, all that happens is that you get older."
—Larry McMurtry, Author and Pulitzer Prize Winner

What are you waiting for? Need an example? I want to make videos of my art processes and Creative Practice wisdom. I don't know how nor do I have the financial resources to hire someone. So nothing has happened for years. Nothing.

I know I am waiting to become brilliant at it so I can get started. I see the hilarity in this, just like my waiting for the artist gods to bestow upon me the gift of artist, so I could start making art. As I write this my first year of daily art flashes before my eyes—I started out beyond my scope of competence and ended up simplifying so I would show up and ultimately build confidence. How could I apply this to my dream of creating videos?

Often we have dreams and we do nothing because we don't know what to do. Rather than doing something and failing (or even succeeding), rather than asking for help or letting anyone know we need help, we do nothing,

A deadline can provide us a reason to HAVE to get started. Death of a loved one can push us forward because we are reminded life is limited. The new year or a birthday are fertile areas for beginnings. The beginning or end of a relationship, even a change of seasons can be great motivators. We can be propelled forward by emotions that open our heart, use those moments to get started!

Resource: I challenge you to not wait. Take the first step toward something you have dreamt of creating. You don't have to figure it all out, only take the first step in the direction you want to go. Then just like with your art, follow the next impulse. You are not alone. Let's all do this together.

Day 252
A Dying Man's Art Wound

Edward was dying of pancreatic cancer and had a room at the hospice where I was working. When I told him I was there with art offerings he insisted he didn't want to do art, he wasn't an artist. He was glad to talk about art and look at art. Edward loved to talk! He shared with me all his family members who were artists: sister, brother, children, and grandchildren. But no, he didn't do art, he was a lawyer.

I finally handed Edward a piece of clay. Told him to feel the texture, smell it, squeeze it, play with it, and let his hands do what they wanted with it. As he squeezed the clay, he became unusually quiet. A few moments passed and he told me this story.

"I was interested in art when I was younger. In fact I signed up for a drawing class in college, figure drawing. The first day I showed up I saw that the models we were going to be drawing had no clothes on. I was so shocked I ran out of the room and never went back. I never did art after that." When I asked him what was hard about seeing the nude model he answered, *"I had never seen a woman naked and I just didn't know what to do."*

Edward made a simple little saucer with his clay. Art was our connection that day, talking about it. We talked for 40 minutes, before I handed him the clay and he remembered that confusing moment from the past. I believe the two elements that helped Edward find that memory were the relationship we created by talking, and the simplicity of hands working the clay helped him relax.

I wonder if Edward had been able to deal with his embarrassment or shame back when he was eighteen, how his life might have been different. Would he have been a creator of art rather than only an observer?

Resource: It is through the doing where we find the opening.

Day 253
No Desire?

Some days, the desire is gone. There is not an ounce of energy to put toward creative expression of any sort. AND you have committed to this process. There are many formulas out there for breaking through creative blocks, find what works best for you. My tried-and-true exercise is to begin where you are. Begin with the message going through your head:

"I'm too tired."
"I don't feel creative."
"I don't know what to do."
"I am too worried about money."
"I don't have time."
"I am feeling too depressed."
"I have nothing to give."

Whatever the message, excuse, or reason, start there. Give this message a voice in your painting, in your dance, in your photography, your writing, your music. Part of being an artist is being true to yourself in the creative process. You can even amplify the message or feeling so it is exaggerated. Sometimes giving the "no" a voice can be the most inspiring work we do. Other times it is as boring, unimaginative, and uninspiring as the real moment is feeling. The outcome doesn't matter, it matters you gave it a voice and you showed up to your practice.

The added benefit—when we express, we sometimes feel relief. We may still be blocked creatively, but we have expressed the block and have something to show for it.

Resource: Express the reason you don't want to show up, amplify it, and see if going louder with it shifts anything.

Day 254

No Desire? Deeper Meaning?

There are going to be times when the desire to create is absent and we don't want to show up. And, if we show up despite not wanting to, we may get more information about why we are feeling resistant—why we don't want to create. If we give voice to the negative, unhappy messages as suggested yesterday, it may lead to some new understanding of what may be going on under the surface.

"I'm too tired." Could end up being, "I hate what I am working on and don't want to do it anymore."

"I don't feel creative." Could be code for, "I don't know what I am doing and feel at a loss for the next step."

"I don't know what to do." Could mean, "I am worried what others will think about my project."

"I am too worried about money." Could be a way of saying, "It is not okay to take time out for myself when I am not earning enough."

"I don't have time." Could reveal, "I am scared I cannot be creative."

"I am feeling too depressed." Could translate to, "My feelings are not matching the project I am working on."

"I have nothing to give." Could be, "I am taking care of everyone else and not taking care of myself."

Our Creative Practice is a constant reflection of our life and an opportunity to grow and heal, if we allow it. What is our resistance to showing up telling us? When we feel resistant it can mean we haven't found the right offering, we may feel vulnerable or out of control. Listen to this deeper self.

Resource: Look below the surface for more information about what you need and make adjustments until it gets better.

Day 255
Art as Response to Life

I have written about how I use my Creative Practice to respond to life, to process it, to make peace with it, and to celebrate, too. Tonight at our Writer's Open Mic, I witnessed someone's poetic response to their relationship, in real time. They wrote small poetic responses daily to the dance they did in their rollercoaster life.

To witness someone else's poetic response to daily life was a gift. To be invited into the intimate moments of the heart. A few sentences a day captured a whirlwind of life.

Sometimes we think our creative time needs to be epic, yet distilling our life to a sentence or two can be more profound than a book or a full-length movie. And who knows, the little snippets could lead to a book or movie.

When we respond to our life through art, we also get to see our life as art. It becomes more than everyday, our life becomes moments alive with color, emotion, and metaphor. A rainy day becomes "the sky dropping tears of sorrow on the earth who is disappointing her." The visual artist may capture a moment of this tearful sky while a performative artist expresses its journey.

Art in response to life can be both simple and complex. The simplicity of the moment and the complexity of how we want to view this moment. The angle of our camera, our eye, or our heart can change ordinary into exquisite.

If you think your life is too boring or too depressing, or your talent is too remedial or untrained, allow yourself to look through new eyes and see it differently. Look through the lens of a cinematographer, a photographer, or a Buddhist monk. Create as if you are a child and you see only what is most important.

Resource: Let go of the idea your life needs to be extraordinary and find the extraordinary in the ordinary.

Day 256

Kindness and Creating

The theme in my groups this week was self-love, or more directly, self-kindness. In this exploration some noticed they say unkind things to themselves they would never say to someone else. Even in thought, those unkind words or attitudes can be damaging and carry on the voice of the oppressor in our life. A parent, teacher, or other unhelpful person. Our Creative Practices are fertile ground for our unhealthy critic, for unkindness.

What happens when we bring kindness to our Creative Practice, to our process, and to how we move or how we play? When in the sphere of kindness, we make room for ourselves at the creative table and inspire others. Kindness is slow and gentle versus fast and rough. Kindness meets us where we are and builds us up, lets us know we are okay, encourages us to strive for more.

I am thinking of a moment during COVID, when I went to my local grocery store. We were all standing in line masked and six feet apart, waiting to go into the store a few at a time. There was this sweetness where people offered others to go ahead of them, or we asked each other how we were doing through it all. And then someone started playing a guitar and singing. It was a memorable and kind experience.

The arts are full of critics, from the outside telling us what is good or not good, and from inside, what we tell ourselves. Notice what is different when you get on the kindness path, when you encourage yourself with kindness, and when you are gentle and encouraging toward yourself.

Resource: Bring kindness to your creating—make art about kindness, make art with kindness, and speak to yourself kindly. You could even give away your art as a random act of creative kindness with no expectations of a return.

Day 257
I Feel VERY Stuck

After being on a roll with my writing, I have just been showing up to do the bare minimum these last days. I feel very stuck.

I realize I did it to myself. I broke one of my own rules, not to share something with others when I still feel vulnerable from the creating. It was an entry for this book where I got a personal insight into my mother. It was emotional and I cried as I wrote. I wondered though if it made sense and if it was appropriate for this book. I read it aloud in one of my writing groups and asked for honest feedback. And got it.

This becomes a lesson on two levels. One, start where you are at. As soon as I typed "I feel VERY stuck," I realized what was going on, I had shared my work too soon. I was not ready for feedback, even the good feedback I received.

Second is the reminder to not worry about editing or getting feedback on work that feels vulnerable until some time has passed. Even though it was my idea to read, I had not taken the time to check in with myself fully.

And even in these moments of feeling stuck, my *show-up muscle* gets me here. ONLY by showing up did I get through my block. I didn't get through by thinking about it. It is in the action where things move.

I sound like a broken record about this because it works. When you are feeling stuck, don't wait to get unstuck so you will show up, show up whether you want to or not and things could shift.

In situations like this, a little reward can be helpful. Like right now, it is time for a treat—my famous lemon cake treat.

Resource: When you are feeling blocked or stuck, show up anyway, do something, start where you are and maybe you will get more information about your stuckness as you express.

Day 258
My Famous Lemon Cake

Yesterday I mentioned my famous lemon cake treat. There is a story to tell. My first Daily Art project began a year into my Expressive Arts Therapy Masters studies, so by the time I began writing my thesis, I had two years of daily art experience and my *show-up muscle* was strong. I realized I could transfer the same idea into writing my thesis. I committed to showing up 5 minutes a day so I could stay in relationship with my topic.

As you might imagine, writing a thesis is not as much fun as painting. Being a big lemon cake lover, I decided I could allow myself a teeny, tiny sliver of lemon cake as a reward for showing up and spending time on what seemed like a heroic writing project. So, this is what I did. If I showed up, I got my sliver of lemon cake and enjoyed it as my reward. Believe it or not, one lemon Bundt cake lasted me the entire three months it took me to write my thesis. (I kept the cake in the refrigerator to help it last.)

In the last months of writing this book I am reverting to the lemon cake reward. To get cake, I need to devote a good chunk of time, like an hour, or finalize at least one entry. It keeps me going, keeps me showing up, and adds to the fun quotient.

We do what works to strengthen our *show-up muscle* and to make our creative dreams come to life. A mini-celebration for our greatest good can be helpful.

Resource: Create a way to celebrate and give yourself a reward when you show up—if you need one. Our time creating is often enough of a reward, yet sometimes we need a little extra good cheer.

Day 259
Continuing in Pieces

I am over halfway through my 365 Days of Kick-Ass project and to be honest, I am not sure how it is going to work out. I have been working in a book I got at the thrift store. I guess you would call it an altered book. Well, it is very altered. It is now three or four times thicker than when I started, the binding has come undone, and it is currently in seven pieces. I am going to have to get the book rebound and have no idea how—this is way out of my area of competence!

I am not one to figure everything out before I start. I have never done an altered book like this and I like figuring things out as I go. I have some bookbinding friends I am sending help messages to—maybe you will see the results by the time this book is published. (Number one rule I am learning, use a book with sewn binding, not glued!)

I am telling you this to encourage you along. Do NOT stop because you are not sure how to do something. Keep going while you figure out the next step. Or, don't wait to start being creative because you don't know how to do something. Figuring it out as you go is a great way to learn. We can even end up somewhere we wouldn't have gone to if we knew how to do it when we started.

Often the not knowing what to do becomes an EXCUSE to not move forward—it is fear planting seeds. Don't let fear get in the way of continuing. If you have to, do something else while you are figuring out the next step. In other words, KEEP GOING! As for my altered book, it now has a lovely box to call home, in all its lovely pieces!

Resource: When you don't know what you are doing, ask for help or settle into the not knowing—it could be a great lesson on perfectionism and letting go.

We learn as much or more from what doesn't work as from what works. The best part of things not going as planned is that we can then take bigger risks because we are less invested in the outcome.

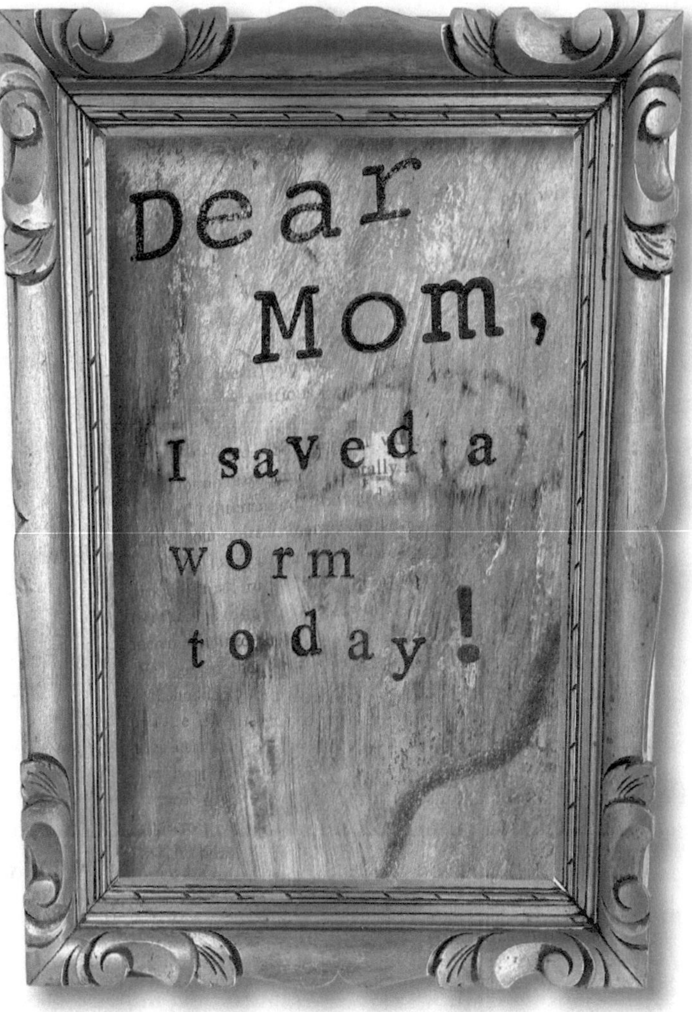

365 Days of Kick-Ass Moments

I have a journal where I keep track of the big kick-ass moments in my life. Bigger stuff. One day I thought about looking for the kick-ass moment in each day. This was a huge kick-ass project because I had lots of challenges. Mostly I was creating an altered book (using an existing book as the basis for it) and I had never done this before, or researched it. The book ended up falling apart in about 20 pieces. Someday I will kick ass by rebinding it!

Day 260

Follow the Impulse* Reminder

My tried-and-true offering to people is to "follow the impulse." You don't need to know where you are going, or how it will turn out, or even what will happen next after the initial impulse. Simply begin.

If the impulse is to use blue, dip your paintbrush into blue. Then listen for what the paintbrush wants to do with the blue. As a writer of music or words, same thing. When I sit down to write sometimes I have an idea and sometimes I need to wait for an impulse, before I can begin.

The secret is, there is never NO impulse. "I don't know what to do" is still an impulse. Start with not knowing what to do. Or maybe there is a new NO to doing something you agreed to do earlier. If you allow this *I don't know* or the *NO* to be where you start, you will probably be off and running. Voice all the reasons you don't want to write or dance or paint. Follow the not wanting to show up and you might get new information or at least you showed up!

Often when we don't follow what is coming to us we are worried what someone else will think. *They* become so important we can't move. *They* will say we are wrong. *They* are telling us to do something different.

An important learning in following the next impulse is deciphering what belongs to us and what belongs to someone else. You *should* do this or you *have* to do that is probably someone else's voice. Finding your own voice, your own impulses, your own personal style, your own creative path, takes deep listening.

Resource: Practice exquisite listening when you get an impulse to do something. Are you following your own creative ideas or is someone else's internalized voice stronger than your own?

**Follow the impulse as long as it doesn't hurt yourself, another, or property.*

Day 261
The Birth of a Way of Life

After yesterday's entry I was wondering where the idea to follow the next impulse in art was born for me. Maybe in my Expressive Arts studies? Or was it born from my own investigation working with people who are afraid of making art? I have no solid memories to put my finger on. I know though, I am grateful.

Today in my writing workshop I wrote a story of being with my mom right before she died. I knew she was going soon; she had just shown a telltale sign. She saw my father, and on taking off her glasses said she would not need them anymore. I remember clearly my impulse was to climb into the hospital bed with her and spend her last night on this earth lying next to her, holding her if I could. For a moment I struggled. Would I instead go home and find myself in my childhood bed with my longing to be with her, just like the night a few months prior, after my father's memorial where I heard her crying in her room and I was crying in mine? I did not have the courage to follow my impulse of climbing into bed with her then. Would I once again allow this impulse to be unrequited? What would I do?

As I wrote this story, I realized this was a moment where I clearly heard the next impulse and followed it. I crawled into bed with my mother, and it *was* her last night on this earth. Maybe this was one more skill my mother helped me grow.

Every day we are offered impulses we follow or ignore. Maybe these creative forces are at work from the day we are born—think of children playing. Maybe we have to re-remember how to follow the impulses that bring us pleasure?

Resource: Join me for the next week and be aware of the impulses that come to you, creative and non-creative. Notice the ones you follow and the ones you put off and do not act on.

Day 262

This Is Not What I Signed Up For

I do not have a private space to do my writing. I do my best to carve out time when I am alone. But today I need to be at the studio while a repairman is here. And there are others here, so my writing time has conversation in the background, and it is frustrating because I cannot concentrate. Rather than wallow and play the victim or give up, I am pushing through and starting where I am at—I am writing about what is happening in this moment.

I write down the bits and pieces of the conversations I am hearing, maybe for future writing prompts.

I feel like I am more of a woman than a man...
My older brother is in a slow death...
I am just trying to manage right now...
I broke it, now I need to go get a new one...
I can't get pulled down into that black hole...

Suddenly I am seeing the creative possibilities of random conversation around me. They could also be painting prompts, dance prompts, improv prompts, or music prompts.

We can always find reasons to not show up. The real test, can we find a way to show up when it doesn't seem to be working? Don't let circumstances become a negotiating point to not show up. Take what you have and make it work. It may not be optimal, but it is something. You may be surprised.

Resource: Notice those moments when the circumstances aren't perfect and you start negotiating your way out of showing up. How can you still show up in the imperfection of it all and make the best of it?

Day 263
Art and Aging

A dear friend and I were talking today about aging and dying. He suggested when he stops being useful and grateful, let him leave this earth. When he is using up resources without giving back, his time is done.

Later thinking about this I remember when my mother was suffering, I prayed for her to be relieved of this life, but then the next day she sang me a beautiful song she said she sang to me as a baby. It was then I realized we never know when the last gift is given. How do we truly know when we aren't useful any longer? At my mother's funeral many of her caregivers told stories about how she left her mark on them, in their hearts.

I have worked with many who are aging and dying and I offer them the idea of acceptance of their new style as their abilities change. I think about my life and wonder will it be possible for me to make art until the end? Will I continue as my abilities fail? Will my art be a sign of my usefulness? Will my art help me to continue to feel grateful for this life?

Often we hold onto the way it was so tightly we do nothing rather than try a different way. We then suffer from the not letting go, not being able to understand how something new could come and nourish us. When artist Claude Monet began to lose his eyesight, he found a new way of painting that changed art forever by birthing impressionism.

Let's commit now to make art right to the end. Plant the seed with our loved ones, put it in our advance directive, a creative life until the end. Long live our muse!

Resource: Create a vision of a long life of creating. How do you want to see yourself in your elder years? Set the stage for adapting as you age. You are never too young to start imagining!

Day 264
The Inside Out of Fear

You might say I have made it my life work to study fear and art making. A heuristic exploration, studying my own process of art-making and finding what works for me to get through my fears. Then helping others walk through their fears so we can all learn together. Finding the easiest way in and the path to keep going.

The most frequent encounter with fear I have experienced personally and professionally is the worry of what others will think. *It won't be good enough, I will get criticized, someone will laugh at me...* Fear tied to an outside source can be immobilizing. It keeps us from trying new things in our art and in our life.

Sometimes we never start because the fear of what someone will think is so strong. What if we fail and the world sees us failing?

Much study is happening with the brain and our reactions to outside stimulus as we look at PTSD, embodied therapies, and trauma. Studies show the body feels something first, which then causes the thought. With this in mind, if we are exquisitely aware of our body as we create—to notice when we feel numb, tightness, stress, or other sensations—we can get more information.

For example, as I write this, I am feeling tightness in my belly. My mind says, "You do not know what you are talking about. You are not an expert." I want to get up and eat something so I don't feel. I do get up and walk around the house for a minute, and while doing this, my inner *Good Parent Self* steps in and says, "You know what you have experienced, and it is important. Keep going. Nothing is written in stone. Stay with it. Don't give up."

Resource: Be with the sensations in your body, listen, make art about it. Meet the fear, the sensation, or the thought with love, kindness, and curiosity. Be open to learn something new.

⇨ *If traumatic memories or sensations arise, be sure to get therapeutic help.*

Day 265
Can I Become an Art Addict?

Someone asked me recently, "If you do it every day, couldn't your art be an addiction?" I think of an unhealthy addiction as something that *separates* us, *takes us away from engaging in healthy relationships and life, with negative effects.*

If we use our creative expression to hide out, stay away from others and avoid our life, it could have adverse effects and become unhealthy, like being a workaholic.

Ultimately though, I see our Creative Practice as a place to process what is going on in our life. Rather than running away, we are running toward and through our challenges with the help of our art form. Then we can come back to our relationships and life with new insights and feeling more connected to ourselves.

My Sweetie and I moved in together two weeks before the COVID shutdown. We share 300 square feet—a huge adjustment for both of us. Because my *show-up muscle* was strong, I would go to my art daily. It became a safe place to answer my internal desire for space. Sometimes to escape my life, to take a vacation from the challenges, and sometimes to work through a strong emotion. My art saved me from reacting hurtfully, helped me get perspective, and respond from a more centered place.

We go to our art every day and yes, it is a ritual, a habit, a regular activity. Rather than an addiction, it may become an irresistible attraction that does not take away from our life or ruin it, but enters our daily life and makes it better. Art helps.

Resource: Allow your Creative Practice to help fill your cup so you can be more available and balanced in your life. And if you do have challenges with addictions, let your art support you in your journey to get healthy. Reach out for help. You do not need to do it alone.

Day 266
A Healthy Addiction

Our Creative Practice can take the place of unhealthy addictions and become a healthy addiction, or even better, a life-affirming practice. The hope is to build a Creative Practice so inviting you can't wait to get to it each day—a space to express the feelings and sensations when you want to turn to less healthy behaviors.

Our Creative Practice can become a place to turn to instead of going to our devices, drugs, alcohol, food, gambling, or whatever we crave that does not serve our greatest good. It can also be the place where we express the sometimes intense, sometimes subtle feelings we have when we want to escape to unhealthy behaviors.

Engaging in addictions can hijack our endorphins and our production of dopamine. Creativity helps the brain create and release these without damaging our body, bank account, relationships, and other areas of our life. When creative expression is a part of daily life, we can feel the authentic sensation of living bigger and taking up more space in our world.

If you have been an artist who used mind-altering substances to help you create, coming back as your raw self can feel challenging. Growing a different relationship with your art and your creating is possible. Acknowledging it is a challenge to show up unaltered is a good start. Let your art hold you through these difficult moments. In other words, express the discomfort through the art, don't avoid the art because of the discomfort.

Whether addiction is a challenge in your life or not, see how your creative expression can be life altering for the good.

Resource: Turn to art when you want to turn to something you know isn't for your greatest good. Let art be the place you express what you would rather avoid or to regulate and calm yourself. And get support from others, too. Your happiness matters.

Day 267
Follow the Next Impulse Experiment

A week ago, I talked about following the next impulse and wondering where it was born in me. I invited you to join me in a weeklong experiment to notice when you get an impulse or idea—to notice when you follow it and when you don't, or simply to notice the impulses when they come.

For me this was a deep dive into a more conscious time noticing my mind, my thoughts, and my impulses. I went to spiritual places and enjoyed pleasure. I noticed when I didn't follow the impulse and I was sorry, or when I did follow the impulse and was sorry (ice cream). And when I was happy.

I noticed small things like when driving somewhere, the thought to turn left here instead of the usual route. Maybe I was avoiding something in my path or maybe it was a curious mind.

I was going away for a day and needed to pack art supplies. "Just bring a few materials so you don't have a lot of choices." I listened and it worked, it was a vacation to have less to choose from.

Impulses came with food choices daily. Yes, this is what I want—very clear messages. If I was not sure what I wanted, I sat quietly till something came to me. I realized I don't have to work so hard, just listen closely.

I am reminded of a story I read years ago about a man who was driving down the highway and the thought came to him to pull over. Just after he pulled over an airliner crash landed in the waterway to the side of him. He jumped out of his car and immediately swam to begin rescuing people. When asked how he got there so fast he replied prayer taught him to listen to the small inner voice. Similarly, our Creative Practice can help us to listen.

Resource: Maybe we have all the answers, in art and in life. We only need to listen to the impulses that are for our good.

Day 268
The Most with the Least

My most satisfying expression can come when I don't have much time. I know I have to distill what I want to express to the essence. A 5-line poem can cut to the quick while a full page can meander here and there.

When we have less time and need to get the idea out quickly, we do what says the most with the least. Take stick people. Art makers are often apologetic that it is the best they can do. Personally, I love a good stick person because they say the most with the least. A few swipes and we can see the head is hanging and the mouth is turned down. We can always make our stick people more unique when we add a little weight or give them our own personal flair. Still, we say the most with the least.

Do you ever get a song stuck in your head? Rarely does the whole song repeat over and over, it is one line, often the opening line that stays with me, sometimes relentlessly.

Maybe when we have less time we have less expectations, too. If I only have 5 or 10 minutes, how can I judge myself? In my Expressive Arts groups, something might come up, and we spend more time talking so we have less time to create. I am blown away by the art when this happens. Yes, we may not have the time to get into the amazing "flow" space like when we have more time, but we get to name what is most important in the moment.

If I only had a moment to visit a loved one, I probably wouldn't make small talk, I would go direct to the heart. *I love you. You are so important to me. Thank you.*

Resource: Practice saying the most with the least. Then when you don't have much time, you are proficient at getting your expression across. You can go back and do more another day. Remember, you make the rules.

Day 269

From Nothing to Something

The moments when I don't know what to do, and I show up to do SOMETHING, can still be creative. How can I move from nothing to something and find it satisfying?

Yesterday we looked at how the gift of not having much time gives us the opportunity to say the most with the least. Something similar can happen when nothing is there. I have no ideas, no inspiration, and I show up anyway. Frustration, fogginess, or anger might be present, or there is a letting go into nothing and a sense of peace—any of these can become my muse. My muse can arise as much from what's not there, as from what is there. I begin because I have grown my *show-up muscle* and I do something.

Like I mentioned yesterday, not having expectations can be freeing. I have nothing and am grateful for anything that shows up.

Doing the same thing over and over can be a solution for the nothing. I show up and there is nothing, so I revert to something I have done before. My personal go-to is a blind contour portrait. What is your go-to when you don't know what else to do?

You can also prepare for the days when your creative bank is empty by keeping a file of ideas you can refer to when needed. Sometimes nothing leads us to trying something we have been putting off.

Again, I see the most important ingredient, even more than talent and inspiration, is the *show-up muscle*. We show up, and because we show up, we do something. Something from nothing can hold its own rewards.

Resource: If you show up and there is nothing, relax into nothing and see where it can take you. This could be training for being more improvisational in your life.

Day 270
Let's Bring in Nature

Nature for me is the ultimate equalizer. It can bring my body, mind, and spirit into balance without having to work at it. Even my own backyard can work magic if I allow it. Get me out to the mountains, the ocean, the forest, or under the night sky in the desert and stress falls away and inspiration arrives.

I was talking to a friend last week who is helping to landscape a new healing center for people who are unhoused and need aftercare once released from the hospital. It will offer the much-needed time for healing, nursing, physical therapy, and other needs, ultimately finding them housing when they are ready to leave. My friend had studied how effective nature can be to healing. She was so clear nature needed to be an element in this project, she volunteers her time to make it happen.

I write and remember the year after my parents died my son and I took a vacation to the Sequoias. Being with these giant trees, and the wildlife that lived in the forest—the fox that visited our campsite each night, the deer that wandered through often—was so healing. In just the remembering I feel my body relax.

Maybe nature needs to be essential in our life and in our Creative Practice. Can we lie in the grass, look to the sky, the clouds, or the stars? Pick flowers, make land art (bring natural items together and create an art piece) or take photos to inspire us later? Allow our senses to open.

Knowing the imagination is such a strong tool, could creating art from nature, or looking at art depicting nature be healing, too?

We don't have to take a vacation, though vacations are important. Ten or fifteen minutes with the intention to be with nature can do us a world of good. Breathe it in.

Resource: How can you bring nature into your Creative Practice?

Day 271
Pay It Forward

Once we begin to feel like an artist (musician, dancer, writer, actor, sculptor, painter, photographer, chef...) and reap the rewards of growing this identity, we have an opportunity to pay it forward, to make it possible for others to find their way to creative expression.

Not selling anything, but a free gift of kindness. An offering of help for people to find their way to their own personal expression so they can live a more creative life.

People may see your life changing and this could be enough for them to become curious. Sometimes we see someone suffering and know how a creative path could support them, and sometimes we invite whoever is nearby to join us as we create, and the kindness becomes random.

When people wander into my studio, curious about what we do, I try to bring the curiosity back to them and have a conversation around their own creative expression. Often the answer is something they did long ago but haven't done recently. We imagine a place for it to fit today. Even just to try it out. If possible, I want them to leave with a plan. Even send them off with materials, until they can get to the art store. I don't know if anything comes of it, but I do know I have planted a seed.

Even our internet repair person gets an opportunity to share about their creative life and to be encouraged to get back to art, complete with materials to get started.

I am supportive of having classes where we are compensated for our creative gifts. And I like beginning the conversation as an act of kindness—casual support to get people started.

Resource: How can you support others to grow a creative life? Where can you share your path to inspire others?

Day 272
Creative Practice as Companion

My son left in the early hours of the morning when darkness still lay quiet. Back to San Francisco where he lives and goes to school. I crawled back in bed after waving goodbye, watching the taillights of his car round the corner to head north. This morning I am feeling sad and vulnerable. The missing fills my whole body. Reminding me of the days when divorce felt like it ripped him away weekly as our shared custody sent him from mom to dad too often.

When our divorce first happened, I had not yet found my art or Creative Practice. Those first two years it was just me, wandering through an empty life after he was gone. Throwing myself into work. I jokingly told friends I was going to become a voluntary alcoholic so I could fill these hours of absence, which wasn't really funny after growing up in an alcoholic home.

Once I found my art and my Creative Practice, we became dear friends. I put the grief of weekly loss into my painting, and also to express the freedom I felt having self-care time. My art became my confidant, my sister, my lover, my therapist, my diary, and my lifesaver. My art helped me work through my feelings rather than numbing the feelings, the passion, the living of life. I am never alone when I have my art. It is truly my companion.

How would you describe your relationship with your Creative Practice? Friend, foe, teacher, lover? Are you intimately involved or are you keeping each other at arm's length? What would it take to bring you closer?

Resource: What would be a good descriptor for your relationship with your Creative Practice and your art? Honor your relationship and notice if you would like the relationship to change. What could be different?

Day 273
Creative Practice to Learn Discipline

I have heard many times artists are not particularly disciplined in their lives. We have a reputation of being free-spirited and undependable. Personally, I have been very deadline driven in my life, the closer a deadline came the more effort I put forth. A last-minute sprint to the finish line was often a heroic effort. There was a certain amount of adrenaline my Type A personality loved.

My daily Creative Practice helped set me up for a new way of living and working with projects. Having an idea and chunking away at it 5 minutes a day. It is now a way of life for me.

I was so accustomed to showing up 5 minutes a day for my art, when it was time to write my master's thesis I used the same strategy, a minimum of 5 minutes a day. Using the same approach as with my art, I stayed with the process and didn't worry about the end product. I had a great time. Each day I showed up for 5 minutes and usually worked longer. If I only had 5 minutes, it kept me connected so I would not forget what I was doing.

I have used this same strategy writing this book, for overwhelming tasks like clutter clearing, my taxes, and exercise. And I hope to use it on the monumental task of marketing this book which is so overwhelming, but I imagine I can handle 5 minutes a day. Don't underestimate the power of 5 minutes a day of creativity or anything.

Resource: Whenever you notice overwhelm or procrastination in your life, see if 5 minutes a day toward whatever is overwhelming can help you get started and keep going.

Day 274
Creative Practice as Dream Keeper

Our Creative Practice can be a place to process our dreams, both sleeping and waking. This morning my night dreams were thick and unsettling after waking. Dreams of water pipes breaking in the house and the person I was with did not want to take care of it. Then a $3700 fender bender in my car and my insurance company threatened if I didn't pay it out of pocket my rates would go so high I would not be able to afford insurance. I woke with a knot in my stomach and roaming anxiety in my body. Bringing my dreams to my art helped transform my anxiety into creative energy.

The visual journal Creative Practice I did for more than three years revolved around my daydream of bringing my life partner into my life. I used it to work through unfinished business in past relationships, attend to parts of me I knew I needed to grow stronger if I was going to be successful in a relationship. This practice helped me feel like I was doing something toward my future relationship, not just waiting to find it. I was so actively involved in the process, I wasn't lonely or even longing for relationship because I was in relationship with my visual journals and my Creative Practice. Together my journals and I moved toward finding sustainable love.

Whether it is a night dream that needs to be processed or a daydream you want to come to fruition, our Creative Practice is a natural place to bring our musings and to keep them at the forefront of our minds. If we know we are going to create art about our night dreams, we are more likely to remember them. If we are going to create art about our daydreams, we are more likely to stay with those dreams even when faced with challenges and setbacks.

Resource: Life is constant processing and learning. Let your Creative Practice support you as you learn and grow.

Day 275
Creative Practice as Confidant

A daily Creative Practice can be our confidant. It is the place we bring our feelings, spill them out through the art. Our art can be a witness and an expression of our life. Our art can hold it all so we can stand back, look, or listen with a new eye, a new ear. Our art holds power to help alchemize our life events and the feelings attached to them.

Though this process happens to me almost daily, I recall a time early in my Creative Practice when I had just driven my son to his dad's house for his time there. We had been divorced for three or four years but the changing of the guards was still emotional for me. That evening I did a blind contour portrait painting of my son, adding words to describe the unnatural feeling of being separated from him. I spent a couple days working on it, and when I came out the other side, I felt more trusting of my son's life and process. My art was like a two-day retreat with a dear friend, a confidant who listened with exquisite patience until I could find my way through.

The arts can help us hold the incongruences of life, and the space for more than one truth, the duality that shows up. Finding the expression of the joy and the pain, the anger and the love, the disappointment and the promise.

As we use our art as confidant, we then have evidence of our process we can share with others, which can create more intimacy with them. Art helps us find our authentic response to life.

Resource: Allow your Creative Practice to act as confidant. If you do not feel safe or comfortable expressing details, express the feeling sense of your day. If you need more support, get help through traditional therapy, or try Expressive Arts Therapy, Art Therapy, Dance Therapy or other creative therapies. Find a good fit for YOU.

Day 276

Creative Practice as Journal of Journey

I still have a notebook of poems written when I was in 8th and 9th grade. Sad poems about not fitting in or belonging. I look at those poems and I can remember exactly where I sat while I wrote. I can remember the events that were my muse. My current visual journals tell the stories of my intentions for the year and what is happening in my personal world and the bigger world.

A daily Creative Practice can be a diary, showing us where we have been. We live in a time when it is easy to document our lives. Most of our devices take photos with a date and time attached so we can track our progress on our projects. I try to date all my work. My first year I only dated the first few months and later was disappointed because I couldn't put the work in order. Even better is when I document something about the day, at the minimum, a title, and even more satisfying is writing a brief description of what was happening this day. "The studio officially shut down for COVID after what seemed like performance art."

Dating our work adds a personal journey element so we can look back on the stories of what was happening in our life—small daily happenings and larger global events.

For the arts that are not visual, keeping a daily journal or calendar to track your days can be satisfying. Writing one sentence a day is enough, just to remind you what dance, song, recipe, or other creative endeavor took place each day.

To know my life has been witnessed, even by myself, is satisfying in a way I don't fully understand. Maybe it is human nature. Maybe it is leaving evidence that I exist and am an art maker. Whatever the reason, it works for me. What works for you?

Resource: Remember to date your work or document it in some way that is meaningful to you.

Day 277

Art, Grief, and Resilience

Resilience is our ability to bounce back after stressful situations. We need resilience to handle our day-to-day challenges as well as big life changes, losses, and traumas.

Even before I felt like an artist, I used art to help me bounce back. Mostly angry art that was not pretty but it said what I needed to say. It kept me from turning the anger in on myself.

This is why I reached for art on the anniversary of my mother's death. Her death had been the culmination of a big year—I needed to move my home, my father died, my beloved dog died, and finally my mother died.

When I was deepest in my losses, writing was my savior. I wrote letters each night for the weeks leading up to my mother's death that I shared with close friends so I would not feel so alone.

In retrospect I see the simple act of showing up to create is an act of resilience. When we pick up our instrument and make a sound or mark, dig our shovel into the earth, or sing the song that needs to be sung, we are saying, I am here, I grieve, and I am still here.

Our grief and trauma can even be a gift that gives back to us, as we see, hear, or feel its expression. This tragedy, big or small, happened. I made it through and not only am I here, I am here to express it. I will not carry this alone, my art will carry it with me. My art validates my loss and the process of my bounce back—resilience in action.

Resource: Allow your creative expression to be your companion and helper through tough times. If you are holding back, are you afraid to see it or afraid someone else will see? Create a safe place to let your art help you express, memorialize, and bounce forward into the new life which waits.

⇨*If traumatic memories or sensations arise, be sure to get therapeutic help.*

Day 278
Control and the Creative Process

It can be hard to accept we are not in control of the creative process. We can't make things happen, can't make ideas appear on demand or be creative on command. With a Creative Practice though, we know we will be showing up, so there is the chance of catching the creative impulse when it does come.

What happens if there is no impulse? What if nothing comes? Lael Greenleaf, one of my mentors, uses the example of a beach ball in a pool. The more you reach for it, the further it moves away from you. But if you stay still, and wait, it will eventually come to you. So it can be with creativity. The more desperate we get to find an idea or a solution, the further away it gets or less successful it will be because we are trying to make something happen. When we let go and allow, the answer will come.

We may need to be quiet so we can listen for the impulse. My best ideas can come when I am washing the dishes, brushing my teeth, hiking in nature, or driving on the open road. I have learned once the impulse comes, to take action quickly before I forget.

Sometimes the impulse asks for action that may take some serious muscle or courage. We might need to muscle through our critic who is telling us it is not the way to go, it is too hard, you might fall on your face or make a fool of yourself, or it isn't really what you want to do. We might think we got the wrong answer, we push it away because if this was really the answer it would be easy. Sometimes what is best for us isn't easy.

Resource: If you are not sure what is next, be still so you can listen. Honor what arrives. When you hear the impulse, act as quickly as possible. Or write it down before it gets lost. Take baby steps to move forward or even a big step if you are inspired.

Day 279
No One Will Know

Even after all my years of creating art every day, I find myself negotiating again. The negotiator can be a constant visitor, especially when I am not taking good care of myself and my time.

Tonight my energy is low, I am ready for bed, and I still need to write and paint. I negotiate. *No one will know if I don't show up. After so many years of daily art, I can miss a day here or there. I get to make the rules, right?*

I have talked about this before and I feel it is worth another reminder. If we let ourselves negotiate we could lose—our Creative Practice, going to the gym, meditating, or the class we are taking—whatever it is we've decided matters to us enough to make a commitment. Missing once makes it much easier to miss again, and then again. It can also make it harder to get back into the rhythm. I have heard many stories from creatives who missed a few days and fell out of the habit. Then it was necessary to build their *show-up muscle* all over again.

For me the answer is to notice the negotiation conversation, stop it, and get to my practice. And honestly, I have NEVER been sorry I showed up. I have never wished I hadn't, I am always grateful. So, here I am, writing. Yes, I am still tired. I still want to go to bed. And I still need to paint. One brushstroke of paint. Could I do one stroke of paint? Of course. And I'll probably do more.

If you aren't aware of the negotiator's voice inside you, listen closer so you will be able to stand up to that part of yourself when it arrives. And also beware of external voices from family, friends, and work. *Oh come on, you can miss a day.* Showing up is care for yourself. The negotiator wants us to forget.

Resource: Another reminder, if you negotiate you lose. And you lose time negotiating. Just get to it. You could be done already!

Day 280
Awaiting the Arrival of the Idea

We hope to live the life of the creative. The hard work has been learning to show up. The *show-up muscle* is the deepest necessity. Without showing up, nothing can happen. Getting ourselves there to begin the process of creating and staying put once we arrive. Even if we show up and sit, write one word, play three notes, or dance for 30 seconds, we have done the essential.

Waiting for the arrival of inspiration though can feel even harder on some days. Like being imprisoned in blankness. Glory to the idea of starting where we are at. Taking the blankness and turning it into something just by acknowledging it exists; expressing the I don't know what to do or where I am going. We can express the feeling of frustrations at the blankness or describe and express creative emptiness through metaphors.

Maybe a rushed day becomes a day like a dog chasing its tail. Or the worries that overtake our thinking become a vicious dog, not letting go. Maybe we express the feeling sense of the rushing or the worries and the emptiness becomes something.

It all becomes the arrival. It all becomes a possibility for living the life of the creative, if we can let go of the idea there will be something award-winning or a grand epiphany that makes our expression special.

Let the normal everyday common things become special. Stay out of the results and simply be in the process of expressing whatever is there or not there. Stop worrying and create or express the worry as your creation.

Resource: If you feel blank, check in, is there really nothing there or does what is there feel like it won't be good enough? Allow yourself to express what is there, even the blankness. Allow that every day is not going to be a big-idea day and that is okay.

Day 281

Art as Support Through Tough Times

Just moments ago I found out a dear friend died. Annie always called me "baby" in her Texas way. "I love you, Baby." At eighty years old, her spirit was young and vibrant in her last days. She had made it through months of deep depression and was now happy.

She was back making her sweet art, sparkly bobbles that she would adhere to painted canvas boards. Helpers at her living center were lined up wanting her to make a piece for them. It was good exercise for her arthritic hands to pick up the small pieces and squeeze the glue from the bottle. Though her process seemed random, on days we would visit I would assist her with tweezers picking up sparkly beads as Annie directed me where to place them. She would point saying, "No, Baby, that doesn't go there, it goes here." Again I hear her voice clear and loving in my head.

In my grief my immediate impulse is to turn to my art. I want to find a blind contour portrait I did of Annie a year or so ago—complete with a pink pussy hat, modeled after a photo she had sent me. I want to look through my photos of her showing her art at my studio. And do my own art in response to her sudden death.

The first thing I do is come to my writing. What can be more comforting for me than to write about Annie and share her with the world. She was an example of finding art in her seventies, and creating until the end. It is NEVER too late to begin!

My writing comforts me. Not only does it hold her story, but also holds my story in real time. My art helps me slow down and feel my grief. This entry is for you, Annie. Wherever you are now. I hope you know how much I love you.

Resource: Turn to your art when life happens. Let it hold you and comfort you. May it help you express what needs to be expressed so you can feel supported and keep going.

Day 282
My Art Is a Patient Lover

"My art waits for me, all day, like a patient lover. Ready to receive me when I arrive. Usually late at night we sit together in a lover's embrace." —Tish McAllise Sjoberg

I found this quote today in an old diary I kept of my daily art experience. Happily, it still holds true. Often, I live my day for my art time, it dangles in front of me like a carrot, knowing when work is done, we will spend time together. This is when I can let go of everything and be with myself. It is anti-work. I do not have to do anything right, make any major decisions, I simply show up and follow the impulses.

My art is also a great listener. It is where I review my day, work out any unfinished business through expressing, or let go of what does not need immediate attention.

If my art feels like work, or is not pleasurable, I know I need to make a change so it will feel good again. Just like in my human relationships sometimes we need to adjust. We need a heart-to-heart or something to spice up our relationship.

I am grateful for so many lovers, so many Creative Practice projects, through these years. Each project teaches me a new way to love. When we reach day 365 and have to part, it is with joy and a heavy heart. On occasion, we can't live without each other, so I sign up for another 365 days with maybe a little different focus or practicing a different style. Allowing the relationship with my art to change and evolve with me as an artist.

Resource: Are you committed to your relationship with your Creative Practice? If you are in love with your art, let the world know. If you need to deepen your relationship, figure out how before you break up.

Day 283
Okay, There Have Been Breakups

Most of my daily art relationships have been successful. A few have ended in breakups before they reached the finish line, usually early in the process. None were knock down drag out, vicious, or hateful breakups. They were early in my daily artist life when I didn't know myself as well as I do now. The times I gave up completely were because it was too much work or too stressful and I didn't identify this early enough to create changes, but I could see it all clearly after I had some distance.

With experience I have learned to listen along the way, notice things early and to make adjustments. I put less pressure on myself and problem solve the challenges.

Some breakups were forever, some were rekindled and went the distance when I tried it again with adjustments. My Manikin Project was one. When I began the first time, I was taking a photo a day of my beloved art Manikin doing something in the world and then posted the photo on social media. What I didn't realize until after I gave up and years later when I wanted to try again, was the need to post every day took it over the edge and made it un-fun, stressful, and too much pressure. The second try when I only had to take the photo went the distance. I did post the photos on occasion, when I felt up to it. This simple letting go helped me fall in love.

Ultimately my short-term lovers hold a sweet place in my heart. None of them have been given up forever. Maybe someday we will be reunited, or not.

Resource: If you are not in love with your project, what needs to change? Communicate with each other, listen for what is not working and see if you can make changes to find love. If not, allow yourself to try something new.

Day 284

Don't Wait for Inspiration to Visit

For more than half my life I waited for a moment of inspiration to come, and when it arrived, I would start making art, I would become an artist. If the inspiration had come, I would probably not have had the resources or creative confidence to move forward. In fact, I probably had many moments of inspiration I never acted upon, because I wasn't ready, I wasn't showing up yet.

Beginning my daily Creative Practice I made the space, the time, and showed up to do something, to do anything. My creative confidence grew, and eventually the bigger inspirations came and I was there to catch them and create.

Thinking about the 1990 Oscar-nominated movie, *Field of Dreams.* Kevin Costner's character heard a voice say, "If you build it, he will come." It was a crazy idea but the impulse was to mow down his cornfield and build a baseball diamond, complete with bleachers for fans. I won't tell the ending in case you haven't seen it, but there was one guest who was the most important, the real reason for the field.

We begin our Creative Practice, make a place in our life for the visitors who will come, and because the table is set and ready, when the special guest arrives—the inspiration we have awaited—we will be ready to welcome them.

We don't create the space, sit, and wait. We create the space and fill it with our presence and our expression. We grow our *show-up muscle* and our confidence so we are ready for the arrival.

Resource: If you are still sitting on the fence, waiting for the inspiration to arrive so you can get started making art, turn this around and get started so you will be strong and ready when the inspiration does arrive. It takes energy to answer the creative call, if you prepare, you will be ready.

Day 285
Is It Sabotage?

Do you make plans to show up and then sabotage your plan by saying *yes* to something else? When the other *yes* gets in the way of doing what we really want to do, we have a challenge. A *yes* to one thing becomes a *no* to another. When the *no* to our creative time is continual this could be sabotage.

Granted, important things come into our life that we must say yes to. When something important comes, how do we make this decision consciously? My son needs help on his homework, so I will not take time to do my art. Name it.

Then ask, is this true? Could you say "yes, and..." Yes, I will help you with your homework and, I need to play music, I will get you started and then play for you as you work. Or, I will help you for 30 minutes and then I will get to my art. If you need more, I will help you in the morning.

As I am writing this entry, I am in the end phase of this book. I have a deadline and I am aware I must say *"no"* to anything that will take time away from my book.

Having a project that allows you to take just 5 or 10 minutes on the days when you have to work late or be there for someone else is helpful. When we notice we are doing this too often, it might be time to reevaluate life and commitments. Or is there something about our art we are avoiding?

Why is our creative time, our chance to fill our own cup, often cut out of our life first? What if your Creative Practice becomes the essential activity that needs to be worked around?

Resource: Look for sabotage moments. Are you avoiding something? Is your critic trying to keep you from your art? If you choose something else over your creative time, make it a conscious choice to not do your art. Even better, learn to put your art first.

Day 286

Another Reminder to Celebrate

How long has it been since you celebrated? I am noticing my level of celebration is low and wondered if yours is. When I first started my Creative Practice, I was so grateful I remembered to show up my celebration looked more like relief. Then I graduated to a little dance with a few words like, "I did it, I did it. I really, really, did it."

Yet with time I forget, it becomes routine. Sure, I have the good feelings of showing up, but celebrating takes it a step further and consciously honors my effort.

As I think about this, I feel a bit sad. I don't ever want my Creative Practice to feel routine. I want to always feel grateful for not only showing up but also for the mark I make, the small contribution to my creative life. Celebrating is a form of gratitude.

On my best days I would give gratitude before I begin, for having a life that allows me to have a Creative Practice, and take a moment for celebration when I finish. I want to continually remember so I never take this path for granted. My art has helped me live what I would call a quietly extraordinary life. When I die, there will be plenty of evidence I was a creative, an art maker, an expressive human.

Resource: How can you honor your life that allows creative time and how can you celebrate what you do with your creative time? Even a small contribution is worth a little celebration.

Day 287
A Spark of Creative Fire

We had a house concert at the studio tonight. It was a convergence of many things. Importantly, it was our first concert since the pandemic shutdown. The packed studio felt alive and even normal.

Next, Marc Delgado, our singer, songwriter, and musician for the evening told the story of when we first met. I saw him on the street walking his dog. I stopped my car and yelled, "Hey, you play music don't you?" and asked him if he would come play at our Artists of North Park Show opening that week, featuring artists from our neighborhood. I didn't know it kickstarted a new level in his music career. We never know when we influence someone.

I left the concert feeling inspired in a way I hadn't in the last two and a half COVID years. I am not a musician or singer, but the evening sparked a fire that showed up in my painting and now my writing.

I am thinking of *The Artist's Way,* author Julia Cameron's suggestion to have artist dates. Getting into the play zone. Feeling the vibe of other artists invites us to be creative, too. Earlier today a friend read a story out loud for the first time. It was a heart wrenching and beautiful account of an experience when they were in prison. Again, my heart doors flew open and I too want to write.

Creativity can be like wildfire. We catch the inspiration and it spreads into other areas of our life. When we have a regular Creative Practice, when we show up regularly, we can take the inspiration and run—with little effort. We are prepared and ready.

Resource: Allow yourself experiences that nourish and inspire you, even make you hungry for more. This may mean getting out more, trying new things, and being ready to respond through your own expression when you return.

Day 288

Trapped by Unfinished Projects

As creatives we may have so many ideas and desires, we do a little of this and a little of that and never finish anything. We may bounce from one project to another, sometimes we eventually finish yet more often we may abandon things completely—yet we continue to hold ourselves responsible for not finishing.

When I first opened my studio, I received donations from friends to help me get on my feet. Everything from chairs and tables to financial donations. It was so heartwarming to know I was being supported by my community. I wanted to create a meaningful thank you—a beautiful picture book showing them how their donation had helped. Well, I made this project complicated and it never got done. Though I would tap into it over and over, I never finished. Yet I have never stopped holding myself responsible for not finishing. This was over eleven years ago. Do you have unfinished projects that are still alive in the back of your mind?

We may not finish because we get overwhelmed, stuck, bored, or don't feel competent. Our critic might tell us it isn't good enough, and we don't want to fail. Can we learn to push through, risk doing something poorly? It has been shown the most successful environments for innovation allow people to make mistakes and fail, which means they are trying new things.

Maybe instead of criticizing ourselves for not finishing, we celebrate we tried something and have compassion for this part of us who had an idea but couldn't make it happen. Maybe in forgiving ourselves we will unlock more creativity?

Resource: Do you have unfinished projects that weigh heavy on you? Messages you can't start something new without finishing the old? Can we all just let them go, let ourselves off the hook, maybe say a short eulogy before we send them on their way?

Day 289
Take Responsibility

I am a fairly positive person and I also have a well-developed "woe is me" side. Because my brain works different from the standard brain that school was developed for, I spent many years telling the story that life was harder for me. I tried, I worked hard, but I could not excel. I even imagined the words on my gravestone would be "She Tried."

What I was doing was blaming my life, my brain, and the system for my inability to succeed. To some extent all this was true. When I was young, I did not know this was going on so I believed I was not smart. But then there was the point where I did know different. I learned I had Attention Deficit and learning disabilities. The psychologist who tested me said I had learned to adapt well, come up with many strategies on my own to get along in the world. For example, if I don't write things down, I will forget. So from there, I could choose to write it down, put it on my to-do list or I could choose not to and forget, then later kick myself.

This is ongoing. It isn't a one-time fix. I constantly have to remember to take responsibility.

When it comes to my art, I cannot make excuses for myself. I must take responsibility. Currently I am unhappy because I am not allowing myself enough time to do art—when I go to this "woe is me" place, it does nothing to build me up or to create change. When I take responsibility, I start thinking of what I can change and carve out more time. I commit to setting an alarm on my phone to remind me it is time to do my art and I feel better already!

Resource: Notice when you are making excuses. How can you turn this around to take responsibility? For example, shifting slightly from, I don't have enough time, to How can I make enough time?

Scribbling could be the native art form
of the entire human race.
As children it is
our first visual language.
Scribble with a pen, with music,
with dance, with writing,
with improv, with recipes,
in other words, don't think!

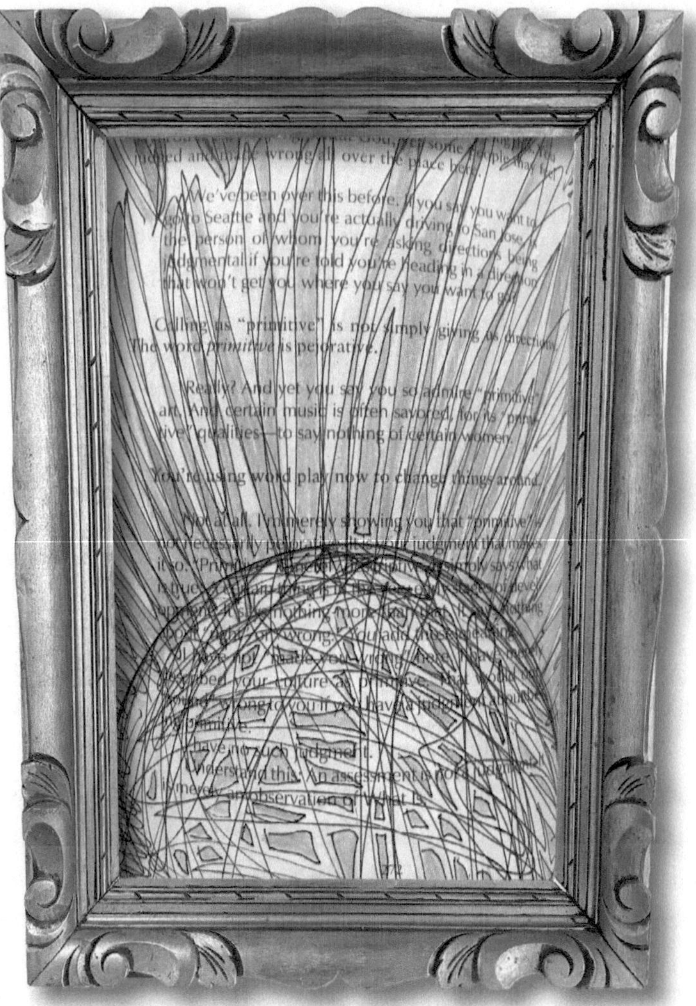

365 Days of Scribbling with the Scribble Kit

After a year of Scribble Art I created a Scribble Kit that helped make scribbling easy, fun, and aesthetically pleasing. (What could be easier than scribbling?) My scribble book and scribble kit were born from the idea that everyone can make art, we don't need to have any experience or talent. This year was an altered book where I read a page in the book then scribbled on it, and added colored pencils. The entire year fit into one book!

Day 290

Don't Like it? You're Not Finished

If you don't like your art, don't throw it away or abandon it, do something different. When you don't like it, you have nothing to lose and it can become an opportunity to try something new or do something that scares you. Even disassemble and reassemble it in a new way. If you don't like something it can feel less precious so you can think further outside the box. At my studio we have examples of how to repurpose art and give it a different life. A painting becomes a book, a weaving, or even gift wrap.

Often we don't like what we are working on because we are unsure what to do next. It is easier to say, "I hate it" than it is to stay with the discomfort of not knowing the next step. Or we don't like our work because we compared it to someone else and feel lesser than. Learn to stay with the uncomfortable feelings rather than avoid them, don't act on the impulse to throw it away or quit.

As creators it can be common to not like what has been done, take a break and come back a day or week later and have a whole different view of it. Sometimes we need space from the creating to appreciate more fully what we have done, get an idea for the next step, or see what is working and build from there. One small change and it could all look or sound different.

This idea goes for life, too. If you don't like your life, don't quit, throw it away, or settle. Do something different. Do what scares you, disassemble and reassemble it in a new way. Or look for what is working and build on it. Maybe just one small thing needs to change and it will all look different. Even a new attitude can change everything.

Resource: Stay with the discomfort of not liking your creative expression and try on the idea you are not finished. Take a break if you need to and come back with curiosity that keeps you going.

Day 291
Direction Versus Destination

When we head in the direction of our hopes and dreams, we can enjoy the journey. We might wander here or there, take unplanned trips, rest awhile, have a change of plans, but we are still moving forward in the direction of our hopes and dreams. We follow what feels good, feels pleasurable.

Conversely, if we get wrapped up in the destination, we go, go, go taking step after step toward our destination, not really taking the time to check in and see if we are enjoying ourselves, and when we arrive we may realize we don't like where we ended up. This can happen with college. We declare a major, work hard, take the classes, graduate, and realize we don't like the work. We might also realize we picked our major to please someone else, not ourselves.

When I struggle the most with my creative process is when I am trying to force an outcome. Afraid of failure I lock down harder and enjoy myself less.

Maybe it is the difference between *making something happen* and *allowing something to happen* with gentle progress. Following what brings pleasure, what is enjoyable, until we arrive somewhere. Maybe we arrive someplace we didn't know existed.

I could not have predicted I would someday be sitting writing this book, having done daily art for twenty years, and entertaining a weaving project for next year. I knew nothing about weaving until a month ago! Thank you to Lael Greenleaf who first taught me about *direction rather than destination.* I promise to wander in the direction of living an artful life, until death when I part.

Resource: Try it on. Feel the difference between having a destination in mind, and powering through; versus having an idea, heading in the direction, and following what feels good.

Day 292
The Heart of Creating

There is the craft of making art, and there is the heart of creating. In the art world, both are important.

The craft is the doing, the lines that are drawn, the notes played, the way our body moves to the music. We keep showing up and practicing our craft and we become better at it. Something changes. Maybe we try different pens on paper, we memorize a song, or our legs get stronger as we dance. We show up regularly and our *show-up muscle* gets strong, too. We allow ourselves to relax as we create, or get excited, or zone out. We are creators.

And then there is the heart of creating. The arts become our love language, our gift to the world. Yes, we draw the line and we also live that line we draw. We don't just play the music, we become the music, as we dance, we are the dance. When the heart arrives in our expression we don't only show up, we are exquisitely present, our senses are open and experiencing the world and our process. We express our longings and our emotions. We may stay longer when we are in this heart zone, lingering, not in a hurry. Yet when we only have 5 minutes, we can create from this heart place, too.

The gift is when we can have both at the same time. We work our craft as we open our heart to be vulnerable and connected. I notice a difference when I paint the portrait of someone I want to know better, I am connected from the start. Versus when I paint a generic portrait. The generic begins as eyes, nose, and mouth, crafting shadows and light source. Then I realize the face is expressing an aspect of myself, and I cross a bridge from craft to heart.

Resource: Notice where you are in your creative process. Is it more about craft or heart? Can you explore the side that is less familiar to you? Can you find your connecting bridge?

Day 293
Repetition Works

Doing the same thing over and over can be comforting. Not having to think, just being able to draw a flower over and over and over. Or maybe it is a repetition of a movement or playing the same notes over and over. The repetition can become a meditation, a place to get lost, found, or to call us back to ourselves.

Think of the mother beat in drumming. The mother beat is the strong beat that holds the drummers together. The rhythm can change, solos come and go, but this base beat remains the same. It repeats over and over, and holds everything together.

This can happen in any style of expression. Our work is held together by a theme that follows through. Whether that theme is image, shape, word, color palette, scale, or key, we create a style for ourselves through repetition.

When I was young, I drew a horse and I got so much attention for drawing the horse, I drew it over and over. The response got me going but ultimately it was my love of horses at the center. Eventually I outgrew the horse and transitioned onto something else. Today I do blind contour portraits over and over.

Don't be afraid of repetition. Don't worry someone might judge you or critique you for doing the same thing over and over. Allow yourself to fall into the comfort of the over and over repetition. Like right now, I fall into the mesmerizing place of the word *over* and repeat it, *over and over* as I write, with no worries. Sometimes the over and over is the starting place, the launching ground for something new that will be coming. Until it comes, we can repeat what works, over and over.

Resource: If it feels good, do it over and over as many times as it continues to feel good, until a new impulse comes. Own what you love to do and allow yourself the gift of repetition.

Day 294

Are You Afraid of Your Creativity?

When I found my way to painting in my second year of daily art, I was on fire—feeling a surge of passion about finding my way into painting that was not stressful, so I could show up.

There is nothing quite like being in the flow with my creativity, when time falls away, and it is just me and my art. My planned art weekend retreats can be like this when I wander from one creative project to another. It can also happen when I think I only have 5 minutes in me and I realize an hour has passed.

And yet, sometimes the intensity of emotion can be hard when we are creating. The sense of freedom of expression can feel great and also overwhelm us. Keeping the channel open can be scary. Because sometimes when the channel is open, we have feelings we may be trying to keep pushed down. Or maybe we get in touch with how powerful we are when we are creating.

This reminds me of my experience in church. I was raised in a fairly liberal spiritual setting and going to church was often an emotional experience for me. I would feel a deep sense of connection well up inside me. But then I wouldn't go again for a year. Over and over, this happened. I realize now, my channel was open, and this scared me. The same could be true for a creative path.

With a Creative Practice we do not have to figure it out. Instead, we keep showing up regularly so things will be revealed. If the showing up causes stress, we express the stress through our art and grow our capacity to hold the discomfort. Maybe the reasons appear, or maybe it won't matter anymore.

Resource: Could you be afraid of your creative power? It could show up as a love-hate relationship with your Creative Practice. Stay with it and see what is revealed, rather than stopping until you figure out what is going on.

Day 295
Art as Storyteller

"Telling our stories is a way to share whatever meaning and joy we have found along the way, the depth of our love for others and for life itself. It is a way of saying not only that we the storyteller matter, but even more so the beloved listener. To share our story with someone is to say you matter to me."
—Steve Leder, *For You When I Am Gone*

The arts are vehicles for us to tell our stories. Whether literally or metaphorically, each time we show up we are revealing something about ourselves. We invite the viewer to witness what is important to us. Through the expression of our own story we find connection through shared experiences.

Years ago, I attended the Collection de l'Art Brut, an art museum in the city of Lausanne in Switzerland that exhibits art created in psychiatric hospitals, by people with mental illnesses, neurological differences, and people who are marginalized. Friends told me to allow a couple hours, but it took me much longer, the staff needed to usher me out so they could lock up for the night. What was it about this exhibition that kept me there, wanting to look at every single piece? It was the stories written about each artist. The museum created windows into each artist's life and through this window our hearts connected.

When I opened my own studio/gallery I was adamant about including story with the art. Let the artist speak to the viewer. Story can bridge the gap between artist and audience and invites us to share the human experience. Let's tell our stories, however they get out into the world and to whom. Even if it is just to one person.

Resource: Do you see the value in your life story? What wants to be told through your Creative Practice?

Day 296
Creative Atrophy

My brother and I live four thousand miles from each other and try to talk on the phone once a week while we walk.

Yesterday we were joking about how long it takes to get in physical shape, the mental commitment, the physical work, and the effort to finally get feeling good, but how little time it takes to get out of shape. Just a few weeks away and our bodies begin to atrophy. Returning can feel like starting all over and take a huge effort.

This can be true for our creative endeavors, too. It takes time to build our *show-up muscle*, to feel comfortable with the materials and find our footing. If we stop, it can be an even bigger commitment to get going again because our art muscle may atrophy, we may have to rebuild again.

This is why a daily practice works so well for me and maybe for you, too. I don't have to worry about one missed day turning into two then five, then weeks, months, or even years. Every day helps me show up, every day. I am astonished at how hard it can be to reengage regularly after stopping something. I would rather deal with the pain of not wanting to show up and showing up anyway, than atrophy and have to start all over.

Resource: Remind yourself when you don't want to show up: it may feel hard, but it will be even harder to show up after missing. What small thing can you do when you don't want to be there, to keep your *show-up muscle* strong?

Day 297
Shake It Up

Doing the same thing every day in a Creative Practice can breed familiarity and boredom. Today I challenge you to do something different. Not just a little different but change it up big. It doesn't need to be forever, just for today, or a week.

Recently I changed things up in my painting. It was a sort of self-dare. I began painting designs in my backgrounds before I drew my blind contour portrait on top. Being honest I don't like it. Or, being more specific, I am struggling. It is pushing me to do something different and I know it could lead to something good, but right now it is hard.

When my discomfort is big, I know I walk a dangerous line. If it is too uncomfortable, I may stop showing up. Yet my *show-up muscle* is strong, and I know I can go back to "normal" any time. So, I continue knowing I am not on a timeline to figure it out.

This is different than the first year of my Creative Practice when I wanted to paint but it was too stressful, so I changed to oil pastels. My *show-up muscle* was not strong, in fact, I had only been working it out for a few weeks, so it barely existed. I had to shift to something more comfortable so I would keep going. Now though, I can push myself to do the difficult because my *show-up muscle* is strong.

At some point I might call off this dare and go back to what feels more easily authentic. I will know I tried something new, and if I am bored, I can shake things up again.

Are you game to shake it up? To do something bold and different today? Maybe copy a style of someone you admire or put your work in a metaphoric creative blender and see what happens. Be bold, you can always go back to easy.

Resource: Keep it fresh. Every once in a while, throw yourself a curve ball so you will keep growing as a creative.

Day 298
Limping Toward the Finish Line

I have done many years of daily art practices. It is hard for me to believe I first started almost twenty years ago. Each year had its own joys and sorrows, pains and pleasures, learning and ego, trust and distrust.

My current project of writing this book is the most difficult. I am primarily a visual person. I love to write, but it does not come easy to me. The first draft, the download, can often flow easily as I show up and see what is there. The process of shaping and creating something substantial from my musings is much harder. I am an idea person, the ideas come easy—turning the ideas into something—this is harder. I have found it true in this project and also in life. So, there have been many days along this journey where I have wanted to quit, to say it is not working. I am getting nowhere. Let's move on to something else.

There is also a wise voice who responds, "It doesn't matter how long it takes, you want this, you can do it." And so, I continue.

Know if you are having challenges, I understand, I too have challenges. And, because you are holding this book in your hands right now, it means I made it across the finish line. Maybe not in a year, but through consistent moments of showing up over one year, three years, ten years. I didn't give up. Every time I show up, I get closer to the finish line. I say to you, from my not-yet-finished, questioning and self-doubting self, "Keep going!"

Resource: For the days when things aren't looking good in your life or with your project, how can you keep going? What kind of plan can you create? Call a friend? Do some anger work? Make art about how hard it is?

Day 299
What Does It Mean to Be Unfocused?

People tell me they can't make art because they are feeling unfocused. I have felt it. It doesn't keep me from my practice though because my *show-up muscle* is too strong to let me skip. I am proof we can make art when unfocused and have learned it can be a great time to make art, if I let go of needing it to look a certain way.

When I feel unfocused there is a softness to my life, I am not driven or directed, my energy is dimmed. Unfocused, low energy days can be good for wandering toward what I really want to do. Like right now. I have been feeling under the weather for a few days. I napped and tried to read a book but couldn't. I wasn't really thinking I could write but here I am, typing out a few lines.

The challenge comes when I feel the need to do something productive when I am in this place. It is not the time for me to start a big project or do my taxes. It is not even a good time for me to edit or come up with something new. What works for me is popping into something that has already been started or doing things that are repetitive and don't require thinking, like gluing pages together in my visual journal. And as always, starting where I am.

Maybe unfocused days are days to receive. To allow ourselves to be immersed in music, wander, and make art in a slow, quiet way. Being with our body rather than our brain. Noticing our senses. Expressing feelings.

Unfocused days offer me a chance to look at my art with soft wandering eyes. If I do not criticize this state of being unfocused, I can celebrate its grace of blurring out details and slowing down. I can hurry and be productive another day.

Resource: Don't let the unfocused or off days be a reason to not show up. Bring your curiosity and find how this time could offer you a different way to be with your creativity and your life.

300 days of showing up!
300 days of growing
your show-up muscle.
300 days of growing a body of work.
300 days of showing up for yourself.
Celebrate!

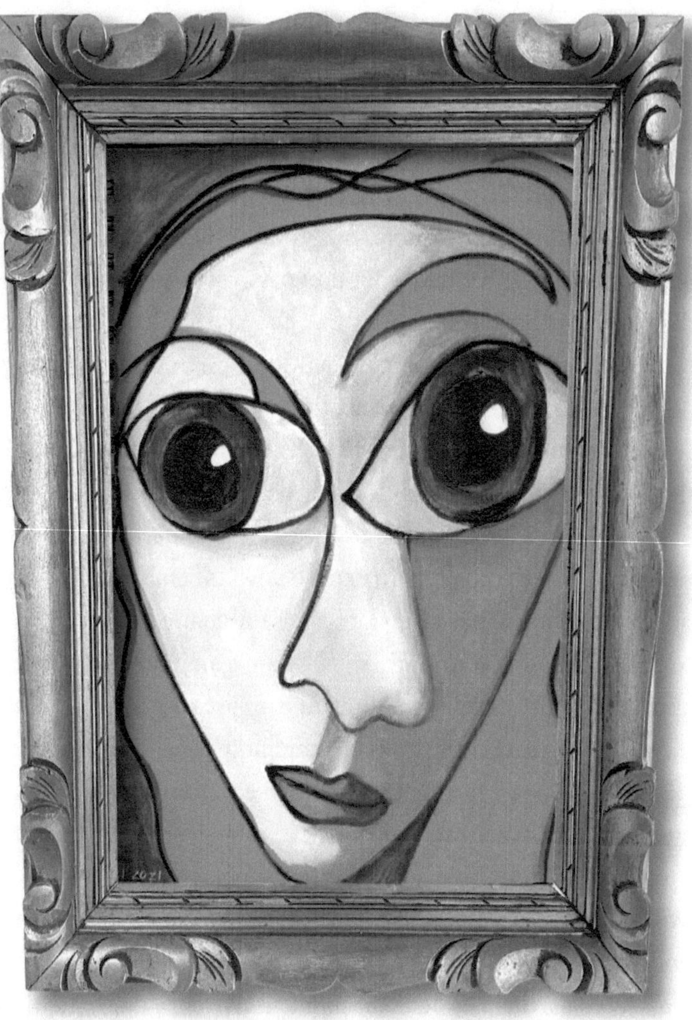

365 Days of Blind Contour Portraits

After years of not painting regularly except at my paint classes, for special projects, or in my collage journals, I needed to find a way to bring my love of blind contour paintings back into my life more fully. I had tapered off when I downsized into a 300-square-foot home. I relinquished my large format to go smaller if it got me back to painting regularly. It worked so well I did not want to stop at the end of year one and continued.

Day 300

Use Art to Grow Through Trauma

We have looked at how our art wounds can shut down our creative process. We receive a message, direct or indirect, that our expression is not acceptable, not good enough, or not appreciated. In response we may shut down and stop expressing so we don't get hurt, made fun of, or lose the love of someone important. Honoring those moments and rewriting our story through our Creative Practice can be healing.

Other life wounds and traumas can have their effects, too. We may have experiences that tell our body it is not okay to relax, play, and express. We must stay vigilant and alert. We must not put ourselves in a position to expose any vulnerability. These are not usually conscious decisions, but automatic body responses to a lack of safety. Our body says, "I am going to keep you safe, and to do this, certain feelings and expressions need to shut down. If we relax for a moment, something bad could happen."

Our Creative Practice can help us heal from our traumas and stresses. First, when we are feeling activated, anxious, scared, or upset, we can turn to our art to calm us, to help us regulate our body. We bring our attention gently and slowly to our art-making, and notice what we hear, see, and create. The arts are our doorway into our senses that help us be in the moment. We slow our fight, flight, freeze, or collapse and slowly return to feeling safer in our body.

Second, when we do feel safe, the arts can help us express and tell our truth. Our Creative Practice can be the place where we tell our story in a creative way, make sense of our life, and even rewrite our story by creating a new outcome through our imagination. Allow your Creative Practice to support you to grow forward.

Resource: Use your Creative Practice to calm and safely express.

⇨*If traumatic memories or sensations arise, be sure to get therapeutic help.*

Day 301
Will I Hurt Someone with My Art?

In storytelling, whether it be verbal or visual language, there can be a concern, if I tell the story it could hurt someone, or they will get upset. Or we will reveal something personally embarrassing or something we feel shame about. The worry there may be a negative reaction can keep us from beginning or finishing a project.

Express the story that needs to be told. Don't worry about protecting anyone, or yourself, tell the story you need to tell, for you.

After you create, the art and your heart will tell you if it wants to be more. If it wants to be published, read or sang out loud, or viewed by others, then you can decide if you want to change it to protect the guilty or innocent. Change names, likeness, turn it into fiction, or find alternatives without losing the power of the story. If your concern is safety in your immediate surroundings, you could write the story and paint over it or rip it up and reconstruct it into visual art. Or, you could write a "once upon a time story" where the characters may be animals or archetypal figures like kings and queens.

When we get the impulse to work with a part of our life, I think it is important to follow the thread. There can be healing in getting the stories out. Worrying what others will think is a roadblock to expression.

When we tell vulnerable stories it is important to take extra care of ourselves as we go through the expression process. Take your time and get support.

Resource: Sometimes the stories that are scariest to tell are the ones we need to express the most. Get support, tell the story YOU need first, then see what the next step will be. No need to worry ahead of time.

Day 302

Protecting the Dead (and the Living)

In my writing support groups, people have shared their worry about how deceased family members, lovers, or friends would feel about them telling a story about their life. I don't know if we can hurt the dead. I have a sense they would be happy when we tell our truth and release them from holding us back in our life. They would want us to experience healing.

Often in abusive relationships there is a spoken or unspoken agreement—do not tell. Even in families where there is not abuse but there is mental illness, unwanted pregnancy, addiction, disabilities, or any topic that may hold shame, there can be a family allegiance to not let the outside world know.

As we age and process our life, we may need to express the stories that were once taboo or secret. The telling of the story through creative expression can take our healing to a new level. When we share the story through the arts, we can find important metaphors, surprises, and new endings because we are now in charge. If we tell our story from the third person, become the narrator, or see it through another character's point of view, we can have more distance, feel safer telling, and see it in a new light.

Express the stories for yourself first. Share them in trusted and confidential relationships with a therapist or friends. If you decide to take it to a bigger audience you can then look at how to do that and protect yourself or others if needed. Maybe it becomes fiction or fairytale. It is important when working with vulnerable events in your life to be well supported and take care of yourself.

Resource: What have you been reluctant to express? Are you protecting someone at the expense of your own well-being? Get support and remember to breathe, drink water, and go slow to help stay regulated and balanced. Your story is important.

Day 303
Life as Art—Seeing the Story

Our life can be filled with amazing inspiration if we can stand back and see it as story. Country singer Trevor McSpadden played a house concert at our studio years ago. In this intimate setting he told stories and shared about his life as a songwriter, husband, and stay-at-home dad. One was about a road trip back from Texas to visit family, and the kids needed to get out of the car and move. At a rest stop with a playground he overheard his wife say to their young one on the slide, "Hold my hand, if we're gonna fall, let's fall together." The rest of the road trip Trevor turned those words into a heartfelt song, "Let's Fall Together." A moment of life on a long and boring drive became inspiration.

A client was dreading a trip home to see their dysfunctional family. Filled with anxiety, they created a plan to look at their family through the eyes of a writer. They brought a notebook to jot down moments of the dysfunction and in the evenings would turn them into third-person stories. They became an observer of the craziness and crafted it all into hilarious and heartwarming stories.

Dance and music are powerful storytellers—we can embody and express story in ways that transcend everyday language. Recently a client told the story of a challenge through drumming and dancing. Their body felt victorious in this wordless expression.

Through our expression, we can see our life from a different vantage point. We become witness to the hero's journey we have walked, and rewrite the ending from this new perspective. Our stories can beg to be witnessed by another, see the light of day, and sometimes it is only for us.

Resource: If you think you have nothing to say, look at your life or your day as a story. Follow it, express it, change it, or release it through your Creative Practice.

Day 304

Life as Art—Seeing the Beauty

We can easily get caught in a life of dullness, routine, and hard work. When we look at our life through the eyes of our artist, our zombie-like world is awakened and a whole different world unfolds as we travel through our day. Our senses are open, and another grey day becomes an entire palette of subtle colors that make many greys. We might notice the melodic sound of traffic trapped by the fog or a subtle wetness on our face as the clouds hover low. The bright orange flower we have passed each day becomes a doorway to wonder. The banter we overhear on the bus becomes dialogue for our story or poetic inspiration; the sounds of feet on stairs become a steady drumbeat; our unassuming dinner becomes a living sculpture to create on our plate. Through our artist eyes the mundane can become special.

Then there is the beauty art can bring to the worst of the world. Thinking about Billie Holiday singing "Strange Fruit." Life does not get darker than the lynching and murder of innocent humans who are black. Holiday sings the poetry of songwriter Abel Meeropol aka Lewis Allan and brings this dark history into haunting beauty. Through her voice we become witnesses to this ugly truth in a way we may not have been able to before.

When we have permission to express the darkness of our life, the unfairness, the depression, the grief, and the mundane, we can stand back to see what we have created. Beauty can arrive because it came from us, it becomes something other than the moment it expresses. Our expression is a release, we become a witness to a life moment transformed into a gift.

Resource: View your life through the eyes of an artist. Invite beauty to touch your heart and wake your spirit. How can your Creative Practice be an alchemist into an aesthetic life?

Day 305
Life as Art—Seeing the Humor

When we look through the lens of art at our life we can find beauty, depth, wisdom, and even humor. Recently at our Writers' Open Mic a studio regular read their story of mental health challenges through the lens of finding the funny moments. The audience not only laughed but also received a unique and intimate look into the writer's world and the bigger world of depression and mental health.

Comedy and humor are often at the forefront of presenting difficult information in a way that is easier to digest. Looking at life through laughter can be less of a threat, we can see a new point of view while laughing, and the information can become a pathway to compassion.

Laughing at ourselves, in a loving way, can be cathartic. Finding humor in our own drama can be healing. Finding the humor in the bigger world of social issues can open people's minds to another way of being.

We can write our story through the third person and see all our quirks that may be funny when we are not taking them so seriously. We get to experience our life from the outside. I have a collection of writing where I view myself from the outside and poke loving fun at my everyday neurotic behaviors. The moments are not always funny in the moment but when I look at them from the outside, they can become funny and I can even see some new ideas for dealing with those difficult moments.

A small warning here, be careful not to cross the line into sarcasm. Sarcasm can be cutting and cruel. We do not want to hurt ourselves, but to love ourselves with a smile.

Resource: Look at your life as art and see the humor in your stories, humor with love can be a great healer and a fun ride as well.

Day 306

Life as Art—Bigger Than Life

When we exaggerate the elements of our story and make the characters bigger than life or see the players as superheroes and monsters, we can feel empowered and rewrite our story. Exaggerating our story becomes a creative expression, we can get a kick out of what may be exasperating. We find images that speak to us, metaphors to guide us, offering relief through the expression.

Bigger than life can be metaphorical—our mean boss becomes a monster who eats employees for snacks, or maybe we are human size, and our boss becomes a cockroach who we can crush. Or, bigger than life can be literal—we create a portrait of our boss six feet tall, or turn a simple sentence that was uttered into an entire monologue.

A change in dimension can be satisfying, take us into our imagination where anything can happen. We can feel strong and in control, and even get distance to realize it is about them, and then tend to our part we can control. We use the arts to step back and view our life from the outside.

Bigger than life can also bring in helpers so we are not alone. I am thinking back to college, living in a house of seven women. When there was a breakup, our favorite breakup songs would begin playing, and we would all start singing them dramatically, at our loudest volume. The person in pain, and all of us, would laugh until we cried.

A while back a friend was going through a challenging time and we threw a comfort party. We each brought a comforter and our favorite comfort food, so we could wallow together. Life is easier when shared, and as entertaining as theater.

Resource: Art is a constant companion in championing our life. Let it help you get a new perspective.

Day 307
The Starving and Suffering Artist

All my life I have heard the idea of the starving artist. Then we have icons like Vincent van Gogh struggling from mental illness and cutting off his ear, Amedeo Modigliani who died of alcohol and disease. Street artists who need to steal their paint because it is so expensive, and prison artists who make art with whatever is at hand like coffee or tea. Must artists suffer?

I have heard many stories from people whose parents would not let them major in what made them happy in college like art, music, dance, theater, or creative writing because they feared their child wouldn't be able to earn a living. My undergraduate degree was in graphic design because it was the one art profession that promised a possible income. Little did I know I would end up starving for self-expression.

Even in my Expressive Arts Therapy Masters training a teacher stated if you want to make money you have not chosen the right field. Being a single mom at the time, there was no other choice but to earn a living where I could support us. Why do we doubt the ability to thrive and be creatives?

So are we suffering and starving? Maybe we are drawn to the arts to reduce our suffering and maybe the arts feed our soul's hunger. I say hallelujah to you the art makers of the world. For the strength it takes to carve out time for self-expression. Celebrate you, the artist who continues to show up to hone your craft, feed your spirit, and *reduce your own suffering and maybe that of the world.* And may we imagine a time where we value and compensate artists for keeping the world alive and real.

Resource: May your Creative Practice lessen your suffering. May it be a place to express your suffering. May it nourish your life for as long as you shall live.

Day 308

Play Versus Game

When we play a *game,* there is usually a winner and loser. There are often rules and usually a goal to be reached and a score, a tally, or a judgment to see who wins. Someone is better or worse than another. And sometimes there is a tie. We have goals we are trying to attain, usually winning.

We live in a competitive world. We may have played games of win and lose since the beginning of time. The winner may eat the animal for dinner, the loser is eaten. The spirit of competition can motivate us to be better, yet being goal oriented can also be tiresome and get in the way of enjoyment.

In *pure play* there is no winner or loser. Play is goalless and random. There are few rules, maybe around safety, where and how long we will play. The only goal is to be in the moment, be curious, and enjoy. Play is wandering through an activity. Think about kids in the sandbox.

Play can be hard for adults. No rules and infinite choices. We are so used to being told what to do and following the rules, letting go into pure imagination can be unfamiliar.

Creativity craves to wander without rules, to be goalless and curious. Can we write without working toward a product? Can we paint just for the fun of painting? Can we create music to be in the moment of each note? Can we play like children and be messy and imperfect? Can we be moved forward by our love of creating without being competitive or needing to win or be the best? If the world was play based rather than competitive what would be different? Would there be the need for wars, classism, or racism?

Resource: Is play hard for you? Try it for one week in your Creative Practice. Notice if anything is different when in play mode. Is there anything you could carry forward?

Day 309
Inspiration Versus Competition

I had my Saturday phone *walk and talk* with my brother today, and we discussed yesterday's piece on play versus game. It brought us to a musing of inspiration versus competition. Is one better than the other? Do they work in tandem? I have to laugh, just the title "Inspiration Versus Competition" feels competitive!

What is the difference between inspiration and competition? For me inspiration *calls me forward,* it feels like an internal call inviting me to do something. There are times when inspiration is insistent and does not want to be ignored. Yet someone or something can inspire me from the outside, when it matches my inside desire.

Competition *pushes me forward,* says I need to make this happen so I don't lose. Sometimes there is a deadline or a rivalry that is set by something outside myself. Competition can push us to be better, it is essential for sports, to win, to do better than. Does that work for our creative life? Creativity needs safety to try new things, to fail, and to be imperfect to learn what works and what doesn't. And, artists often enjoy deadlines to get going!

I think about my studio. I marvel at the community spirit here. Seldom is there an "I am better" attitude. If there is, it is in a helpful way—"I know a little more than you so I would love to help you."

My brother says the best competition is with yourself, to continue to be a better you. Maybe there is only one degree separating competition and inspiration and we each need to decide what is best for our own process and progress. Whatever motivates you and helps you create is valuable, if it is supportive, healthy, and loving.

Resource: What keeps you moving forward? Notice the role of inspiration and competition in your life. Surround yourself with people who honor your style of motivation. And maybe look at who you think you are *competing* with, to see if they can *inspire* you.

Day 310
An Unexpected Retreat

Today I received the gift of what I would call an everyday miracle. A friend needed a cat sitter for a couple days and here I am, in what I now see as a creative retreat. Nothing to distract me, it is just me and Otis* the cat.

I have two days to commit to my art. I am going to pretend I am off the grid so I can only write and paint. And tend to Otis, of course.

When I first arrived here it was a strange feeling. I did not know what to do with myself. The quiet, the beauty of the light as the sun sets. My friend's home, so beautiful and minimal compared to my shared 300-square-foot home filled to the brim. Did I say how quiet it is?

The miracle of this is I have been in a little slump with my writing practice. Not sure what to write and not feeling connected to my writing. And here, I grab my computer and begin. Otis the cat lays nearby, we are temporary creative companions.

Suddenly I am excited to fill the quiet with fingertips hitting the keyboard and I am putting these sentences together. I am a writer, and I am writing. I am back!

Granted, tomorrow I may read this and decide it is not worth saving. Funny thing about moments of inspiration, sometimes they work and sometimes they don't. We still need to catch them while we can and enjoy the great feelings of the ride!

Resource: How can you get away so you can feel the internal and external space to create? A change of place is often an ingredient for increased creativity, whether a big getaway, a weekend house trade, heading to the park or the coffee shop, or just moving to another chair at the kitchen table. Make it happen.

**In hopes of a slightly bigger miracle, maybe one of my long-lost summer childhood friends, niece, and nephew of Uncle Otis, in Granby, CT is reading this.*

Day 311

I Am Glad I Caught the Wave

Here I am just 24 hours after yesterday's entry in my delightful mini-miracle retreat. Well, all did not go as planned. Life found its way into my time. My tax person reminded me I need to get things in by next week. How can I have an art retreat when I must get my taxes done? And then emails sucked me in, so my time was not all my own. I made those choices. I didn't unplug as promised.

Being honest, the quiet can be uncomfortable for me. Taking a day off during my workweek is not easy. Even though it sounds dreamy, not having distractions is hard. Squeezing my art in when I have time is somehow easier.

I remind myself, when I go on vacation it takes me a few days to settle in. I need time to adjust to the new, quieter world where I get to do what I want, like create and relax.

The good news, I am back. I have a free evening ahead to paint and am committed to not look at emails and to silence my phone. Creating boundaries around creative time is hard and growing that muscle is necessary. There is no *show-up muscle* without boundary setting.

I reread what I wrote yesterday and it isn't as fabulous as it felt while writing, yet it is a success. I rode the creativity wave not worrying where it took me. If I show up, I could catch another great wave. If I don't show up, I will get nothing. I am unplugged, here I go.

Resource: If quiet is uncomfortable for you, if having time to yourself to create wants to be filled with other activities, you may need to set boundaries with yourself. Learn to be in the discomfort of *me time* and walk through it so it can become more comfortable, even enjoyable!

Day 312
From Struggle to Joyful

Years ago, I struggled with feeling unlovable, and I was euphoric. It was a strange sensation to be dealing with this heavy issue and simultaneously feeling joyful. My therapist wondered if the sense of joy I was feeling was my soul celebrating I was doing the work I came to do.

We all have stories that help us keep going. This is one of mine. When it is time to work on myself, I see it is a good thing, not bad. I get excited because a part of myself is revealed for healing and change.

I also notice when my art feels hard and I walk through the hard, there is pleasure in the process. I am thinking about this book. With only fifty-five entries to go until I am finished writing, last week I felt terror in my body with the idea of finishing. Once I finish, I will need to do something WITH the book. Find a publisher or indie-publish, promote, and market it. This asks me to step out of my introverted comfort and into discomfort. I am willing, because I have experienced the joy of growing before, and want to do it again.

As I write this, in the other room I have a blind contour portrait painting I have worked on for weeks. Everything I seem to do makes it worse. Part of me says, let it go, move on. And, if I follow my own rule—if I don't like it is not finished—I know I have to keep going. Through this reminder I feel the gift of the challenge.

Back to feeling unlovable. Through the help of the therapeutic processes, I had a major revelation. I realized I only THOUGHT I was unlovable. The gift arrived.

Resource: When life and art get hard, instead of backing away, how about embracing the challenge as an opportunity to find the joy in growing and becoming better at life and your craft?

Day 313
The Vulnerability Hangover

You decide to out yourself as an "artist" and read your short story at an open mic, play your first gig, show your first painting, or perform in your first play. There are probably as many day-after responses as there are creators. In my art processes I have noticed sometimes there is a contraction after, or as I call it here, a vulnerability hangover. I open and expand to share this new and vulnerable part of myself, and then I contract and withdraw after.

Contraction is a natural response to expansion. It doesn't mean there is anything wrong with you, just be aware it might happen. Sometimes it is merely a chemical response to the adrenaline rush of the sharing of your work.

Or maybe you got one unhelpful response that overpowered all the supportive feedback. Maybe you are caught in an old message cycle saying it is not okay to share or be happy. Contractions can also happen after we have had an exceptional creative surge.

Vulnerability hangovers don't just happen when we are new to sharing our work, it can happen to seasoned artists, too. It is a part of the human experience to expand and contract in life.

The gift of having a Creative Practice is when we show up with big feelings, with numbness and a lack of feelings, or we feel uncomfortably vulnerable and want to curl up in bed, we can turn to our art to investigate these feelings or respond to them. A Creative Practice is a gift of support, always there for us.

Resource: When you stretch out of your comfort zone take time to celebrate the success, don't gloss over it. It is a big deal to share your art or have a breakthrough with your project. If you are having a vulnerability hangover, what needs to be expressed? Be curious. If there is something you would do different if you had a do-over, bring love and compassion to your exploration.

Day 314
Aging with Art

Michael came to my open art night for hospice patients. He had been a painter throughout his life. He loved oils and landscapes. Tonight, though, he was a frail man with a shaky hand. He did a small watercolor piece and was frustrated because his hand was so shaky. His painting reminded us of a Chinese brush painting. I had some frames with me and framed his piece.

A few days later when I was doing my art rounds I stopped into Michael's room. I played music and gave him some oil pastels with the directive to fill the page with shape and color. He said he loved to paint sunsets at the beach, which is what he proceeded to draw. Michael got frustrated again. He said his picture looked like a second grader did it. We talked about his style changing. That every artist changes their style and sometimes it has to do with physical changes, as with Monet losing his eyesight.

The next week when I visited Michael, I brought with me an article from a magazine I had found about a Japanese painter whose work looked very much like Michael's new style. I framed his newest sunset and heard people comment on it when they came into his room. Michael asked me to get it, so he could do a little more work on it. Again, he expressed frustration and gave up. He said no one will even know what he just drew. I put the drawing back in its frame and within minutes a nurse walked in and noticed his drawing.

"Michael, you added a sailboat to your sunset!" Which was exactly what he had done. He was satisfied at that point. He accepted his new style, his last style.

Resource: The art we create is alive and ever changing. Allow for change in your abilities as you age—find what works so you keep going! Ask for help if you need it.

Day 315
I Have Come a Long Way

Today I cried when I told a friend the story of my first art studio. I was in my mid 20s and we had just moved into a 1950s house. There was an addition in the backyard off the garage, maybe 150 square feet, no water or heat but electricity, lighting, and French doors that looked out at a huge pine tree. We decided it would be my art studio.

At the time I had the desire to be an artist but had been thwarted by fears and not knowing what to do or how to do it. This first moment, standing in this potential art room, hope surged through me. Yes, this would be the beginning I had been cautiously imagining. I even bought an antique typewriter at a yard sale to symbolize my desire to write, too.

Three years later I moved out of this house, without ever using my art studio. I didn't unpack the boxes. They still sat in the corner where I had put them when I moved in. I never sat and looked out at the grand pine tree. This was how afraid I was of doing art.

It took me another fifteen years before I was finally able to slay this dragon. My tears today are tears of compassion. Seeing the thread of my journey as I write this book helping others find their way into a creative life. Tears for my mother's surprise dying regret for not becoming an artist that began this journey, and tears wishing she was here to see the rest of my story.

Resource: If you are still looking for your way, don't give up. Keep following your pleasures. If you have found your way, honor the journey you have taken to this moment.

Day 316
Was It Divine Inspiration?

Thinking about what I wrote yesterday, about my path to this point in time. The moment where I committed to an art piece every day for a year to honor my mother and now being in my 20th year of daily art making. Was it divine inspiration? A moment of enlightened wisdom? Or, is it just the luck of the idea? I have had many ideas in my life, some appear for a moment and some, like this one, stay a long time.

At the time, except for poet friend, Diane Gage, creating a haiku poem a day project, I had never heard of people creating art every day as a practice. I just knew I did not want to die not fulfilling this dream to live the life of a creative. The entire trajectory of my life changed with this decision.

I didn't know it would become a way of life for me, I was simply following an idea, an impulse. This is part of the magic of the creative life. We don't know when our YES to something will change our life or if it will lead us to something else that will be important.

I wasn't saying yes to doing art every day for twenty years, offering workshops and mentoring others to do the same or to write a book to reach an even greater audience. I was answering a call in the moment. Being aware of what I am saying yes to and following through is huge. Day after day, saying yes to taking time to make art.

Resource: What can you say YES to? In improv they call it *accepting the offer.* Fear and anxiety can stop us from saying YES. Even though it is scary it could be divine inspiration! Sometimes taking action toward our calling can be the scariest! If you are not ready for a big YES, can you take little YES steps in that direction? You never know what step will become a life changer.

Day 317
I Am a Daily Artist

"I am a Daily Artist." Came out of my mouth without thinking, without premeditation before the words entered the room. This was it. This I could own with complete confidence, "I am a daily artist." This was me, and it took a long time to arrive.

It wasn't until finishing fourteen years of daily art-making the title Daily Artist slipped out effortlessly. I had grown into this new skin in my evolutions as an art maker.

Prior to this I would refer to myself as an art maker, a painter, and on some occasions an artist, but the word artist alone never felt like it fit.

The gift of a creative path is we are constantly evolving and changing. We get to make it up and identify who we are being in the world. Experimental musician, improv sculpture, landscape dancer, garden chef, collage poet, meditation singer, or whatever we want to create and own. How interesting we become when we get to share ourselves with a curious world.

When people tell me they have not found their way with their art or owning their path and place in the art fields, I get it. It takes time to grow into who we are and even more time to recognize who we have become.

There may be moments when our critic shows up and blasts us with unhelpful thoughts like, "Who do you think you are fooling?" or other equally unkind messages. If this happens to you, stay the course, and ask questions. Whose voice is this? What is the fear? And make art about it!

Resource: What title would you give yourself at this place in your creative journey? Maybe you are feeling like a daily artist or have some other descriptor. Try it on within yourself and out in the world. How does it feel to say it out loud, to own it?

Day 318

I Am a Passion Seeker

In my late 20s I was wrestling with the desire to be an artist and art-maker and my fears kept me from trying. I felt fortunate to find a 12-Step meeting for artists called A.R.T.S. (Artists Recovering Through the Twelve Steps) Anonymous. It was an eye-opener to learn I was not the only one who was challenged by fear and my critic.

In the group I identified as a "Passion Seeker," as I was trying to find my creative passion. I couldn't understand why it seemed everyone else knew what their creative path was, often from a young age. Why didn't I have *"it"* and what could I do to find *it*?

I was devoted to learning how others found their passion with hopes of finding mine. I even interviewed artists who seemed to have this creative fervor in hopes to find my way. I see now that I was passionate about finding my passion! I was not going to roll over. I was not going to let the art gods pass me over. I wanted art. What was my way in?

Through my Creative Practice I learned showing up was the necessary ingredient. I kept showing up and then, through strengthening my *show-up muscle*, I began to feel more passionate about what I was doing. I began noticing what felt good and building on it. I learned I didn't need to know how to do anything, except to show up and play, do something, do anything.

Today I am a Passionate Daily Artist. I have arrived, and I am still seeking new ways to express my passion. My younger self is very happy.

Resource: If you are not feeling passionate about your art, keep showing up to see if the passion will build as you continue to show up. For some great tools check out A.R.T.S. Anonymous: www.ArtsAnonymous.org

Day 319
A Witness and a Recipient

Today I witnessed and experienced the gift of art-making when stressed. At this point in the world COVID has captured our attention. It is not yet in our immediate circle, but the concerns are here and the prediction is it is getting closer. The fears and stress have arrived ahead of the virus. Add to this, a challenging political season and you have a recipe for extreme tension. My studio is an Expressive Arts Studio where we not only make art, but we also use the arts to navigate life.

Today I was able to witness the shift in the room as my group began making art in community. Arriving constricted and uncertain we began to breathe. Our mood lifted, knowing we were connected to our art and to this community. We brought all our feelings to the art for others to see. We found images that helped us express even deeper concerns. We met through the art and it opened us to each other.

It occurs to me when we are feeling stressed, we often isolate. That is probably the worst thing for us. Add to this a highly contagious virus and the natural inclination is to stay separate from others. What if we learned instead when the desire to isolate comes up, it is the signal we need to be with others the most. We need to come together to share our aloneness, our stresses, and our fears.

We can't always be there in person like during a pandemic, but we can stay connected over the phone, video chatting, text, email, and art-filled snail mail. When we share our worries and concerns through art, we reveal more of ourselves than the standard, *I am fine* or *I am stressed*, we open the door for a fuller sense of expression.

Resource: Find your tribe, the people to connect to when you want or need to isolate. Have an emergency plan with them when the bigger world or your inside world gets hard.

Day 320
Art and Isolation

"Isolation exists only in isolation, once it is shared it no longer exists."—Similar to a quote by Irvin Yalom in *When Nietzsche Wept*

This quote has hung above my desk for years. Whether isolation is created by something outside like a pandemic or by something inside like depression or shame, it can be emotionally, spiritually, and even physically painful. The world was in isolation during COVID. Many had family or friends in their bubble, many did not, and their isolation was overwhelming and debilitating.

There is also self-isolation. Usually when I experience self-isolation it is because I am going through something I believe no one will understand, or I feel too tender to share it with others. I am protective of myself, and I am trying to keep myself safe. Being seen may be what I need most, but I can't recognize this in the moment. My self-isolation grows from a place of not thinking I will be fully accepted, fully loved, and that I will be critiqued or judged harshly. Behind this is a longing to truly be seen and accepted just as I am.

Does our art witness our isolation, so it no longer exists? When I am with my art, creating, I do not feel alone. I am in relationship with my art. I can work through things with my Creative Practice I may not be ready to speak about with other humans. My art becomes my witness and confidant. I am expressing, not holding it in, and if I choose, I can share my art with a bigger world when I feel ready.

Sometimes my art is a vacation. I use it to isolate from the world, to go into my own private world of expression to fill my cup. Here my isolation becomes self-care.

Resource: When you can't reach out, reach for your art.

Day 321
Balance Your Devices with Art

In this world where we know so much of what is happening because of the instantaneous devices we have, there is a need to balance life with creative expression and creative nourishment for our well-being.

Technology works hard to get and keep our attention and we are all part of the experiment in this electronic world. Who knows what the long-term effects are on our body and spirit?

What I know is when I am away from my electronics—computer, phone, tablet, and television—it is good for me. As a creative I am sensitive and can be overloaded easily by the world. Add to this, not knowing what is true, what is sensationalized, and what I can do to help. This can be a recipe for emotional overload, one notification at a time. With this constant influx of information, we might fall deep into a rabbit hole or crawl into bed with no desire to be in the world.

Filling our creative cup becomes essential to keep the channel of creativity open and clear. Using our hands, bodies, senses, and imagination are a prescription for balance. Being sure we have non-device creative time is a responsibility we need to take seriously. If you do your art on a device, you may think about balancing with some no-tech art time, trade in your technology for old school tools once a week. Write with pen and notebook, play your acoustic guitar, or sing a cappella. Pick up a pencil if you usually draw digitally. Think power outage for your well-being!

Resource: Be sure your life is balanced so you can keep your creative channel open. Rather than following the notifications on your devices—follow your creative impulses to create something totally yours that you can trust and helps you unplug. Use creative time to process info you do take in that throws you off balance.

Day 322
Life Before My Creative Practice

I can't remember what I did before I began my Creative Practice. I know art was important to me. I was motivated by special occasions. My art would be gifts and cards. Usually a last-minute mad dash to an event, a birthday, or holiday. Graphic design was my work, and it was creative but for me it wasn't art.

What did I do before art? I guess it is like asking what I did before becoming a mom, or what I did before emails? I can't remember the details of the before. But I can feel the difference inside me. There is an aliveness, a passion, the passion I spent so many years hoping to find.

What I know now is my life is art. I look through my artist eyes at everything. And everything becomes a possibility. Shadows on the sidewalk become photo backgrounds for my visual journals. Found objects await a future mixed media project. Sounds become backgrounds for videos. Music becomes themes for a workshop. Ideas lay in wait for a project not revealed yet. My life is a constant following of creative impulses. and is filled with creative people, too. I live an inspired life.

Yes, everything has changed since I started my Creative Practice. I know I will never have the time in this life to do everything that inspires me, yet just having the ideas are a payoff, I can appreciate the moments of inspiration.

As you grow your Creative Practice notice what changes. Is it only the time with your craft or are new aesthetics finding their way into other areas of your day? Are you living a more inspired life?

Resource: If you did a portrait of yourself on Day 24, get it out. What has changed for you? Take notice of how your life is changing and if something more is calling you. The artist life can be filled with new ideas and inspirations. Create a new portrait!

Day 323
From Dull to Daring

Dare to do it. The thing that scares you. Being caught in the same old, same old, can be a life crusher. Leading a flat life may be safe, but it isn't pleasurable in a way that keeps us fully alive.

If our art is dull or a drudgery, something has to change. The same is needed if life is a drudgery. What have you wanted to do? What new thing whispers to you? What scares you can be what you need. The change may be little, with big impact.

Following your pleasures is not only for your art-making, but also for your life. And we need to discern the pleasures. Vegging out as you binge-watch a show may seem great, yet do you feel more alive after? Some activities might be fine now and then, yet used all the time, they may suppress our life force.

I am thinking about the kind of pleasure that opens you and gives you a sense of aliveness. Our Creative Practice needs change to keep it fresh. So does our life. What might you dare yourself to do to get out of your comfort zone? What continues to call for your attention?

Maybe you answer the call to write stories from your life. You realize your stories want to be shared. You read one at an open mic. The open mic experience is scary, but you do it again and again. Now the stories want to be combined into a book you publish for your family. You keep following the thread, daring yourself to take it further. I know for myself, when I dare to do new things, I feel enlivened.

The idea of pushing ourselves out of our comfort zone and daring to do what scares us is personal evolution. *(Disclaimer: as long as it doesn't hurt yourself or another.)*

Resource: We need things in our life to get us out of bed in the morning. What can you do in your life to feel more alive?

Day 324

Don't Compare Yourself to Others

One sure way to stop the creative process is to compare ourselves to others. It can happen easily when we are creating art in community. Maybe we are dancing happily with our eyes closed and decide to open our eyes to look around the room to see what others are doing. Suddenly everything changes when we see others we perceive as better and we become embarrassed, or feel inadequate. We may doubt ourselves. We shut down. Our critic wants us to run for our life so we are safe. It may not be this dramatic, but even small comparisons can halt our creativity.

What if instead we scanned the room to find what we liked the most, and let it inspire us? Noticing what we are attracted to in someone else's movement. We might even walk over and begin to mirror what they are doing, follow their steps. Granted, not everyone will be generous with their techniques, but you can get a closer look, start a conversation, and tell them what you like about the way they move.

At my studio we have a culture of inspiring and sharing what works for us. You will surely hear me say, "If you see someone doing something you like, take it and make it your own in some special way." We encourage people to ask how we did something and get excited to see where they take it. We don't experience this kind of fertilization—this living, breathing inspiration from others—when we work alone.

Next time you notice you are comparing yourself or your work to someone else, shift your perspective a degree to notice what inspires you. Likewise, if you are critiquing someone else, how can you shift to being inspired and supportive?

Resource: When you find yourself comparing or critiquing, shift your perspective to looking for inspiration and inspiring others.

Day 325
The Roots of Comparing

Are the roots of comparing in competition? Historically, *success* is based on grades, performance, income, popularity, and hierarchy. A system has been created to put some at the top and others below. This is the system of kingdoms, the military, of most schools, sports, corporations, and governments.

We might be born with natural talent, born into wealth or into the top of the hierarchy. Others have to work hard to get half as much, or don't have access to the same resources. We might even follow what we are winning at and not what we enjoy.

I imagine comparing and competition is born from survival, and still comes from perceived survival. We needed to size up our fellow cave person to make sure we were safe. Perhaps today the idea of winners and losers in life and creative exploration is a flawed system. It puts us on a treadmill of comparison, whether we are at the top comparing ourselves as better than those beneath us, or we are at the bottom feeling less than. Or maybe we are hiding in the invisible in-between. The comparison of putting one human over another is not helpful.

What if instead we see each person as inherently creative, and the offering is to help each other grow our creative talents? I heard many times in school, "If you only tried harder, you would get better grades." This made things feel impossible. What if instead my teachers said, "You had a great start to your story. Let's brainstorm ways to make it even better?" Let's create a world of being inspired and inspiring. Where the human experience and building community are valued over the separation of competition.

Resource: When you find yourself comparing or critiquing yourself or another, gently bring your attention to what this moment or person can inspire in you. Or how could you help inspire them?

Day 326

Compare, Criticize, or Be Inspired?

Today I had an opportunity to practice what I preached—in yesterday's entry I ended with a resource suggesting when we are comparing or feeling critical of ourself or another, to bring our attention to how we could be inspired by the moment instead.

And here I stood in those exact shoes. I was critiquing someone. I was thinking they were not doing something right. Just having written about this, I needed to put my theory into action.

So I softened my gaze with the intention of finding what they could inspire in me. I noticed they were swaying in their chair, just slightly. Okay, I can do that, I thought. So I began to sway slightly, also. As I swayed back and forth I could feel my judgment melt away. I instead was feeling calmness, something I hadn't felt all day. It had worked. My critical thinking had been replaced with calmness and even compassion for myself and for them. The rest of the time we spent together was soft and enjoyable. It was a gift to feel my rough edges sanded away.

Since I wrote the above story I have had many opportunities to practice. When I feel my sharp eye at another or myself I soften my gaze and look for an opportunity to be inspired. Sometimes it doesn't seem like it is working, but after I let it settle in the inspiring moment becomes taking better care of myself, speaking up, or making my own changes. Once I see *what I need,* I can be more compassionate to myself and others.

I realize criticism shuts down my creativity and shuts the door on others—while looking for inspiration opens doors!

Resource: Maybe we can all make this a lifelong experiment. When you are feeling critical of yourself or another, whether it is in the arts or in life, see if you can soften your gaze to looking for what might be inspired by this moment. And take it in!

Day 327
Is It Engaging Enough?

My friend, colleague, and fellow daily art explorer Donna Otter was telling me about a one-second-a-day challenge she tried. She lasted one day. She had been inspired by Cesar Kuriyama who began shooting one second of video every day and plans to do it for the rest of his life. (Check out his app 1 Second Everyday!)

This got us musing over why did something so simple only last one day? At first it seemed hilarious, and then I began to understand and remember my own one-second-a-day story.

It was my 365 Days of Manikin project where I took one photo a day of my treasured college manikin. It only took me a second. I missed a LOT of days that year. I kept losing him and forgetting.

My aha came years later when I was printing a small selection of the Manikin photos for show-and-tell at my Daily Art Workshop. I got so much pleasure from holding the photos in my hands I realized taking the photos was not satisfying enough for me—holding them in my hands was supercharged.

The learning from this story is that we must stay engaged. And part of engagement is satisfaction in the process. Printing the pics along the way may have kept me engaged and also honored the project. Or saving all the Manikin photos to an album for a once a month slideshow. Or creating a 3-sentence story with each. Having a special bag to carry him in would have helped me keep track of his whereabouts, and honored him, too.

A one-second practice could work, if it is engaging or meaningful enough so you stay with it! And you can't say you don't have enough time for it! (The app 1 Second Everyday strings the videos together for you!)

Resource: Stay engaged so you keep going. You could play with a one-second process in your art form. Try it out, it could be fun!

Day 328
Listen for the Next Impulse*

Listening for the next impulse in art might mean noticing what color, word, or musical note you are attracted to. It is the idea for the next step. You don't need to know where you are going, how it will turn out, or how you are going to get to the end. You just need to listen for the small impulse that calls you. And sometimes you need to listen very closely.

The same can go for our life. We don't have to figure our whole life out. We need to listen for the next impulse and follow it. It really makes life easier. Often, we expect the impulse to be big, for the entire answer to be handed to us with all the bells and whistles. With no uncertainty. And when they are small next steps, we reject them because they don't feel big enough or they don't fit where we think we are going.

Following the small impulses can help us stay out of being overwhelmed by the big picture, the whole project. If we saw all we needed to do, we may never start. If I had known the process of writing this book before I started, I may not have begun. Following the next impulse helps our creative expression and our life be original, authentic, and maybe more manageable in the process.

A common stress in life is in making decisions. People tell me, "I don't know what to do." I can only offer my personal experience. When I don't know what to do, it is not time to decide. When it is time, I will know. The next impulse will be there. If you don't have an impulse for the next step? Then maybe it isn't time. You will know when the time comes.

Resource: Listen. Make space to listen. And listen more.

**The impulse we follow does not want to harm self or others. It is a small voice for our greatest good and the greatest good of all. If you do get impulses wanting to hurt or harm, get professional support. Allow the attention and healing.*

Day 329
A Sense of Urgency

I am a Type A personality. I am a doer. In my twenties I identified my doing through work as a way to avoid my life, a bit of work addiction or workaholic tendencies. I spent long hours at a job I loved yet was also stressful and deadline driven. This was at a time when I was young and energetic, productivity was exciting, and I was also using my work as a way to not go home to my relationship.

I pulled back, eventually left the job (and the marriage), and started my own business committing to do what I loved for the betterment of my life. I have been gratefully self-employed since.

Recently I had the wondering, am I an art addict or an art-aholic? I am driven. In a discussion with my somatic therapist yesterday, she suggested the word "urgency," I have a sense of urgency to get things done. Being in the later years of my life, I do feel a sense of urgency. There are things I want to complete before my time in this body ends. Completing this book is one of them. I feel grateful for this sense of urgency as it helps me get up and get going in my life.

Is it an addiction? Am I an art-aholic? (The idea makes me laugh.) My daily Creative Practice is where I find meaning in my day and the world. I show up for myself, I learn from it, I become a better human being because of it. My Creative Practice improves my relationships, improves my quality of life, and is integrally woven into the fabric of my day. I turn to my art to better understand myself and my world, not to avoid it. Yes, I am driven. Yes, I feel a sense of urgency. Yes, I am in love with my life. Art helps.

Resource: Is there something in you that feels urgent to express? Can you answer its call for attention?

Day 330
A Sense of Patience

The sense of urgency I mentioned yesterday gets me going. Right next to this urgency is a growing understanding of patience. I must get this done, and I must allow time for things to percolate. The slow, thoughtful life calls.

My mother was a slow and thoughtful one, she drove me crazy as a teenager but became my Zen master in her later life. Yet, she never became the artist she always wanted to be. She put other's needs before her own longings. Virtuous, yet at the end of her life it became her one regret. What if she had cultivated urgency around creating art?

I do know patience and slowness are essential for listening to what it is I want and need. Essential for living fully, feeling life happening in my body. When I am slow and patient, I can live through my senses, not just barrel along jumping ahead in my mind to the next thing to do.

Here enters my Creative Practice once again. It is through my art-making my mind stills, the to-do list falls away, and I am listening only for the next impulse that wants attention. "Choose teal blue next." or "Paint a portrait of Charleena Chavon Lyles," or "Go write about being a Type A personality." Through my art I listen.

Ultimately this deep listening prepares me for life itself. If I can learn to listen to the whisper of "Choose teal blue next," I may then learn to hear the other whispers of life like, "Call your brother," or "Say yes to this offer."

Maybe I show up with urgency to express myself because my mother didn't, and when I arrive, I breathe and find the exquisite gift of her patience as I paint, write, or dance.

Resource: How are you at slow and patient? Is there a way you can slow yourself down, even a little?

Day 331
Urgency + Patience = Growth

The gift of writing this book is getting to look at my life, my Creative Practice, and my creative expression with a magnifying glass. Each time I follow the next impulse I am taken deeper into myself. These past weeks I have been looking at urgency and patience. And simultaneously the writing of this book that I now see as a *Calling* has become more difficult. I question this. Shouldn't it be easy if it is my *Calling*?

Though the process of writing is meaningful, it is not easy, and is harder as I venture toward finishing. Last week I was up against my critic at a level that was excruciating.

The urgency and my strong *show-up muscle* keeps me going. Patience and slowness help me take my time, feel my feelings, and soothe myself rather than give up and run. I show up, I make art about how hard it is to show up. I appreciate my critic who is trying to keep me safe from failure and assure this part of myself we will be okay. I soothe myself so I can continue, this teaches me to trust myself more, not because I am becoming a better writer, but because I can soothe and regulate myself more easily.

If I use the history of my daily art progression as an example, as I grow as an author, I will be able to handle what comes my way. If I fail (whatever fail means) I have done what I love and is meaningful to me. I do this for myself first and the world second. And, if it has a life beyond me, you will be reading this right now. And you will know I have grown through what is hard, and so can you.

Resource: Sometimes when things are hard, it doesn't mean it isn't working, it means keep going because you are working through important issues or growing beyond your comfort zone. Take time to pause, soothe yourself, make adjustments, ask for help, and keep going!

The arts are at the forefront of change in the world. Once your show-up muscle is strong, use your art to express and support what is important to you, what you care about.

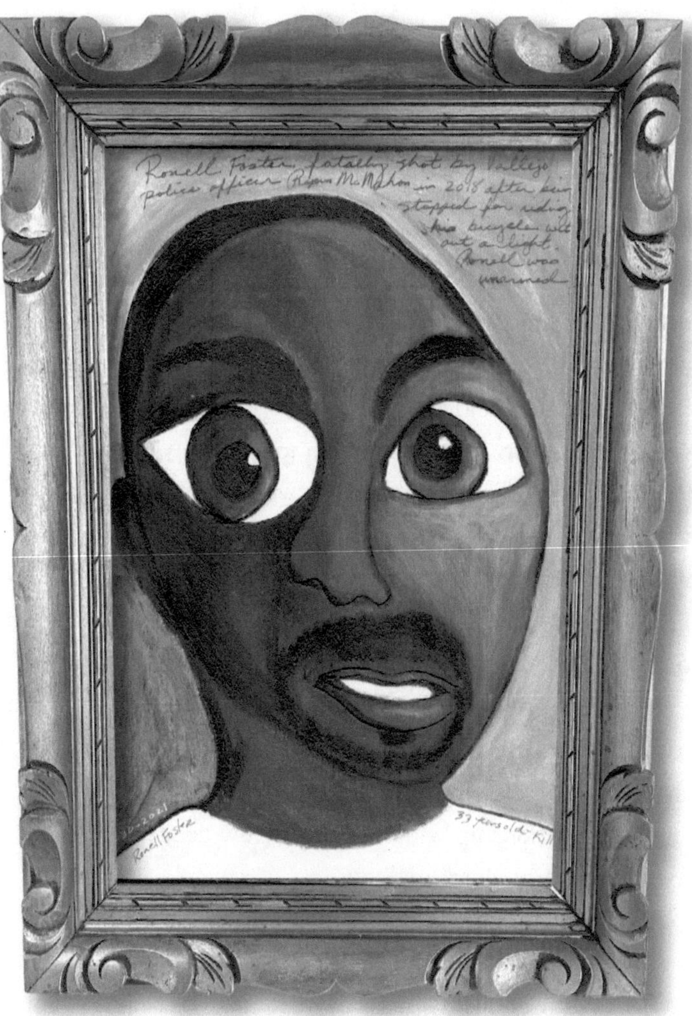

365 Days of Blind Contour Portraits

At the end of year one of Blind Contour Portraits I did not want to stop because I loved painting them. I decided to continue, but in the second and third years I would go back and give more attention to some of the portraits that felt incomplete. (I had been doing one a day and even if it wasn't done, I moved on the next day.) It also gave me a chance to give attention to social activism issues I am involved in through my painting.

Day 332

Honor Your Creative Practice Story

Years ago, a mentor in my life told me I needed to grow my roots deeper. I needed to have a greater dedication to my life, to where I was, right then in space and time, and to the people in it. I had just lost both my parents and I think he knew if I did not grow my roots deeper, I might be untethered and find myself lost. With deep roots, I would not get blown over or uprooted by life's happenings.

What I didn't realize at the time was my Creative Practice would become my roots. I started it to honor my mother and her desire to be an artist, and it became where I processed my life. I was the tree, barren of leaves in the winter of death. The process of creating was nourishing fertilizer for my life, for my tree, and the art I created became the buds, leaves, and flowers that began to appear and signal spring's arrival.

My roots grew deep, my Creative Practice was the taproot that reached deep down into the earth, able to reach water, to be strong in the gusts of loss and chaos. Ultimately this taproot became my relationship with myself, it grew deeper as I explored my interior through art-making.

What has your Creative Practice become for you? Maybe it is your place to process your life, or it is your place to escape day-to-day life and feel a sense of freedom. Maybe it is your time to hone your craft or be in an art meditation.

However your Creative Practice serves you, take a moment to honor its place in your life. Even if you are still finding your footing or taproot, you are breathing life into it. This is worthy of a nod, a celebration, a moment of appreciation for following the call to be here right now.

Resource: Look at your own Creative Practice story and take time to honor it. Maybe it becomes your muse for today.

Day 333
Honor Your Effort

Just Do It, Nike screams all over the advertising world. I have not been a fan of the phrase, the word "just" seems to minimize the effort. Just do it, just show up. I am guessing they are giving us permission to jump in, and maybe a two-syllable phrase isn't as sexy, "Do it!"

At my studio I hear the word "just" all the time when people are presenting their creative talents. I just did this painting, I just wrote a few sentences, I just showed up once, or I just did the same thing I always do. And then I realized I say it, too! It feels like a minimizing of the effort and maybe if we say "just" before what we did, it protects us from criticism. I know from my own experience showing up is not as easy as "just." It is most definitely an effort, maybe a feel-good effort, but still an effort.

I look up the definition and see the other kind of "just," which becomes justice, truth, fairness. It isn't until the end of all the definitions I see the word "just" in relation to the word "joust." Yes, this fits with the "do it." The doing can be filled with jousting, a jousting match between my creator self and all those parts of me who don't feel confident. In jousting we are trying to knock someone off balance, even inflict pain. So would this mean, do it despite the pain, do it despite getting knocked off your feet, do it because every fiber says it needs to be done?

Ultimately, let's learn not to diminish our work with the word "just." Let's do ourselves justice and admit where it is hard and where it feels great. Let's joust with our critic, take away the word "just" and own it—I painted today! I wrote a few lines! I showed up once! I did what I love to do!

Resource: Notice if you use the word "just" and if you are minimizing something. Practice owning your efforts outright.

Day 334
Can I Hate What I Am Doing?

My mother used to say "hate" is a big word. "Is it true you hate it?" She would ask. She would say it is not okay to hate people; you can dislike someone's behavior, but not hate them. Wise words of the day.

In my art-making journey, I have tried things I thought I would be really good at or would really like and to be honest, I hated it or disliked it very, very much and would never do it again. Sometimes things look so good in theory, like when I used to look at photos in the many art-making books I owned, but then when I actually tried them, it became a no-go. It wasn't me.

I am remembering my paper-making journey years ago. I was so excited with the idea of making paper. I bought a book. I talked about it all the time. And finally I was gifted the things I needed to make it happen. (Probably because they were tired of hearing me talk about it.) I tried it and dare I say, I hated it. And, I wouldn't have known if I hadn't tried.

If it isn't pleasurable, why do it? There may be parts of the process that aren't pleasurable, but because it is part of the whole, we get satisfaction out of the completion. Or we find a new way. I love mosaics but I do not like the process of grouting. I found a style I could do that did not require grouting.

It is not a fail if you don't like something—it is information. You do not have to suffer. You do not have to pay creative dues. You get closer and closer to what you love by trying things and ruling out what isn't a good fit. This goes for art and for life.

Resource: Let your expression time help you identify what brings you pleasure and what doesn't. (You can probably feel it in your body.) If you don't like something, alter it, change it, explore different processes, or move on to something else.

Day 335
How Can I Make Art When...

In this world where news is available all the time, a voice in my head says making art is a first-world ability, for the privileged. I could use this time to change the world. I sit in my safe kitchen writing while on the other side of the world, yet not far away, tanks line up, bombs fall, and evacuations add to the already excruciating number of worldwide refugees.

All around the world people have to do things they hate so they can live or stay alive. And I sit wondering what to write about next. I sit trying to block out these realities so I can find peace in a privileged life.

Even in a world where war threatens us or lack of safety is a way of life, we must create. We need to have mastery over something. It could be in the stories we tell to remember where we came from or songs we sing to offer us a moment of freedom. Art-making can become part of our survival and the survival of our story.

People are generally compassionate, and even if we are not in the line of fire, our hearts break for those who are. We can feel helpless and inadequate to create the change we want. Going to the arts can help us take a vacation from the awfulness of life, and it can also give us a place to put the horrors. Let the paper hold the pain, let the song transform our relationship to the pain, let the dance allow our body to express it. We all need relief, and the act of creating can be our reprieve while the creation holds our pain.

Resource: No matter what life presents you, find pockets of creative pleasure, time to express and *make things special,* so maybe you will survive longer and even thrive.

Day 336

Feel Like an Artist or Be an Artist?

"We don't become an artist and then do art, we do art and then begin to feel like an artist." —Tish McAllise Sjoberg

I was challenged today by a reader, "You frequently refer to feeling like an artist in this book. Why don't you own that you are an artist and help others say they are an artist?" I take this in, after all, the title of my book is *Artist is a Verb.*

If we go back in any of our lineages we will find that our ancestors were art makers—they told stories around the fire through word, song, drum, and dance. They were artisans who made everyday things special, like pottery, weaving, and pictographs which left evidence of their existence.

Then art became commerce. Collectors, galleries, and museums decided what was worthy—new levels of beauty and comparison were born. We moved from being artisans to artists and a hierarchy was born. Critics began to place value on art. Society limited the title of artist, allowing it only for the few.

I see the act of growing a Creative Practice as an inside job, a deeply personal journey of finding our way by following what brings us pleasure. In this context, to FEEL like an artist is the most valuable compensation for our devotion.

For me, this inside feeling is more important than being seen on the outside as an artist, the label. The feeling sense of artist can't be taken away with a negative comment or critique. I want people to feel the expansion of creative play, ultimately, live an artful life. And yes, the confidence to say, I am an artist can become an exciting by-product.

Resource: We each come to feeling like an artist at our own pace. Have you had that feeling? Do you want to claim a title?

Day 337
Dear Mom

Last night I wrote a letter to my mother. She died twenty years ago, yet writing it still felt helpful. I followed the impulse. My mother was my inspiration to begin my first daily art project, and she continues to be my muse. I asked her for any help she could send to finish this book as my creative confidence was wavering.

As creatives we sometimes think we need to figure everything out on our own. We need to drive solo on this creative journey, as if asking for help is cheating. What do we do when we are driving solo and our creative confidence is low?

I am one who thinks I have to figure things out on my own. Yet it is in being with others and sharing my plight, where I get input and new insights that are helpful. Just being around people can put me in a different frame of mind, give me a new perspective, and help me not feel so alone. We are creatures who need each other. We need to know we are loved and cared about and yes, that we can ask for help.

It makes me laugh to think it is easier to ask my mother, who died many years ago, for help than to ask living people to give me a hand. Writing to her did help in the moment and now it is time to ask for *living* help.

Thinking of how she wanted to be an artist and then died with the regret she didn't make it happen, I wonder, was this an example of her having trouble asking for help? Who could she have talked to? I wish she had told me before it was too late. Maybe we could have figured it out and stumbled forward together.

Resource: What do you do when your creative confidence is low or you are feeling stuck? How do you keep your creative channel open? Make a list and put "ask for help" at the top. (When we are in the stuckness, we can't always remember what is helpful.)

Day 338
Thrown Off Balance

In creative expression, comparison and doubt can lead us down negative roads. If I notice I am in fear or worry about my expression I am usually imagining what someone else will think. Or I'm comparing myself to someone else, and judging mine as not as good. Comparison and doubt stop momentum and kill joy.

Creative expression is not a competition. Yes, there are competitions in the arts like applying to a show or a program, but in the context of our Creative Practice, this is not the place for comparison. It is a place to try new things, be inspired, explore what works and doesn't work, to relax and be ourselves.

Even with all my years of daily art-making, I can still get thrown off balance. Currently I am in the end stages of writing this book and doubt has found its way into my process. Is it good enough? What will you think of it? I imagine you thinking, "Who do you think you are fooling?" Yikes, the voice of my fourth-grade teacher has arrived in my head, I can't believe she still haunts me.

I take a moment from writing to look out my window, take a deep breath. I remember, I am writing for me first. What happens next is not here yet. Once again the words from Martha Graham to Agnes de Mille on creativity come back to me:

"It is not your business to determine how good it is, nor how valuable it is, nor how it compares with other expressions. It is your business to keep it yours clearly and directly, to keep the channel open. You do not even have to believe in yourself or your work. You have to keep open and aware directly to the urges that motivate you. Keep the channel open."

My doubting heart is nourished by these words, I can continue.

Resource: If comparison, doubt, or other unhelpful thoughts creep in, how can you rebalance and keep your channel open?

Day 339
Ordination Versus Germination

I often witness onlookers seeing my art and declaring their own lack of creative confidence. "You are so creative, I could never do THAT," or even harder for me to hear, "I am not an artist and never will be." Other expressions include clichés like, "I don't have a creative bone in my body," or "I couldn't draw a straight line if my life depended on it." Thankfully, I have graduated from letting these comments take away my joy in my own art (thinking my creativity is causing them pain) to hearing these statements as code for, "I wish I could do art, I wish I were an artist."

Before I started creating art regularly, I too would look at art and participate silently in negative internal chatter. I even felt a bit of resentment: THEIR *artist ordination* had arrived and MINE was lost in some karmic bureaucracy. Maybe tonight the artist gods would hear my prayer, visit me in the night, and I could wake up an artist.

Once I went through my own learning, *Artist is a Verb—I don't become an artist and then do art, but I do art and then begin to feel like an artist,* I found a new way to respond. When someone says they are not creative, instead of offering assurances that they really are creative, I engage them in imagining if they could be an artist, what would they imagine themselves doing? There is always an answer. "I would paint," or "I would write," or "I would play the drums," or "I always wanted to sing."

As the longings surface, the artist seeds have an opportunity to germinate. I believe we all have longings for more in our life, waiting to be acknowledged and watered. Sometimes we need someone a few steps ahead to help us get started.

Resource: Germinate your own longing, and once it takes root, help someone else germinate their longing to become a creative.

Day 340

Today I Bring the Earth

Today I decided to write outdoors. I sit at my small garden table, late morning light dappling my fingers and keyboard. I rest my hands on the black keys and feel they have been warmed by the sun. My fingertips lightly trace all the keys and I open to noticing my senses.

The light breeze sounds the wind chimes in the distance. Dogs begin to bark as they announce what is probably the mail carrier traveling down our street. The neighbor's cat brushes against my leg and my old blind and deaf pup noses his way in for attention, too. The barking stops and I hear the birds singing. My coffee is still warm as I sip between sentences. I am in a small corner of my city oasis, power lines above me but beyond is a clear blue sky. The bright green weeds at my feet say, don't pull us, we are lush.

This is the creative life. This is taking a moment to be fully immersed in the world with my senses. A quiet moment, not a manic get-things-done swirl. I think of this as a living meditation; it is welcome relief from the busyness of the day starting to nip at my heels.

The concept of people having a "nature deficit" is a growing idea. We are spending less time in the natural world and more time indoors and on our devices. The arts can help us find balance in our life. The arts plus nature can be an inspiration.

Resource: What can you do today to slow down and open your senses? Maybe you grab the tools of your trade and go to a neighborhood park, sit outdoors where you get a different view of the world. A patch of sky or a tree, or even the native weeds can be your muse. Or maybe you go out into the natural world and then come back to do your art. Notice what is different.

Day 341
Today I Bring Fire

Today I am writing in the studio of my dear friend, Pamela Underwood, who lost her previous house to fire. Everything she owned burned—all her art, her supplies, and her creative history except what had been documented by others or given away. Even her thesis that she had just finished and was making final edits to, went up in flames. What did she do? She made art from the rubble. She made art from the ashes. She made art to face all the emotions that screamed for attention and to transform her loss into something tangible.

Working here in her new space has me wondering, what if today you brought fire into your practice? What could this mean? How could you turn the heat up on the way you work or on what you are creating? Would this mean going deeper into a subject matter that scares you? Something personal or vulnerable? Can you hold your feet to the fire and begin something you have been putting off or finish something you have been unsure of? Turn up the heat, add color, change the tempo, think hot.

The element of fire lets the old burn away. Bringing fire may transform something. Think of the phoenix rising from the ashes or glass as it hits intense heat or the sun always rising once again. The sun is fire, the sun lights our way—we cannot look it straight in the eye or get too close or it will burn us, yet we can let it warm us and keep us in the light.

Maybe fire is our muse, active and giving. We don't have to lose everything we own, but we can let go of what we have outgrown, that which isn't serving us any longer. Maybe fire wants us to stop being so comfortable and take chances, make decisions, or alchemize something. What will rise tomorrow?

Resource: What might fire ask of you? Follow its light.

Day 342

Today I Bring the Moon

I found the moon late in life. Though it has always been there, my father was part of the team who put humans on the moon so I was well aware of its proximity and existence. I also had a vague connection to it guiding me through my cycles, its magnetic effect on the ocean tide, and the connection of a full moon to strange behavior.

It was not until I began my Creative Practice and noticing the world through my artist eyes that I truly began to be in relationship with the moon. My new art eyes needed to locate it each evening. I would watch it change, and feel the magic of its presence. This ball in the sky reflects the sun, is not the sun, powerful and bright, yet it absorbs the sun's rays and becomes an expression of where the sun and earth are on this night. The sun, earth, and moon all dance together in creation.

As I sit to write we are on the cusp of a lunar eclipse which has me thinking more about our beloved moon. I see the sun and moon as metaphors for my Creative Practice. I cannot look directly into the sun or it will burn my eyes. Yet the sun can be my muse and the moon an expression I can easily look at. In my life I may have a moment I cannot look at directly, but I can look closely at this moment through my creative expression. My art then, like the moon, can hold a magnetic push and pull in my world.

The moon also teaches me I am allowed to ebb and flow in my expression. I do not have to burn bright in every moment. I get to be full and I can also wax and wane, even have a rare momentary eclipse. I know I will always return to fullness.

Resource: Stand in your life and absorb it, be receptive and listen. What do you want to reflect back through your art? Allow yourself to wax and wane and have creative cycles.

Day 343
Today I Bring Water

I was recently gifted my first visit to Hawaii. In my work I encourage people to let go of their everyday life as they enter into the imaginal world of art where anything is possible. There I was in the reality of paradise, and I wasn't yet able to let go of my everyday life and enter into this enchanted world.

Freedom was finally found in the water, in the bay near our friends' home. On a shore surrounded by hardened lava, a small inlet was passageway to this magical sea. Once I let go of my fears about cutting my feet on the sharp lava bottom, staying upright on a paddle board, or trusting my first kayak ride, I found peace in the ocean. My worries washed away.

When my son was young, I would take him surfing on Sunday mornings and watch him sitting on his board waiting for a wave and think, "This is his church." Floating silently in this Hawaiian bay, I entered into the world of possibilities. I was baptized by nature—I found my church.

The letting go into paradise seems bigger on my return. I didn't spend hours in the water, but moments. Yet since my return I have spent more time floating in the silence of the water in my imagination than I did while I was there. I hear the gentle lapping of water, taste salt on my lips, squint my eyes to see what I am sure is a dolphin. This is the gift of the imagination.

What can happen when we bring the idea of water to our practice, metaphorically allowing ourselves to float in creating? No hurries, no worries. Can we allow ourselves to enter the magical place of creative flow, where time stands still and there is nothing but us and creating? Can we simply remember to row, row, row our boat, gently down the stream?

Resource: Allow yourself to float in the waters of creativity.

Day 344

Today I Bring Breath

I sit to write and I feel my confidence sliding south. Familiar unwanted messages fill my head: *It is not good enough. I really have nothing new to say. Others have done it much better. Why did I commit myself to this project and tell others that I am doing it?*

I decide to look at my life to see what else might be happening. I learned years ago that when I am upset, it is often not about this exact moment, but about a thought or event that took place just before this moment. I remember to breathe.

Our lives need to be viewed as a whole, not compartmentalized. When we are challenged in life with work, relationship, or money, these challenges spill into our Creative Practice. When our life is touched by loss, fear, or uncertainty, our ability to think and be creative is affected. Breathing deeply helps.

As I write, I feel the truth of these words. I have an event tomorrow at my studio and am filled with unknowns. "Will anyone come? Will it be interesting? Why did I say I would do this?" I am astounded by the similarity to my worries about my writing. I take a deep breath and a sense of compassion comes to me. My attention is redirected to what is going on under the surface. My writing becomes my helper. I start where I am, worried about tomorrow, and I begin to see a different picture, a kinder, gentler picture.

Sometimes our art becomes a magnifier for life, both the joys and the sorrows. The gift is given when we can show up even for 5 minutes and see where it takes us. Our Creative Practice becomes a possibility for relief from our challenges.

Resource: Remember to breathe. When you are feeling down about your creative endeavor, look at your life to see if there is something else affecting your mood or feelings at this moment. Make art about what is going on, and breathe.

Day 345
To Show or Not to Show

Is your art only for you or is it for a bigger world? At some point it has probably crossed your mind to share your art—a show, live event, or getting published. We each have to follow our own path and decide, do we want to take our practice outside the personal? Two years into my Creative Practice I sent a proposal to a small local gallery to show my first 365 Days of Art for their monthly art walk event. They accepted my proposal and we spent many hours hanging hundreds of pieces. It was a labor of love.

The night my show opened I stood in the center of the room, surrounded by all this work I created and had what I might call a spiritual moment. It felt like this was my greatest accomplishment. I was 100% responsible for what I was seeing. Yes, I had graduated from college and given birth to my son, but this was a different kind of graduation, a different kind of birth. Tears welled in my eyes as I took in what was happening. It was truly a life-changing experience, I felt like an artist.

When we create, it is to serve ourselves first—to answer the call of our creative hunger. When we share our work, it has a life of its own. Others can experience what we create and it affects them, even inspires them. Its life multiplies. A few years back I had a show, 5,985 Days of Art. This time I was not showing so much to celebrate myself and my accomplishment, but to inspire others to begin their own journey. My place in the world had changed and I was having another life-changing experience, owning a new role—I am a mentor.

Resource: Your art will tell you what it wants, if it wants to become a book or a show or a performance, it will tell you. Take your time as you follow the inspirations so you can grow into your new role—artist, mentor, or teacher.

Honoring our work
is an important step
in owning our creative power.

What can you do
to honor the work
you have done this year?

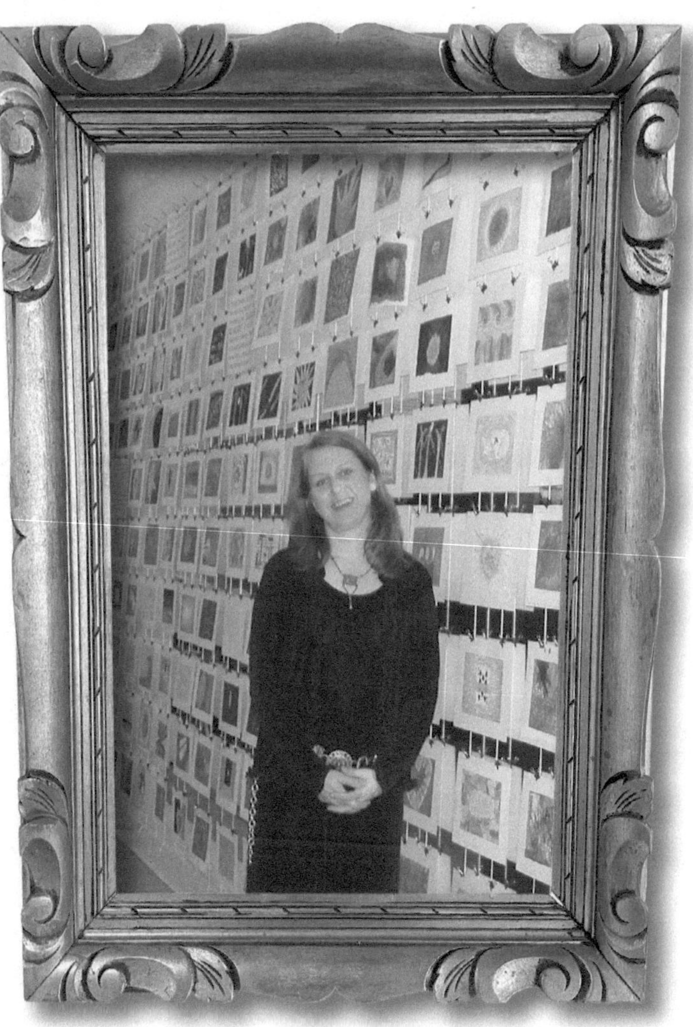

Showing My Art

Here I am at my one-woman show, 365 Days of Art, with my first year of art, mostly oil pastels on paper, because I didn't feel confident enough yet to paint. It was an exuberant experience to have what were simple rudimentary pieces of art exhibited all together. The gift was realizing the true art was the whole year together, not the individual pieces.

Day 346

To Sell or Not to Sell

As an art maker there always seems to be a time where we wonder if we could make money with our art. Could it become a career, a way of making a living?

I pursued this question for a few years in the beginning of my Creative Practice life. I entered shows, participated in local art walk events, created press releases and yes, sold art. I realized it took a lot of promotion to get work out in the hands of buyers. It can be a full-time job just promoting. I eventually decided it wasn't for me. I wanted to create art because I loved to create art for me, not to sell. And, who knows, I may revisit it again in the future.

While selling my work I made great contacts for my Expressive Arts Therapy practice. If you want to teach, sharing your work can be a helpful way to attract students.

Things can change when our art moves from being for ourselves, to consumer-oriented art-making. We can become sales oriented, creating what sells or what we think will sell rather than creating for ourself. My artist friends who make a living from their art create and promote eight hours or more a day. It is a business.

All this said, if you want to be in the business of making art, try it. Maybe start part-time to see if it works for you and if you want to grow it into more. The most important consideration is to make the choice that keeps you showing up, keeps you enjoying the process and expressing. And maybe you separate your Creative Practice from your business, so creating for yourself still has a place in your day.

Resource: Each of us needs to find our own path in living a creative life and deciding whether we want to monetize our art. Remember to follow your pleasure. If it feels good, keep going, if it doesn't feel good, listen and make changes.

Day 347
Your Creative Practice Superpower

We all have an area in our creative life where we are strong—what is yours? I grew the superpower of showing up every day.

Trust me, this was not innate in me. I spent my life putting things off until the last minute, being a deadline driven creator. Doing a little a day was born from having a daily Creative Practice. Learning to show up every day helped me write my master's thesis, create and promote a successful Expressive Arts Studio, write this book, and live a less stressful life. I had no idea having a Creative Practice would help me in other areas of my life. It has become a superpower for me.

Even after all the years I have been showing up, there are a few other superpowers I would like to grow. I would love to become a master at changing things up and experimenting. I tend to stay on the well-worn path. Could I grow into being bold, unafraid of trying something new? I admire artists who have the ability to play with color and make it look so easy. I would love to grow the patience to do work that takes time or is detail oriented.

My writer friend, Jen, went through over one hundred rejections, and then finally found a literary agent and publisher for her book. I totally trust her to be successful because she will not give up on her dreams. This quality is her superpower.

If you know what your superpower is, you can use it to build your confidence. For example, I may not be the best craftsperson, but I know I am a show-up-every-day superhero, so eventually, my craft will grow.

Resource: Think about your own superpower. If you can't claim one, ask someone who knows you well. Others sometimes can see us better than we see ourselves. You could create a superpower symbol, theme song, or title for yourself! (If you do, send it to me!)

Day 348
Dream Life and Your Art Life

"I realized it was time to leave and I told my mother, I did not want to go. She told me I had to and gave me a long hug."
—Dream snippet, January 2018

Our dream life or our "other life" as I call it, is rich with images and strange stories that can be told through the arts. Even when we only remember a snippet, sometimes those few words can be rich and powerful. They can inspire bigger stories for books or movies, poetry, dance, or visual art. Dreams can also be like puzzles filled with metaphors and learnings to untangle.

I keep a dream journal by my bed and write down what I remember, as soon as I wake. I can't wait. Night dreams can disappear as quickly as I enter my day life.

If we begin to look at our dreams as inspiration for our art, they can become alive with potential and spur ideas that take us out of our usual creative routine. Dreams that stay with us may be asking for attention. The arts are a way to attend to them and reveal more.

Creating art around bad dreams could give them a place to live or allow us to get some distance from them. It could be a relief to express them and even to share the expression with another.

After the dream of seeing my mother and getting a long hug from her, I did a page in my visual journal expressing the good feelings of her beautiful hug. It had been over fifteen years since she died, and our hug was a gift. Even now as I write about it, I can feel it.

Resource: Put a dream notebook and pen next to your bed. Write what you remember, immediately. If you already keep a dream journal, read through and pull out anything you might want to play with in your art form.

Day 349
Is This Therapy?

There can be many trying days along the way to building our *show-up muscle*. It can be surprising though when we are deep into our commitment and hit a rough patch. Why is this? We have been showing up day after day, yet after all this time we are met with resistance.

Sometimes standing behind our 5-minute commitment is doubt about our talent, or concern we are not measuring up. Will others like what we have done or even worse, brutally critique us? Or maybe we have been diving deep into healing our life through our art and it seems too much and we need a break.

Maintaining the *show-up muscle* could be comparable to years of therapy, even slaying 365 dragons—a new one arriving each day, taunting us, *"Do you really want this? Do you really want to express yourself creatively? Do you really want to tell your story or face the truths of your life?"*

Today in my Women's Writing Support Group we checked in with what frightens us. It was all there, all the worries about talent, being critiqued, and measuring up. We opened our heart doors to each other and felt closer as we shared the voices that taunt us to stop, to not show up, or even give up. Being witnessed by others was helpful. Ultimately, we could see each other's paths as sacred—moving through these messages that are strong and loud.

After being with others in my group I find myself more committed than I did hours earlier when I was alone. I feel encouraged, with strength to stand up to my internal aggressors and do the next bit of therapy being offered. I am encouraged to keep going.

Resource: If you haven't, start a *Creative Practice Support Group* where you can be honest about your process, be supported, and support others. See the Follow-Up Resources for ideas to get started.

Day 350

Where Does Creativity Come From?

Last night in my writer's support group we were discussing that feeling when you create something you like and there is this moment of, "Where did that come from?" It happens to me when I see something I have written or painted that I have not seen in awhile, and wonder, "Did I do that? Where did THAT come from?"

My best work seems to come when I realize I am just a conduit for the creative expression. When I am not trying too hard but showing up and acknowledging my role. What do I need to say to tend to myself? What do I need to say to be of service to the bigger world?

When I get caught up in ME, my ego gets in the way and then there is sure to be a critical moment and self-made ruins. When I show up and acknowledge that I am just a conduit for this creative expression, it offers me a respite to be in the process and create, to not worry how it looks or what I might do with it.

My friend and sister traveler Martha is a qigong teacher. She leads us in an exercise, organizing the qi field, which connects us infinitely to the qi (energy) as far as we can imagine out into the universe and back into our selves. Maybe being internally organized helps our channel to be open to creative flow. Or maybe it is the desire to be internally organized that turns us to the creative process. Through being present to our instrument, our voice, our body, our hands, we are organizing our internal world and in that place, creativity flows. Something to ponder.

Resource: Where do YOU think creativity comes from? Take this question to a discussion with other artists and friends. Notice in yourself what is happening when you are in the flow of your creative experience. Appreciate those moments of surprise and delight of, "I did that?"

Day 351
Toward the End

Though it did not begin this way, most of my 365 daily art projects are based on the Gregorian calendar, starting January first and ending on New Year's Eve. At this writing the days get shorter, holidays approach, and the year and my project will end soon.

There can be a magic to the ending days of a project. For me this is when I feel the depth of the relationship I have built with my art—to be so intimately connected with it that I grieve its ending even though I am sure a new project will begin the day after this one ends. In all my years there have been a few times when I was happy when it was over but those are the rare and few. Usually, like today, I can already feel myself missing my project.

I have been doing a minimal amount these last weeks because my life has been so busy, but now with the reality that the year is closing I want to recommit so I can go out feeling strong. Each day I want to show up with gratitude and reverence for the creative path I have walked this year.

Tomorrow I have a whole day to be with my art. I will get out my year of blind portrait paint journals and review what I have done. I will check back with you after I have done my review to let you know what I notice.

This isn't the last chance you will have to review your practice, but if you start now, you will have these last two weeks to implement any changes you might want to make so you too will end on a strong note.

Resource: As you draw toward your year's end, take note as to how you would like to honor the ending of your own one-year journey.

Day 352
An Early Review

Today is day 352 of my daily Creative Practice, doing a blind contour portrait every day. As I mentioned yesterday, I have the desire to look back at my work. I am taking time to review what I have done this year because I am feeling the need to begin planning next year's project. More accurately, I am feeling anxious because I don't know what to do next. Here are a few things I am noticing:

- The pages stick together! I need to coat them so they don't become a continual disaster!
- I have some brilliant and satisfying pieces.
- Many paintings say to me, come back and do more!
- I have new ideas I could bring to some of the pages.
- There are many pages I was not able to paint but just draw the blind contour portrait.
- Those unfinished pages WANT my attention.
- This was a very ambitious project and I am feeling proud.
- Out of seven journals only three have painted covers, I would like to paint the covers of the others.
- Except for a few moments, I loved this daily art process.
- I loved the process most when I allowed myself more time.
- Painting every night was a great avenue to "me time."
- If I did it again, I would do more painting in silence.

After doing this year review, I think I want to stay with this project for another year. Go back and finish incomplete paintings. Why do I have to create something new? And along with painting, I can work on writing this book daily, maybe even finish!

Resource: When you don't know what to do, review what you have done. This can fill you with new ideas, and gratitude, too.

Day 353
You Get to Make This Up

I remember the day when I left my small hometown in Ohio. I drove a used blue Dodge station wagon with a bad paint job filled with all my belongings to move to Los Angeles. I tearfully waved to my family as my new husband and I headed south and then west. It is a similar feeling at the end of my 365 projects. I have lots of anticipation for what will be next, but first there is the heartfelt sadness of ending.

What do you need to do to say goodbye to this year and say hello to what is next? What is calling you? Remember, you get to make this up and do whatever you want. *If you want to do the same project every day for the rest of your life, do it!* It is all about following your pleasure in your creating and having a great relationship with the process.

After yesterday's review and as I write this, I feel a firm conviction to spend another year, my nineteenth year of daily art, with my blind portraits. This will offer me a chance to leisurely look for the portrait who calls to me, and we get to spend more time together. This feels good and right. I am not ready to say goodbye. There is so much left I can still do, and so much I want to do!

Note: I just entered my twentieth year of daily art and am now on year three of working on these portraits and writing! Will I do it for the rest of my life? Stay tuned!

Resource: You are making this up, so you get to do whatever you want. Start thinking about what you will do next. Please yourself first, follow the next impulse and what feels good.

Day 354
This Is All Just Made Up

Really. I am not here quoting experts. I am not doing quantitative research that shows if you do *this,* the result will be *this.* I am making things up as I go. I'm following ideas that come to me as I sit to write, or I jot down as I do my own art or lead groups.

In my ninth year of working on this book, some days like today I wonder if I could be an impostor. What do I have to say that anyone would want to hear? Am I a fake? Am I a pontificator, someone who thinks they know something but really knows nothing? Am I a wannabe? Am I cheating or fooling myself? (There is my fourth-grade teacher again.)

Even with nineteen years of daily art-making, doubt still visits me. Could I be more original? Am I doing enough? Is it really such a big deal? After all these years, after all this writing, I have felt doubt to a point where the idea to quit seems like a good idea.

The truth of this all? I am *IN* the creative process and that includes questions and doubts. Will this work? Has this been done before? Can I do it? This book is filled with what I have learned and what I continue to learn. Doubt keeps me humble and helps me make things even better. It is only bad if I let it stop me.

The creative process pushes us beyond what is comfortable, sending us to new places we never thought to go. Being out of our comfort zone can be scary, and it is also necessary if we are going to do new things. It is for me—if I am going to finish this book.

Maybe we are all experts. Experts of our own process, showing up every day to create, even when doubt creeps in. And so I pass the baton to you—the expert at what works for you. You get to make things up, and be the author of your own life!

Resource: If it is hard, know this is the creative process. Simplify to follow the next impulse to keep going and growing.

Day 355
Things I Do Know

Having said yesterday that this is all made up, here are some truths I do trust. All by practicing the idea that *Artist is a Verb.*

A Creative Practice can be exciting and scary. Anything new can be both. Keep going. You may be disappointed, or you may be inspired—you won't know until you do it. And sometimes the disappointment becomes the inspiration.

Once you grow your show-up muscle, you can apply it to doing anything in life. The key ingredient is to show up.

Listen for the next impulse. Listen to that voice who offers a small next step, a next idea. You don't need to know where you are going, you just need to know the next step.

Sometimes you need quiet to hear the impulse.

Follow your pleasures to find your way, if it feels good and doesn't hurt anyone or yourself, keep going!

Sometimes when it gets hard, you are on the verge of a breakthrough. Don't give up, stay with it until you experience the breakthrough. (Often it is the critic making it hard.)

Show up. Don't worry about what happens next. Find your way through your challenges by *doing* and facing your critic.

Your Creative Practice IS a relationship. If you are having challenges with commitment, you might have challenges committing to yourself. YOU are worth it. Allow yourself the human need for creative expression.

You know more than you think. You have all the answers inside you. Making art helps finding those answers easier. You will still need help from others, but art helps, too.

With art, you have a constant companion and confidant.

If you give up, you will NEVER know where you could have gone. Keep going.

This book is not just about art, but about living life!

Day 356
Make Good Trouble

How do we become more daring in our art-making and what we do with our art? How do we stretch ourselves and maybe make some good trouble? Tell the stories that need to be told, change the world, or change our inner world by expressing what needs to be expressed? How do we find our way into taking risks with our art that push us to be bigger in our life, or even push the world to be a better place? Can we use our art to deconstruct what is, so we can reconstruct something new?

What is keeping you from doing something amazing, brave, bold, or life changing? This life is short. Even if you are young, trust me, it goes by in the blink of an eye. What can you do today to show the world your gift, your unique point of view? Follow your dream and send out a proposal for a show or performance of your work. Sit in the park with a sign that says, *"Join me for scribbling."* Sing "Here Comes the Sun" by the Beatles in a crowded elevator or some other place you have a captive audience. Begin to write your story and share your hero's journey.

Maybe you will gather other artists together to become an even stronger voice. Organize group shows that voice different points of view on relevant topics, or create an arts-based foundation or fundraiser for the needs of your local community.

As you grow your artist self take that out into the world to make good trouble. In the words of John Lewis, "Speak up, speak out, get in the way. Get in good trouble, necessary trouble..." Remember, the arts are at the forefront of change.

Resource: Begin to think of how your art can create something bigger in the world. Whether it is for yourself or for your community, small or large. What is a cause that you could imagine supporting with your art to help create change?

Day 357

Will I Ever Stop Showing Up?

I am currently in year nineteen of having a daily Creative Practice. People ask me if I will ever stop, take a day off, a year off, or even end this journey. My best answer is, I don't know. I talk about following the next impulse with our art. Well, this is how I live my life. Following the next impulse, the next idea, the next offering that fits. And so far, I have not had the desire to quit. I currently can't imagine stopping. This would be like saying, I am going to stop brushing my teeth or stop eating, or I am not going to love anymore.

Taking time for an intentional creative act every day is part of who I have become. It is essential to the life I have created for myself. Maybe at some point I will not have to work and my entire day will be devoted to creative acts. For today, I need to work and my Creative Practice supports my life.

The truth is, I am more creatively motivated than I have ever been. Most days I am writing an hour or more a day and spending an hour or more painting. My commitment is still 5 minutes, but 5 minutes rarely feels like enough. I have recently increased my monthly art retreat weekend that I have done for over seven years to two weekends a month, because I have simplified my life. I am diligent about carving this space for myself. If I am not, life creeps in to push out my art and my sanity.

I can't imagine a life where I do not show up every day for a *creative act of expression.* Maybe a musical instrument or a documentary film becomes a daily practice. Who knows where the next impulse will take me. How about you? What is calling you?

Resource: If you can't wait to end your daily Creative Practice, look to see if there is something you can change to create a better fit, so maybe you can't live without each other, too.

Day 358
Dear Art, Thank You...

Dear Art, thank you for waiting for me. I know it took me a long time to get here. I had to wrestle through lots of demons. They weren't mean or hurtful, but they gave me lots of doubt. I didn't believe I was an artist so I couldn't show up to make art. Though I dabbled here and there, I never felt any sense of confidence or good feelings to keep going.

I thought someday I would wake up and realize it was my time to be an artist. The gift of artist would be bestowed on me. I had fantasies of living an artist's life someday when I was an old woman. I would be surrounded by my art, finished and unfinished. Art would be my life.

Thank you, Mom, for revealing to me before you died that you, too, had the desire to become an artist. You were on your deathbed and it had never happened. My life might have turned out the same way. I too might have died before I realized my artist dream.

About halfway through my first year of daily art to honor my mother's wish to be an artist and my own fear I might never be one, I discovered the secret.

Artist is a verb. I don't become an artist and then do art. I do art and then begin to feel like an artist.

Thank you art, for waiting for me until I could learn if I make art regularly, then I can feel like an artist.

And thank you art for planting the seed for this book in my heart. You helped me feel like a writer so I could share my Creative Practice wisdom with others. This is a perfect marriage. Until death do us part, I will continue to create.

Resource: Now it is your turn, write a letter to your art. Maybe you start with "Dear Art, thank you..." or maybe you create your own beginning.

Day 359

In the End—A Review

We are coming to the end of our year—now could be a good time to review how it went. If you haven't already, gather your work in front of you so you can see how much accrued over the year. If you have been working on the computer, maybe print out what you have. Or print photos you took. Or simply bring everything together in one place so you can see or hear the entire body of work. You might want to have someone with you when you do it, to witness you, not to critique the work. (Tell them ahead you want them to help you celebrate.)

I did this process after my first year. I had done 365 pieces and with the help of my colleague and mentor Pamela Underwood, laid them all out on the floor of her studio to see what I had done. In the moment when they were all there showing their colorful selves, rather than in their boxes, I got a huge surprise—each day wasn't the true piece of art—individually each was mediocre, but it was the totality that was the real work of art. It was all the pieces lined up next to each other, the sheer size of the project impacted me, seeing it in its totality. I was stunned.

My process from there was to choose my favorites and whittle the favorites down to the one I liked the most. From 365 to twenty to ten to three and finally, the one I loved the most. When I got to the final piece, a blind drawing of my cat, I knew what my next year would be. I would finally start painting. After years of wanting to, I finally felt confident enough. I felt more like an artist. I could draw blind contour portraits with my eyes closed and then paint them, eyes open.

In my review of the year, I also decided I *must* have a one-woman show, so others could see it in its totality, too.

Resource: Gather your work to honor it, be with it. Any messages?

Day 360
More End-of-Year Review

Once you have looked at or listened to the product(s) you created over the year so far, you may want to look at the process and what you have learned. Here are some questions you could ask yourself in a review of your year. I suggest writing down the answers so you will remember.

Did the year and the project go the way I wanted?

What could have made it more satisfying?

If I did it again, would I do anything different?

If so, what? What did I learn along the way?

What surprised me?

What helped me the most?

What was not helpful?

Does something more want to happen with the body of work I created? (If you don't know what to do with it, ask the work what it may want.)

What wants to come next? Any ideas for a next project?

What would it take to get the next year started?

Where may I need more support or help?

Resource: Take the time to do this review. You may think you will remember it all forever, but you probably won't! Do it while it is fresh in your mind. And if you had any great learnings, I would love to hear from you!

Day 361

What If the Work Feels Unfinished?

Today in doing a review of this past year I notice I found my groove at about month four. The art I made earlier in my process is not as aesthetically pleasing as the later work. I also have some entries where I did the absolute minimum to show up, and I see I could take them further. What do I do?

In past years I have had this dilemma and had the best of intentions to go back and fix and finish in my own time, when I was in the mood. Well, the mood never came. Once I started a new project I was freshly absorbed. I still have those "unfinished" pieces.

The message here is to be forgiving. Remember, the goal is to have a Creative Practice, to show up regularly, not to be an award-winning artist. The unfinished days or those that seem less than "worthy" have their own story. It is up to you if you want to change their story. I have even considered one year of my Creative Practice will be going over old projects and taking them to the next level. Yet, right next to this is the desire to keep them authentic and leave things the way they are. Some pages where I spent hours or days will shine—while some pages stay minimal.

Once again, this is YOUR practice, you can do anything you want. You get to make it up, change it, redo it, or move on. Mostly, make it simple yet engaging so you will continue! There is no right or wrong answer, only *your* answer—you can continue to work on a project for *the rest of your life*!

Resource: In your year review decide, for this moment, is it okay to move forward and leave this year behind, or does it call to you for more?

Day 362

What's Next—Curiosity Meets Reality

Today is day 362 in my year of scribbling with the Scribble Kit. I have ideas for my next project, but feel stifled, or is it scared? I want to get back to painting my blind contour drawings, yet my life does not feel conducive to paint anymore, or so I think. But I long for it. I stopped painting as a regular practice eight years ago when I moved into my tiny 300-square-foot home. My projects became smaller and more manageable in materials and process. And now my Sweetie lives with me, so my art space is even smaller.

Can I show up with enough time for a painting project? If I take myself back to my first three years of daily painting, my commitment was "one stroke of paint a day, with no painting taking more than a few days."

I have been doing daily art where I completed something every day for so long, the idea of not finishing something feels odd. Yet, I know it isn't. I want to paint because I miss the feeling of putting paint on brush, brush on paper. I miss the vibrant colors of my palette. If this is true, the end product is less important than showing up to paint. Now I am getting excited!

If you have questions or doubts when you are in the planning stages, keep in mind, after all my years of daily art-making, I am still curious and unsure! The only way we really squelch those worries or wonderings is by DOING. It is through the doing we work out the bugs. It is through the doing we find what we enjoy or don't like. It is through the doing we can reflect on our process. When it is in our head, it is all conjecture.

Resource: Be curious and open. Create a plan to move forward with your idea. You can even allow yourself a few days of trial and error to "practice" your potential new Creative Practice.

Day 363
Icing on the Cake

When I took the big step of handing off my first draft of this book to my developmental editor, Cherie Kephart, I suggested she participate in a Creative Practice while she did the editing. I knew she was a painter, so I had the idea that she would pick up a paintbrush every day. When we met for our meeting at the end of her editing process, she filled me in on her experience.

Cherie has had a career in editing but her first love is writing. She has authored several books including a memoir. She told me as an editor she is so tired by the end of the day she can't even look at another word, so her own writing projects are put on the back burner.

As she read and edited this book, she said I gave her permission to show up for herself first. And that is exactly what she did. She started a Creative Practice in writing—set a timer for one hour every morning to do her own writing BEFORE she began editing.

It worked! She was more energized for her editing because she had done her own writing first. And one day she was having such a great time with her own writing project that she stayed with it all day and never got to my book!

My doubts faded hearing her story. *Maybe I really do have something to say. And other people besides myself can benefit from this book.* In this moment I feel like my job is finished. My book has helped someone to be in relationship with their art, their passion—everything moving forward is icing on the cake.

I hope your experience with this book will add more icing to the Creative Practice cake! Just one new action can change your life.

Resource: If you haven't already, put yourself first by putting your Creative Practice first. Don't let life and work pull you away from your creative center, your longing, your expression. And, if you have a success story with this book, please let me know!

If you held yourself to only 5 minutes a day, you have been creative for 30 hours more than if you did not show up. And, I am guessing you went longer many or most days because it was irresistible! Congratulations for anything and everything you have done!

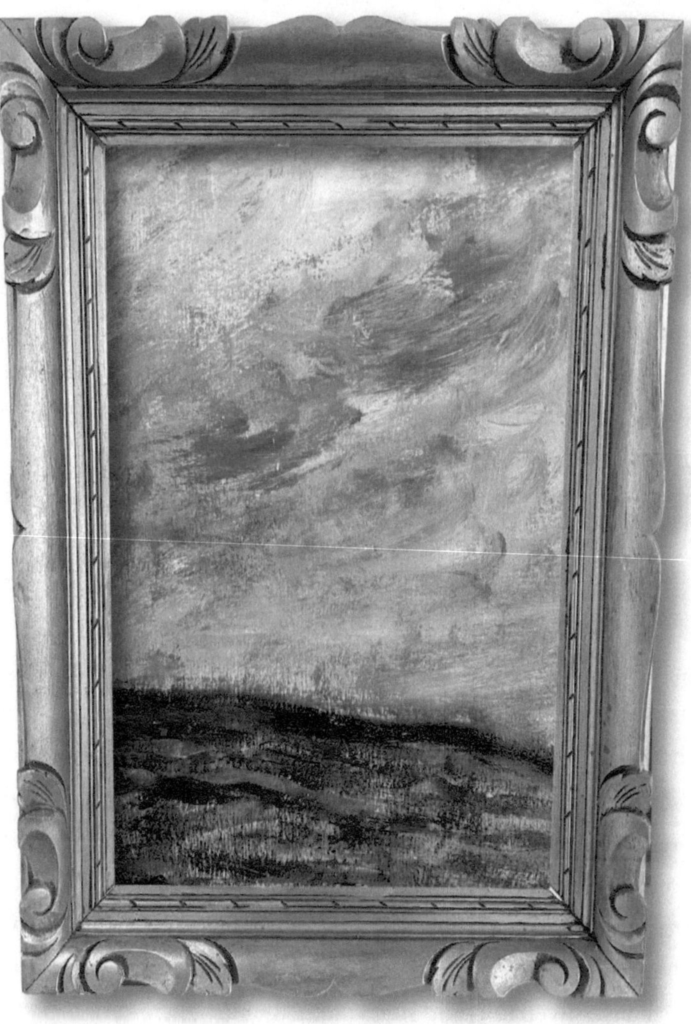

Clean Off the Brushes Paintings

I began my clean off the brush and palette paintings because I hate to waste paint. And it quickly became one of my absolute favorite parts of my painting process! I am not thinking, or trying. I am simply cleaning off the brushes or using up the leftover paint. It is liberating! I create either abstracts or abstract landscapes. It feels like improv jazz with a paintbrush. This last year I started doing this process on my couch! Stay tuned!

Day 364

Learn from What Doesn't Work

I have shown up one day at a time for twenty years of daily art making. I had no idea when I started that I would continue this long. I was doing a one-year project to honor my mother who died wishing she had been an artist. The surprise was I liked it so much I kept going.

And yes, there have been pauses, what I call *false starts.* When I realized a project was not working and I needed to re-group and figure things out.

If you are reading this and things didn't pan out the way you hoped, I encourage you to keep going.

I adopted the idea of *false starts* instead of *failed* because I realized how helpful it was to learn from what doesn't work. I have an idea, it doesn't evolve as I hoped, but I made an attempt. It happens to all of us. The idea may not translate in real life like the perfection in our head. In our imaginings it does not include our human limitations. Maybe we were too ambitious or chose the wrong medium for our lifestyle, or an idea is too big for our confidence level. We don't know until we try. So bless the *false starts* as creative action taken, a step into something new. And a chance to learn why it didn't work and carry the learning forward.

I have saved my *false starts* along the way and I even picked up a couple for a second go, incorporating what I learned and it worked!

If you didn't make it all the way to one year, learn from what you did or didn't do. No worries. Listen for the next impulse and get going again. *Artist is a verb.*

Resource: Take it one day at a time. Learn from what works and what doesn't work so you can keep going. Remember there is no need for perfection. Follow the next impulse for as long as you live and you will live a very creative and inspiring life!

Day 365
The End, or Is It the Beginning?

Maybe you have arrived at this page because you started a project or process and have seen it all the way to the end, to day 365. Or maybe you have turned to the last page to see how the process ends, before you even start. Or maybe you have been using this book as a daily reader with no project.

No matter how you got here—congratulate yourself for the desire to live a more creative, inspired life. Appreciate the journey you have taken. Celebrate that you showed up. You might even need to grieve the end of a long intimate relationship with your project.

And tomorrow? You may also want to finalize a plan for what you will do—will you be starting a new project? Will you be continuing what you have already been doing? Will you be taking a break, and for how long?

Whatever is next, mark this linear ending with some celebration, get up and do a little dance, let out an audible "woohoo!" Or make a final piece today that proclaims, THE END of year one.

May this book be a lifelong companion of reminders and resources to help you continue moving forward on your creative journey. May this journey never end. KEEP GOING!

Resource: How do you want to mark the end of one year of your Creative Practice? Do something! (See the next entry for some ideas.) Think about tomorrow, what will you do tomorrow? Read the extra leap-year day included, or start again from the beginning at Day One? Let this book be an ongoing source of support. You can read it again day by day, pick a random page each day to read, or use the index when you are feeling challenged or are looking for the next impulse.

Day 366
A Leap Year or Not Ready to Leap

For those years where there is a leap year, you might have an extra day, or you may need an extra day if it is not a leap year, to transition or celebrate. Feel this big HIGH FIVE coming to you from me, and from everyone else who has finished 365 days of making their life more creative and inspired. You did it!

Celebrate and honor yourself, share your success and even your challenges with yourself, with others. And continue to ask, "Now what?"

Resource:

- Journal about your process this last year, the challenges, and the successes.
- Create one last piece as an artful response to the entire year.
- If you haven't already, share the work you have done with someone you trust. Remember to be specific about the kind of feedback or response you want.
- Plan a *celebration party, performance, or show* to bring your project to your bigger world. (Something simple, don't make it such a big deal you don't do it!)
- Frame one piece from your Creative Practice so you can honor the effort. With visual art, writing, or poetry projects you may pick a favorite to frame, or maybe it is the last piece you create that is an artful response to the whole year.
- If your practice was in dance, theater, or other performing arts, take a photo that captures you and the overall feeling or theme of the year and honor it with a frame.
- Musicians could frame a piece of music written or played.
- Take time to honor your journey and the results—it is a big deal!

Last Words

Am I Finished or Just Starting?

As I finish the writing of this book, and it is my time to say goodbye, sadness comes. Though I write this now and you read it later, I feel as though we have been on this journey together. I have expressed and problem solved my own challenges thinking maybe it will help you, too. We are ultimately so similar, being human. We bring our unique history with us, yet we are connected through the human desire to express, the human reality of having a critic, and the human need to be seen and heard.

Trust that I have held you in my heart as I write. I honor the successes and challenges you have experienced. I imagine it may not have always been easy. I hope there were openings, steps forward, new confidence, or that a deeper knowing arrived.

It feels important to say as we end, be kind with yourself on your creative journey. Know for most, showing up to our creative expression does not come naturally. We live in a time when creative thinking is not fully valued. Our creative expression is a growing, evolving part of ourselves and the world.

I am thinking of my journey with singing, my deepest art wound, where I did not sing for most of my life because I was told I had a terrible voice. I will never sing a solo concert, and probably never record a song. But I can do what I never thought was possible: I can sing sentences I want to speak. I can improv silly rhyming songs that don't need music memory, and as my greatest teacher Paolo Knill taught me, when I hit a wrong note, I don't stop, I hold it as long as I need until it becomes the right note.

Have compassion for yourself and where you are in your creative journey. When it seems like it is not working, keep going, until you find the right note. Keep *making things special* until you find your unique voice and beyond. Maybe we do another year together? Thanks Mom, for getting us started!

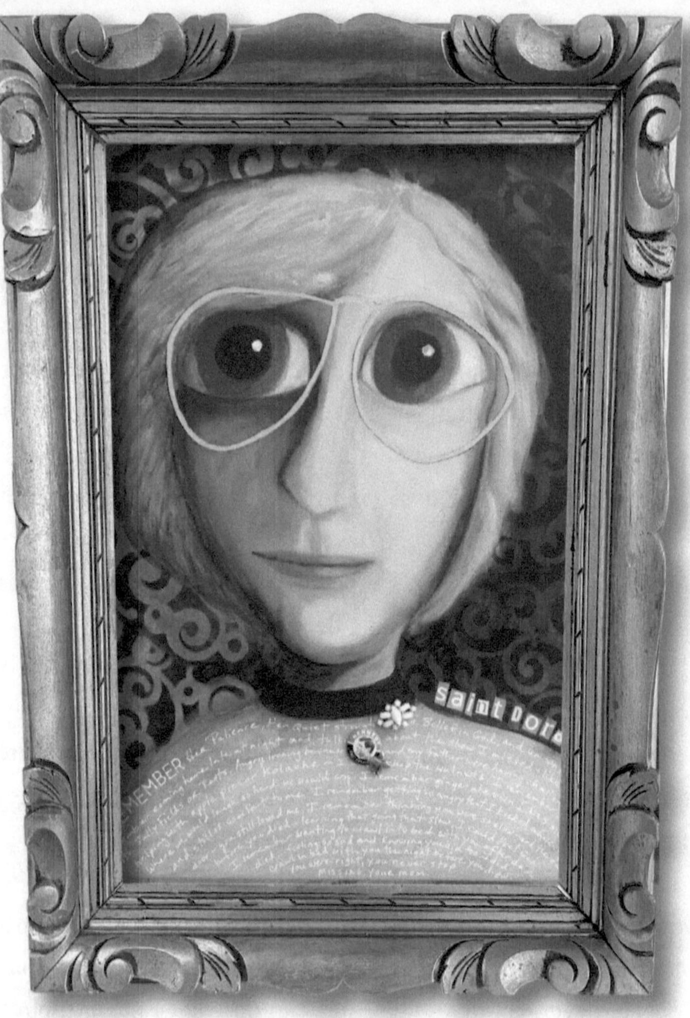

My Mother My Muse

My mother is my muse and the instigator of this Creative Practice path I have been on. Once again my deepest gratitude goes to her, for trusting me with her regret about not becoming an artist. Though her death was over twenty years ago I have felt her here with me writing this book. I wonder if she feels some sense of satisfaction now too. I gratefully carry forward her dream of being an artist and live it as her descendant, and now pass it on to you.

Deep Gratitude
Acknowledgments

Gratitude for all the dots connecting so I could have this amazing journey that is my life. All the people who have influenced my life and this book. I can't name you all but I can say, "Thank you!"

The Expressive Arts Institute of San Diego and Judith Greer Essex who caught me just on the other side of my mother and father's death to grieve and learn about this amazing world of Expressive Arts, including the tools and safety to walk through my fears around art-making. The European Graduate School masters program and Paolo Knill who gave me the confidence and freedom to go out and create the life I wanted as an Expressive Arts Therapist. (And five great summers in Switzerland!)

And then there is my earlier adult life that prepared me for this. Lael Greenleaf, who was a master educator of human development and how we can go back and recover our childhood and become beautiful adults. You helped change my life.

All the community I grew from my life path, my family is huge. My Los Angeles peeps who re-grew up with me. My San Diego Tribe who continues to do the healing work alongside me. My Expressive Arts colleagues who are the sisters I never had, I love how we continue to support each other.

My son Shea who witnessed the early days of me finding my artist self, and you have become a prolific creator yourself. Gregg who is the best big brother ever, thank you for walking this path together of losing our parents in such a brief time and for your wise and encouraging counsel. And my Sweetie, Michael, who so many years of my daily art prepared me for and today my art is helping me learn to love you even better. Thank you for supporting me every day to live this daily art dream.

And then my book helpers! Donna Otter for being a great reader, editor, and cheerleader, your daily diaries are inspiring.

Deep Gratitude
Acknowledgments

Cherie Kephart for your editor eye and heart, asking great questions and walking the daily art path as you edited this book, to prove it works. Keith Robbins for your eagle eye. If there are any errors it was because I kept changing things after you saw the "final" draft. Thank you Michele, Pamela, Donna, Martha, and Mary who offered your beautiful homes so I could create the deep space of writing retreats. And Somatic Therapist Gloria Gonzalez for your huge support in helping my body and heart be ready for the ride of being an author.

Thank you to my Monday night writing group family who has seen this book grow over many years. My Wednesday morning women writers who encouraged me to be more vulnerable and include my story. And all those who have come through my Expressive Arts studio door—you have been my greatest teachers.

And finally, I want to acknowledge my fourth-grade teacher, Miss Rosebrooks, whose unkind message, "Who do you think you are fooling?" still visits me when I am stretching and growing. Today I can firmly stand before you and say, "I am not fooling anyone, I am living my beautifully imperfect and inspired life." You are forgiven, rest in peace.

As I finish this book, I want to acknowledge the most amazing fourlegged rescue friend, who is at the end of his life as I write this. Thank you, Jack dog, for over fifteen fabulous years together. May you meet Sandy, Buffy, Mink, and Friday in doggie heaven.

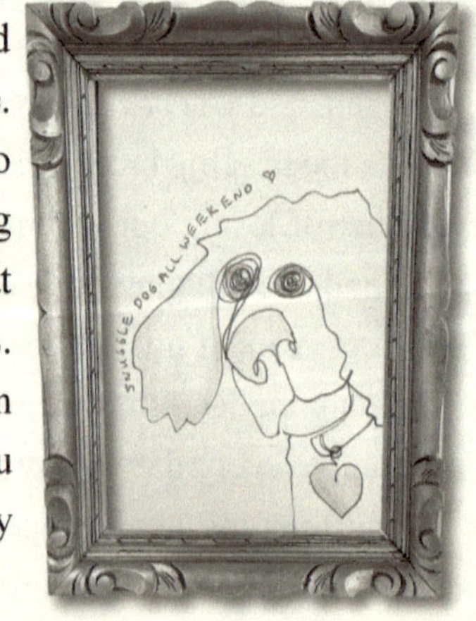

Follow-Up Resources

More Support for Your Journey

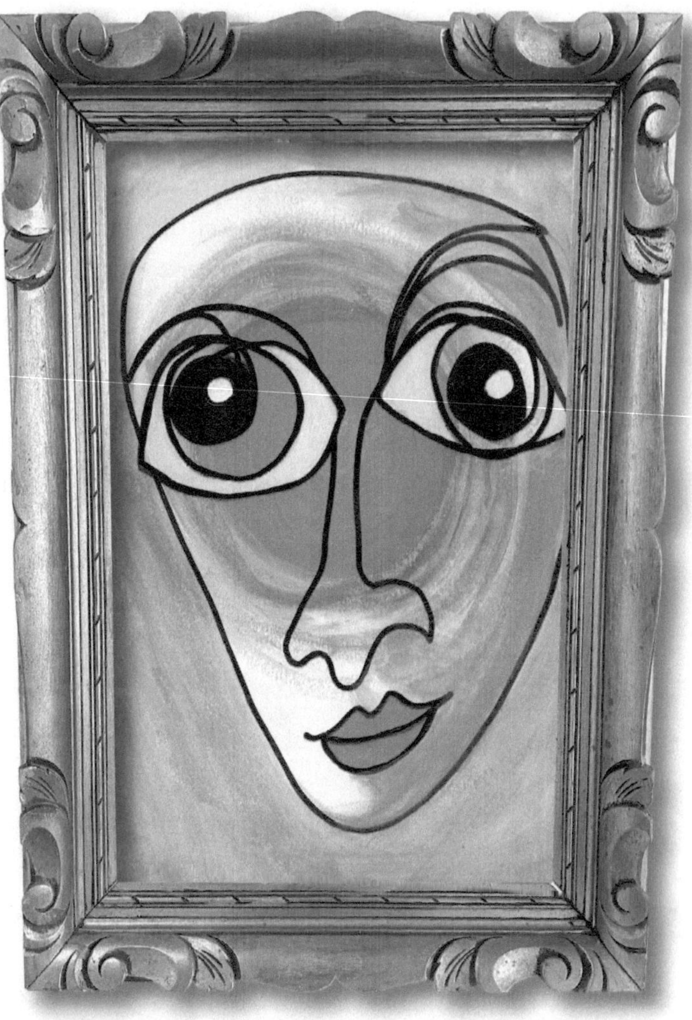

You don't need to do this alone! Continue to use the help here in this book and reach out for help from others. As you grow stronger and more confident in your art discipline, pass it on to another by being a mentor in the arts and sharing your gifts with the world.

Follow-Up Resources

Creative Practice Support Group

It can help to have the support of other like-minded people. The creative process can be lonely. Having others to walk through successes and challenges with can be encouraging, even life giving.

Put out a call to friends and family to find creatives who might want to be supported and supportive. You can decide whether you want your group to be open to all disciplines of creativity or just visual artists, musicians, dancers, writers, actors, gardeners or...

It could be good for everyone to use this book as a foundation for the group, but that is not necessary.

Following are questions to answer and ideas for a meeting format that you can use if you would like, or come up with your own.

- Will we meet online or in person?
- How often will we meet?
- How long will we meet?
- Adjust share times by number of people to allow equal time for all.
- A timer is helpful. Let participants take turns being timekeeper.
- Rotate the "leader" role each time you meet so everyone gets a chance.
- Does the leader get to make up the group when it is their turn or do you stay with a basic format?

You get to make this up as a group. Try different formats to find what works as a group. Maybe you make art together or share your progress. Maybe you do an open mic and art show quarterly for just the group, or you invite family and friends too.

Follow-Up Resources
Support Group Meeting Format

Here is an example for a creative support group meeting format:

Opening:

Pass around *Creative Practice Group Reading* each meeting, each person reading aloud a section if they choose. This is a good reminder to create safety in the group. (See next page.)

Inspirational reading, poem, and/or exercise. Maybe you choose a day from this book either randomly or in advance, and let it be your topic.

Check-in Round:

2 minutes each participant (or adjust for your group size) What am I feeling scared, worried, or concerned about? What seems hard? What is working or feels exciting and inspiring? Or sharing around the opening reading topic.

Support Round:

Each participant gets to share for 5 minutes about their process and how they might need support. May include show and tell.

Listeners follow with supportive feedback for 1 minute each.

Closing Commitments:

Next steps. Each person says what they are inspired to do next.

Closing Reading:

The *Creative Practice Blessing* (page 33 and 448) or other chosen reading or poem.

Final Word:

Each person gives a word or a phrase to answer "What are you taking with you from our time together?"

Follow-Up Resources
Support Group Reading

(You can pass the reading around the group and have each participant voluntarily read one paragraph. If someone doesn't want to read they can pass it along to the next person.)

Welcome to our Creative Practice support group. We are here to support each other to create and take regular actions toward our creative dreams.

We are here to create a safe environment, where we can support and learn from each other. We are here to be accepting of ourselves in this moment. To create "shitty first drafts" (thanks, Anne Lamott!), not be concerned with doing it right or perfect. Practice being in the process and follow what feels good as we fill our creative cup.

If our inner critic rears an ugly head, we will not accept its general statements like, "This is awful. I hate it. You don't know what you are doing." Instead, we can ask our critic what is specifically going on. Are we afraid of what others will think? Are we worried what we have done is not good enough? Are we revealing something vulnerable?

Often our critic is trying to protect us. We can stand up to our critic because our work and we the creators are important.

As individuals and as a group we come together to create an environment which is non-critical and encourages us to take risks and grow. This includes not critiquing each other or ourselves, and honoring the process of creating and sharing.

Which also includes NOT minimizing our efforts with language like, "I ONLY did…I JUST did…I didn't really do much…It is not very good…" We will share our work without apology, knowing whatever we have done has value.

We are here to be good listeners. Listen to what is being shared. "Listening to the person who is speaking rather than to our mind which is chattering away with instant solutions" (Lael Greenleaf). Not comparing or critiquing—when we find ourselves comparing or critiquing, we can gently bring our attention back to listening.

We will celebrate we showed up. Ask for help when we need it. Remember we become better at our craft by creating, and the more we create the more confident we get. We can also remember we have the rest or our lives to learn and grow creatively.

Finally, we will listen to our heart, appreciate the process of creating and the community which is created as we share our work. Don't worry, have fun!

Follow-Up Resources

Creative Practice Blessing

(Can be read before creative meetings or before you begin your art each day.)

May you have a love affair with your art.
May you wake each day with desire to spend time together.
May you begin slowly yet commit to know each other deeply.
May you bring enthusiasm and caring to each meeting.
May your time together be mostly pleasure
with just the right amount of risk.
May you keep each other company in darkness,
as well as dance when the light shines bright.
May you be honest and forgiving, knowing today's mistakes
can become tomorrow's new ideas.
May you show up consistently and not allow others,
or yourself, to pull you from your commitment.
May you honor each moment spent together
as the gift or the challenge it is,
and continue to show up for both.
May you share your anger, disappointment,
and sadness with each other
as well as your joys and delights.
May you listen to your art with an open heart
and follow the steps that are illuminated by it.
May you breathe in courage, exhale doubt, and know
just after things get hard, they usually get easier.
So don't quit.
Keep showing up.
Leave ample evidence you existed in this relationship,
in this marriage of creation.
Till death do you part,
or at least until you reach day 365.

Follow-Up Resources
Books

Outliers: The Story of Success, by Malcolm Gladwell, copyright © 2008. Reprinted by permission of Little, Brown and Company, an imprint of Hachette Book Group, Inc. (Day 14)

Trust the Process, by Shaun McNiff. Shambhala Publications, Inc. (Day 15)

The Power of Daily Practice: How Creative and Performing Artists (and Everyone Else) Can Finally Meet Their Goals by Eric Maisel. (Day 19)

Bird by Bird: Some Instructions on Writing and Life by Anne Lamott. Pantheon Books (Days 17, 38, 106, 152, 165)

The Artist's Way by Julia Cameron. copyright ©1992, 2002, 2016, tarcherperigee an imprint of Penguin Random House. (Day 63)

Steal Like an Artist by Austin Kleon. Workman Publishing. (Day 63 and 118)

Studio Art Therapy by Catherine Hyland Moon. Jessica Kingsley Publishers (Day 105)

Your Brain on Art by Susan Magsamen and Ivy Ross. copyright © 2023 Penguin Random House. (Day 145)

Writing Down the Bones by Natalie Goldberg. Shambhala Publications, Inc. (Day 202)

What Is Art For? by Ellen Dissanayake. University of Washington Press (Page 26, Day 203)

For You When I Am Gone: Twelve Essential Questions to Tell a Life Story by Steve Leder, copyright © 2022 by Steve Leder. Used by permission of Avery, an imprint of Penguin Publishing Group, a division of Penguin Random House LLC. All rights reserved. (Day 295)

War on Art—Break Through the Blocks and Win Your Inner Creative Battles by Steven Pressfield. Black Irish Entertainment, LLC

A Writer's Book of Days: A Spirited Companion and Lively Muse for the Writing Life by Judy Reeves. New World Library

Scribble Art: A How-to Guide and Coloring Book by Tish McAllise Sjoberg. Art Helps Art Heals Press, available on Amazon.

Use this index as a resource
to find help, get unstuck and get inspired.

It is also a fabulous word list that could
be used for creative prompts!

Like, blindly pick three words and use
those words to create something!
A poem,
a song,
a story,
a collage,
a dance,
a painting,
an improv scene,
or...

Follow-Up Resources
Index

C

I

J

K

T

Who Is This Daily Artist?

About the Author

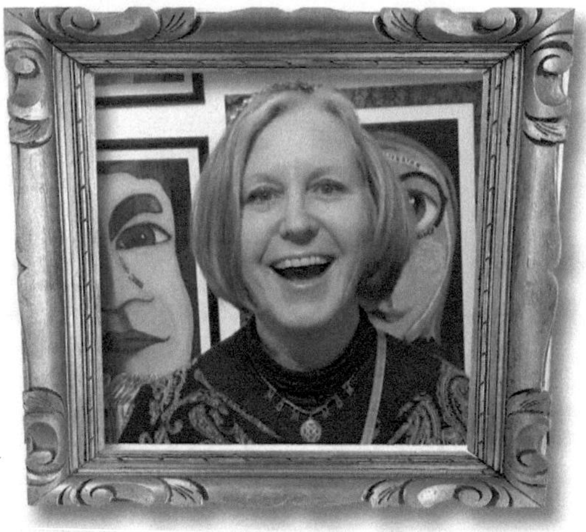

Tish McAllise Sjoberg has been creating art daily for over twenty years at the time of this publication. What began as a one year honoring of her mother's death ignited a lifelong passion of using the arts to live a more inspired life. She received her Masters in Expressive Arts Therapy, Coaching and Education from the European Graduate School in Switzerland and the Expressive Arts Institute of San Diego. Her Studio, Expressive Arts @ 32nd & Thorn in San Diego, is a vibrant safe space for creative expression with offerings in all the art disciplines: visual art, movement, music, writing, and drama.

This book is an extension of her desire to create safe spaces for all to express—reaching out to creatives everywhere.

Tish hopes to create every day for the rest of her life so she and the world know that she lives the life of an artist, and her life is the evidence. Tish is a painter, writer, and photo historian. She also loves improvisation through music, dance, performance, and even singing a few lines when she feels courageous.

You can learn more at:
ArtHelpsArtHeals.com
ExpressiveArtsSanDiego.com

“It is never too late to have a happy creative life!”

Tish McAllise Sjoberg

www.ingramcontent.com/pod-product-compliance
Lightning Source LLC
LaVergne TN
LVHW091246150826
845673LV00006B/1335

9798989137312